REMAKING THE CHINESE EMPIRE

REMAKING THE CHINESE EMPIRE

Manchu-Korean Relations, 1616–1911

Yuanchong Wang

CORNELL UNIVERSITY PRESS   **ITHACA AND LONDON**

First published 2018 by Cornell University Press

Library of Congress Cataloging-in-Publication Data

Names: Wang, Yuanchong, 1979– author.
Title: Remaking the Chinese empire : Manchu-Korean relations, 1616–1911 / Yuanchong Wang.
Description: Ithaca : Cornell University Press, 2018. | Includes bibliographical references and index.
Identifiers: LCCN 2018023443 (print) | LCCN 2018029151 (ebook) | ISBN 9781501730511 (pdf) | ISBN 9781501730528 (epub/mobi) | ISBN 9781501730504 | ISBN 9781501730504 (cloth ; alk. paper)
Subjects: LCSH: China—Foreign relations—Korea. | Korea—Foreign relations—China. | China—Foreign relations—1644–1912.
Classification: LCC DS740.5.K6 (ebook) | LCC DS740.5.K6 W335 2018 (print) | DDC 327.51051909/03—dc23
LC record available at https://lccn.loc.gov/2018023443

Contents

Illustrations

Acknowledgments

In the course of the fifteen years that I have worked on the project presented in this book, I have incurred deep debts to so many mentors, supervisors, colleagues, friends, and family members in China, South Korea, Japan, the United States, and other countries that I cannot list all their names here.

My thanks must first go to Jian Chen, Haijian Mao, Sherman Cochran, and Julien Victor Koschmann for their matchless academic guidance and strong support over the years. My sincerest gratitude is due to those senior researchers who have helped me to develop my project and enrich my ideas, including Young-seo Baik, Shangsheng Chen, Zhihong Chen, Yinghong Cheng, TJ Hinrichs, Douglas Howland, Isabel Hull, Nam-lin Hur, Chin-a Kang, Shin Kawashima, Seonmin Kim, Mio Kishimoto, Dorothy Ko, Bum-jin Koo, Kirk Larsen, Hun Lee, Dezheng Li, Yunquan Li, Ping Liu, Tianlu Liu, Zhitian Luo, Tobie Meyer-Fong, Yūjirō Murata, Mary Beth Norton, Takashi Okamoto, Myung-lim Park, Kenneth Pomeranz, Xiaoyan Rong, Naoki Sakai, Chengyou Song, Osamu Takamizawa, Yuanzhou Wang, Yuanfeng Wu, Jiashen Yang, and Zhiqiang Zhao.

My learned colleagues in the Department of History, the Program of Asian Studies, and the Center for Global and Area Studies at the University of Delaware have provided a stimulating academic environment from which I continue to draw inspiration. In particular, I have to thank Alice Ba, Anne Boylan, James Brophy, Eve Buckley, Jianguo Chen, Jesus Cruz, Rebecca Davis, Lawrence Duggan, Darryl Flaherty, Alan Fox, Christine Heyrman, Barry Joyce, Hannah Kim, Daniel Kinderman, Peter Kolchin, Wunyabari Maloba, Rudi Matthee, Mark McLeod, Arwen Mohun, John Montano, David Pong, Ramnarayan Rawat, David Shearer, Steven Sidebotham, Patricia Sloane-White, David Suisman, Douglas Tobias, Owen White, and Haihong Yang.

Numerous friends in different countries have supported my research over the years. Among them are Christopher Ahn, Eriko Akamatsu, Claudine Ang, Harutoshi Aoyama, Zhilei Bie, Michael Carpentier, Shiau-yun Chen, Jack Chia, Deokyo Choi, Danielle Cohen, Mari Crabtree, Brian Cuddy, Haibin Dai, Chennan Ding, Feng Feng, Xuefeng Gu, Kate Horning, Noriaki Hoshino, Zachary Howlett, Xiangyu Hu, Junliang Huang, Qixuan Huang, Hongwei Huo, Aimin Ji, Chen Ji, Huajie Jiang, Christopher Jones, Dong-hun Jung, Jason Kelly, Elli Kim, Hanmee Kim, Amy Kohout, Tinghui Lau, Peter Lavelle, Pyong-soo Lee, Seok-won Lee, Baoming Li, Gang Li, Shan-ai Li, Wenjie Li, Minling Liang, Joshua Van Lieu,

Bensen Liu, Oiyan Liu, Wenli Lü, Jorge Marin, Hajimu Matsuda, Mayuko Mori, Huixiang Pan, Trais Pearson, Yuanyuan Qiu, Zhiyong Ren, Victor Seow, Nianshen Song, Ming Sun, Shichun Tang, Lesley Turnbull, Bo Wang, Haitao Wang, Qingbin Wang, Sixiang Wang, Dong Xu, Heng Xu, Jiguo Yang, Sungoh Yoon, Wei Yu, Hairong Zhang, Jianjun Zhang, Lei Zhang, Ting Zhang, Tingting Zhang, Jian Zhou, and Taomo Zhou. For more than a decade, Danielle Cohen, Zachary Howlett, and Nianshen Song have always read my chapter manuscripts and offered superb and interdisciplinary feedback, and I cannot thank them more.

It was an honor to be a fellow of the Korea Foundation and of the Japan Foundation, which funded my research at Yonsei University in Seoul and the University of Tokyo in Tokyo, respectively. Cornell University and the University of Delaware generously supported my overseas archival research in East Asia. The University of Delaware also offered strong support for the publication of this book. The staff members of the many archives, libraries, and research institutes that I visited in East Asia and the United States provided much-appreciated assistance. The publishers of two earlier articles kindly allowed me to include those articles in this book; they are "Claiming Centrality in the Chinese World," *Chinese Historical Review* 22, no. 2 (2015): 95–119, and "Civilizing the Great Qing," *Late Imperial China* 38, no. 1 (2017): 113–54. The critical comments of the anonymous reviewers of the two articles helped me improve the quality of this book.

I am delighted that this book found a home at Cornell University Press. Emily Andrew offered wonderful guidance and advice throughout the entire process. Bethany Wasik and Susan Specter helped me deal with many issues connected to the publication. The two dedicated anonymous reviewers read my manuscript with great care and provided outstanding and thought-provoking comments. Alice Colwell, Hanna Siurua, and Eric Levy provided brilliant suggestions in the process of polishing the manuscript.

Finally, I must express my heartfelt thanks to the members of my family, who resolutely supported my career during the years in which I studied and worked in different countries across the Pacific. This book is dedicated to all of them, in particular to my wife, Na, and my daughter, Yujia.

Note on Romanization and Conventions

This book follows the Pinyin romanization system for Chinese, Möllendorff for Manchu, McCune-Reischauer for Korean, and Hepburn for Japanese. The abbreviation "Ch." refers to Chinese, "Ma." to Manchu, "K." to Korean, and "J." to Japanese. A few established Wade-Giles spellings of Chinese figures, such as Sun Yatsen, remain unchanged. Several key Chinese, Manchu, and Korean terms, such as *Zongfan*, *Zhongguo*, *Dulimbai gurun*, *Zhonghua*, and *Junghwa*, are capitalized. The names of Manchu figures are spelled either in Möllendorff (when the Manchu characters are available) or in Pinyin (when they are not available). A core indigenous Chinese term, *fan*, which is often rendered as "tributary state" in English, always appears in italics. The Chinese and Korean dates of primary documents using the lunar calendar have been converted into their counterparts in the Gregorian calendar based on *Jinshi Zhong Xi shiri duizhao biao* (Cross-reference lists of modern Chinese and Western historical dates), edited by Hesheng Zheng.

Chinese and Korean Reign Periods, 1600–1911

CHINA (LATE MING AND THE QING)		KOREA (LATE CHOSŎN)	
REGNAL TITLE	PERIOD	REGNAL TITLE	PERIOD
*Wanli	1573–1620	Kwanghaegun	1608–23
Tianming	1616–26		
*Taichang	1620–21	Injo	1623–49
*Tianqi	1621–27		
Tiancong	1627–35		
*Chongzhen	1628–44	Hyojong	1649–59
Chongde	1636–43		
Shunzhi	1644–61	Hyŏngjong	1659–74
Kangxi	1662–1722	Sukchong	1674–1720
Yongzheng	1723–35	Gyŏngjong	1720–24
Qianlong	1736–95	Yŏngjo	1724–76
Jiaqing	1796–1820	Chŏngjo	1776–1800
Daoguang	1821–50	Sunjo	1800–1834
Xianfeng	1851–61	Hŏnjong	1834–49
Tongzhi	1862–74	Ch'ŏlchong	1849–63
Guangxu	1875–1908	Kojong	1863–1907
Xuantong	1909–11	Sunjong	1907–10

* The Chinese regnal titles marked by an asterisk are those of the Ming Dynasty.

REMAKING THE CHINESE EMPIRE

Introduction

Day dawned on April 25, 1644, in the seventeenth year of the reign of the Chong-zhen emperor of the Ming Dynasty of China. As the first rays of the sun struck the walls of the Forbidden City in Beijing, a large group of rebels stormed the gates. Right before the rebels swarmed the imperial halls, the emperor managed to climb up an artificial hill behind the palace and hang himself from a tree. His loyal servant, a eunuch who had cared for the desperate thirty-three-year-old emperor since the latter's birth, hanged himself from another tree. The Ming Dynasty, or the Great Ming, which had governed China for 277 years, came to a sudden end.

The Ming's unexpected demise put one of its generals, Wu Sangui (1612–78), who was fighting on the front lines of an unrelated conflict about 190 miles east of Beijing, in an awkward position. General Wu was defending Shanhai Pass, a strategic military outpost of the Great Wall connecting inner China with Man-churia, in the war with the Qing, a regime founded in 1616 by the nomadic Manchus in Manchuria. The war had lasted for almost three decades, during which the Manchus had decisively defeated the Ming troops in Manchuria, sub-ordinated neighboring Mongol tribes, and conquered the Chosŏn Dynasty of Korea, a loyal tributary state of China. Shanhai Pass became the last fortification preventing the formidable barbarians, as both Ming Chinese and Chosŏn Kore-ans regarded the Manchus, from entering inner China. As Beijing fell into the rebels' hands, General Wu lost his country overnight. In Manchuria, the Manchu emperor seized the opportunity to send his troops under the leadership of Prince

Dorgon (1612–50) to the outskirts of Shanhai Pass, where the army waited to cross the Great Wall to enter inner China. Meanwhile, the rebels in Beijing began to march toward the pass, with General Wu's father as a hostage, in order to annihilate Wu. In this life-or-death situation, Wu chose the Manchus as his allies. He opened the giant gate to allow the Manchu forces to pass through the Great Wall and help him defeat the rebels.

Among those who entered the pass along with the Manchu forces was the crown prince of Chosŏn Korea. The prince had been living with the Manchus for seven years, since 1637, when the Manchus had conquered Chosŏn and taken him and his younger brother hostage.[1] The guardians of the pass, General Wu's army, also included people of Korean origin. Among them was a young Korean officer, Ch'oe Hyo-il, who had joined General Wu's anti-Manchu fight after 1627, when the Manchus first invaded Chosŏn. Ch'oe was not to live long, but he did not die at the hands of the Manchu conquerors. On June 6, 1644, the Manchus took over Beijing without a fight. In a hall standing amid the debris of the Forbidden City, which had been burned by the rebels, Prince Dorgon accepted the capitulation of the Chinese officials of the Ming, witnessed by the Korean crown prince. Ch'oe, however, refused to prostrate himself in front of the Manchu prince, who in his mind was a barbarian. Instead, dressed in a Ming-style robe, he went to Chongzhen's tomb to mourn for the Ming—the civilized Middle Kingdom, or *Zhongguo* in Chinese. Ch'oe died near the tomb after a seven-day hunger strike. General Wu buried his body and commemorated him in an elegy.[2]

A Korean subject, Ch'oe died not only for the Chinese emperor but also for a civilization embodied by the Chinese dynasty and his homeland. Yet when he sacrificed himself, he did not realize that the Manchu regime was transforming itself by embracing the ideological, political, and cultural norms of the same civilization. More importantly, before it crossed the Great Wall in 1644, the Qing had begun to use its hierarchical relationship with Chosŏn to fashion itself as the civilized center of the world. As history unfolded, this relationship lasted for 258 years until the end of the Sino-Japanese War in 1895, and it continued to exert a strong influence over China and Korea thereafter. From the early seventeenth to the early twentieth century, the Qing used its relationship with Chosŏn as an ideological tool to consolidate its identity as the Middle Kingdom and to manage its relations with other neighboring countries and the newly conquered polities that stretched from Manchuria and the Mongol steppe to Turkestan and the Himalayas. By the time the Eurasian empire fell apart in 1911, Qing China had evolved into a multiethnic and multicultural modern state, providing a solid foundation for state building in the rest of the twentieth century. Among the factors that helped the Qing remake the Chinese empire, what stood out in particular were the politico-cultural discourse and imperial norms drawn from the

Manchu-Korean contacts. These took place within a hierarchical framework I call *Zongfan*, a term I will explain below. The microhistory of Manchu-Korean relations vividly reflects the macrohistory of China's transformation during the course of the three centuries, making Sino-Korean relations distinct from China's relations with other countries.

This book reveals the development of China from an empire into a modern state through the lens of the dynamics of Sino-Korean political relations from 1616 to 1911. It incorporates Chosŏn Korea into the historical narrative of Qing China by examining the high politics of the two countries. The book shows that the Manchu regime used its constant relations with Chosŏn to establish, legitimize, consolidate, and present its identity as the civilized center of the known world, as a cosmopolitan empire, and as a modern sovereign state. By employing a long-term historical and cross-border perspective to observe the bilateral relationship, this book casts new light on the rise and inner changes of the Chinese empire during the Qing period, the clashes between the Chinese foreign-relations system and its Western counterpart, and the formation of modern sovereign states in East Asia.

Revitalizing the Concept of *Zongfan* in the Narrative of Late Imperial China

I use the Chinese term *Zongfan*, or in some cases the English phrase "Chinese world order," rather than the oft-adopted English translation "tributary," to refer to the nature of the hierarchical relationship between late imperial China and its subordinate countries, which included Korea. I reserve the term "tributary" for related aspects of this system.[3] "Late imperial China" in this book refers to China from 1368 to 1911, namely, the Ming (1368–1644) and Qing periods following the collapse of the Yuan Dynasty (1271–1368) of the Mongol Empire. As I argue below, the Zongfan system was central to establishing the political orthodox legitimacy of China and its subordinate countries. As a key concept of Confucianism, political orthodox legitimacy (Ch., *Zhengtong*) refers to the universal ideological, moral, cultural, and social rationale behind the legitimate status of a political entity in the hierarchy of the Chinese world. In late imperial times, this legitimacy entailed "name and status" (Ch., *mingfen*) and "great unification" (Ch., *da yitong*) and found its dedicated audience in the ruling elites and Confucian scholars of Ming and Qing China, Chosŏn Korea (1392–1910), and Tokugawa Japan (1600–1868).[4]

As a politico-cultural structure, the Zongfan system is believed to have been established in the Western Zhou Dynasty (1046–771 BC). It was associated with the kinship-based feudal system (Ch., *zongfa fengjian*) of the day. This system was practiced between two sides, *Zong* and *fan*. *Zong* refers to the royal lineage of the Chinese monarch, who claimed to be the "Son of Heaven" (Ch., *tianzi*) residing in the Middle Kingdom with absolute patriarchal authority and exclusive orthodox legitimacy as the human agent of the "Mandate of Heaven" (Ch., *tianming*). *Fan* originally meant the clan(s) of the royal family who established outposts on China's borders, where the rulers' legitimacy was dependent on investiture by the Son of Heaven. The two sides of the kinship constituted the familistic hierarchy and the order of "all-under-Heaven" (Ch., *tianxia*)—the known universe to the people within this political entity.[5]

The connotation of China's periphery evolved within this feudalistic model by incorporating all countries or polities outside China into the category of *fan*. According to the ideal tenets, on a regular basis the *fan* dispatched emissaries, "ministers of ministers" (Ch., *peichen*), bearing taxes or tribute to the central court, where they would offer appropriate obedience to the Son of Heaven and receive largesse or gifts. In return, the court would not only send envoys to the *fan* to invest the rulers with legitimate titles but also protect the *fan* whenever necessary. This reciprocity was the foundation of the double policy of "serving the great" (Ch., *shida*) and "cherishing the small" (Ch., *zixiao*). The exchanges of emissaries following ritual codes dictated by the Middle Kingdom kept the Zongfan system running. This model later evolved into the basic philosophy of the foreign policy of late imperial China.[6]

In addition to being defined by its geographical distance from the central court, the *fan* could also be characterized in kinship terms as inner *fan* and outer *fan*. The inner *fan* maintained a strong blood relationship with the emperor, but the outer *fan* did not. In the case of Korea, the situation was complex. The imperial norms of the successive Chinese dynasties preferred to ascribe the beginning of Sino-Korean kinship to Jizi (K., Kija), a royal member of the Shang Dynasty (ca. 1600–1046 BC) who was believed to have been invested by the Western Zhou court with the lands of ancient Chosŏn. This legend produced an assumption of a unique cultural homogeneity that the Chinese side deeply endorsed and that helped unified Chinese dynasties see Korea as belonging within China's territorial perimeter.[7] The Han Dynasty (206 BC–AD 220) and the Tang Dynasty (618–907) invaded Korea and integrated parts of the Korean lands into China. In the 1260s the Mongol forces of the Yuan Dynasty gradually came to control the Koryŏ Dynasty of Korea (918–1392), and in the 1270s the Mongol court invested King Ch'ungnyŏl (r. 1274–1308), who married the Princess of Qi of Kublai Khan, as the consort of the imperial princess and the king of Koryŏ (K., *Puma Koryŏ kugwang*).[8] After the Ming overthrew the Yuan, it ceased practicing the Yuan's policy toward Koryŏ, which had been based on strong personal ties between the Mongol and Korean courts through state marriage.

After its establishment in 1368, the Ming followed the feudal principles of the Zhou Dynasty and the Zongfan practice of the Yuan in establishing the Zongfan system within its domain, but it had no desire to extend the system to Koryŏ. The founding father of the new dynasty claimed that Ming China would never invade Koryŏ or fourteen other neighboring countries. In 1392 a new Korean regime replaced Koryŏ and immediately sent emissaries to China to pursue imperial investiture of the kingship. Although the Ming conferred the title "Chosŏn" on the new regime, after Jizi Chosŏn, it did not endow the Korean king with investiture until 1401, when Emperor Jianwen (r. 1399–1402) invested the third king of Chosŏn (T'aejong, r. 1400–1418), formally extending the Zongfan arrangement to the kingdom. In the imperial mandate, the Ming underlined that the king should serve as a fence of the civilized kingdom and "assist China forever" (Ch., *yongfu yu Zhongguo*).[9] In 1403 Emperor Yongle (r. 1402–24) awarded the same king an official robe commensurate with the rank of first-degree prince (Ch., *qinwang*, a brother of the emperor), further integrating Chosŏn into the Ming Zongfan system.[10]

In the transition from the Yuan-Koryŏ relationship to the Ming-Chosŏn one, the Ming made a consequential shift in China's policy toward Korea: China allowed Korea independence as a foreign country in practice, but it continued to regulate the bilateral relationship with reference to Zongfan norms in the domestic feudal sense and on the ideological level. In the familistic and culturally homogeneous Zongfan context, the Ming depicted Chosŏn as an outer *fan* descending from Jizi, while Chosŏn identified itself as a "vassal" (K., *chehu*; Ch., *zhuhou*) of the Ming court and viewed their relationship in father-son and monarch-subordinate terms.[11] Simultaneously, Neo-Confucianism (K., *Chŏngju hak*), which celebrated Confucian social hierarchy, had become the ruling ideology during the Yuan Dynasty, and had lately been introduced to Korea, helping to institutionalize and stabilize this bilateral relationship.[12] After the Ming rescued Chosŏn from a Japanese invasion in the 1590s, Chosŏn became even more committed to the Ming, regarding the Ming as its "parent nation" (K., *pumo chi pang*).[13] This arrangement seemed similar to the feudalism practiced in medieval Europe and Tokugawa Japan, but as a cross-border framework it possessed features unique to the Confucianism-supported Chinese world. As part 2 of this book demonstrates, in the nineteenth century the nature of the Sino-Korean relationship built on these features confused European and Japanese diplomats, who could not find historical precedents for it within their own worlds. However, as scholars have pointed out, applying the Ming-Chosŏn hierarchical relationship to Sino-Korean contacts or China's foreign relations before 1400 would be ahistorical.[14]

The Qing inherited the Ming Zongfan mechanism in its contacts with Chosŏn, but the Manchus' kinship relations with Mongol tribes complicated the outer *fan* spectrum of the empire. This point is illustrated by the multilayered nature of the outer *fan* and the varied usage of the term in Qing political discourse, particularly in referring to political entities within the Qing pilgrimage system (Ch., *chaojin*) and to countries in Southeast Asia, such as Siam (Thailand).[15] The Manchu court nevertheless understood Chosŏn and other subordinate entities as members of the Qing-centric family, in which the position of these entities was similar or even equal to that of their Mongol counterparts.[16] As the Ministry of Rites (Ch., Libu) described it to the Qianlong emperor in 1768 in the context of investing the Korean king's grandson as the successor to the throne, "The outer *fan* are the same as Zongfan in terms of their relations with the central court" (Ch., Waifan zhi yu zongfan, shi shu xiangtong). Similarly, in 1790 the Qianlong emperor awarded the Vietnamese king, Nguyễn Huệ (r. 1788–92), a golden leather belt that only Zongfan of the royal family could use.[17] The term "Zongfan" aptly encapsulates the relationship between the center/patriarch and the periphery/family members during the Qing period, and for this reason I have revitalized it in this book.

Reinterpreting the Rise of the Modern Chinese State through the Lens of Qing-Chosŏn Relations

The involvement of Chosŏn in the Ming-Qing war led to two fierce Manchu invasions of the country in 1627 and 1636. After conquering Chosŏn in early 1637, the Qing established a Zongfan relationship with it by replacing the Ming in the patriarchal position. Scholars have widely regarded Sino-Korean relations in China's late imperial period as the quintessential manifestation of the Sino-centric order.[18] Some scholars have tended to attribute the uniqueness of the relationship to the parties' shared Confucian culture, especially Neo-Confucianism, while others have preferred to emphasize China's political or military influence or control in the hegemonic sense.[19] This book embraces the cultural perspective, but it simultaneously underlines the significant effect that the Manchu use of violence had on the establishment and maintenance of Qing-Chosŏn ties in the early seventeenth century. More importantly, I avoid enshrining the Qing-Chosŏn relationship in the pantheon of Chinese narratives of Sino-Korean relations since the Western Zhou, and I refrain from conflating the Qing-Chosŏn relationship with that between the Ming and Chosŏn. Rather, I explore the unique and crucial role of these bonds in providing the Qing with the political, intellectual, and ideological sources with which it reconstructed itself and the Chinese empire and eventually gave birth to a modern Chinese state.

A key term in analyzing the Sinocentric hierarchical arrangement between Qing China and other countries imagined in Qing imperial discourse is *yi*. Like so many abstract terms in Chinese (or indeed any language), its meaning varies according to context, but I have generally translated it as "barbarians." As the following chapters show, *yi*, which was often used to describe outsiders in Sinoforeign contacts, did not necessarily carry a pejorative connotation. I also demonstrate a change in the meaning of *yi* from the perspective of the Manchu regime. The story of the Qing-Chosŏn relationship unfolds within the broader process of the Qing's efforts to meet the unprecedented challenge of proving its orthodox legitimacy in the politico-cultural setting of the "civilized vs. barbarian distinction" (Ch., *Hua–Yi zhi bian*; K., *Hwa–I ŭi chai*).[20] It was against the background of this civilized–barbarian dichotomy that the Korean warrior Ch'oi sacrificed himself in Manchu-occupied Beijing, and it was in light of this distinction that his homeland strengthened its identity as "Little China" (K., So Chunghwa) in the post-Ming era, while the Qing positioned itself within the pedigree of the Middle Kingdom as the civilized center and the "Heavenly Dynasty" (Ch., *tianchao*).

The establishment of the Qing-Chosŏn Zongfan relationship in 1637 was a watershed event in the history of the Qing's prodigious enterprise of redefining itself and remaking the Chinese world. Scholars have commonly dated the Ming-Qing transition to the Manchu occupation of Beijing in 1644, but the Manchu regime in fact had initiated its bid for status as the Middle Kingdom at least a decade earlier, by employing the politico-cultural discourse embedded in the Zongfan structure. After 1637, the Qing progressively converted Chosŏn into a prototypical "outer subordinate," known as *waifan* (outer *fan*) or *shuguo* (subordinate country) in the Chinese language and *tulergi gurun* (outer country) or *harangga gurun* (subordinate country) in the Manchu language. Very significantly, the Qing imperial terms abruptly reversed the Manchu-Korean hierarchical arrangement in the Ming period by portraying Chosŏn as a country of barbarians on the periphery of the Qing.

In its frequent contacts with Chosŏn from 1637 to 1643, the Qing strengthened the new bilateral political arrangement and developed a mature model for managing its relations with other newly conquered or subordinated entities. I call this model the "Chosŏn model" (Ch., *Chaoxian shili*, lit. "Korean cases/examples"). As part 1 explains, the model constituted a pattern by which a country or a political entity could follow Chosŏn into the Qing-centric Zongfan system primarily by receiving imperial investitures from the Qing, adopting the regnal titles and calendar of the Qing, and sending emissaries and tribute to the Qing on a regular basis. The idea behind this model was to encourage outlying regions to embrace the Qing as the civilized center of the world and to affirm its supreme political and cultural position. After 1644, as the Qing continued its conquest of inner China by marching west and southwest, it used the Chosŏn model as a handy soft-power weapon to manage its political relations with other entities and to consolidate its new identification as the center of all-under-Heaven.

The Qing-Chosŏn hierarchy was far more than just the final chapter in the long Sino-Korean Zongfan history. Rather, it buttressed the rationale of the entire Zongfan system by keeping the periphery of the Chinese empire informed and regulated while the Manchu regime controlled and remade the empire at the core. The Qing's dynamic relations with its first Confucian outer *fan*—Chosŏn—played a vital role in establishing, institutionalizing, and nourishing the entire Qing-centric system of foreign relations. By the end of the eighteenth century, the Qing had constructed a new imperial order within and beyond its Eurasian empire. It had simultaneously labeled Britain and other European states "countries of barbarians" and posited them on the periphery of China. These states, however, changed their status vis-à-vis China through gunboat diplomacy and treaties in the nineteenth century, when they encountered the Chinese world through such outer *fan* as Annam (Vietnam), Ryukyu, and Chosŏn. The introduction, translation, and dissemination of international law in the Chinese world put China, China's outer *fan*, and the European states on an equal footing in terms of their state sovereignty. Nevertheless, the relationship between Qing China and its outer *fan* remained unchanged until the very end of the nineteenth century in that they still needed each other to acquire mutually constitutive and mutually defined orthodox legitimacy in their own world.

What confused the Western states in their contacts with the outer *fan* of China in the late nineteenth century was the nebulous nature of the Zongfan mechanism that constantly shunted them into perplexing negotiations with Beijing, the only place where diplomacy with outsiders could be conducted in accordance with Zongfan conventions. The disputes emerging at the periphery of China were thus transferred to the center of the empire, where they converged as an accumulative force to trigger certain reforms within China that in turn spread to and deeply influenced the periphery. Although this model may seem similar to contemporary relationships between European powers and their overseas colonies, it had a fundamentally different structure, as later sections and chapters will elaborate. The most typical case among the manifold and interwoven disputes regarding this mechanism arose in Chosŏn Korea.

The political and diplomatic conundrum of the international status of Chosŏn led the Qing and Chosŏn into legal quagmires and prompted both sides to modify their time-honored relations in the context of both the inner and the outer dual networks, as chapters 5 and 6 explain. But the various adjustments made to the relationship on both sides in the chaotic decade of the 1880s kept the Zongfan fundamentals untouched, as neither side could overcome the ideological dilemma caused by their mutually constitutive legitimacy at the level of high politics in the Confucian world. This double bind meant that colonizing Chosŏn was not an option for China in the turbulent period before the outbreak of the Sino-Japanese War in 1894. The growing controversy between China, Korea, Japan, and Western states finally resulted in the termination of the Sino-Korean Zongfan relationship in 1895. Accordingly, the cosmopolitan Chinese empire withdrew its political and cultural reach from its subordinate countries and became identical with the Chinese state defined by the norms of international law. After the war, China and Korea negotiated a new treaty for an equal state-to-state relationship, but the new arrangement lasted only a few years before both the Chosŏn Dynasty and the Qing Dynasty ceased to exist in 1910 and 1911, respectively. This book describes the trajectory of this varied relationship and shows its significance for the development of modern China and East Asia.

Revisiting the Chinese Empire under the Qing

This book defines the Qing as an empire and as a Chinese empire. As I explain below, this empire included Chosŏn in a politico-cultural sense. The term "empire" as a European concept that was always traced back to the Romans did not exist in the Chinese political lexicon until 1895, when the Sino-Japanese Treaty of Shimonoseki addressed the Qing as the "Great Qing Empire" in Chinese characters (*Da Qing diguo*), as a counterpart to the "Great Japanese Empire" (*Dai Nippon teikoku*).[21] None of the ruling dynasties before the end of the Qing ever claimed to hold an empire, either in Chinese or, when the ruling house was not Han Chinese, in any other language. Even nowadays, describing a Chinese dynasty as an empire remains rare among historians in China. Nevertheless, if we define an empire broadly as a political entity in which different peoples are governed differently, Chinese history from 221 BC, when the Qin Dynasty (221–207 BC) unified China as a multiethnic polity, to the present is clearly a history of empires.[22] In this book, the Chinese empire (Ch., *Zhonghua diguo*) refers to a multiethnic and multicultural polity in which the Middle Kingdom represented the political and cultural core against the background of the civilized–barbarian distinction and for which the concepts of "Mandate of Heaven" and "all-under-Heaven" served as constitutional ideologies to establish its political orthodox legitimacy and Confucian orthodox legitimacy (Ch., *daotong*). This definition may not fit all the dynasties that claimed the name of the Middle Kingdom, because, as R. Bin Wong observes, "the ideas and institutions of this empire were neither constant over time nor uniform through space."[23] But it applies to the dynasties in Chinese history such as the Tang, the Northern and Southern Song (960–1279), the Liao (907–1125), the Xixia (1038–1227), the Jin (1115–1234), the Yuan, the Ming, and the Qing.

The Manchu ethnicity of the imperial house was not a barrier to the Qing's presentation of itself as a Chinese empire, in particular after 1644, when the term "Chinese" (Ch., *Zhongguo ren*) took on a multiethnic character. The Qing had presented itself as a Chinese empire as early as 1689 in the Treaty of Nerchinsk with Russia. The original treaty text, written in Latin by the French Jesuit Jean-François Gerbillon (1654–1707), who was serving the Manchu court, called the Qing *Sinicum Imperium* (Chinese Empire) as a counterpart to *Ruthenicum Imperium* (Russian Empire). The French version of the treaty rendered the term as *l'Empire de la Chine* (Empire of China) as a counterpart to *l'Empire de Moscovie* (Empire of Muscovy).[24] In the Manchu translation of the treaty, the Qing court used the term *Dulimbai gurun* to define itself as China/Zhongguo; this term is equivalent to "Chinese Empire" in the other versions of the text.[25]

When "Chinese" became a multiethnic descriptor, the Qing also became the representative of Chinese culture, in particular the Confucianism that lay at the core of imperial political discourse. In 1712 Emperor Kangxi instructed the Manchu official Tulišen (1667–1740), an envoy to the Turgūt Mongols in Russia, that if the "khan of Russia" (Ma., *Cagan han*) asked what was esteemed in China, Tulišen should respond that "our country takes fidelity, filial piety, benevolence, justice, and sincerity as fundamentals."[26] All of these concepts came from Confucianism, not from Manchu ideologies. After all, it was this Confucian identity and politico-cultural discourse informed by Confucianism, not the Qing's Manchu characteristics or its realpolitik practiced along the newly conquered frontiers in Inner Asia, that determined the Qing's political orthodox legitimacy as the Middle Kingdom and enabled it to obtain and justify Confucian orthodox legitimacy. This Confucian identity on the state level later helped the Qing display its Chineseness and win strong support from Han Chinese scholars, who assisted the dynasty in weathering the storm of anti-Manchu rebellions in the nineteenth century. This book broadly defines "Chineseness" as the state of being the legitimate Middle Kingdom, thus referring to statecraft, not ethnicity.

I interpret the Chinese empire under the Qing in two dimensions: the territorial empire and the politico-cultural empire. The territorial Chinese empire was equal to the Great Qing, composed primarily of the Manchu court, the inner provinces (Ch., *zhisheng*, "directly controlled provinces"), and the first group of outer *fan*, which were under the management of the central institution of *Lifan yuan*. These outer *fan* included regions and groups such as the Cahar Mongols, Tibet, and Mongol and Muslim tribes in Xinjiang. The Chinese name *Lifan yuan* means "the ministry of managing the affairs of the *fan*," and it differs from the

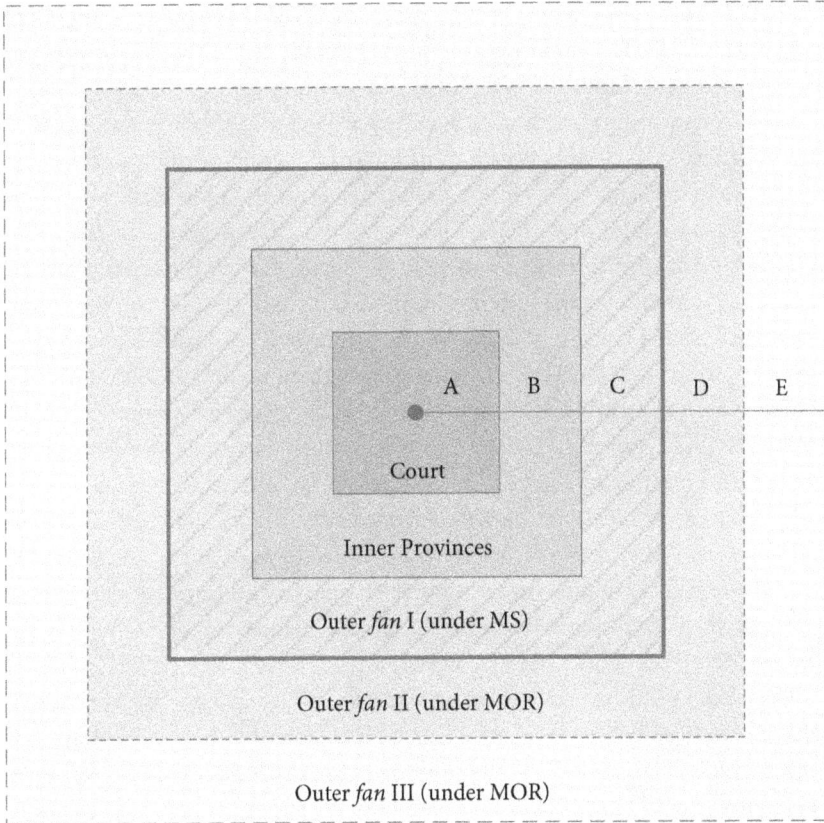

FIGURE I.1. The structure of the Chinese empire during the Qing. *A* = the court; *B* = inner provinces; *C* = outer *fan* under the Mongolian Superintendency (MS); *D* = outer *fan* under the Ministry of Rites (MOR), primarily Chosŏn, Ryukyu, and Annam; *E* = Western countries listed by the Qing as outer *fan*; *AB* = inner China, or China proper; *ABC* = the Great Qing, or the territorial Chinese empire; *ABCD* = the politico-cultural Chinese empire; *ABCDE* = all-under-Heaven.

organization's Manchu name, *Tulergi golo be dasara jurgan*, which means "the institution in charge of the outer provinces." Scholars have generally translated it as "Court of Colonial Affairs" or "Mongolian Superintendency." This book adopts the latter rendering. The politico-cultural Chinese empire encompassed not only these political entities but also the second group of outer *fan*, whose contacts with China took place via the Ministry of Rites and whose shared characteristic was their identification of the Son of Heaven in China as the highest sovereign in the world (see figure I.1).

Three key issues in the relationship between China and its outer *fan* within the politico-cultural Chinese empire invite elaboration: sovereignty, borders, and subjects. These issues were woven together in imperial times by the cosmopolitan idea of all-under-Heaven and were critically questioned within the context of the nation-state order of the late nineteenth and twentieth centuries. China, or Zhongguo, had historically always been mutually defined by its relations with the countries on its periphery—that is, by a combination of the country's own perception of itself and the devotion of its neighbors to Chinese civilization. The nebulous dual nature of China's identity posed a challenge to Chinese scholars who sought to define China anew in the late nineteenth and early twentieth centuries by comparing it to European states. These scholars could not find an established and consistent name for their homeland in history. For example, Huang Zunxian (1848–1905), a distinguished diplomat and scholar, reviewed the conventional civilized–barbarian discourse and preferred to call China the "central civilized country" (Ch., *Huaxia*). In his treatise exploring the reasons for China's weakness, Liang Qichao (1873–1929), an intellectual leader of China's modernization, pointed out that for a long time the Chinese had seen no difference between "state" and "all-under-Heaven" or between "state" and "court."[27] Huang's and Liang's arguments reflected the cosmopolitan nature of the Chinese world, in which sovereignty, borders, and subjects manifested themselves in ways distinct from those of its Western counterpart.

The nature of the sovereignty of an outer *fan* in the Chinese world was twofold: it was fully independent in terms of the territorial Chinese empire but fully dependent in relation to the politico-cultural Chinese empire. An outer *fan* enjoyed the right of independence, that is, autonomy or self-rule—*zizhu* in Chinese—within its boundaries. As Jean-Baptiste Grosier (1743–1823) in the 1780s and George N. Curzon (1859–1925) in the 1890s observed, the king of Chosŏn was an independent and supreme sovereign in his own lands.[28] The kings of the Nguyễn Dynasty (1802–1945) of Vietnam went even further, claiming to be "emperors" and calling Vietnam the "Middle Kingdom" in the first half of the nineteenth century.[29] The kingship of the *fan*, however, was ultimately subjugated to the emperorship of China. As demonstrated by Emperor Qianlong's deposition of the king of Vietnam, Lê Duy Kỳ (1765–93), and his investment of a new king in 1789, the emperor possessed absolute patriarchal power over the kings. This was particularly true for the Confucian kingship of Chosŏn.[30] What determined this relationship was not China's military power or geopolitical gravity or its "suzerainty," as Western and Japanese diplomats understood it in the nineteenth century, but the mutually constitutive legitimacy of each side of the bilateral arrangement that was undergirded by Zongfan tenets and Confucian ethos. As a consequence, in the 1830s and the 1870s, the king of Chosŏn refused to negotiate with Western representatives on the grounds that "subordinates of a *fan* have no right to conduct diplomacy" (Ch., *fanchen wu waijiao*).[31]

Vietnam adhered to the same ideology until the early 1880s.[32] Within this system, a Korean king did not have his own regnal title during his lifetime but gained a posthumous title or temple name, which is why I tend to refer to Korean kings as, simply, "the king," or to use their names ("Yi Chong," for example) rather than their temple names ("Injo," Yi Chong's temple name). Although the awarding of temple names to the kings could suggest a portrayal of Korea as independent of China in an abstract sense and in an intellectual sense, in practice China's patriarchal and divine imperial power was always real and effective.[33]

The differences between peoples on either side of the borders that separated Qing China and its outer *fan* were clear, but these distinctions were not translated into the language of nation-states, as illustrated by the Qing's cartographic survey in the Kangxi period and the Qing's juridical negotiations with Annam and Chosŏn over legal cases.[34] The territorial border between China and the outer *fan* could be diluted and blurred by the shared ideology of all-under-Heaven within the Zongfan framework. In this cultural context, the Qing court treated *fan* such as Chosŏn as a part—even an indispensable part—of the "imperial dynasty" (Ch., *huangchao*) or the "Heavenly Dynasty." For the most part, scholars do not consider countries such as Chosŏn to have been components of the Chinese empire during the Qing. This view results from the dissemination of nationalist historiography in East Asia since the late nineteenth century and cleaves closely to a territorial definition of the Chinese empire. The Chinese empire as a politico-cultural unit, however, encompassed its outer *fan* beyond China's borders, where China's centrality was further constructed by local manifestations of the divine authority of the Chinese sovereign. Believing that all lands of the outer *fan* were under his rule in this sense, Emperor Yongzheng demarcated a new border with Annam in 1727 that allowed Annam to extend its territory 12.45 miles (40 Chinese *li*) farther into China in order to end the territorial disputes between the two sides.

Chosŏn never ceased trying to redraw its borders, as reflected in its prolonged negotiations with China over border demarcation in the Tumen River area from the 1710s to the 1880s, yet the Korean court had endorsed the Chinese imperial discourse of all-under-Heaven since the Ming period.[35] In 1593, for example, the king of Chosŏn (Sŏnjo, r. 1567–1608) claimed that Chosŏn was a vassal (K., *chehu*) of China and had been regarded by the Chinese dynasties as an "inner subordinate" (K., *naebok*; Ch., *neifu*) since Jizi. The king further emphasized that Chosŏn "is actually China's land and China lets our country manage it."[36] In the 1730s the Qing historians in *History of the Ming* commented that "Chosŏn was the Ming's subordinate country, but it was not different from an inner part of China [Ch., *yunei*]."[37] The position of Chosŏn as part of the Chinese empire remained unchanged during the Qing in terms of imperial norms. In 1784 and 1788,

Emperor Qianlong noted that Korea was almost the peer of the Qing's "inner subordinates."[38] In the rituals that marked imperial edicts, the Qing imperial ritual code made it clear that the local officials of Chosŏn should perform the same rituals as did "those in directly controlled provinces" (Ch., *ru zhisheng zhi yi*).[39]

Another indicator of Chosŏn's position was the annual calendar of the Qing (Ch., *Shixian li* or *Shixian shu*; Ma., *Erin forgon i ton i bithe*), issued every year by the Imperial Astronomical Bureau (Ch., Qintian jian; Ma., Abka be ginggulere yamun), which Korean emissaries had to retrieve from Beijing. The calendar included charts of the sunrise and sunset times and charts of the solar terms in "each province" (Ch., *gesheng*; Ma., *yaya golo*) and "each Mongol and Muslim tribe" (Ch., *ge menggu huibu*; Ma., *geren monggo be, hoise i aiman*) under Qing jurisdiction. From 1645, when the Qing inaugurated the calendar, Chosŏn was included in the list of inner provinces such as Shanxi and Shandong and later showed up alongside Mukden, Nerchinsk (Ma., Nibcu), Sanxing (Ma., Ilan hala), Bodune (Ma., Bedune), Heilongjiang (Ma., Sahaliyan ula), and Jilin. Following Chosŏn, Annam was added to the lists in 1789 and Ryukyu in 1810.[40] As Johan Elverskog has pointed out, "A fundamental role of the emperor was to control the flow of time properly by creating the calendar and propitiating its cultural force through ritual and ceremony."[41] Many maps of the known world produced by the cartographers of the Qing and Chosŏn in the eighteenth century, such as the *Huangyu quanlan tu* (Map of a complete view of the imperial lands, known as the *Kangxi Atlas*), also presented and substantiated this cosmopolitan ideology by including Chosŏn as part of the empire.[42] The Qing thus subtly but unmistakably incorporated the group of outer *fan* into the Chinese empire.

Cosmopolitan ideas strongly shaped the Qing's understanding of the subjects within and beyond its borders, even after international law reached China in the 1860s. In 1643, for instance, the Qing emphasized to Chosŏn that "the two countries have become one family" (Ch., *liangguo yijia*) and that "the people of Chosŏn are also ours."[43] In 1882, when the Chinese governors in Manchuria reported to Beijing that many poor Korean peasants had crossed the border to cultivate Chinese lands, Emperor Guangxu noted, "In the eyes of the local officials, there is certainly a line between them and us [Ch., *bici zhi fen*], but in the eyes of the court, there is originally no difference between the inside and the outside [Ch., *neiwai zhi bie*]."[44] A group of Korean students learning Western technologies in Tianjin in 1882 were also treated by Chinese officials as "loyal children of the Heavenly Dynasty" (Ch., *tianchao zhi chizi*) and were granted free tuition.[45] In 1886 the Guangxu emperor emphasized that Chosŏn was close to Beijing and had "no particular difference from other provinces in the inner land" (Ch., *you yu neidi xingsheng wuyi*).[46] For Qing China, Chosŏn was equal to a "domestic subordinate" (Ch., *neichen*), which might have been the impetus behind the proposals made by a large number of Chinese officials in the 1880s to convert Chosŏn into "prefectures and counties" of China—an approach I call "provincialization"—in order to save "our Chosŏn" (Ch., *wo Chaoxian*).

Within the Zongfan framework, these factors—sovereignty, borders, and subjects—were not complex issues between Qing China and its outer *fan*. But when international law and the norms embedded in it, such as sovereignty and suzerainty, reached East Asia in the 1860s and acted as a catalyst for the independence (Ch., *duli*; K., *t'ŭngnip*; J., *dokuritsu*) of the outer *fan*, these issues became controversial and began to be reconsidered and redefined in accordance with the imported legal terms in both China and its outer *fan*. Nevertheless, as part 2 of this book shows, the politico-cultural Chinese empire connecting the Middle Kingdom and its outer *fan* remained unchanged at that time, because international law could not endow the two sides with the necessary political orthodox legitimacy.

What drew China into the wars with France in Vietnam in 1883 and with Japan in Chosŏn in 1894, therefore, was not the territorial Chinese empire but the politico-cultural one. Similarly, what Japan defeated in 1895 was the tangible former rather than the invisible latter. In this regard, this book reveals the complexity of the dual presentation of the Chinese empire under the Qing, in particular in the late nineteenth century, when China and Korea tried to deliver a legal definition of their relationship to Japan and Western states. After 1895 the politico-cultural empire began to draw back from its extended frontier in its subordinate countries to China's geographical borders, eventually becoming identical to the territorial empire. Through the decline of the politico-cultural empire emerged a modern Chinese state.

In his study of empires and states, Frederick Cooper argued that "France only became a nation-state in 1962, when it gave up the last vital element of its imperial structure, Algeria."[47] Although China is not France and Korea is not Algeria, Korea had served for centuries as a key part of the politico-cultural Chinese empire, and under the Qing it acted as an "outlying province" of the empire in the Qing imperial norms.[48] It is thus not an exaggeration to say that China became a modern nation-state only once it recognized the absolute independence and sovereignty of the Korean state after World War II, especially after the Korean War in the 1950s. It was also in the 1950s that the People's Republic of China officially endorsed the independence of the Mongolian People's Republic, which had been part of the Chinese empire under the Qing, while at the same time integrating the northwestern region of the empire—Xinjiang and Tibet—into the territory of New China. At that point, the Korean side finally accomplished the prolonged process of decentering China and became equal to its Chinese counterpart.[49] Within this conceptual framework, this book traces the historical process through which both China and Korea detached themselves from the Chinese empire and moved toward modern state building in the postimperial era.

Renegotiating Qing Imperialism

Scholars of China and East Asia have commonly identified imperialism (Ch., *Diguo zhuyi*) with the West or Japan. As a concept, imperialism refers to a system that was underpinned by a series of aggressive political, economic, or diplomatic policies carried out by Western and Japanese powers against other states. Through these policies, the imperial powers attempted to reap the highest possible profits from the countries they subjugated via unequal treaties, while competing with each other for primacy. Imperialism is thus seen as a holdover of Western capitalism (Ch., *Ziben zhuyi*) and colonialism (Ch., *Zhimin zhuyi*) that reached the Chinese world aggressively after 1800.[50] This interpretation also reflects a phenomenon that scholars have called the "great divergence" between China and the West in world economic history.[51] The Sino-Japanese War of 1894–95 marks the rise of imperialism in East Asia, a regime under which Qing China, too, suffered heavily. Historical narratives along these lines have promoted a Chinese victim mentality and nourished Chinese nationalism in the twentieth century, in particular after the Leninist definition of imperialism as the highest stage of capitalism became popular in scholarship.[52]

Since the second half of the twentieth century, two groups of scholars have questioned and complicated this received wisdom. The first group comprises students of the High Qing (that is, from the Kangxi to the Qianlong period in the seventeenth and eighteenth centuries), who have promulgated the paradigm of "New Qing history" that is characterized by an Inner Asian and ethnic approach to interpreting the multiethnic and multicultural Qing.[53] The second group consists of students of Sino-Korean relations who have depicted Qing China's policy toward Chosŏn in the late nineteenth century as imperialism. The approach of the first group might be called "High Qing imperialism," and that of the second group "Late Qing imperialism."

The High Qing imperialism school describes the High Qing as an institutional agent of imperialism, a system of coercive instruments aimed at extending the core area of the empire and keeping the empire functioning. This Qing imperialism manifested itself in geopolitical and global competitions between the Qing, the Mongol khanates and Muslim tribes in Inner Asia, the indigenous and cross-border tribes in southwestern China, the Russian Empire, and the British Empire.[54] Chinese and European colonialism and capitalism found their place in these intense competitions.[55] What fundamentally supports this argument of Qing imperialism is the fact of the Qing's territorial expansion by force, followed by the political and cultural hegemony that it introduced to the newly conquered borderlands. However, if the High Qing was an agent of imperialism, all Chinese regimes that extended China's borders would fall into the same category, including the Han, the Tang, the Yuan, the Ming, and the People's Republic of China. In this sense, the thesis of High Qing imperialism risks detaching its interpretations of the Qing Empire from the pre-Qing Chinese historical context and being construed as a complement to Eurocentric narratives of imperialism in the broader context.

The argument of Late Qing imperialism, by contrast, distinguishes the Qing from its predecessors in Chinese history by asserting that the Late Qing exercised imperialism through coercive means characterized by power politics and economic expansion in the late nineteenth century. The leading proponents of this approach concede that the Late Qing was a victim of Western and Japanese imperialism but claim that it simultaneously practiced its own imperialism over weaker countries. This overseas imperialism fits the general definition that historians have drawn from the history of the Roman Empire: "an unequal power relationship between two states in which the dominant state exercises various forms of control, often forcibly, over the weaker state."[56] Whereas the theory of High Qing imperialism does not take the Manchu conquest of Chosŏn in 1637 into consideration and leaves Chosŏn largely off the list of victims of that imperialism, Chosŏn is typically the only identified victim of Late Qing imperialism, which was embodied by activities such as sending troops to Chosŏn and obtaining treaty ports and settlements through unequal treaties that granted the Chinese extraterritoriality. The concept of "informal empire," originally coined to refer to the powerful economic expansion of the British Empire in the nineteenth century, provides this argument with further intellectual support.[57] In retrospect, the argument of Late Qing imperialism bears a remarkable resemblance to the interpretation of China's behavior in Chosŏn put forward by Western diplomats and observers in the nineteenth century. As M. Frederick Nelson has pointed out, "Under the assumption that China had nothing but a religious and ceremonial connection with Korea, Westerners viewed her growing *de facto* control of Korea as pure and unjustified power politics directed against an independent state."[58] By likening the Qing to its Western imperial counterparts, the thesis of Late Qing imperialism homogenizes Qing China as a major participant and a powerful predator in Eurocentric global history, therefore strengthening the approach of interpreting the histories of others with reference to that of the West instead of contextualizing these histories in their local milieus. As this book shows, the Qing activities in Korea in the late nineteenth century were a manifestation not of imperialism, but of Zongfan empiricism.

The argument of Qing imperialism, including both High Qing imperialism and Late Qing imperialism, serves as a normative tool for interpreting the constant changes undergone by China in its various forms. In order to explain those changes, this book renegotiates Qing imperialism by presenting the Qing as an empire that used ideological tools—the Chosŏn model and a set of imperial

norms embodied by the model—to establish and consolidate its political authority and cultural superiority in the Chinese world. What I call "Zongfanism" in this
book can provide us with a different perspective for observing the rise and fall
of the Eurasian Chinese empire under the Qing Dynasty and the rise of modern
sovereign states in China and its neighboring countries. Zongfanism refers to a
Chinese system of political and diplomatic communication conducted between,
on the one hand, a political entity that culturally identified itself as the exclusive
civilized center of the world, and, on the other hand, the political entities on its
periphery that the center considered less civilized or even barbarian. The sovereign of the center possessed absolute patriarchal authority over the monarchs
of the subordinate entities, while the two sides enjoyed mutually constitutive
legitimacy informed by their shared politico-cultural norms.

Zongfanism transcends the entrenched divide between premodern and modern Chinese history. Historians have generally identified the Opium War of
1839–42 as the twilight of premodern China and the dawn of modern China.
Along these lines, the mainstream narrative of Qing China holds that the premodern system of China's foreign relations was incompatible with the modern
treaty system, with which it was finally replaced. The principal problem with
this paradigm lies not in its Eurocentrism per se (indeed, "modern" is a crite-
rion rooted in European history) but rather in its neglect of constant factors
within China's foreign policy that bridged the premodern and modern periods
without conspicuous changes. In other words, the factors that historians have
widely identified as having led to the "stagnation" of China before it encountered
the industrialized West constitute the very key to understanding late imperial
China.[59] The Chinese empire lived with its indigenous norms, not imported ones.

The Zongfan perspective does not aim to replace that of Qing imperialism,
nor can it completely account for the Qing's activities during the high tide of the
Manchu conquest in the seventeenth and eighteenth centuries from Manchuria
to the Korean peninsula and from Xinjiang to Tibet.[60] It instead aims to reveal
the crucial relationships between the construction and dissemination of imperial ideology from the center to the periphery on the one hand, and imperial
top-down statecraft in practice on the other. In the early twenty-first century,
China has begun to exploit sophisticated ideas drawn from its recent history to
preserve the legitimacy and unity of the multiethnic and multicultural Chinese
state and to manage its relations with neighboring countries and the world. In
this contemporary context, it may be helpful to examine the trajectory of changes
in the Chinese world from an inside perspective, and the following chapters seek
to do just that.

Part I

KOWTOWING TO OUR GREAT EMPEROR

1

CONQUERING CHOSŎN

The Rise of the Manchu Regime as
the Middle Kingdom, 1616–43

As the Manchu regime consolidated its power in Manchuria between the late 1610s and the early 1640s, it reshaped the perceptions of other polities and eradicated its longstanding barbarian image. The regime derived its political and cultural resources in large part from its relations with Chosŏn, which validated and reinforced the Manchu dynasty's position as the Middle Kingdom within the newly established multistate hierarchical system. In this process, the Manchus appropriated the Ming's Zongfan discourse to designate other political entities as barbarians, initiating a prolonged process that I call the barbarianization of others. By crossing the Great Wall in 1644, the Manchu regime had fundamentally reconceptualized its own identity and position in the Chinese world.

Barbarians, Rebellions, and Wars

The Jurchen Uprising in Manchuria

On February 17, 1616, the lunar New Year and the first day of the Forty-Fourth Year of Wanli of the Ming Dynasty, a number of high-ranking Chinese officials assembled at the Meridian Gate of the Forbidden City with tributary emissaries from Chosŏn and China's other outer *fan*. They waited to enter the imperial hall to present the emperor with their congratulations on the New Year. Finally, realizing the emperor had no desire to grant them an audience, the officials and emissaries carried out their ceremonies in front of the gate.[1] This scene was not surprising, as the emperor had long been uninterested in such ceremonies. Many high-ranking officials in Beijing had not seen the hermit-like Son of Heaven for almost thirty years.[2] The Middle Kingdom and its lethargic human agent seemed to have fallen asleep.

The day was significant, however, in Hetuala, a small Manchurian town about seven hundred miles northeast of Beijing, where a tribe called the Jianzhou Jurchens announced the establishment of its own country under the leadership of Nurhaci (1559–1626; r. 1616–26). Proclaiming himself the "brilliant khan caring for all countries/peoples" (Ma., *abka geren gurun be ujikini seme sindaha genggiyen han*), Nurhaci accepted the congratulations of Jurchen and Mongol officials and generals, took the regnal title of Tianming ("mandate of Heaven"; Ma., *Abkai fulingga*), and named his country Houjin ("the later Jin").[3] He thus defined his regime as the successor to the Jin Dynasty established by the Jurchen ancestors.[4]

Nurhaci's political ambitions extended far beyond unifying the local tribes. In May 1618 he attacked the Ming forces after announcing the "Seven Grievances" (Ma., Nadan amba koro; Ch., Qi dahen). Nurhaci had visited Beijing three times to present tribute and had been appointed by the Ming court to govern the Jianzhou Jurchens, whom the Ming considered "northeastern barbarians" (Ch., *dongbei yi*).[5] In the Seven Grievances, Nurhaci identified the Jianzhou as a subordinate that had guarded the Ming's border for generations, and declared that various conflicts between his tribe, other tribes, and the Ming's local leaders had led to his rebellion.

The Ming was confident about suppressing Nurhaci. To do so it enlisted the aid of the tribe of Yehe, an old and powerful enemy of the Jurchens, as well as the support of Chosŏn. As a loyal *fan*, Chosŏn had followed the policy of "serving the great" (K., *sadae*) for more than two centuries. It regarded Nurhaci's rebellion as intolerable and its military assistance to the Ming as a "legal and moral duty" (K., *ŭibun*). Although the king, Yi Hon (Kwanghaegun), was worried that his men would be defeated, he nonetheless ordered Gen. Kang Hong-rip in early 1619 to lead thirteen thousand soldiers across the Yalu River to join forces with the Ming army in Manchuria.[6]

In the battle of Sarhū on April 17, 1619, more than six thousand Korean soldiers were killed, and General Kang surrendered to Nurhaci. Ending Chosŏn's military engagement in the war, the surrender provided Nurhaci with a golden opportunity to open an official channel of communication with the Korean sovereign. In addition to seeking a peace agreement with Chosŏn to reduce the military threat on his eastern flank, Nurhaci wanted to change his relationship with Chosŏn by identifying his newly founded regime as a state equal to Chosŏn rather than as a state of lower status, as presupposed by the longstanding framework of Jurchen-Chosŏn relations.[7] This political ambition posed a grave challenge to Chosŏn in the context of the civilized–barbarian distinction and initiated an invisible but intensive struggle of political discourse between the two sides.

Chosŏn's Role in the Jurchen-Ming War

The bilateral communications between the Jurchens and Chosŏn started with an exchange of letters. In May 1619 Nurhaci sent a captured officer to Chosŏn to present a "sovereign letter" (Ch., *guoshu*; K., *kuksŏ*) and a copy of the Seven Grievances to the king. After explaining why he fought against the "big country" (Ch., *daguo*; Ma., *amba gurun*), that is, the Ming, Nurhaci asked the king to make common cause with him against the Ming. Chosŏn had contacted Nurhaci by letter in the 1600s through a local officer in the town of Manpo on the northern border, but now Nurhaci's "barbarian letter" (K., *hosŏ*) reached the court directly and posed a thorny problem for the king.[8]

After fierce debate among officials, the king appointed Pak Yŏp, governor of P'yŏngan Province, to write back to Nurhaci, but the format of the reply, and in particular the question of how to address Nurhaci, remained a challenge. In Nurhaci's letter, the Mongolian characters of his stamp read "Emperor Tianming of the Houjin" (K., Hugŭm ch'ŏnmyŏng hwangje), which greatly shocked the king and the Border Defense Council (K., Pibyŏnsa) because they believed the Ming emperor to be the sole emperor in the known universe. It was highly likely that the characters defined Nurhaci as a "khan" in the Mongol sense, rather than as an "emperor" (Ch., *huangdi*; K., *hwangje*) in the Chinese and Korean sense. Chosŏn had always called Nurhaci "old chieftain" (K., *roch'u*), "barbarian chieftain" (K., *ich'u*), "chieftain of slaves" (K., *noch'u*), or "chieftain of thieves" (K., *chŏkch'u*), so endorsing Nurhaci's self-proclaimed imperial title was out of the question. The king, pretending he could not understand the characters on Nurhaci's seal, instructed Pak to send a letter to the "assistant general of the Jianzhou garrison" (K., *Kŏnjuwi mabŏp*; Ch., *Jianzhouwei mafa*).[9] The Border Defense Council had learned the word *mabŏp* from previous letters sent by the Jurchens and assumed that it referred to an assistant general (K., *p'ŏnbi*). In fact, it came from the Manchu word *mafa*, which means "grandfather." In addition, the letter addressed its recipient in the second person using the form of "you" (K., *chokha*) that officials who were equal to each other used among themselves, not for sovereigns.[10] Finally, the letter bore Pak's official stamp instead of the king's. In this way, the king downgraded the communication with the Houjin to a provincial level and sidestepped the sensitive issue of the political legitimacy of the Jurchen regime.

The Korean letter noted that Chosŏn and the Houjin had been subjects (K., *sin*) of the "Heavenly Dynasty" for two hundred years and suggested that Nurhaci pledge allegiance to the "Imperial Ming," an action that would also yield reconciliation between Chosŏn and Nurhaci. This strong pro-Ming stance made the Houjin bristle.[11] In his reply, calling himself *gu*, a Chinese term used only by a sovereign to refer to himself, Nurhaci inferred that the Heavenly Dynasty to which Chosŏn referred must be the "southern dynasty"—the Jurchen appellation for the Ming, which indicated that the Houjin no longer endorsed the divine position of the Ming. Nurhaci clearly asked the king to form an alliance with him and suggested that the two countries kill a white horse and a black bull to offer to Heaven and Earth and burn incense to swear an oath.[12] Nurhaci had conducted this ritual with the Yehe, Hada, Ula, and Hūifa tribes in 1597 and with the Ming in 1608 and later started wars with these entities on account of their reneging on the oath.

Chosŏn was uninterested in Nurhaci's offer, particularly in light of the Ming's potential reaction to Korean-Jurchen contacts. Ming officials such as Xu Guangqi (1562–1633), a close friend of the Italian Jesuit priest Matteo Ricci (1552–1610), suspected that Chosŏn would join the Jurchen rebellion against the Ming and considered it advisable to rein Chosŏn in. In August 1619 he proposed a new policy toward Chosŏn in a memorial to Emperor Wanli. Xu argued that Beijing should follow historical precedents set by the Zhou and Han Dynasties by sending a commissioner to Chosŏn to "supervise and protect" (Ch., *jianhu*) the country. Xu enthusiastically volunteered to take up this position, but the emperor, who had sent Chinese forces to Chosŏn to defend the country against Japanese invasions in the 1590s, did not grant his request.[13] As a matter of fact, Chosŏn was not collaborating with the Jurchens, whom it still called "barbarians" (K., *orangk'ae*), but maintaining its political and moral allegiance to Beijing would not alleviate the risk of a Jurchen attack. Under the circumstances, the king took a practical approach by tactically maintaining connections with the Houjin but confining them to the local level.

In the meantime, the outlook for the Ming-Chosŏn alliance was not sanguine. Two Ming emperors died within two months in 1620, and the new emperor, Tianqi, showed more interest in carpentry than he did in statecraft. On the battlefield, the Ming was losing more lands to the Houjin. In May 1621 the Jurchens occupied Liaoyang, a key military fortress in Manchuria, and made it the Houjin's new capital, cutting off the overland route of communications between Chosŏn and the Ming. Facing a series of dramatic changes, the king made the risky move of sending Nurhaci his first sovereign letter in October 1622 through a civil official of the Ministry of Rites in Hansŏng (today's Seoul). In the letter, he referred to Houjin as "a neighboring country" and Nurhaci as "khan of the

Houjin country" (K., *Hugŭmguk kahan*). The letter adopted the same format as letters sent to Japan in accordance with Chosŏn's policy of *kyorin*, communicating with a neighboring country.[14] By acknowledging the statehood of the Jurchen regime, the king elevated his communications with Nurhaci to the level of a sovereign addressing another sovereign.

The pragmatism of this policy called into question the king's loyalty to the Ming, which the king's nephew, Yi Chong, used to justify a bloody coup that he launched in May 1623 to dethrone the king. Assuming power as the new king (King Injo), Yi Chong blamed his uncle for failing to embrace his monarch-subordinate and father-son relationship with the Ming. He himself took a different tack: in addition to ending the exchange of messengers with Nurhaci and imposing trade sanctions on the Houjin, Yi Chong mobilized his followers to prepare for a war with the Houjin and even planned to lead an army himself to attack the Jurchens.[15] Being a usurper, Yi Chong used his fervent pro-Ming attitude to obtain the Ming investiture that legitimized his rulership. The new king also helped Mao Wenlong (1576–1629), a Ming general who had escaped to Chosŏn after the Jurchens' occupation of Liaoyang and had stationed his forces on Ka Island, close to mainland Chosŏn, carry out a guerrilla war to prevent the Jurchens from entering Shanhai Pass. Chosŏn's new policy posed a considerable military and economic threat to the Jurchens, but it did not stop the Jurchen expansion. In 1625 the Jurchens occupied Shenyang, the political heart and economic center of Manchuria, and made it their new capital. After Nurhaci died in 1626, his son Hongtaiji became the new khan with the regnal title Tiancong ("Heavenly wisdom"; Ma., *Abkai sure*) and quickly decided to invade Chosŏn.

Becoming the Elder Brother of Chosŏn: The Jin and the First Manchu Invasion

In the spring of 1627 Hongtaiji launched an attack on Chosŏn. The forces of the Jin, as the Jurchen regime now styled itself, swept into northern Chosŏn and captured P'yŏngyang within two weeks, forcing the king, who had escaped to Kanghwa Island, to sue for peace. As a precondition of withdrawal, the Jin commander, Amin (?–1640), required the king to swear an oath to Heaven to sever Chosŏn's relations with the Ming and establish an elder brother–younger brother relationship with the Jin, the latter taking on the dominant role. In Chosŏn, many Confucian officials and students pleaded with the king to stop negotiating with the barbarous invaders, kill their messengers, and fight to the death. Although the king told his subjects that the peace talks with the "Jurchen clowns" were only a stalling tactic, or a conventional "loose rein" (K., *kimi*) policy, he had no choice but to continue the negotiations.

In his letters to Hongtaiji, the king endorsed Hongtaiji's political position by addressing him as "Khan of the Country of the Jin," but he purposely selected neutral terms for the Jin and Chosŏn. While he called the Jin "your honorable country," the king referred to Chosŏn as "our country," instead of "our humble country" or "our small country," as he would say in his palace memorials to the Ming. No honorific expressions for Hongtaiji appeared at the beginning of the letter.[16] The king conveyed that Chosŏn would follow the policy of "communicating with a neighboring country" vis-à-vis the Jin and that of "serving the great country" vis-à-vis the Ming. By deliberately using the Ming regnal title "Tianqi" to express the date in his letter, the king implied that he would not betray the Ming. This act of adhering to Ming time led to a deadlock in the negotiations. The king later switched to a "notice" format for his communications, since this format did not require a regnal title. The new format helped the two sides reach an agreement regarding Chosŏn's oath.

The oath-swearing ceremony occurred at the palace on Kanghwa Island on April 18, 1627. The king burned incense and swore the oaths to Heaven after one of his officials read them aloud. Despite the king's reluctance, the substance of oaths was what Hongtaiji had demanded. The nine highest Chosŏn officials and eight high-ranking Jin officials also read their own oaths. However, the performance of these ceremonies between the king and the Jurchen officials was not mentioned in either Manchu or Korean records.[17] Another oath-swearing ceremony took place later in P'yŏngyang between Amin and a brother of the king. The P'yŏngyang oath included several additional terms imposed by the Jurchen invaders, emphasizing that the king should present gifts to the khan, host the Jin's emissaries as he did those of the Ming, and not reinforce the city walls or conduct military drills.[18] The two ceremonies ushered in a decade of peace between the two countries.

In political and ideological terms the Jurchens benefited substantially from their invasion of Chosŏn. Chosŏn officially endorsed the Jurchen regime as a country with a supreme sovereign, helping to foster the regime's political legitimacy in the geopolitical arena. With the support of Chosŏn, the "Little China" that now regarded the Jin as its elder brother, the Jin's politico-cultural self-identity changed from that of a barbarian, imposed by the discourse of the Ming-centered cosmopolitan order, to that of the civilized. Although resentment of the Jurchen "barbarians" soared in Chosŏn after the war, the Korean court was unable to escape the newly established brotherhood. Economically, too, Chosŏn yielded to the Jurchens' terms by opening markets in several towns on its northern border and paying "annual tribute" (K., *sep'ye*) to the Jurchen court.

Constructing a Jin-Centric, Quasi-Zongfan System: The Jin's New Position

The Rise of the Jin-Chosŏn Quasi-Zongfan Order

As he withdrew from Chosŏn, Hongtaiji sent the king a letter, explaining why he fought with the "southern dynasty"—the Ming—and attacked Chosŏn. He said, "The southern dynasty regards only itself as Son of Heaven and views people of other countries as inferior servants. . . . The Mandate of Heaven is truly righteous by assisting us with punishing the southern dynasty. . . . In the future, our two countries should be brothers forever and never bully others as the southern dynasty does."[19] By quoting the theory of the Mandate of Heaven, the khan challenged the Ming's centrality in the universe and justified his war with the Ming. Over the following decade, his construction of a Jin-centric, quasi-Zongfan system in the Jin's contacts with Chosŏn and other neighboring entities gradually changed the Jin's position.

In the face of serious economic difficulties brought on by the war, the Jin required Chosŏn to open markets for trade in a border city, Ŭiju. Chosŏn yielded to the Jin's pressure but agreed to hold the markets only twice a year, in the spring and the autumn, rather than three times per year, as the Jin had wished. On March 31, 1628, the Ŭiju market opened for the first time, and the Jin emissary Inggūldai (1596–1648) came to Ŭiju accompanied by eight generals and more than a thousand people. As the Ŭiju market fell short of the Jin's needs, Hongtaiji urged Chosŏn to open another one in Hoeryŏng, a northeastern border city.[20] In the midst of the shortage, the Jin relied heavily on the yearly gifts provided by Chosŏn and conveyed to Shenyang by one emissary in the spring and another in the autumn. From 1627 to 1636, the required gift comprised up to eighty-five categories of goods, but the amounts in each category kept changing to reflect the Jin's needs or Chosŏn's concerns, becoming a barometer of their relations.[21] The Korean emissaries brought commercial opportunities to Shenyang. In 1631 the Border Defense Council of Chosŏn complained to the king that "the dispatch of emissaries to Shenyang was no different from opening markets there."[22] On the other hand, the development of the market in Shenyang, like that of the markets in Ŭiju and Hoeryŏng, suffered from significant differentials in the prices of the consumer products offered by the two sides. The black cotton cloth and ginseng sold by the Koreans were expensive, whereas the animal skins and furs that the Jurchens traded were not. This difference made it difficult for the Jurchen side to turn a profit. The Jin's military hegemony could not subordinate Korean capital, which contributed to the Jin's second invasion of Chosŏn.

Given the military and economic situation, the Jin did not force Chosŏn to end its contacts with Beijing. Hongtaiji had the option of concluding a peace agreement with the Ming through which he could win the latter's political endorsement. In a memorial to Hongtaiji in 1630, Gao Hongzhong, a Han Chinese scholar serving the Jin, suggested that the Jin "follow the Chosŏn model to receive the [Ming] investiture with kingship and to use the regnal title [of the Ming] to count the date" (Ch., *bi Chaoxian shili, qingfeng wangwei, cong zhengshuo*).[23] This proposal reflected a popular perception among the Chinese about Chosŏn's exemplary tributary position in the Ming-centric world. Had the Ming agreed to negotiate for a Chosŏn-like status for the Jurchen regime, the Jin could have followed Chosŏn to become an outer *fan* of the Ming. Nevertheless, the war persisted, and the Jin moved toward a broader objective of replacing the Ming. For that purpose, the Jin started to transform its hierarchical relationship with Chosŏn.

After 1627 Chosŏn continued to embrace the centrality of the Ming in its contacts with the Jin by applying its *kyorin* policy to the Jin; this put the Jin on an equal footing with Chosŏn. The king called his emissaries to the Jin "messengers" (K., *sinsa*), not "tributary emissaries" (K., *kongsa*), as he did those dispatched to Beijing. The goods brought annually to Shenyang were "gifts" (K., *yemul*) rather than "tributes" (K., *kongmul*) like those presented to Beijing. As the king noted in 1633 to Hongtaiji, "It is the proper principle [K., *ye*; Ch., *li*] that our two countries give each other local products in communications via emissaries."[24] These terms reflected befitting modesty and suggested that Chosŏn treated the Jin as a country lower than the Ming.

In stark contrast, the Jin developed a new discourse to nourish its self-identity as a political entity superior to Chosŏn. In documents written in the Manchu language beginning in 1627, the Jin downgraded the Korean monarch from "khan of Chosŏn" (Ma., *Solgoi kan*) to "king of Chosŏn" (Ma., *Solgo i wang*, or *Coohiyan gurun i wang*).[25] With the steady rise of the Jin's military power, especially after its triumph in the battle at Dalinghe in late 1631 and early 1632, Hongtaiji enacted considerable reforms to the Jin political structure, abolishing the power-sharing system at the highest level of the court and making himself the exclusive sovereign.[26] From 1632, in his letters to the Ming and Chosŏn, Hongtaiji began to call himself "brilliant khan of the Manchu country" (Ma., *Manju gurun i sure han*) rather than "khan of the Jin country" (Ma., *Aisin gurun i han*), the title he had used before.[27] More importantly, he imitated the Ming bureaucracy by establishing a six-ministry system in Shenyang and instructing Manchu officials such as Dahai (1595–1632) to translate Chinese classics into the Manchu language.[28] From then on, the regime substantially accelerated the Sinicization of its imperial norms from the top down, a process carried out through the institution-building efforts of a group of Han Chinese officials and scholars such as Ning Wanwo (1593–1665), Fan Wencheng (1597–1666), Gao Hongzhong, and Bao Chengxian (?–1645). One of the most significant acts of these elites was to persuade Hongtaiji to produce the annals of the monarch and the regime in both the Chinese and Manchu languages.

The Chinese terms that these Han Chinese savants adopted to describe the exchanges of emissaries and diplomatic relations between the Jin and Chosŏn were crucial to revising the Jin's political identity. According to the Manchu-language records written by the Manchu scholars, the emissaries of Chosŏn (Ma., *Solho i elcin*) "arrived and delivered the local products as gifts" (Ma., *baci tucire doroi jaka benjime isinjiha*) in Shenyang. When they left, the khan "gave" (Ma., *unggihe*) or "awarded" (Ma., *šangnaha*) them and the king gifts.[29] Although these Manchu terms were largely vernacular and had no strong political meaning, their counterparts in the Chinese-language records offered a very different portrayal. The visit of the "tributary emissaries" (Ch., *gongshi*), who brought "tribute" (Ch., *gongwu*) or "local products" (Ch., *fangwu*), was described as "the coming to the court to present themselves before the sovereign" (Ch., *laichao*), suggesting that the emissaries' visit was prompted not by the Jin's formidable military might but by its outstanding merits.[30] These terms invoked a hierarchical relationship between the sovereign—an emperor in the Chinese sense—and his subjects, which in this case included Chosŏn, Vietnam, Ryukyu, other *fan* of the Ming, and the Central Asian political entities.[31] Meanwhile, the Jin applied the political and diplomatic discourse it had developed toward Chosŏn to forces and political entities that sought shelter with or surrendered to the Jin, such as Bar Baturu, Nomun Dalai, Coir Jamsu from Alakcot of Cahar, and the Ming general Kong Youde (?–1652).[32]

In 1634 Hongtaiji changed the name of Shenyang to Mukden in Manchu and Shengjing (lit. "prosperous capital") in Chinese, and the following year he instructed his people to call the country "Manzhou" (M., *Manju*; "the Manchu state"), not "Jurchen" or other names. The regime's institutional construction was thus facilitated by a clear ethnic identification, but the rationale behind this framework focused more on politico-cultural factors than on ethnic ones. In this period, Jin officials, particularly those who were Han Chinese, started to address Hongtaiji as "emperor" (Ch., *huangshang*, or *huangdi*). Some suggested that Hongtaiji perform conventional rituals established by the Han Dynasty, through which he would claim to be the Son of Heaven in the Chinese sense. More significantly, these officials invoked the principles of the civilized–barbarian distinction to brand the Ming "southern barbarians" (Ch., *manzi*) and those Chinese who surrendered to the Jin "Han Chinese barbarians" (Ch., *hanyi*), thereby appropriating and completely reversing the Ming's language regarding the center of the world.[33]

With this change in its worldview, the Manchu regime began to play the role of the exclusive institutional agent of the Mandate of Heaven, to which "all barbarians in the four quarters of the world willingly come in submission" (Ch., *siyi xianfu*). When the Ming generals Kong Youde and Geng Zhongming (1604–49) surrendered to Hongtaiji in 1633, the Jin jubilantly described the event as "people from afar willingly coming to our court for civilization" (Ch., *yuanren laigui*).[34] The euphoric adoption of this phrase demonstrated that the Manchu regime was purposely constructing its identity as the center of the world, with cultural superiority over "barbarians from afar" or on its periphery, which now included the Ming.[35] These momentous changes in the Jin's political discourse were rooted in orthodox Chinese political theory as articulated in Confucian classics, such as *Analects of Confucius* (Ch., *Lunyu*) and *Doctrine of the Mean* (Ch., *Zhongyong*), and they demonstrate the deep significance of both the Sinicization of the Manchu regime and the barbarianization of others by the regime. The use of Chinese political rhetoric of this sort was no mere imitation of the Ming's discourse to please Hongtaiji. Rather, it was aimed at achieving a political goal by transforming the regime into a new center of gravity in a Jin-dominated world, a goal that the young and vernacular Manchu language—including the New Manchu (Ma., *ice manju hergen*) developed in 1632—was incapable of securing.

The Manchu regime conducted its relations with Chosŏn in accordance with hierarchical principles within a quasi-Zongfan system. Some historians have argued that at this time the Manchus derived their political concepts of imperial rule mainly from their Mongol allies rather than from the Chinese.[36] Yet the transformation of the Manchu regime's understanding of its relations with neighboring nomadic and Confucian states, which took place concurrently with the transformation of the Manchu-Chosŏn relationship, indicates that the regime was enthusiastically constructing a new politico-cultural self-identity by appropriating and exploiting the Chinese politico-cultural discourse. Scholars have also long debated the theory of the Sinicization or Sinification of the Manchus. The mainstream explorations of this issue so far have focused either on how the Han Chinese culturally assimilated the Manchus or on how the Manchus tried to retain their ethnic identity.[37] What this chapter explores is how the Manchu regime, rather than the ethnic Manchus, promoted itself as the exclusively civilized Middle Kingdom—Zhongguo—and it is in this sense that I use the term "Sinicization" in this book.

The Manchu Regime's Strategic Goal of Transforming into Zhongguo

While the quasi-Zongfan discourse helped to refashion the self-image of the Manchu regime along Chinese lines, the Manchu language offered an international setting for this reconstruction by framing the Jin's relations with other political entities as state-to-state interactions. In Manchu records the Jin, the Ming, Chosŏn, and such Mongol polities as Korcin were all defined as *gurun*. The term *gurun* has several meanings, including "country," "tribe," "people of a tribe," and "race." Two of these meanings are primary: "people" and "country." For instance, *amba gurun* could mean "big country" or "adults," and *ajige gurun* could mean "small country" or "children," while *haha gurun* refers to "men" and *hehe gurun* refers to "women."[38] In political contexts, *gurun* denoted primarily "country," as in *Aisin gurun* (the country of the Jin), *Nikan gurun* (the country of the Han Chinese, that is, the Ming), *Daiming gurun* (the country of the Great Ming), *Solho gurun* or *Coohiyan gurun* (the country of Chosŏn), *Korcin gurun* (the country of the Korcin Mongols), and *Cahar gurun* (the country of the Cahar Mongols).[39] The Mongolian equivalent of the term in the Mongol records of the day is *ulus* (country).[40]

The Manchu rulers drew clear geographical, social, and cultural lines between the Manchu regime and other countries, even as they emphasized commonalities. Nurhaci underlined to the Kalka Mongols in 1619 that "the Ming and Chosŏn have different languages, but they share the same styles in clothing and hair, so the two countries look like a single country; similarly, our two countries look like a single country."[41] The consciousness of being a state became progressively more transparent in the regime's political norms, in particular in the Chinese-language records. In 1628, for instance, Hongtaiji called the Cahar Mongols a "different country" (Ma., *encu gurun*; Ch., *yiguo*) and a "far country" (Ch., *yuanguo*).[42] The following year Hongtaiji treated the prince of "the country of Korcin" to the music and dances of "four countries," including the Jin, the Korcin Mongols, the Ming, and Chosŏn.[43] In a letter to Ming officials in 1632, Hongtaiji named his country and the Cahar Mongols as two "countries outside of the border [of the Ming]" (Ma., *jasei tulergi gurun*; Ch., *bianwai zhi guo*).[44]

The new political discourse fundamentally transformed the worldview of the Manchu regime from within by representing the regime as a state at the center of a multistate community. The strategic goal of this transformation, as Ning Wanwo indicated in 1633 when he suggested that the Jin compose an institutional code (Ch., *Jindian*) by modifying that of the Ming, was to break with Ming conventions and "gradually develop the institutions of Zhongguo" (Ch., *jianjiu Zhongguo zhi zhi*). In other words, the Jin intended to develop its own "institutions of Zhongguo" to replace those of the Ming. According to Ning, only in this way could the regime manage its great enterprise after conquering the "place of the southern barbarians" (Ch., *manzi difang*), that is, the Ming. Ning justified his proposal by stressing that "a new monarch and his officials must have their own institutional works."[45] This strategic plan shows that Zhongguo, as a politico-cultural identity, was available for the Manchu regime to embrace and claim. What is more, it suggests that control over the central plain (Ch., *Zhongyuan*) was not necessarily a prerequisite for a regime to claim to be Zhongguo, as has been assumed.

Nurhaci wished to preserve the ways of his ethnic nation, or Manchuness, by enshrining Shanhai Pass and the Liao River as the border between "the Chinese and Jurchen countries" (Ma., *nikan, jušen meni meni gurun*). He tried to avoid "turning to the Chinese way" (Ma., *nikan i doro de dosimbi*; Ch., *xiao hansu*)— or becoming Sinicized—as the Liao, the Jin, and the Yuan Dynasties had done after their founders left their own homelands for the "Chinese inner land" (Ma., *nikan i dorgi bade*; Ch., *handi*); they had "changed ways and all became Chinese" (Ma., *doro forgošoro jakade, gemu nikan ohobi*).[46] Although the Manchu leaders exhorted their ethnic cohorts to keep to the "old way" (Ma., *fe doro*) in daily life by wearing traditional garb and practicing Manchu archery and horseback riding, the regime was unavoidably following the "Chinese way" in its rapid transformation in the 1630s. The Manchu regime could have become Zhongguo even if it had remained in Manchuria and not crossed the Great Wall in 1644.

By employing the newly adopted Chinese political discourse, the Manchu regime gradually absorbed the Chinese political philosophy of the Zongfan order into its understanding of its place within the constellation of polities. Aside from the Ming, other countries served as the Jin's outer *fan* by presenting tribute to the khan, who occupied a position akin to that of a Chinese emperor. This quasi-Zongfan system matured to the point that in 1636, in their Chinese letter to Chosŏn, forty-nine princes of sixteen countries of Mongols under the Jin's leadership termed themselves "Mongols as the outer *fan* of the Jin" (Ch., *Jinguo waifan menggu*), equivalent to the Manchu term *tulergi goloi monggo* ("Mongols as the outer *fan*").[47] In the same year, the Jin founded Menggu yamen (M., Monggo jurgan, lit. "the ministry of Mongolian affairs") on the basis of Chinese civil administrational concepts. As an institution parallel to the Ministry of Rites, this ministry enabled the regime to transform its relations with the Mongols and to build and govern an emerging empire.

The construction of this quasi-Zongfan discourse occurred primarily within the Jin's borders, but the Jin found Chosŏn the best external resource to support its discursive revolution. Within the bilateral relationship, the Jin held the role of the supreme power, and it converted Chosŏn from a younger brother into a subordinate or outer *fan*. Students of Sino-Korean relations tend to assume that the Manchus adopted hierarchical discourse in 1637 after the second Manchu invasion, when the Manchu side imposed clear Zongfan terms on Chosŏn. However, in practice the process had begun much earlier. In the 1630s the scholars of the Jin had mined Chinese history for intellectual resources with which to manipulate the civilized–barbarian distinction in order to establish the centrality of the Jin.

Within the Zongfan framework, the "central civilized country" (Ch., *Huaxia*) and its counterpart, "barbarians," were the two key concepts addressing the status of the Middle Kingdom and that of its outer *fan*. The two terms were derived from the notion of all-under-Heaven, developed in the Xia (ca. 2070–1600 BC), Shang (1600–1046 BC), and Zhou periods, through which the three dynasties sought to legitimize their rule as divine. At the same time, the political entities spanning China's lands identified *xia* (referring not to the Xia Dynasty but to a larger area in which the regime once resided) as the symbol of a civilized community possessing the Mandate of Heaven, namely, Zhongguo, *Zhongyuan* (the central plain), or *Zhongtu* (the central lands). At that time, the term "barbarians" referred primarily to groups that resided along the periphery of the central plain and were reluctant to identify and embrace the concept of "civilized China," as exemplified by the state relationship between the Qin and the Chu in the third century BC.[48] The originally geographic notion of "barbarian" became an instrument used by political forces to deprecate their antagonists during the movement of "revering the court of the Zhou and expelling the barbarians" (Ch., *zunzhou rangyi*) in the Eastern Zhou (770–256 BC), a chaotic time that led Confucius (551–479 BC) to call for restoring the ideal order of "proper conduct" (Ch., *li*) of the Western Zhou. Due to the fierce interstate rivalries, the civilized–barbarian distinction evolved into a politico-cultural ideology that the dynastic regimes of China continuously reinterpreted for the next two thousand years, until 1911.

After the Han Dynasty, with the official institutionalization of Confucianism and the expansion of the concept of all-under-Heaven, the civilized–barbarian distinction became a critical theoretical framework for the Chinese court's management of its foreign relations. As "northern barbarians" gained ascendancy in the Northern Song (960–1127), the distinction presented itself as an essential cultural instrument with which Chinese elites endowed certain regimes with the pedigree of "legitimate historical narratives" (Ch., *zhengshi*) by expelling competing polities from these narratives.[49] Some scholars, such as Shi Jie (1005–45), the author of *A Treatise on the Middle Kingdom* (Ch., *Zhongguo lun*), and Ouyang Xiu (1007–72), the author of *A Treatise on Orthodox Legitimacy* (Ch., *Zhengtong lun*), depicted the Song as the exclusive civilized center of the world and the polities on the Song's northern border as uncivilized. One of the most influential histories, *A Comprehensive Mirror to Aid in Government* (Ch., *Zizhi tongjian*), edited by Sima Guang (1019–86), drew a clear lineage connecting states identified as "China" from 403 BC to AD 959. The efforts of these scholars to conceptualize the narrative of orthodox legitimacy eventually paid off, for their rhetoric triumphed over that of the northern regimes, especially when Neo-Confucianism, created and elaborated by such Song intellectual vanguards as Cheng Hao (1032–85), Cheng Yi (1033–1107), and Zhu Xi (1130–1200), became China's official ideology under the Yuan Dynasty.

This intellectual history can help explain why the official historical narrative of the People's Republic of China still celebrates the Song for its legitimate status as Zhongguo and marginalizes the Liao, the Xixia, and the Jin as regimes established by "ethnic minorities" (Ch., *shaoshu minzu*). It was against this historical backdrop that the scholars of the Manchu regime in the 1630s began to construct the regime's orthodox legitimacy, which laid the foundation for the Manchu enterprise of governing a vast empire as the legitimate Middle Kingdom, Zhongguo.

The Practices of the Manchu-Chosŏn Quasi-Zongfan Order

The Manchu regime implemented its quasi-Zongfan discourse through the rituals that accompanied the exchange of emissaries with Chosŏn by imitating Ming-Chosŏn contacts. In Mukden, the Korean emissaries kowtowed five times to Hongtaiji. They were comfortably lodged in the city and enjoyed a welcome banquet (K., *hama yŏn*, lit. "banquet for getting off a horse") and a farewell banquet (K., *sangma yŏn*, lit. "banquet for getting on a horse"). Hongtaiji dispensed gifts to the Korean king, emissaries, interpreters, and servants.[50] In exchange, the Jin sent Manchu emissaries to Hansŏng in the spring and autumn of every year. Before they entered the Korean capital, the Manchu emissaries were housed at the Hall of Admiring the Central Civilized Country (K., Mohwa gwan), a place that had previously accommodated Ming emissaries. The emissaries also had an audience with the king in the palace and were treated to official welcome and farewell banquets. Although Chosŏn did not want to treat the Manchu representatives like those of the Ming, the general ritual procedures of greeting were practically identical. The Manchu emissaries lacked only their Ming counterparts' standing as "imperial envoy" or "Heavenly envoy."

This de facto Zongfan relationship conflicted with the de jure one of equality between the two brothers, a contradiction strikingly manifested in the different formats of their sovereign letters to each other. In its letters to the Jin, Chosŏn placed the two sides on a fully equal political plane, which was hierarchically lower than the status of the Ming. According to the Chinese convention, whenever the characters for Heaven or the Ming emperor appeared, they were placed at the top of a new line, two character spaces higher than the characters for Chosŏn and the first characters of other lines. This honorific elevation acknowledged the emperor as the supreme human agent of Heaven with the highest spiritual position in the world. Hongtaiji also used honorific elevation in his letters, but he adopted a different arrangement of the hierarchy, as shown by his letters to the Ming general Yuan Chonghuan (1584–1630). Hongtaiji divided the hierarchy into four levels, among which his position was lower than that of Heaven and the Ming emperor but higher than that of Ming officials (see figure 1.1). For his part, General Yuan followed Ming custom in his letters to Hongtaiji (see figure 1.2). Frustrated by Yuan's usage, Hongtaiji exclaimed that he was "the monarch or the khan of another country" (Ma., *encu gurun i ejen han*) and "son of Heaven and the Buddha" (Ma., *abka fucihi i jui*). He declared that he would not accept any letters from the Ming that addressed him with a status lower than or even equal to that of the Ming officials.[51] Nevertheless, in his communications with the king of Chosŏn, Hongtaiji was more pragmatic, addressing the king as a near equal in order to avoid offending the Korean monarch (see figure 1.3).

The king followed the same format in his responses to Hongtaiji but avoided mention of the imposed brotherhood (see figure 1.4). Although Hongtaiji called the king "younger brother," the king never referred to Hongtaiji as "elder brother."

					Heaven	1
				Emperor		2
			Khan			3
		Ming officials				4
X	X	X	X	X	X	5
X	X	X	X	X	X	6
X	X	X	X	X	X	7
f	e	d	c	b	a	

FIGURE 1.1.   The format of Hongtaiji's letters to Yuan Chonghuan in 1627. In this and the three figures that follow, the Arabic numerals represent horizontal lines from the top down, the English letters represent vertical lines, and the direction of the writing is from right to left. "X" represents a Chinese character. *MWLD*, 821, 847; *MBRT*, 4:28, 72.

				Emperor	Heaven	1
		Khan	Ming officials			2
X	X	X	X	X	X	3
X	X	X	X	X	X	4
X	X	X	X	X	X	5
f	e	d	c	b	a	

FIGURE 1.2. The format of Yuan Chonghuan's letters to Hongtaiji in 1627. *MWLD*, 821; *MBRT*, 4:28.

					Heaven	1
	Your country	Jin	King	Khan		2
X	X	X	X	X	X	3
X	X	X	X	X	X	4
X	X	X	X	X	X	5
f	e	d	c	b	a	

FIGURE 1.3. The format of Hongtaiji's letters to the king of Chosŏn, 1627–36. *Kakyu gobu*.

					Ming	Heaven	1
	Your country	Our country	Khan	King			2
X	X	X	X	X	X	X	3
X	X	X	X	X	X	X	4
X	X	X	X	X	X	X	5
g	f	e	d	c	b	a	

FIGURE 1.4. The format of the letters of the king of Chosŏn to Hongtaiji, 1627–36. *Chosŏnguk raesŏ bu*, vol. 1.

When Hongtaiji questioned the king about this discrepancy in 1629, the king shifted to friend-to-friend expressions: "The king of the country of Chosŏn," he wrote, "presents this letter to the khan of the country of the Jin" (K., Chosŏn kugwang pongsŏ Kŭmguk han; Ma., Coohiyan gurun i wang ni bithe, Aisin gurun i han de unggimbi). This usage matched Hongtaiji's wording: "The khan of the country of the Jin sends this letter to the king of the country of Chosŏn" (Ma., Aisin gurun i han i bithe, Coohiyan gurun i wang de unggimbi). Later, the king changed the verb "present" (K., *pong*; Ma., *jafambi*) to "send" (K., *ch'i*; Ma., *unggimbi*), eliminating the hierarchical connotations of the former term. This subtle change provoked the Jin, but Chosŏn explained that both terms were used between "neighboring countries."[52] To the Jin, Chosŏn's pronounced pro-Ming attitude meant that the brotherhood was unstable. The Jin's security would not be guaranteed so long as Chosŏn was a loyal subject of the Ming. The only way to solve this problem, the Jin believed, was with another war against Chosŏn.

From Elder Brother to Father of Chosŏn: The Second Manchu Invasion

Manchu-Chosŏn Conflicts over Orthodox Legitimacy

In the middle of the 1630s, many Han Chinese and Manchu officials of the Jin sought to persuade Hongtaiji to take the title of emperor. On February 4, 1636, these officials presented memorials to prompt Hongtaiji to follow the Mandate of Heaven by claiming the emperorship. Following Chinese ritual conventions, Hongtaiji ostensibly declined and suggested his officials send emissaries to Chosŏn to discuss the matter with the king, his younger brother.[53] Hongtaiji's true motivation, as the Korean official Hong Ik-han (1586–1637) shrewdly recognized, was to use Chosŏn's identity as Little China to assert before other countries that Chosŏn revered him as the Son of Heaven.

The Manchu officials Inggŭldai and Mafuta (?–1640) arrived in Hansŏng on March 30, along with forty-seven Mongol princes, thirty generals, and ninety-eight soldiers. They brought with them five letters. The first three letters extended Hongtaiji's condolences on the death of the queen of Chosŏn. The fourth letter, written by eight Manchu princes (Ma., *hošoi beile*) and seventeen high-ranking Manchu ministers (Ma., *gūsai amban*), and the fifth letter, by forty-nine Mongol princes under the Chinese name *Jinguo waifan menggu* (Mongols as the outer *fan* of the Jin), aimed to persuade the king to submit a memorial urging Hongtaiji to follow the Mandate of Heaven (Ma., Abkai gūnin) and to claim the "great title" (Ma., *amba gebu*)—namely, that of emperor. The letters emphasized that the Jin now possessed "virtues" (Ma., *erdemu*) that enabled it to manage the world.[54] But on March 31, 139 Korean Confucian students presented the king with a petition, calling on him "to kill the barbarian emissaries and burn the barbarian letters." Inggūldai and his followers were thrown into panic and fled the city.[55]

Chosŏn's stance was strengthened when the king dispatched Na Tŏk-hŏn as the spring emissary and Yi Kwak as the response emissary to Mukden in late April. On May 15 the Jin held a grand ceremony in which Hongtaiji assumed the title "emperor of lenience, kindheartedness, beneficence, and brilliance" (Ma., *gosin onco huwaliyasun enduringge han*; Ch., *kuan wen ren sheng huangdi*) and adopted the regnal title Chongde (Ma., Wesihun erdemungge, lit. "worshiping virtues"). The Jin renamed itself the "Country of the Great Qing" (Ma., Daicing gurun; Ch., Da Qing guo). Gathering on Hongtaiji's left and right flanks, the Jin's Manchu, Mongol, and Han Chinese officials knelt down three times, each time making three prostrations (Ma., *ilan jergi niyakūrafi uyun jergi hengkilembi*; Ch., *san gui jiu koutou*)—the highest level of kowtow during the Qing period. Although Na and Yi had performed a ceremony of four kowtows before Hongtaiji upon their arrival, they called this second ceremony a "usurpation of the imperial title" (K., *ch'amho*) and refused to perform it, expressing their strong opposition to Hongtaiji's political ambitions.[56] Chosŏn was the only Confucian country that lay beyond the Manchu regime's political control but maintained regular and official diplomatic communications with it. Since Hongtaiji had made his claim to be the Son of Heaven in observance of proper Chinese conduct, he desperately needed the support of Chosŏn to counteract the designation of the Manchus as barbarians and to legitimize his emperorship in the Chinese sense. The ritual conflict with the Korean emissaries thus posed a grave identity crisis for him. Without endorsement from Chosŏn, the Manchu regime's political transformation would remain largely confined to its borders and would not significantly influence regional politics.

Hongtaiji sent Na and Yi back to Chosŏn with two Chinese-language letters to the king. In the letters Hongtaiji called himself "emperor of the country of the Great Qing" (Ch., *Da Qing guo huangdi*) rather than "khan of the Jin" and referred to Chosŏn as "your country" (Ch., *erguo*) instead of "your honorable country" (Ch., *guiguo*), signaling the end of the bilateral brotherly relationship. Invoking the time-honored notion that "the Heaven does not belong to one person, but to all people under the Heaven" (Ma., *abkai fejergi emu niyalmai abkai fejergi waka, abkai fejergi niyalmai abkai fejergi*), Hongtaiji sought to demonstrate that his regime could govern the space of all-under-Heaven (Ch., *tianxia*; Ma., *abkai fejergi*) by following the precedent set by previous dynasties: namely, the Liao, which had been founded by the "northeastern barbarians" (Ch., *dongbei yi*; Ma., *dergi amargi jušen*); the Jin, founded by the "eastern barbarians" (Ch., *dongyi*; Ma., *dergi jušen*); and the Yuan, established by the "northern barbarians" (Ch., *beiyi*; Ma., *amargi monggo*, "northern Mongols"). By chronicling the rise and fall of these dynasties, Hongtaiji located the Qing, the dynasty of the Manchu "barbarians," within this lineage of rulership, with himself as the Son of Heaven. The Qing's rule was justified, he argued, because the Qing possessed the virtue that the Ming had lost.[57] This assertion was based on the Chinese political view that "the Great Heaven has no partial affections and it helps only the virtuous" (Ch., *huangtian wu qin, wei de shi fu*), a theory articulated in *The Classic of History* (Ch., *Shangshu*), which had endowed more than thirty dynasties with legitimacy. In short, Hongtaiji hoped that Chosŏn would become the Great Qing's outer *fan*, just as it had served the previous dynasties of China.

Chosŏn became the first external target of the Qing's new, Qing-centric Zongfan doctrine. Yet Hongtaiji's position was unpopular in Chosŏn because it conflicted with the orthodox legitimacy on which the Confucian country based its political and social principles. With the exception of several high-ranking officials who preferred the Manchus, the majority of the ruling elite resolutely called for "revering China and expelling the barbarians" (K., *chon Chungguk, yang yichŏk*) in accordance with "the doctrine of revering the Zhou Dynasty" (K., *chonju ŭiri*).[58] In the face of tremendous pressure, the king reaffirmed that Chosŏn would not endorse Hongtaiji's emperorship. The Qing thus declared war for the sake of its name and legitimacy.

The Establishment of Manchu-Chosŏn Zongfan Relations

On December 28, 1636, Qing troops attacked Chosŏn. They captured Hansŏng on January 9, 1637, without encountering strong resistance. The king had escaped to Namhan Mountain Fortress with the crown prince (K., *seja*; Ch., *shizi*; Ma., *šidz*) and some officials, while the remaining royal family members and other officials fled to Kanghwa Island. The Qing forces surrounded the Namhan Fortress and, as their precondition for negotiations, demanded that the king send the crown prince as hostage. The king refused and mobilized his forces to resist the invasion and protect the "great justice under Heaven" (K., *ch'ŏnha taeŭi*). While Hongtaiji marched on the fortress with reinforcements on January 19, the king and his officials performed ceremonies to celebrate the birthday of Emperor Chongzhen of the Ming. Yet the king realized that Chosŏn's fate was now at a crossroads. Ch'oe Myŏng-gil (1586–1647), a minister who had assisted the king in assuming the throne in the coup of 1623 and served as the king's close adviser since that time, argued for peaceful negotiation with the Qing as he had done in 1627, when the Manchus invaded Chosŏn for the first time. Ch'oe's approach was not welcomed by the majority of his colleagues, but it was undeniably pragmatic. On January 26, the lunar New Year, the king, fulfilling Chosŏn's duty as a subject of the Ming, performed vested rituals in the direction of Beijing. Once the ceremony was over, the king sent two officials to negotiate with the Qing.

Two days later the king presented a letter to Hongtaiji in which he called Hongtaiji "the emperor of lenience, kindheartedness, beneficence, and brilliance of the country of the Great Qing" and referred to the Qing as the "big country" (K., *taeguk*) and to Chosŏn as the "small country" (K., *sobang*). The presentation of the letter was defined as "submitting the letter to the higher authority" (K., *songsŏ*).[59] Hongtaiji insisted that the king should surrender to him in person, so the two sides negotiated for two more weeks, during which the Qing troops shelled the fortress and defeated Chosŏn reinforcements sent from provinces. On February 15 the king presented another letter, in which he called Hongtaiji "Your Majesty" and himself a "subordinate" (see figure 1.5). He dated the letter using the Qing regnal title "Chongde."[60] His letter suggested that the king had decided to surrender before Kanghwa Island was conquered.[61] On February 17 the king submitted a sovereign letter to Hongtaiji, declaring that Chosŏn would "present the humble palace memorial [K., *p'yo*; Ch., *biao*] as the subordinate and serve as a *fan* [K., *pŏnbang*; Ch., *fanbang*] of the Great Qing forever," while "all rituals about serving the big country would be performed in the vested format."[62]

On February 22, 1637, Inggŭldai brought an imperial edict to the king and asked the Korean officials to perform the same rituals that they had done when receiving edicts from the "southern dynasty" (the Ming). This occasion marked the first time that the Qing replaced the Ming in ritual exchanges with Chosŏn on Korean territory. In his edict, Hongtaiji listed ten terms of submission, among which two stood out. First, the king had to surrender to the Qing the book of

		Great Qing			Qing Emperor	Heaven	1
							2
X	X	Chosŏn	X		King	X	3
X	X	X	X		X	X	4
X	X	X	X		X	X	5
f	e	d	c		b	a	

FIGURE 1.5. The format of the king's letters to Hongtaiji in February 1637. The Arabic numerals represent horizontal lines from the top down, the English letters represent vertical lines, and the direction of the writing is from right to left. X represents a Chinese character. *Chosŏnguk raesŏ bu*, 2:26–38.

imperial investiture and the seal that he had received from the Ming, stop communicating with the Ming, and begin to use the regnal title of the Qing instead of that of the Ming to indicate dates in all documents. Second, the king had to dispatch officials to the Qing every year to bring "humble palace memorials," present gifts, and perform rituals to celebrate occasions such as the winter solstice, the New Year, the birthdays of the emperor, empress, and crown prince, and any good news for the Qing, and to extend condolences on the loss of members of the Qing's royal house. The format of these memorials was required to follow the established format of Chosŏn's memorials to the Ming. The rituals of receiving imperial decrees, accommodating imperial envoys in Chosŏn, and paying formal visits to the Qing emperor through tributary emissaries were to dovetail precisely with the "established way of the Ming country" (Ch., *Mingguo jiuli*). Hongtaiji also listed the items and amounts of the tributes required of Chosŏn and specified that tribute submissions ought to begin in 1639.[63]

The king unconditionally accepted all of Hongtaiji's terms. On February 24, 1637, he presented himself before Hongtaiji at Samjŏndo (lit. "three fields ferry"), near the Hangang River, where the Qing had built a massive altar for Hongtaiji to receive the king's surrender. During the ceremony, presided over by the Qing's Ministry of Rites, the king knelt down three times, each time bowing his head three times before the emperor, after which he handed in his seal issued by the Ming. This ceremony marked the official establishment of the Zongfan relationship between the Qing and Chosŏn, as the king confirmed in his palace memorial to Hongtaiji on December 16, 1637.[64] The Qing's forces soon returned to Mukden, taking the crown prince of Chosŏn, Yi Wang (1612–45), and the king's second son, Yi Ho (King Hyojong, 1619–59), as hostages. Beginning on March 24, 1637, Chosŏn used the regnal title of the Qing to express the date, thus incorporating the country into the Qing's temporal realm.[65] Chosŏn became the Qing's outer *fan*.

The establishment of the Qing-Chosŏn Zongfan relationship, which replaced the Ming-Chosŏn relationship that had been officially institutionalized in 1401, was extremely significant for the Qing. The Ming's passionate endorsement of the Zhou Zongfan system meant that under the Qing, the system was likewise directly connected with the classical and ideal tenets of the Zhou. As its political rhetoric developed after 1644, the Manchu court began to define its relationship with Chosŏn's court by using more sophisticated terms that were associated with the Zhou Zongfan system. As early as 1649, Emperor Shunzhi, in his imperial mandate to invest King Hyojong, emphasized that Chosŏn served as an "outer *fan*" for the "central court" (Ch., *wangshi*).[66] In 1659 Emperor Shunzhi began his imperial mandate to invest King Hyŏngjong with the traditional term "dividing cogongrass" (Ch., *fenmao*), a metaphor for the Zhou's Zongfan investiture.[67]

Meanwhile, the Manchu court came to define Chosŏn as a "princely submission" (Ch., *houfu*; Ma., *jecen i golo*) according to the conventional theory of the "five submissions" (Ch., *wufu*) of the Zhou.[68] This definition equated the status of the king with that of China's princely minister, governor-general, and governor.[69] Along the same lines, the Qing side, emperors and officials alike, regarded Korean emissaries as "ministers of ministers of the outer *fan*" (Ch., *waifan peichen*).[70]

These established Zongfan tenets determined the familistic nature of the Qing-Chosŏn relationship, which crystallized in a crisis of kingship in 1768. In August of that year, Yi Gŭm (King Yŏngjo) asked Emperor Qianlong to invest his grandson Yi San (later known as Chŏngjo) as the crown successor to the Chosŏn kingship in the wake of the deaths of Yi Gŭm's two sons, including the crown prince. Because the Qing court had never before encountered this situation, Emperor Qianlong instructed the Grand Secretariat (Ch., Neige) and the Ministry of Rites to consult Confucian books and historical records in search of appropriate precedents for the title of "crown grandson" (Ch., *shisun*). The ministry cited Confucius's interpretations in *The Book of Rites* (Ch., *Liji*) and historical precedents ranging from the Liu Song Dynasty (420–79) to the Ming Dynasty pertaining to the investment of a vassal's grandson as crown grandson. Stressing that "the outer *fan* is fundamentally the same as Zongfan," the ministry recommended that the emperor invest Yi San as the crown grandson, and the emperor did so.[71] As the Ming had done, the Qing regarded Chosŏn as an extended royal family member of the Middle Kingdom where the patriarch—the Son of Heaven—resided.

This ideology continued to exert profound influence over Qing-Chosŏn relations in the nineteenth century. In 1882, under the Qing's supervision and mediation, Chosŏn signed a treaty with the United States that portrayed Chosŏn as an independent state with a sovereign equal to the American president. But regardless of the treaty's legal implications based on international law, in 1883 the Chinese official Li Hongzhang (1823–1901), who had negotiated the 1882 treaty with the United States on Chosŏn's behalf as governor-general of Zhili, superintendent of trade for the northern ports of China (Ch., *Beiyang tongshang dachen*, hereafter "Beiyang superintendent"), and China's de facto foreign minister, cited the Western Zhou's Zongfan tenets to declare that the king was an "outer vassal" (Ch., *wai zhuhou*) of the Son of Heaven in China. Li further pointed out that the king was equal to China's governors-general and provincial governors, who were "inner vassals" (Ch., *nei zhuhou*), while the status of lower-ranking Korean officials corresponded to that of their Chinese counterparts.[72] In 1886, when Yuan Shikai (1859–1916), Li's protégé, who resided in Chosŏn as the Chinese imperial resident, asked Li what level of ritual he should perform in front of the king, Li replied that it would be courteous enough for Yuan to follow the rituals used by Chinese provincial officials when visiting first-degree princes (Ch., *qin-junwang*).[73] On the Korean side, the king, in a pre-1894 humble memorial to Emperor Guangxu, still referred to Chosŏn as China's "princely submission."[74] In their dealings with each other in the late nineteenth century, both China and Korea looked to Zongfan precedents from the Western Zhou down through the Ming, and their country-to-country contacts were subordinate to their familistic court-to-court hierarchy. All of these stories started in 1637, when the Qing formalized its Zongfan relationship with Chosŏn.

At this point it is necessary to explain further why this book prefers the Chinese term "Zongfan" over the oft-used English renderings "tribute system" or "tributary system." In the twentieth century, the promulgation of the term "tribute system," together with the concepts "suzerain" and "vassal," owed a great debt to the popularity of a more neutral phrase, "Chinese world order," proposed by the American historian John King Fairbank. Between the 1940s and the 1960s, Fairbank prompted a constellation of historians and political scientists to explore the rationale behind China's foreign relations in the late imperial period. Although Fairbank was aware of the complexity of Sinocentric cosmopolitanism, or "Sinocentrism," the term "Chinese world order," which he used broadly to denote this system and to highlight its diversity, became a rough equivalent of "tribute system." Acceptance of this English rendering has allowed scholars in a variety of fields to treat it as a counterpart to "treaty system" or "treaty port system." Some scholars have questioned the appositeness of the terms "tributary system" and "suzerain-vassal relations" and criticized them as "a nineteenth- and twentieth-century reinterpretation of an older form of symbolically asymmetric interstate relations," while others, likewise seeking to avoid the possible misunderstandings caused by English terminology, have proposed new terms, such as "Pax Sinica," in a world history context.[75] But their combined efforts have not changed the entrenched renderings or paradigm, and the conventional English parlance still profoundly influences scholars' understanding of late imperial China's foreign relations.[76]

An underlying problem with the term "tribute system," as chapter 2 shows, is that it can convey only some of the connotations of the comprehensive Zongfan system—namely, *chaogong*, or sending emissaries to pay tribute to China, the perennial activity that was the most sensational and visible part of the regular ritual contacts between Qing China and its *fan*. The term "tribute system" thus trims the entire mechanism down to a Sinocentric trade structure. As Peter C. Perdue points out in his study of Qing-Zunghar relations, "Overly simplistic generalizations about the Qing 'tribute system' tend to single out one trading relationship as the orthodox, normative one, neglecting the great diversity of ritual, economic, and diplomatic conditions found in the Qing trading regime as a whole."[77] The submission of tribute should not be used loosely as a master concept to represent the entire structure and its core nature. This is not to suggest, however, that the term "tribute system" has no analytical utility as a conceptual interpretive tool. This is clear in the debate over the question of when the practices of the Sinocentric order became as mature, institutional, and systematic as they were in the Ming and Qing periods.[78]

Cherishing the Small Country: The Qing's Construction of Its Zhongguo Identity

The Qing's Transformation into the "Big Country"

Within the new Zongfan relationship, the Qing was Chosŏn's monarch and the patriarch of the big family principally consisting of the Qing, Chosŏn, and the Mongol states. Given its supreme authority, the Qing could use the subordination of Chosŏn to its advantage. The first and most direct effect of the relationship was the formation of a new military alliance between the two countries. By conquering Chosŏn, the Qing reinforced its home front in the war with the Ming by eliminating the potential military threat on its eastern flank. It also gained material assistance from Chosŏn in the form of warhorses, grain, warships, cannons, and soldiers. Two months after Chosŏn's subordination, the Manchu forces conquered Ka Island, destroying the last Ming military base in Chosŏn. In the next few years, a number of Korean soldiers, particularly gunners, were forced to join the Manchus in their fight against the Ming and to garrison Jinzhou and other cities newly conquered by the Qing in Manchuria.[79]

By transforming its relationship with Chosŏn into one between a monarch and a subordinate, or between a father and a son, the Qing obtained political legitimacy from Chosŏn, a Confucian country beyond the Qing's geographical borders but within its political and cultural realm. Given that the Chinese perceived their Zongfan relationships with other countries or political entities within a model centered on China as the Middle Kingdom, the establishment of the Qing-Chosŏn Zongfan relationship defined the Qing as the Middle Kingdom. In other words, the identities of both China and the countries on its periphery within the Zongfan framework were mutually dependent and constitutive. This rationale provided the Qing with the political and cultural foundations that it desperately needed to legitimize its centrality in the Chinese world.

In practice, the change of the Qing's position was materially corroborated by the intensive bilateral exchange of missions between 1637 and 1643. On May 13, 1637, Chosŏn sent its first tributary mission to Mukden, and in the documents submitted to the Qing the Korean side called the city "capital" (K., Kyŏngsa), a term previously reserved for Beijing. This terminological choice indicated that, at least on the surface, Chosŏn acknowledged Mukden as the new political center of the world.[80] The mission had 315 members, including three primary members: an envoy, an associate envoy, and a secretary. After traveling 517 miles along the conventional overland tributary route between Hansŏng and Beijing, the mission arrived in Mukden on July 8.[81] The next day the Korean officials appeared before Hongtaiji to perform the highest level of kowtow. During the imperial audience, the Qing's officials read the king's humble memorials, written in the hierarchical format once used for the Ming emperor. By praising the admirable virtues of the "big country" that "brought Chosŏn to life again," the text of the humble memorials endowed the Qing with the position of the Middle Kingdom, adding that "all far countries on the periphery [of the Qing] have willingly subordinated themselves" (K., hwangbok hambin) and lauding the Qing for its virtuous act of "cherishing the small." The Qing's position was confirmed by the Qing itself in the emperor's edict to the king, which defined the relationship clearly with reference to orthodox Zongfan principles such as "serving the great" and "cherishing the small." Chosŏn became a "far country," a "small country," and the "remote land" on the periphery of the new civilized center.[82] This framing of the two countries' mutually constitutive identities consigned Chosŏn to the category of barbarians surrounding the civilized Middle Kingdom of the Qing.

At the same time, the frequent visits to Mukden by tributary emissaries from the Mongols and other ethnic-minority polities whose affairs were under the management of the Mongolian Superintendency highlighted the spread of the Qing-centric Zongfan circle. For the previous two decades, the Manchu regime had gradually eroded the Ming's Zongfan network at the periphery and used the dislodged parts to construct a similar model with itself at the center. After establishing the Zongfan relationship with Chosŏn, the Qing sought to institutionalize its Zongfan mechanism by imitating the Ming's policies and improving them to meet the Qing's needs. The institutionalization of the system took place through the Ministry of Rites. Although the Ministries of Revenue, War, and Justice also exchanged official notes with the king over cases involving financial and military assistance or illegal border crossings, the Ministry of Rites constituted the most important channel between the emissaries and the Qing court. It forwarded the king's humble memorials to the emperor, directed the emissaries' visits, treated the emissaries to banquets, accommodated them at a dedicated residence in Mukden for forty days, forwarded imperial edicts to them, and issued official response notes to the king. With the ministry's guidance, the Korean emissaries performed the highest level of kowtow to the emperor, presented tributes, and received imperial edicts and gifts. These highly programmed ritual practices demonstrated, institutionalized, and consolidated the two sides' bilateral relationship and strict hierarchy.

To formalize the Zongfan relationship, the Qing sent ethnic Manchu emissaries to Chosŏn to invest the king and other core members of the royal family with certain titles. On January 4, 1638, the first imperial mission led by Inggüldai, Mafuta, and Daiyun arrived in Hansŏng to officially invest the king. The king greeted the envoys at the Hall of Admiring the Central Civilized Country outside the West Gate of the capital.[83] Later, in the palace, the king received the imperial edicts of investiture, a gold seal, and gifts, and performed established rituals for the occasion. The edicts stated that, with the establishment of "investiture-subordinate" (Ch., *fanfeng*) relations between the Qing and Chosŏn, the latter was expected to serve as a "*fan* and fence" (Ch., *fanping*) of the Great Qing "until the Yellow River becomes as narrow as a belt and Mount Tai becomes as small as a grindstone" (Ch., *daihe lishan*). The emperor's mandate noted that both sides "have an established name and status, which will regulate the relationship and hierarchy for ten thousand years" (Ch., *li yishi zhi mingfen, ding wanzai zhi gangchang*).[84] Following the ceremony, the king visited the envoys at their residence, the South Palace Annex (K., *Nambyŏl gung*), where he treated them to banquets. All of these ritual procedures were identical to those that had been performed between Chosŏn and the Ming. The Qing's investiture legitimatized the bilateral Zongfan relationship between the two countries, an arrangement that would last for 258 years.

The Establishment of the Stele of the Honors and Virtues of the Emperor of the Great Qing

In the precise spot in Samjŏndo where the Korean king had subordinated himself to Hongtaiji in 1637, the Qing forced Chosŏn to erect a stele to commemorate Hongtaiji's achievements. Despite the Koreans' reluctance to memorialize the humiliating invasion, the Qing continued to advance the project, and the Korean official Yi Kyŏng-sŏk (1595–1671) eventually drafted a Chinese-language inscription based on the Korean letters to the Qing side during the war.[85] After the Chinese official Fan Wencheng approved the inscription, the Qing sent interpreters to Hansŏng to translate it into Manchu and Mongolian. In 1639 the stele, inscribed in three languages, was erected as the Stele of the Honors and Virtues of the Emperor of the Great Qing (Ma., *Daicing gurun i enduringge han i gung erdemui bei*; Ch., *Da Qing huangdi gongde bei*) (see figure 1.6).

The inscription reviewed the history between the two countries from 1619 to 1637 from Chosŏn's perspective and exalted the Qing's great virtues in "bringing Chosŏn to life again." It claimed that the king had surrendered in 1637 "not to

FIGURE 1.6. The Stele of the Honors and Virtues of the Emperor of the Great Qing. The stele is now located in a small park next to Lotte World in Seoul. Photo taken by the author in 2015.

[the Qing's] might but to [its] virtues" (Ma., *horon de gelere teile waka, erdemu de dahahangge kai*), given that those virtues made "all the far [people] subordinate themselves willingly" (Ma., *goroki ci aname gemu dahambi*). The stele also stated that the bilateral relationship would last for ten thousand years under "the emperor's goodness." The most significant aspect was the official transformation of the identity of the Manchu regime as manifested in certain terms. The inscription called the Qing the "big country" (Ch., *dabang, dachao*; Ma., *amba gurun*) or the "upper country" (Ch., *shangguo*; Ma., *dergi gurun*), while terming Chosŏn the "small country" (Ch., *xiaobang*; Ma., *ajige gurun*) as well as "a faraway country." The fact that the two countries geographically bordered each other did not prevent the Qing from redefining Chosŏn as "faraway" in the politico-cultural sense.

Among these terms, which had been used between Chosŏn and the Ming and were now grafted onto the Qing-Chosŏn relationship, the Manchu phrase *amba gurun* (big country) was particularly significant. As a literal translation of the Chinese *dabang* or *dachao*, the term had once referred exclusively to the Ming. More importantly, as chapter 2 shows, after 1644 the Qing adopted *amba gurun* as a key equivalent of the Chinese terms *Zhongguo* (Ma., *Dulimbai gurun*) and *Tianchao* ("the Heavenly Dynasty"; Ma., *abkai gurun*). The inscription of the Samjŏndo stele was probably the first instance in which the Qing publicly and officially called itself *amba gurun*; over the following two and a half centuries, this term would refer solely to Qing China.

"Cherishing Men from Afar": Publicizing Qing Centrality, 1637–43

The Manchu invasion of 1636 and the king's surrender to Hongtaiji, known in Chosŏn as *Pyŏngja horan* (lit. "the invasion of the northern barbarians in the year of Pyŏngja"), were humiliating to the Koreans and stimulated widespread anti-Manchu feeling in the country. Korean resentment is evident, for example, in an incident that took place in December 1637, when the Manchu envoys visiting Chosŏn asked Korean local officials to procure courtesans (K., *panggi*), but the women "killed themselves to show their resistance" (K., *yisa kŏchi*).[86] In order to win Chosŏn's loyalty beyond mere lip service, the Qing quickly adopted the traditional Chinese policies of "cherishing the small" and "cherishing men from afar" (Ch., *huairou yuanren*; Ma., *goroki niyalma be bilume gosimbi*).[87]

In addition to providing Chosŏn's delegation with better accommodations in Mukden and bestowing more gifts on the king and his emissaries, the Qing progressively reduced the tribute required of Chosŏn beginning in the early 1640s, when the Qing controlled more resources as a result of its military triumphs over the Ming. In 1640, for instance, the Qing lowered the number of sacks of rice that Chosŏn was expected to offer as tribute from ten thousand to just one thousand. In 1643 the Qing further reduced the annual tribute and furthermore cut by more than half the gifts that Chosŏn gave to the Manchu envoys. Proclaiming that "the two countries have become one family," the Shunzhi emperor also permanently abolished many tributary conventions, such as the requirement that Chosŏn provide the imperial envoys with official courtesans. These exemptions, the emperor suggested, embodied the Qing policy of "cherishing the small with benevolence."[88] Compared with the late Ming, which tried to extract the maximum economic and military benefits from Chosŏn, the Qing took a deliberately placatory approach toward its outer *fan*, represented by the many exemptions. This benign policy substantially facilitated the Qing's historical transformation into Zhongguo.

The Qing was characterized more by its actions than by its pronouncements. Its policy of appealing to the subordinate country was manifested above all in its frequent contacts with Chosŏn. From 1637 to 1643, the Qing sent twelve missions and twenty-eight emissaries to Chosŏn, an average of one and a half missions per year, while Chosŏn sent fifty-six missions and 102 emissaries to the Qing, an average of seven missions per year.[89] In this context, some Koreans changed their established understandings of the Qing. In the spring of 1643, for example, Yi Chŏng-hae from Kyŏngsang Province submitted a letter to the Qing envoys in Hansŏng, volunteering to go to Mukden to serve the Qing and "our emperor" (K., *a hwangje*).[90]

The Qing used its intensive contacts with Chosŏn as a powerful tool to manage its relations with other political entities. In 1638, a year after it converted Chosŏn from a younger brother into an outer *fan*, the Qing changed the Chinese name of the Mongolian Superintendency from Menggu yamen to Lifan yuan, applying the Chosŏn precedent to add the Mongols, too, to the Qing-centric family of nations as a *fan*. This move was part of the Manchu leaders' project of steadily transforming Mongol conceptualizations of their position in the Qing-dominated world.[91] In this sense, it could be argued that the dramatic change in the Manchu-Mongol relationship had deep roots in the Zongfan concepts promulgated by Han Chinese officials of the Manchu regime since the early 1630s. This shift could also indicate that the Qing was streamlining the administration of its outer *fan* in order to strengthen its centrality and pursue an imperial enterprise beyond Manchuria.

BARBARIANIZING CHOSŎN

The Chosŏn Model and the Chinese
Empire, 1644–1761

The year 1644 marked the beginning of a new stage in the Qing's exploitation of the "Chosŏn model" as an institutionalized policy for constructing a new imperial order within and beyond the Qing's borders. Informed by Chosŏn's status as the Qing's prototypical outer *fan*, this model manifested itself in well-established and highly programmed formalities in the contacts between the Qing and its outer *fan*. Through the Chosŏn model, the Qing rulers initiated a twofold transformation by reversing and institutionalizing the discourse of the civilized–barbarian distinction: they enshrined the Qing as the new Heavenly Dynasty at the center of the known universe and converted Chosŏn and other countries into countries of barbarians on its periphery. The Qing accomplished this transformation conclusively in the middle of the eighteenth century, when the court published the *Illustrations of Subordinate Peoples of the Imperial Qing* (Ch., *Huang Qing zhigong tu*).

This chapter reveals the prolonged process by which the Qing gradually reconstructed a Chinese empire in the post-Ming world by legitimizing, enhancing, and practicing its new dual identity as China/Zhongguo and the Heavenly Dynasty through the Chosŏn model in its foreign relations from the first half of the seventeenth century to the second half of the eighteenth century. Over the course of this century and a half, the macrotransformation of the Manchu regime's identity in the cosmopolitan politico-cultural context was deeply connected with its microtransformation in the Manchu-Chosŏn framework. If there was a tendency among China's neighbors to decenter the Middle Kingdom after the Ming, this chapter brings to light the process of recentering the Middle Kingdom undertaken by the Qing.[1]

Establishing a Dual Identity: The Qing as China and the Heavenly Dynasty

On October 30, 1644, Emperor Shunzhi offered a grand sacrifice to Heaven and Earth in the Qing's new capital, Beijing. He asserted that the Qing would "pacify China" (Ch., *sui Zhongguo*) and "set a good example for ten thousand countries" (Ch., *biaozheng wanbang*).[2] For many people, this event marked the rise of the Qing as the equivalent of China/Zhongguo. In 1767, after finding that a magistrate in Yunnan Province had failed to refer to the Qing as the "Heavenly Dynasty" or "China/Zhongguo" in an official note to the "foreign barbarians" of Burma, Emperor Qianlong furiously pointed out that "it is the rule for one to refer to the court as the 'Heavenly Dynasty' or 'China' when one mentions it to men from afar. Our country has unified the central area and external areas, and even the barbarians know the Great Qing's virtue and civilization."[3]

Emperor Qianlong's pronouncement indicates that the terms "Heavenly Dynasty" and "Zhongguo" were interchangeable. Historians of the Qing and modern China tend to follow the emperor, or at least the Qing's political discourse as developed by the emperor, by treating China/Zhongguo and the Heavenly Dynasty as synonymous terms, both referring to the political unit of the Qing. Yet what the emperor did not mention—or was perhaps not able to realize—was that the Qing did not acquire the two titles simultaneously when it replaced the Ming in the early seventeenth century. As the emperor indicated, the two terms were used for the Qing almost exclusively in the context of foreign relations with "men from afar" or "foreign barbarians," which generally referred to foreigners. In the domestic context, these terms were replaced by others, such as "the Great Qing," "our dynasty" (Ch., *wochao, benchao*, or *guochao*), "our country" (Ch., *wo guojia*), and "the imperial dynasty" (Ch., *huangchao* or *shengchao*). In the first years after 1644, some Qing officials described the new regime as the "Qing Dynasty" (Ch., *Qingchao*), a successor to the "Ming Dynasty" in the context of foreign communications; this usage is found in correspondence between officials in Guangzhou (Canton) and Siam in 1653. But *Qingchao* remains rare in Qing documents.[4]

As the Qing took over Beijing in 1644 and consolidated its rule over inner China afterward, it completed its transformation into Zhongguo, but its refashioning into the Heavenly Dynasty had barely started. In the late 1640s, when the Manchu Eight Banners were marching into South China, Southwest China, and Northwest China, the Qing began to use Chosŏn to construct its new image as the Heavenly Dynasty; however, the process turned out to be difficult and even embarrassing. According to early Qing archives, Qing scholars may have called the Qing the "Heavenly Dynasty" for the first time in a draft imperial edict in

1649 investing Yi Ho (King Hyojong) as the king of Chosŏn. The draft edict was written by Fu Yijian (1609–65), a Han Chinese literatus from Shandong Province who had won first place in the Qing's first imperial civil-service examination in 1645.[5] By emphasizing that the king of Chosŏn should be "an important subordinate serving the Heavenly Dynasty" (Ch., *pinghan tianchao*) and loyal to the "central civilized country" (Ch., *Huaxia*), Fu equated the Qing, which had become Zhongguo, with the Heavenly Dynasty and the civilized country. However, the final version of the edict that was sent to Chosŏn omitted the two latter terms and continued to use the term "upper country" to refer to the Qing, suggesting that the Qing was not yet prepared to claim to be the Heavenly Dynasty.[6]

China, or Zhongguo, could be defined in a general geographical sense by the Qing borders, regardless of how the borders were expanded and redrawn, so long as the Qing controlled the Ming's territory, or at least the central plain (Ch., *Zhongyuan*).[7] In fact, after 1644, when the Qing rulers began writing and revising their history, they deliberately deleted some Manchu terms referring to the Ming as Zhongguo. For example, Hongtaiji, in a letter to the Ming on July 29, 1632, had explained that the Jin fought with the Ming because "the Ming officials in Liaodong did not follow the way of China" (Ma., *Liyoodung i hafasa Dulimbai gurun i doroi tondoi beiderakū*), using the Manchu term *Dulimbai gurun* in clear reference to China/Zhongguo. Later, the narrative written in Chinese replaced the phrase "the way of China" (Ch., *Zhongguo/Zhongyuan zhi dao*) with "the way of rightness" (Ch., *zhengzhi zhi dao*). While Hongtaiji in 1632 had called the Ming "your China" (Ma., *suweni Dulimbai gurun*), the post-1644 Chinese edition replaced this term with "your country" (Ch., *erguo*), deleting the word for "China."[8] The changing terminology shows that after 1644 the Qing deeply identified itself with China.

Given the ethnic background of the ruling house of the Qing, many scholars have been interested in establishing when the Qing court officially used the Manchu term *Dulimbai gurun* to define itself as China/Zhongguo. Some cite the year 1689 and the Treaty of Nerchinsk that the Qing signed with Russia. In fact, the Qing court had used this Manchu term to represent its identity much earlier in its negotiations with Zheng Jing (1642–81), the eldest son of Zheng Chenggong (1624–62), who occupied Taiwan in 1662. While Zheng Jing never questioned the Qing's identity as China, he argued that Taiwan was not a part of China in an effort to secure for Taiwan an independent status like that of Chosŏn. Emperor Kangxi, however, reiterated in a decree in 1669 that Zheng belonged to the "people of China" (Ch., *Zhongguo zhi ren*; Ma., *Dulimbai gurun i niyalma*).[9] In the late Kangxi period, the Qing presented itself as China in a favorable and definitive way. For example, in his travelogue, the Manchu official Tulišen, who was dispatched as an envoy to the Turgūt Mongols in Russia in 1712, generally referred to the Qing as *Dulimbai gurun* ("China") or *meni Dulimbai gurun* ("our China"); these terms were rendered into Chinese as *Zhongguo* or *Zhonghua* when Tulišen's journal was published in 1723 in both languages. Tulišen also consistently translated terms such as "our place" (Ma., *meni bade*) as "our China" (Ch., *wo Zhongguo*) and referred to all people of the Great Qing, such as the Manchus, Han Chinese, and Mongols, as "people of China." More importantly, following Emperor Kangxi's instructions, Tulišen emphasized China's Confucian nature to Russia, claiming that "our country takes fidelity, filial piety, benevolence, justice, and sincerity as fundamentals" (Ma., *meni gurun i banjire tondo hiyoošun, gosin, jurgan, akdun be fulehe da obumbi*; Ch., *wo guojia yi zhong xiao ren yi xin wei genben*).[10]

By contrast, the Heavenly Dynasty, or Tianchao, could not be delineated in the same way, since it was based on the notion of all-under-Heaven—a China-centered politico-cultural term with no connection to borders in the geographical sense. Put another way, the Qing could define itself as China from within, but it could not identify itself as the Heavenly Dynasty without support from outside the Qing: the new regime would first have to erect a new, Qing-centric, and multinational Zongfan system. The expectation that the Qing would become a new imperial power required the regime to transform the countries that the Ming had represented as its *fan* into *fan* in the Qing's orbit. The Ming had pursued the same policy when it "became the ruler of China" (Ch., *zhu Zhongguo*) in 1368, immediately sending envoys to the countries that had served as *fan* of its predecessor, the Yuan Dynasty, with the aim of converting them into *fan* of the Ming.[11] However, unlike the Ming, the Manchu rulers in 1644 faced the tremendous challenge of overcoming their previous status as barbarians, as defined by the civilized–barbarian distinction. Compared with the mission to identify the Qing as China and as the legitimate successor to the Ming within the Qing's borders, the quest to construct the Qing as the new Heavenly Dynasty beyond its borders called for extraordinary effort.

From the perspective of comparative philology, the Chinese term "Tianchao" was not initially widely adopted in the Manchu language, in which it was literally rendered as *abkai gurun* ("Heavenly country").[12] The Manchu rulers had difficulty identifying with this term and the Chinese political concepts behind it. In July 1637, for example, after reviewing the draft edict of investiture to the king of Chosŏn, Hongtaiji commented that he did not like to equate himself with Heaven as the Ming had done, suggesting that his officials must have employed the Chinese word *tian* ("Heaven") or the Manchu term *abka* ("Heaven") in the draft.[13] Nevertheless, the task of reconstructing the Qing as the new China in the seventeenth century left the Manchu rulers with no choice but to embrace the term and the rationale behind it.

The intellectual transformation of the Qing ruling house is evident in the visit of the fifth Dalai Lama (1617–82) to Beijing in late 1652 and early 1653. The Qing's Manchu officials supported Emperor Shunzhi's plan to greet the Dalai Lama in Daiga in Inner Mongolia, arguing that the Ület Mongols, who controlled Tibet militarily at the time, would be pacified by the emperor's gracious behavior. But the Han Chinese officials argued that the emperor was "the ruler of all countries under Heaven" (Ch., *tianxia guojia zhi zhu*) and should not violate conventions by meeting with a lama, even the Dalai Lama, in person outside the capital. Still hesitant about going to Daiga, the emperor took part in a grand ceremony commemorating Confucius at the Directorate of Education (Ch., Guozi jian) in Beijing, where he knelt down twice, each time making three prostrations. The ceremony, attended by many high-ranking Manchu, Mongol, and Han Chinese officials and generals, conferred on the emperor the mantle of the supreme agent of Confucianism. Right after the ceremony, two Han Chinese grand secretaries, Hong Chengchou (1593–1665) and Chen Zhilin (1605–66), submitted a memorial to the emperor entreating him not to go to Daiga to welcome the Dalai Lama because astrological phenomena reported by the Imperial Astronomical Bureau suggested that intruders would threaten the emperorship. The two officials emphasized that "the way of Heaven is infinite" (Ch., *tiandao shenyuan*) and could not be predicted. After reading the memorial, the emperor immediately abandoned the idea of visiting Daiga. Instead he welcomed the Dalai Lama in the South Garden of Beijing.[14] As this episode suggests, the Manchu emperor had to adjust to his role as the Son of Heaven in the Confucian sense in the post-1644 politico-cultural and ideological contexts, notwithstanding the Qing's serious religious and military concerns over its western frontier in Inner Asia.

Reconstructing the Chinese Empire: The Rise of the Chosŏn Model

From East Asia to Southeast and Inner Asia: The Qing's Presentation of the Chosŏn Model

The Qing did not stand alone as it sought to construct its new dual identity. Chosŏn, the first Confucian outer *fan* of the Qing, played an unparalleled role in providing the Manchu conquerors with resources to form and articulate the Qing's new identity. As early as 1650, in a palace memorial to Emperor Shunzhi, the king called the Qing the "Heavenly Dynasty," even though the Qing court itself was still reluctant to use the term.[15] The development of Chosŏn's essential role in the Qing-centric Zongfan world can be divided into two historical phases: the seven years from 1637 to 1643 and the 251 years from 1644 to 1894. In the first phase, Chosŏn began serving as the outer *fan* of the Qing by adhering to the clearly formulated and institutionalized discipline of the Sino-Korean Zongfan system, which had functioned between the Ming and Chosŏn for more than two centuries. As chapter 1 described, the Qing was able to make a significant move toward the transformation of its identity by assuming the place of the Ming in the framework of Sino-Korean relations. The frequent visits of Chosŏn's tributary emissaries to Mukden provided the Qing with good opportunities to emphasize and practice its centrality in the known world.

After 1644, with its dramatic emergence as a Ming-style, nationwide regime and the extensive expansion of its territory, the Qing found itself in the position of having to manage relations with multiple neighboring countries, such as Annam, Ryukyu, Lanchang (Laos), Siam, Sulu (the Philippines), and Burma, that had served as subordinates to the Ming. Having inherited these *fan* from the Ming, what Qing China now needed to do was to resume and refashion the Zongfan system according to its own standards. On this front, the Qing had gained valuable experience from its institutionalized communications with Chosŏn since the 1630s and, through these communications, had developed a mature model of a Qing-centric Zongfan arrangement. The Chosŏn model laid out a path whereby a country or a political entity could follow Chosŏn into the Qing-centric system primarily by receiving imperial investitures from the Qing, adopting the regnal titles of the Qing in its calendar, and sending tributary emissaries to the Qing.[16] The Chosŏn model was a pattern centered on rituals.[17] Although the Qing-Chosŏn Zongfan relationship had been inaugurated by the Manchu military conquest of 1637, as a result of which the crown prince, another prince, and sons of high-ranking Chosŏn officials were detained in Mukden as hostages, the unpleasant situation began to change when the Qing released the hostages in 1644. The Qing also progressively reduced the tributes required of Chosŏn until, by the late 1730s, they were less than one-tenth of what they had been in the late 1630s and became a mere symbol of political subordination.[18] What accompanied the tributes was the performance of a set of highly programmed and increasingly elaborate formalities that demonstrated the hierarchical Zongfan order and the Qing's new normative identity.

In the first years after 1644, the Qing found the Chosŏn model the most powerful and practical way of managing its relations with other countries and of extending its influence and authority. Emperor Shunzhi articulated the importance of Chosŏn's model role in 1647 after the Qing army conquered Zhejiang, Fujian, and Guangdong Provinces and prepared to establish relations with Ryukyu, Annam, Siam, and Japan. On March 17 and August 25, the emperor announced that the Qing would "give preferential treatment to these countries

as to Chosŏn" (Ch., *yu Chaoxian yiti youdai*) as long as they "subordinated themselves to 'the civilized' and paid tribute to the court" (Ch., *qingxin xianghua,
chengchen rugong*).[19] In this way, the Manchu rulers publicized Chosŏn's prototypical *fan* status and established the Qing-Chosŏn relationship as the yardstick
for relations between the Qing and other countries or political entities. Rather
than adopting the aggressive colonial policy of the Yuan, the Qing learned from
the Ming's Zongfan mechanism, using the sophisticated and markedly Confucian Chosŏn model to maintain stability on its frontiers and to construct a new
Chinese empire beyond them.[20]

As a result of the Qing rulers' efforts at promoting the Chosŏn model after
1644, political units beyond the Qing's control also came to regard it as an ideal
way of solving conflicts with the Qing while retaining their own privileges.
Between 1662 and 1669, for example, when the Qing was trying to persuade
Zheng Jing to surrender in Taiwan, Zheng insisted on "following the Chosŏn
model" (Ch., *zhao Chaoxian shili*) into the Qing's Zongfan system by "proclaiming subordination and paying tribute" (Ch., *chengchen nagong*) but refraining
from cutting his hair in the Qing style.[21] For Zheng, the Chosŏn model appeared
to offer the most favorable and promising way to resolve the standoff with the
Qing. Emperor Kangxi refused this proposal on the grounds that Chosŏn had
been "always a foreign country" (Ch., *conglai suoyou zhi waiguo*; Ma., *daci bihe
encu gurun*), whereas Zheng belonged to the "people of China."[22] These negotiations show the perceived broad applicability and coverage of the Chosŏn model
in situations in which neither independence nor complete annexation was an
immediate and acceptable solution.

The Chosŏn model provided the Manchu ruling house with a general blueprint for dealing with other political entities. Over the Qing period, two parallel
central institutions were responsible for the affairs of outer *fan*: the Mongolian
Superintendency mainly managed outer *fan* located to the north and west of
Qing China, while the Ministry of Rites was in charge of *fan* in the east, the
south, and the west. This book focuses on the outer *fan* under the management
of the Ministry of Rites rather than those under the Mongolian Superintendency, although the two types of outer *fan* may have been associated through the
Chosŏn model in the early years of the Qing's expansion to Inner Asia and the
development of its Eurasian empire.

This inconspicuous connection between the eastern and western frontiers
of the Qing empire had manifested itself at least by 1653, when the Qing
invested the fifth Dalai Lama and the Gusi Khan of the Ület Mongols by
incorporating them into the Qing-dominated extended family and placing
them under the Qing's jurisdiction. At the time, the Mongolian Superintendency and the Ministry of Rites were administratively still closely connected

with one another: it was a Manchu minister (Ch., *shangshu*; Ma., *aliha amban*) from the Ministry of Rites, Langkio, and a vice minister (Ch., *shilang*; Ma., *ashan i amban*) from the Mongolian Superintendency, Sidali, who together gave the Dalai Lama and the Gusi Khan the books of investiture. The imperial statement in the khan's investiture book bore a remarkable resemblance to that issued to the new king of Chosŏn in 1649. It declared that the recipient must serve as the Qing's "subordinate" or "fence" (Ch., *pingfu*) "until the Yellow River becomes as narrow as a belt and Mount Tai becomes as small as a grindstone" (Ch., *daili shanhe*).[23] In addition, the mechanism governing the "local products" and tributes that the lama and the khan presented to the emperor and the empress dowager in 1654 and the imperial gifts the lama and the khan received in return was much like that used between the Qing and Chosŏn.[24] Finally, the imperial mandates of investiture (Ch., *gaoming*; Ma., *g'aoming*) that the Qing issued to the Dalai Lama and the Panchen Erdeni bore the same imperial seal—"Seal of declaring imperial mandate" (Ch., *zhigao zhi bao*; Ma., *hese wasimbure boobai*)—as had the mandate investing the new king of Chosŏn.[25]

If we compare the imperial codes of the Mongolian Superintendency and the Ministry of Rites, it seems that the former borrowed institutional regulations from the latter to formalize the communications between the Manchu rulers and the Mongol *fan* in Inner Asia. The prototypical role of Chosŏn in the Qing-centric Zongfan system may have contributed to the Qing's policy of integrating the Inner Asian political and military entities into the Qing's extended family.[26] On the surface, the geographical responsibilities of the Ministry of Rites did not overlap with those of the Mongolian Superintendency, as Qing officials confirmed in 1743, so Qing-Chosŏn contacts were ostensibly unrelated to Qing–Inner Asian contacts.[27] But on the political level, soon after 1644 the Qing rulers began to apply the Zongfan rationale behind the Chosŏn model to Inner Asia, along with the Manchu court's promulgation of the discourse of "all-under-Heaven" and "people without difference between the outside and the inside," as part of the long process of subordinating the Zunghar Mongols, whom the Qing rulers treated as people "beyond virtue and civilization."[28] Administratively, the Ministry of Rites was also in charge of the affairs of some lamas in Gansu and Shaanxi until the 1740s, when it transferred this jurisdiction to the Mongolian Superintendency.[29] The Chosŏn model, in this sense, gradually became a normative, standard, and powerful soft weapon in the repertoire of the Qing. It allowed the Manchu rulers to govern the areas conquered by the formidable Eight Banners in Inner Asia, which arguably smoothed the way for the Qing to insert its civil administrative system into these areas during the Yongzheng and Qianlong periods.

Who Were the Barbarians? The Imperial Code and the Qing's Reforms

Under the Qing, the Zongfan order was maintained and embodied by the exchange of emissaries between the Qing and its "subordinate countries" (Ch., *shuguo*; Ma., *tulergi gurun* or *harangga gurun*), which were generally described as "subordinate countries of foreign barbarians" (Ch., *waiyi shuguo*). All exchanges were conducted in accordance with *The Universal Tributary Regulations* (Ch., *Chaogong tongli*) codified by the Ministry of Rites, and the performance of the exchanges was supervised by the Host-Guest Office (Ch., Zhuke qingli si) of the Ministry of Rites. These regulations primarily consisted of the following seven mandates:

1. Investiture (Ch., *cefeng*): The Qing emperor gave the new king of each *fan* a patent of appointment through an imperial mandate of investiture along with a decree (Ch., *chiyu*) and an official seal for use in correspondence.
2. Regnal titles (Ch., *nianhao*): The *fan* adopted the Qing's regnal titles as the way to enumerate years.
3. Calendar (Ch., *shuoli*): The *fan* used the Qing's calendar and celebrated Chinese festivals.
4. The dispatch of emissaries to pay tribute to the Qing (Ch., *chaogong*), with a frequency individually determined by the Qing.
5. The conferral of noble rank on a deceased king or privileged members of the royal house of the *fan* (Ch., *fengshi*).
6. Reporting events to the Qing (Ch., *zoushi*): Each *fan* informed the emperor of important domestic events but did not need to ask for instructions and could assume that the Qing would not intervene in its domestic affairs.
7. Trade (Ch., *maoyi* or *hushi*), including trade at the frontiers and at the Foreign Emissaries' Common Accommodations (Ch., Huitong siyi guan; Ma., Acanjime isanjire tulergi gurun i bithe ubaliyambure kuren) in Beijing.[30]

The Qing made considerable changes to the Zongfan system that it inherited from the Ming. The Ming had also relied on *The Universal Tributary Regulations*, by which the Ministry of Rites managed routine exchanges between China and the "subordinate barbarian countries in the four quarters" (Ch., *fanguo* or *siyi*)—Chosŏn, Ryukyu, Annam, the Jurchens, Mongolia, and other countries and political entities—as well as interactions between the Ming and "indigenous chieftains" (Ch., *tuguan* or *tusi*), including local chieftains in Yunnan, Guangxi, Guizhou, Sichuan, Hunan, and Hubei.[31] But two significant changes distinguished the list of "foreign barbarian countries" in the new Qing regulations from the Ming's list. First, the Qing excluded "indigenous chieftains" from its list of tributaries because of its policy toward "barbarian chieftains" (Ch., *yimu*) in southwestern China. Known as "replacing the hereditary indigenous chieftains with rotating officials" (Ch., *gaitu guiliu*), the policy had been inaugurated by the Yuan and the Ming, but only in the Yongzheng period of the Qing was it carried out on a truly large scale.[32] The areas and populations under the chieftains' control were integrated simultaneously into the Qing's territory and into its household registration system.[33] The indigenous chieftains were thus outside the supervision of the Ministry of Rites. The line between barbarians belonging to these political units and barbarians from other countries was clear in the minds of the Manchu rulers at court and their deputies in the provinces.[34] Second, the Western countries gradually disappeared from the list of foreign barbarians in the tributary regulations. By the late fourteenth century, the Ming had fifteen outer *fan* countries, and the majority of these became the Qing's outer *fan*, including Chosŏn, Ryukyu, Annam, Lanchang, Siam, Sulu, and Burma.[35] From the 1760s to the 1840s during the Qing period, the list also included the Netherlands and the countries of the Western Ocean (Ch., *Xiyang*), but by the 1890s only these seven Asian countries remained on the list.[36]

Whereas in the Qianlong period the Mongolian, Tibetan, and Muslim areas under the management of the Mongolian Superintendency had "all entered [the Qing's] map and registers" (Ch., *xianru bantu*) and were presented "like prefectures and counties" (Ch., *youru junxian*),[37] the "subordinate countries of foreign barbarians" under the supervision of the Ministry of Rites were not integrated into the Qing's core territory. Nor would these countries be treated as parts of the Republic or the People's Republic of China in the twentieth century. By the same token, the dual management system for the outer *fan*—the Mongolian Superintendency and the Ministry of Rites—under the Qing made it difficult for people outside this institutional mechanism to draw a clear line between them. This might explain why, as discussed in chapter 5, some Qing officials in the late nineteenth century responded to complications involving Chosŏn by suggesting that Beijing apply its policy vis-à-vis Mongolia and Tibet to Chosŏn by converting Chosŏn into prefectures and counties, as they supposed Chosŏn had been in the Qianlong period. The rationale behind this suggestion applied the basic structure of the Qing empire on its western frontier to the management of its eastern one, highlighting Chosŏn's prominent subordinate position within the empire.

The role of the Qing-Chosŏn Zongfan relationship is thus significant. This relationship should not be treated simply as a specific instance of the Zongfan system, as scholars have typically done. Rather, it is best understood as a prototype that shaped the formation of the Qing's Zongfan system and helped the Manchu regime transform its political identity for the purpose of claiming centrality and accessing orthodox legitimacy in the process of reshuffling the Chinese world. In short, the Qing-Chosŏn relationship was the seedbed of the Qing's entire Zongfan arrangement, from which the political legitimacy of both sides—the Qing and its outer *fan*—sprang.

Civilizing the Center: The Practice of the Chosŏn Model

Five aspects of the Qing's practice of the Chosŏn model, aspects embodied in and undergirded by ritual practices and documentary discourse, showcased the Qing's identity as the civilized center. These aspects concern the frequency and composition of missions; the overland route and the Sino-Korean geographical boundaries; humble palace memorials, imperial mandates and decrees, and orthodox legitimacy; tributes, gifts, and court-to-court interactions; and receptions and rituals.

The Frequency and Composition of Imperial and Tributary Missions

The exchange of missions between the Qing and Chosŏn started in 1637 and continued without interruption until the Sino-Japanese War of 1894–95. The frequency of Chosŏn's missions to the Qing was higher than that of any other country. Whereas other subordinate countries sent tributary missions to Beijing every other year (Ryukyu), every three years (Siam), every four years (Annam), every five years (Sulu), or every ten years (Lanchang and Burma), Chosŏn dispatched several missions every year.[38] Although the imperial code required Chosŏn to send an annual tributary mission at the end of each year that would simultaneously serve as the mission for the winter solstice, the imperial birthday, and the lunar New Year, Chosŏn never hesitated to send more emissaries under different names, dispatching a new mission before the previous one had even returned in order to nourish its relationship with the Qing.[39] From 1637 to 1894, Chosŏn sent about 698 official missions to the Qing for twenty-six different purposes, an average of 2.71 missions per year.[40] In 1784 and 1788, Emperor Qianlong commented jubilantly that in this respect Chosŏn was a peer of the Qing's inner *fan*.[41]

According to the imperial regulations, a Korean mission was to have thirty members: an envoy, an associate envoy, a secretary, three interpreters, and twenty-four tribute guard officers. The envoy, associate envoy, and secretary were the three key members. As a special privilege to Chosŏn, the number of attendants and servants attached to the mission was not limited. By contrast, the missions from Ryukyu, Lanchang, Burma, and the Netherlands were not to exceed twenty members; those from other Western countries were limited to twenty-two, those from Siam to twenty-six, and those from Annam to thirty.[42] Many Korean scholars and businessmen visited Beijing as mission attendants or servants in order to experience Chinese culture or to seek their fortunes, so a Korean mission often numbered several hundred people. For example, the annual tributary mission of 1653 had a total of 225 members, the gratitude mission of 1777 a total of 310, the gratitude mission of 1803 a total of 213, and the congratulatory mission of 1889 a total of 311.[43] In 1829, two missions with more than six hundred people combined arrived in Beijing at the same time, forcing the Ministry of Rites and the Ministry of Works to borrow twenty large tents from the Imperial Household Department (Ch., Neiwu fu) to house the additional visitors. Until the late nineteenth century, the legions of Chosŏn's missions continued their pilgrimages to Beijing every year with a large number of tributes and horses.[44]

By contrast, the Qing sent far fewer and smaller imperial missions to Chosŏn. From 1637 to 1894, the Qing undertook 172 missions to Hansŏng, an average of 0.67 missions per year. In the early Qing, the Manchu court frequently dispatched emissaries to investigate cases of homicide and smuggling at the border, to negotiate resolutions to these cases with the king, and sometimes to discuss the punishment of Korean officials who failed to satisfy the Qing. As early as the Shunzhi period, the Manchu court began to reduce the number of its envoys, the rationale behind the change being the Zongfan idea of "cherishing the small." In May 1653, for example, in the course of investigating a cross-border case of homicide, the Ministry of Rites proposed to ask the Korean emissary in Beijing to carry the imperial documents to the king instead of dispatching an imperial envoy for the purpose, given that "Chosŏn is a country of men from afar" (Ch., *Chaoxian guo xi yuanren*). Emperor Shunzhi endorsed this proposal, declaring that "hereafter, do not propose to send envoys to disturb the *fan* [Ch., *fanbang*] with minor matters."[45] By the middle period of Emperor Kangxi's reign, such envoys to Hansŏng disappeared entirely.[46]

From this point on, imperial missions to Chosŏn were of two primary types: missions for investiture and missions to confer noble rank, both relating to power shifts that required the Chinese emperor's bestowal of legitimacy. In the early period, an imperial mission contained around a hundred men, many of whom were Manchu bannermen of the Eight Banners who joined the mission for the purpose of trade. In 1658 Emperor Shunzhi significantly trimmed the size of the missions by calling for the end of Manchu trade in Hansŏng. After that, a mission comprised an envoy, an associate envoy, four interpreters, and eighteen attendants.[47] In 1845 and 1846, Emperor Daoguang further reduced the number of core members to four.[48] Taking attendants into account, after the early nineteenth century an imperial mission had fewer than thirty members in total. The mission in 1876 comprised twenty members, and the last mission, in 1890, had twenty-eight.[49]

All imperial envoys to Chosŏn—from the first envoy in 1637, Inggŭldai, to the last one in 1890, Xuchang (1838–92)—were Manchu officials. They included some members of the Mongol and Han Chinese Eight Banners but no non-banner Han Chinese, whereas envoys to Annam and Ryukyu were mainly non-banner Han Chinese rather than Manchus. By at least the 1760s, Han Chinese scholars were fully aware of this ethnic discrepancy, though some of their Korean counterparts were not.[50] The door was never opened for Han Chinese to participate in tributary affairs in Korea. The exclusion was perhaps rooted in the implicit demands of the civilized–barbarian distinction and the Qing's need to transcend the pre-1644 Manchu-Korean relationship: the Manchu court had to demonstrate, maintain, and consolidate its legitimacy as the human and institutional agent of the Mandate of Heaven and to strengthen its claim to civilized centrality and Chineseness through the hierarchical relationship. Still, some Manchu envoys, such as Akdun (1685–1756) in 1717, broadly identified themselves from a cultural perspective as "Han envoys" (Ch., *hanjie*) from the "central civilized country" (Ch., *Zhonghua, Zhongxia*).[51]

The Overland Route, the Willow Palisade, and Geographical Boundaries

In the post-1644 period, the emissaries of the two countries traveled on an overland route, which was about 950 miles (3,000 Chinese *li*) long and linked Hansŏng and Beijing via around eighty-two stations. The route passed through P'yŏngyang, Ŭiju, the Yalu River, Fenghuang City, Mukden, Shanhai Pass, Fengrun, and Tongzhou (see map 2.1). From 1644 to 1894, both Korean and Manchu emissaries were required to follow the overland route, the sole exception being the last imperial mission in 1890, which took a maritime route due to exceptional circumstances. In general, a mission took forty to sixty days to reach Beijing from Hansŏng, and an imperial mission from Beijing faced the same trudge to Hansŏng.[52]

In Manchuria the overland route skirted the long Willow Palisade (Ch., Liutiao bian)—a system of levees and trenches planted with willow trees, their branches tied together—from Fenghuang City to Shanhai Pass, where it almost connected with the Great Wall. The Manchu rulers built the palisade from the late 1630s to the 1680s in order to preserve their economic privileges by demarcating domestic boundaries between Manchu, Mongol, and Han Chinese regions. In the early period of Kangxi's reign, the palisade connecting Shanhai

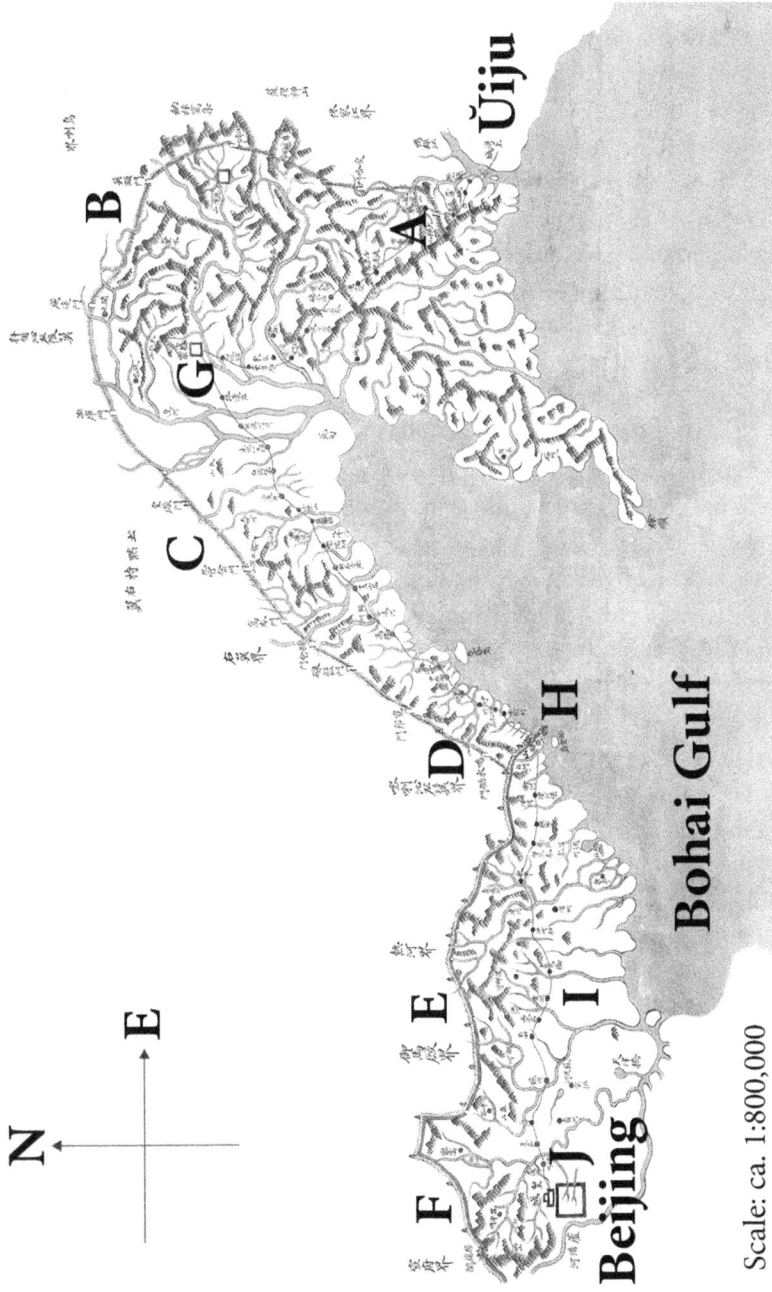

MAP 2.1. The overland route between Beijing and Ŭiju in the late eighteenth century. The line connecting points A, B, C, and D on the map marks the Willow Palisade, which started at Fenghuang City (A) and ended near the Great Wall (the line connecting points D, E, and F). The line connecting points A, G (Mukden), H (Shanhai Pass), I (Fengrun), and J (Tongzhou) forms the overland route that Chosŏn's emissaries took to Beijing after crossing the Yalu River. *Yŏji to*, handwritten map, preserved at the Kyujanggak Institute for Korean Studies at Seoul National University. Copyright Kyujanggak Institute for Korean Studies.

Pass in the west and Fenghuang City in the east, known as the Old Fence, was around 590 miles (1,900 *li*) long and had sixteen fence gates, while in the north the New Fence between Weiyuan Village and Fateha Mountain was 215 miles (690 *li*) with four gates.[53] Fenghuang City, located at the southeastern corner of the east wing of the Old Fence, was under the supervision of the Manchu General of Mukden (Ch., Shengjing jiangjun) and had a gate (K., *ch'akmun*; Ch., *zhamen*), known as Fenghuang Gate, about three miles (eight *li*) to the southeast of the city.[54] The Qing built Fenghuang Gate between 1638 and 1639 and extended it southeast toward the Yalu River between 1685 and 1690 up to a location about nine miles (thirty *li*) from the city.[55] The gate was the only pass through which Korean emissaries could enter the Qing's "ancestral territory" (Ch., *genben zhongdi*) in Manchuria.

Between the gate and the boundary river lay a Qing-controlled area in which no one was allowed to live. In the late seventeenth century, this area spanned about thirty-four miles.[56] The Korean emissaries could pass through this area freely and were not subjected to security checks until they reached Fenghuang Gate. The garrison major of the Manchu bannermen at Fenghuang City did not welcome, check, or send off the missions beyond the gate, which may help explain why Korean emissaries were occasionally robbed by Chinese bandits outside the gate.[57] For the Korean visitors, Fenghuang Gate was thus more like a border-line than the Yalu River was, although the geographical borderline ran along the middle course of the river.

After entering Fenghuang Gate, the Koreans were to proceed to Beijing within twenty-eight days under the escort of Qing soldiers, passing through thirty-nine transfer stations (Ch., *gongshi guanshe*; Ma., *alban jafara elcin i tatara guwan i boo*). In fact, however, the visitors were so familiar with the route that generally no Chinese soldiers accompanied them to Beijing. The absence of Chinese monitors endowed the Koreans with fair freedom to visit places along their route and interview local people, enriching their travel journals, which eventually constituted a voluminous collection known as *Yŏnhaengnok* (The records of the journey to Beijing). All emissaries of the Qing's *fan* were required to follow specific tributary routes and dared not deviate from them. For example, Ryukyu's emissaries were instructed to arrive at Min'an in Fujian, Sulu's at Xiamen in Fujian, those of Western countries at Macau in Guangdong, Siam's at Humen in Guangdong, Annam's at Taiping in Guangxi, and Burma's at Yongchang in Yunnan. After the emissaries reached the designated places, the governor-general and the governor of the province would report their arrival to the Ministry of Rites and instruct subordinate officials to send them on to Beijing. Chosŏn's emissaries had no such relations with officials in the provinces through which they passed, and they communicated directly with the Ministry of Rites. In other words, Chosŏn's contacts with the Qing were under Beijing's direct control, which enabled Beijing to use Chosŏn to portray the harmony of its Zongfan system whenever necessary.

Along the overland route, the high frequency and large size of Chosŏn's missions produced considerable and lucrative commercial opportunities for merchants from both countries. What flowed into the Qing realm in massive quantities, in addition to Korean and Japanese goods, was silver. The mission of 1712, for instance, carried more than two hundred thousand taels of silver to Beijing, while the one in 1777 brought more than ninety-three thousand taels. The bulk of the silver was originally from Japan, acquired through trade between Tsushima and Chosŏn. The Hansŏng–Fenghuang City–Mukden–Beijing overland trade route was an extension of the Kyoto–Osaka–Tsushima–Pusan–Hansŏng overland and maritime trade route, with Hansŏng and Beijing the two major entrepôts on the combined route. Financially, the three nations made up an integrated international silver network, and in the eighteenth century the amount of silver that poured into the Qing from Chosŏn annually could reach five hundred thousand to six hundred thousand taels, which contributed to the Qing's prosperity but aroused serious concerns among Korean officials.[58] In this sense, it is not an exaggeration to say that the Beijing–Hansŏng overland route was the most prosperous and most lucrative long-distance and international trade route in East Asia before Chosŏn opened treaty ports in the 1870s and 1880s.

Humble Palace Memorials, Imperial Mandates and Decrees, and Orthodox Legitimacy

The imperial court in Beijing and the royal court in Hansŏng interacted through meticulously formatted court documents written in accordance with highly institutionalized hierarchical norms. From 1637 on, the most important category among the documents that Chosŏn submitted to the Qing was the king's humble palace memorials (K., *p'yo*; Ch., *biao*). In 1705 the Ministry of Rites in Beijing laid down a set of new criteria for the syntax of these memorials that Chosŏn adhered to for the next 190 years, but the king was still free to use his own terms in composing other kinds of palace memorials.[59] The humble memorials were aimed at strengthening the Qing's authority by reiterating and affirming the reciprocal and hierarchical relationship between the emperor and the king. The memorial submitted by the crown prince and deputy king of Chosŏn, Yi Yun (King Gyŏngjong), on April 14, 1721, in the sixtieth year of Emperor Kangxi's reign, to congratulate the emperor on his birthday, is a typical example. The memorial was written on a sheet of well-made Korean paper in tiny, narrow Chinese characters evenly arranged in twenty-three vertical lines from right to left—although a memorial could, on occasion, exceed fifty lines—and it carefully followed the rules of honorific elevation, exactly as the Qing had mandated in 1705.[60] Refer-ring to himself as "your minister" (K., *sin*; Ch., *chen*) of a vassal (Ch., *fanfu*), who could hardly bear his separation from the court (Ch., *queting*), Yi proclaimed that "Your Majesty raises all people of the world by assuming the Mandate of Heaven. The world is peaceful and imperial civilization extends to all places. Your Majesty has pacified the four seas, and ten thousand countries have come to revere Your Majesty [Ch., *sihai yi er wanguo laiwang*]."[61]

In such highly formalized memorials, the king frequently called himself "subordinate" or "minister," Chosŏn the "small country," and the Qing the "big country," the "upper country," the "big dynasty," the "central dynasty," or the "Heavenly Dynasty."[62] These Qing-mandated terms exploited Chosŏn's subordinate status to highlight the Qing's centrality in the early eighteenth century. Year after year, Chosŏn, as the representative of the others, helped consolidate the Qing's supreme cultural identity as well as Qing hegemony through its performance of such written subservience. Upon receipt of the king's humble memorials, the emperor generally wrote on the cover in red ink, "I have learned of the appreciative memorial that you, the king, respectfully presented. Let the relevant ministry [the Ministry of Rites] know." The com-ments were made either in Manchu ("Wang sini kesi de hengkileme wesim-buhe be saha, harangga jurgan sa.") or Chinese ("Lanwang zouxie. Zhidao liao. Gaibu zhidao.").

On the Qing side, the imperial decrees granting a deceased king noble rank or investing a new king with a patent of appointment also served to consoli-date the hierarchy. The special terms used in these edicts had their own rules, which underwent a process of institutionalization after 1644. When the Qing invested Yi Chong as king in January 1638 (the first investiture that the Qing performed), the decree stated only that Chosŏn would be recognized as *fan* to the Qing forever.[63] But after 1644 the Manchu court began to include additional terms with strong political meanings in the Zongfan context. For example, the decree of investiture in 1649 clearly defined Chosŏn as an outer *fan* in a "remote area" (Ch., *xiahuang*) that submitted itself to the Qing's virtues and civiliza-tion. In 1675 the phrase "cherishing the eastern country" (Ch., *huairou dongtu*) appeared in the decrees.[64] These terms substantially broadened the scope of the Qing's political and cultural ideology and transformed its identity in the context of the civilized–barbarian dichotomy.

On March 6, 1725, Emperor Yongzheng issued a mandate and a decree to Yi Gŭm to invest him as the king and his wife as the queen. The mandate of inves-titure (Ch., *fengtian gaoming*; Ma., *abkai hesei g'aoming*) consisted of five con-nected pieces of dyed ramie cloth in red, blue, black, white, and yellow from right to left. Each of the five sections was surrounded by a pattern of flying dragons (see figures 2.1 and 2.2). In the mandate Emperor Yongzheng stated, "The great strategy is simply to extend civilization [Ch., *jiaohua*; Ma., *tacihiyan wen*] to the countries from afar [Ch., *haibang*; Ma., *goroki gurun*]. . . . Generations of your court have been sincerely loyal and trustworthy and have been paying tribute diligently [Ch., *zhigong qinxiu*; Ma., *tušan alban be kiceme faššambi*]." In investing Yi Gŭm the "king of Chosŏn" (Ch., *Chaoxian guowang*; Ma., *Coohiyan gurun i wang*), the emperor emphasized that the king "shall serve as the fence on the eastern land [Ch., *pinghan dongfan*; Ma., *dergi bade fiyanji dalikū*], devoutly use the imperial calendar [Ch., *qiangong zhengshuo*; Ma., *forgon ton be olhošome ginggulembi*], pacify the land, and assist the imperial house forever [Ch., *jiafu yu huangjia*; Ma., *ejen i boode aisilame wehiyembi*]." The emperor advised the king to "use a pure and genuine mind to serve the Heavenly court [Ch., *tianshi*; Ma., *abkai gurun*]."[65] A decree to the king articulated this point again by stating, "You should be loyal forever and efficiently govern the land as a minister from afar [Ch., *houfu*; Ma., *jecen i golo*], while you should be loyal and obedient and serve as a fence [Ch., *pinghan*; Ma., *fiyanji dalikū*] for the Heavenly house [Ch., *tianjia*; Ma., *gurun boo*]."[66]

The Chinese and Manchu terms of the imperial edicts portrayed the king as a family member of the Qing court, and they became more sophisticated in the Qianlong period. The imperial edicts to the king in 1757, for instance, referred to Chosŏn as a "fence," a "subordinate country" (Ch., *shuguo*; Ma., *harangga gurun*), a "remote submission" (Ch., *yuanfu*; Ma., *goroki i jecen*), and a "lower country" (Ch., *xiaguo*; Ma., *fejergi gurun*) of the "Middle Kingdom" (Ch., *Zhongchao*, *Zhongbang*; M., *Dulimbai gurun*). The edicts also emphasized that the king's court (M., *wang ni boo*) had been loyal to and received special rewards from the "Heavenly court" (Ch., *tianshi*; Ma., *han i hargašan*).[67] By invoking these norms, the Qing explicitly presented itself as the civilized center—China and the Heavenly Dynasty—in both Chinese and Manchu terms.

In his memorials to the emperor, the king used a gold seal received from the Qing. From early 1637 to early 1653, the seal had only Manchu characters, which read *Coohiyan gurun i wang ni doron* (seal of the king of the country of Chosŏn). On April 22, 1653, Emperor Shunzhi, evidently displeased by the absence of Chinese script from the seal, instructed the Ministry of Rites to make a new seal that included "Chinese characters" (Ch., *hanzi*). As a result, the words *Chaoxian guowang zhi yin* (seal of the king of the country of Chosŏn) were added to the seal.[68] The emperor did not explain his rationale for the change, but his decision underscored the new dynasty's Chineseness. On the Qing side, the emperors, in their mandates to Chosŏn, always used the "seal of declaring imperial mandate," which carried both a Chinese text, *Zhigao zhi bao*, and a Manchu one, *Hese wasimbure boobai*, exactly the same text that appeared on the imperial mandates

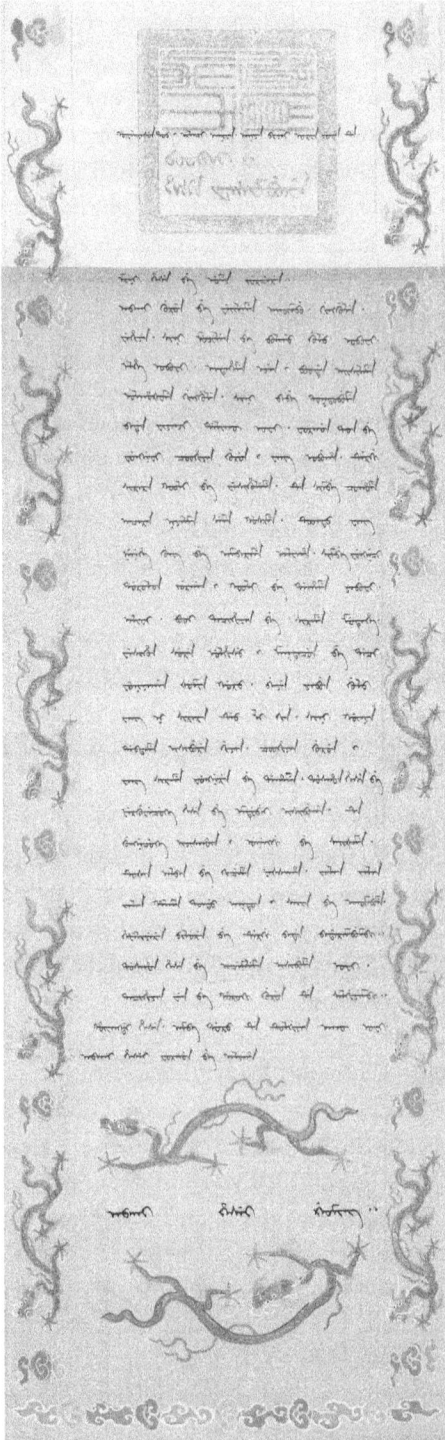

FIGURE 2.1. The Manchu section of the imperial mandate to invest the king of Chosŏn in 1725. *Cefeng Chaoxian guowang Li Qin fengtian gaoming*, preserved at Jangseogak, the Academy of Korean Studies, Korea. Copyright Academy of Korean Studies.

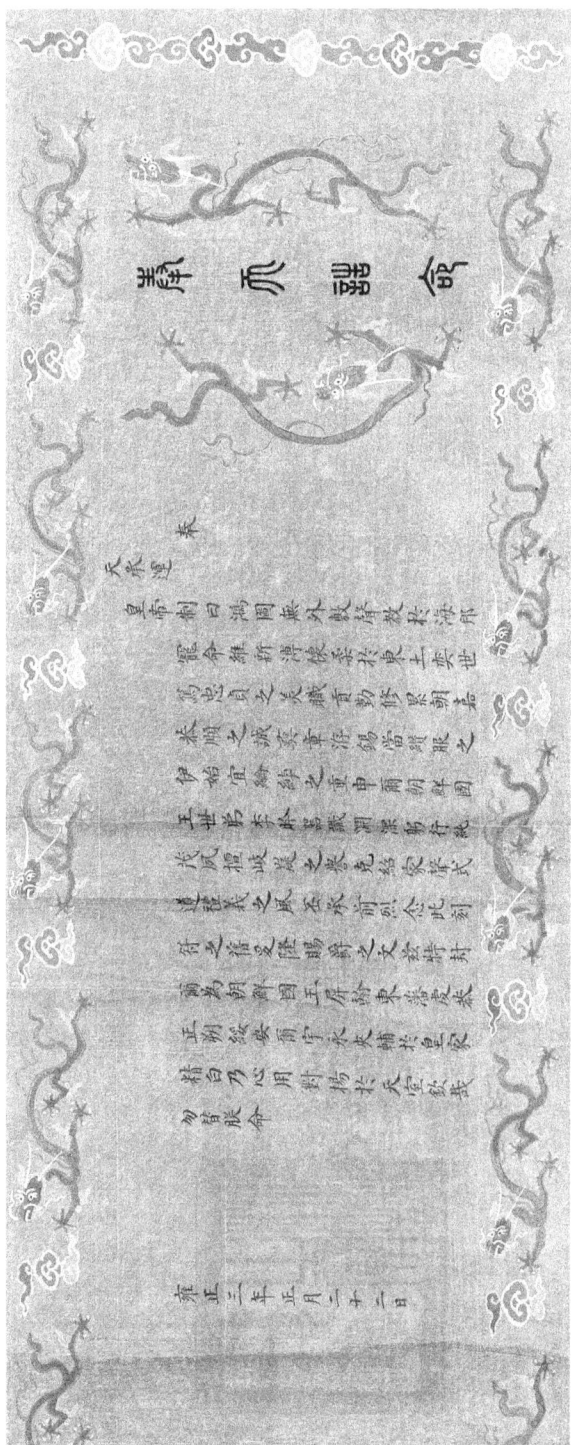

FIGURE 2.2. The Chinese section of the imperial mandate to invest the king of Chosŏn in 1725. *Cefeng Chaoxian guowang Li Qin fengtian gaoming*, preserved at Jangseogak, the Academy of Korean Studies, Korea. Copyright Academy of Korean Studies.

issued to the Dalai Lama and the Panchen Erdeni in Tibet. The combination of languages reflected the polyglot politics of a multiethnic empire.[69]

The imperial investiture of the king helps explain a paradox in the Qing period: certain Confucian countries, in particular Chosŏn and Annam, were privately reluctant to identify the Qing as the supreme representative of Chinese culture, but in practice they never challenged its status as the superior country and frequently sent tributary missions to Beijing to display their deference. The explanation for the apparent paradox lies in the fact that the missions fulfilled a dual purpose in establishing not only the legitimacy of the Qing but also that of the monarchs of the *fan*. The Zongfan relationship between the Qing and its *fan* was an incarnation of this symbiotic and synergistic legitimacy, namely, the orthodox legitimacy embodied in the highly programmed rituals involved in the exchange of emissaries. This orthodox legitimacy was the goal for which King Taksin (r. 1767–82) of the Thonburi regime of Siam sent tributary missions to Beijing to pursue investiture after the fall of the Ayutthaya regime (1350–1767), even though King Taksin's understanding of "paying tribute" (Ch., *jingong*) was very different from that of the Qing.[70] The need for legitimacy could also explain why Nguyễn Huệ, the leader of the peasant rebellion against the Lê Dynasty (1428–1788) of Annam, defeated the Qing army in 1789 but nonetheless accepted the Qing's investiture in 1790. It was also in 1790 that Burma accepted the Qing investiture after winning the Burmese-Qing War in the early 1770s.[71] In addition to pragmatic concerns reflecting geopolitics and China's military might, securing political legitimacy from China proved crucial for these regimes' own rule.

Tributes, Gifts, and Court-to-Court Interactions

The Qing ritual code clearly listed the types and quantities of tribute that Chosŏn had to present for different purposes. After 1644, these fell into eight major categories. Beyond the most official category of annual tribute, designated as "standard tribute" (Ch., *zhenggong*), the king generally referred to the items in the other seven categories, such as those marking the imperial birthday, the lunar New Year, and the winter solstice, as "gifts" or "local products." The Qing accepted all of the submitted items and did not challenge the king's choice of terms, although it preferred to refer to the items as "tribute."[72]

While the annual tribute marked a country-to-country relationship, all other categories of tribute, which were presented specifically to the emperor, the empress, and the dowager empress, suggested a strong court-to-court connection. The Ministry of Rites accepted the annual tribute as a routine matter, but it had to submit memorials to the emperor for instructions on how to handle tribute in other categories. In the early Qing, the Ministry of Rites forwarded all tribute items to the Ministry of Revenue and later to the Imperial Household Department, which was in charge of the affairs of the Manchu royal house and had its own financial system independent of the one managed by the Ministry of Revenue.[73] Therefore, although the Qing-Chosŏn Zongfan relationship seemed to manifest itself mainly in hierarchical country-to-country interactions, in reality it was a dual system involving the two countries and the two courts.

The gifts that the imperial envoys carried to Chosŏn were directed at specific members of the royal family, including the king, the queen, the crown prince, and the dowager queen. Usually the envoys brought first-rate silk for official robes. When imperial missions were dispatched to extend the emperor's condolences on the deaths of core royalty, some gifts were consumed at the funeral ceremonies, while others were converted into 150 to 300 taels of silver by the Ministry of Revenue and delivered to the Korean royal house. Over the course of the seventeenth and eighteenth centuries, imperial envoys followed a precise routine to deliver their condolences and gifts. The last such mission occurred in 1890, and it is explored in detail in chapter 5.

Receptions, Ritual Performances, and the Civilized Qing

Chosŏn's emissaries were well accommodated at each transfer station after they entered China, but they had to prepare food for themselves until they arrived in Beijing. Upon reaching their residence in Beijing, the Foreign Emissaries' Common Accommodations, the emissaries first visited the Ministry of Rites to present the king's memorials and the list of tribute items. All emissaries from Chosŏn and from other countries, as well as the kings they represented, had to submit their documents to the emperor through the ministry, with which they could communicate via official notes (Ch., *ziwen*). In the main hall of the ministry, the emissaries would pass the memorials to the head officials, who would place the memorials in front of the imperial tablet on a table in the middle of the hall. The emissaries would then kneel down once to make three prostrations toward the head officials, who would in turn bow three times to the emissaries with their hands folded in front (Ch., *zuoyi*, a ritual practiced between officials of equal ranks). Once they had finished, the emissaries would kneel down three times, each time making three prostrations toward the tablet.[74] The ministry would submit the documents to the emperor the next day, while the emissaries returned to their residence to wait for the imperial audience.

The Qing's commander general of the Metropolitan Infantry Brigade Yamen (Ch., Bujun tongling yamen) sent soldiers to guard the emissaries' residence.[75]

Three additional institutions were involved in hosting the guests: the Court of Imperial Entertainments (Ch., Guanglu si) delivered daily food and drink, distributed to each member of the mission according to rank; the Ministry of Revenue brought fodder for the Koreans' horses; and the Ministry of Works provided charcoal. These meticulous regulations embodied the Qing's policy of "cherishing men from afar."

During their stay in Beijing, the emissaries had various responsibilities to fulfill. If there was a grand court assembly of officials in the Forbidden City, the emissaries had to attend and pay homage at the end of the wing of the Qing civil officials. A major task was to pay a formal visit to the emperor at either the Summer Palace in Beijing or the Summer Palace in Rehe (Chengde). After the audience, the emissaries would be invited to attend certain events, such as banquets in the Forbidden City, performances of Chinese operas, or fireworks shows at the Summer Palace.[76] All ritual procedures, in particular the highest level of kowtow, were minutely regulated and fastidiously practiced. Such rituals between the Chinese emperor and foreign emissaries had been defined and institutionalized at least since the "great rituals" laid out in *The Rituals of the Great Tang* (Ch., *Da Tang Kaiyuan li*), compiled in the eighth century.[77] In the Ming and the Qing, the rituals became extremely elaborate, and the Korean emissaries were required to rehearse the complicated ceremonies in advance as a sign of their loyalty and as part of the process that would "civilize the barbarians in the four quarters" (Ch., *feng siyi*).[78] Rituals helped maintain the political arrangement and strengthen the identities of all participants.[79] In grand court gatherings, emissaries from Chosŏn were usually the first representatives of the outer *fan* to perform the rituals for the emperor, as on February 9, 1675, at the Lantern Festival, where the Chosŏn emissaries congratulated Kangxi ahead of their Russian, Kalka Mongol, and Ület Mongol counterparts.[80] Chosŏn's role as an exemplar was particularly prominent in the late eighteenth century during the Qianlong period, when the Qing in many cases "followed the model for Chosŏn" (Ch., *zhao Chaoxian zhi li*) in managing its bilateral exchanges with Annam, Ryukyu, and Siam.[81] Chinese scholars at the time also widely regarded Chosŏn as the "model for other countries" (Ch., *zhuguo zhi zhang*).[82]

The emissaries also attended two major official banquets, one held at the Ministry of Rites and the other at the emissaries' residence. An astonishing number of institutions were involved in their organization: the Court of Imperial Entertainments; the Food Supply Office (Ch., *Jingshan qingli si*) of the Ministry of Rites; the Ministries of Revenue, Works, and War; Shuntian Prefecture; and the Revenue Superintendent of Chongwen Gate (Ch., *Liangyi shuiwu jiandu*). Royal contractors (Ch., *hanghu*) were also assigned specific tasks. Each of the three key members of the mission was treated to what was known as a fifth-level Manchu banquet and the other members to a sixth-level one, preferential treatment not afforded to emissaries from any other country. The high cost of the banquets was fully covered by the Qing and, not surprisingly, the banquets were replete with ritual performances reinforcing the bilateral hierarchical order.[83] The imperial code included an "illustration of the banquets for Chosŏn's tributary emissaries" (Ch., *Chaoxian gongshi yantu*) and specified that the seating arrangements for banquets held for emissaries from other countries should follow the Chosŏn pattern (Ch., *geguo gongshi fangci*).[84]

During their sojourn in Beijing, the emissaries, particularly scholars without official status or responsibilities, were enthusiastic about socializing with Qing literati. The tradition of such interactions had started in Ming times but had been suspended in the Ming-Qing transition period because of the anti-Manchu attitudes that were prevalent in Chosŏn. Indeed, before the eighteenth century, the three key members of the tributary mission barely left their residence to meet with Chinese officials or scholars because many Korean scholars embracing Neo-Confucianism saw the Qing as a barbarous country and regarded the tributary mission as a humiliation.[85] In the 1760s, however, literary social gatherings involving Korean emissaries again became frequent and continued until the 1890s. In the 1860s, many Chinese officials, such as Dong Wenhuan (1833–77) of the Imperial Academy (Ch., Hanlin yuan), who was known for calligraphy and epigraphy, actively socialized with Koreans.[86] On the Korean side, Pak Kyu-su (1807–76), an emissary who visited Beijing in 1872, befriended more than a hundred famous Chinese scholars through social gatherings.[87]

Versed in the same Confucian classics, adhering to the same Neo-Confucianism, and using the same Chinese characters, the Qing and Chosŏn scholars could easily identify one another as men of the same caliber. They met for drinks, composed poems, and exchanged their own compositions and calligraphy. That Chosŏn was known as "Little China" might also have lent these transnational literary social gatherings a homogenous cultural identity. These savants formed an informal perennial club in which they exchanged ideas about history and literature and improved their perceptions of each other's countries. According to Key-hiuk Kim, their communications also "assured Korea of a constant stream of information and knowledge concerning the latest intellectual trends in China."[88]

When they gathered with their Han Chinese friends, the Korean guests usually showed an aversion to Manchu customs, such as the Manchu-style official robe and hairstyle, and were very proud of their Ming-style robes and hats, in keeping with the civilized–barbarian dichotomy. But in 1766, when Hong Tae-yong (1731–83) expressed contempt for the Manchus' control of China, he found to his surprise that his Han Chinese counterparts, such as Yan Cheng (1733–67), did not appreciate his anti-Manchu sentiments; instead, Yan and his colleagues applauded the Qing's support for civilization. After intensive conversation with his Chinese friends, Hong conceded that Koreans on a fundamental level still belonged to the "barbarians by the sea" (K., *haesang chi iin*). By concluding that "the civilized and the barbarians are the same" (K., *Hwa–I il ya*), he acknowledged the Qing's civilized status.[89] Through such interactions, many Korean and Chinese scholars became close friends and continued to correspond even after the emissaries returned to Chosŏn. When Yan Cheng was on the brink of death, he laid a letter from Hong on his abdomen to indicate how deeply he treasured their friendship. When news of Yan's death reached Hansŏng, Hong burst into tears and commented that he had lost a brother to whom he was as attached as he was to his right arm.[90]

Like the emissaries from Hansŏng who experienced a combination of hardship and comfort as they made their way to Beijing, Qing imperial envoys also had to endure discomfort until they passed through Fenghuang Gate on their journey toward Ŭiju. There they were welcomed and treated well by the Korean side. Although the land between the gate and the Yalu River was Qing territory, the Korean prefect of Ŭiju was able to dispatch Korean officers, Manchu interpreters, and servants to welcome the envoys at the three stations in this area: Congxiu, Mazhuan, and Sanjiang. At each station the Koreans would set up temporary houses for the envoys and provide hearty meals that could feature more than thirty different dishes. In Ŭiju the prefect treated each envoy to a banquet with more than 130 kinds of food.[91] Receptions along the way from Ŭiju to P'yŏngyang and then to Hansŏng were even more luxurious, and the cost was significant.[92]

In contrast to their Korean counterparts in Beijing, the Manchu envoys in Hansŏng confined themselves to ritual exchanges. Beijing-style literary social gatherings did take place in Shuri, the capital of Ryukyu, but not in Hansŏng, where the envoys, along with their assistants, never left their lodgings to converse with local officials or scholars.[93] No transnational literati club like the one in Beijing ever formed in Hansŏng. After 1658, when Emperor Shunzhi put an end to Manchu trade in Hansŏng, the imperial envoys were always temporary visitors who returned home as soon as their mission was accomplished. In addition, almost all imperial envoys before the early eighteenth century made a point of visiting the Samjŏndo stele in a southern suburb of Hansŏng. The Koreans regarded the stele, with its inscriptions celebrating the Manchu conquest of Chosŏn, as a humiliation, and some Confucian scholars and students argued that it should be destroyed, so the envoys' visits were sensitive and made the stele a barometer of the two countries' relationship. In 1723 the Qing's two envoys made a formal visit to the stele with a number of Korean officials. At the site, the vice envoy knelt down three times, each time bowing his head three times.

In 1724 and 1729, the imperial envoys also paid formal visits to the stele, again accompanied by a group of Koreans. On these occasions both the Manchu envoys and their Korean interpreters kowtowed to the stele. In 1731, however, instead of visiting Samjŏndo, the envoys simply asked for copies of the inscriptions on the stele, and after 1762, they no longer even requested transcripts. By the late nineteenth century, Qing officials had only a vague understanding of the stele and were uncertain whether it featured a Manchu inscription.[94]

During their sojourn in Hansŏng, the Qing envoys performed four major ceremonies in which the king participated. The first was the welcome at the Gate of Receiving Imperial Favors (K., Yŏngŭn mun) outside the West Gate of the city. The king bowed once to the imperial documents, then returned to his palace in the city. The second, conducted inside the king's palace, was the transfer of the imperial documents and other items to the king. The king kowtowed four times to the imperial edicts. In addition, the king and the envoys bowed once or twice to each other with their hands folded in front. The king, on his own territory, did not need to perform the highest level of kowtow toward the imperial decrees or other documents and gifts, as his ministers would do in Beijing. The third ceremony was the king's visit to the envoys at their residence, the South Palace Annex, where the Koreans honored the envoys with several tea banquets. Finally, there was the send-off at the Hall of Admiring the Central Civilized Country on the city's outskirts, where the king provided a tea ceremony for the departing envoys. Contact between the two sides was always conducted through the Korean Ministry of Rites. All of the procedures in these ceremonies were regulated by ritual codes and were executed until the early 1890s. The Korean side had no obligation to report any domestic affairs to the envoys, nor would the envoys intervene in such affairs. Rather, this stylized interaction in Hansŏng endowed the monarch of Chosŏn with political legitimacy, continuously consolidating the reciprocal and hierarchical Zongfan relations between the two countries.

Celebrating the Relationship: The Qing Emperor's Roles in the Zongfan System

As the institutional agent at the highest level of the Zongfan hierarchy, the emperor could exploit the occasions of imperial audiences and his patriarchal authority to modify and lubricate the mechanism from the top down. As the following sections show, he could freely endow tributary emissaries with various extra gifts, supervise and admonish the Manchu envoys to Chosŏn and the Manchus along the border in Manchuria, and make final decisions about border conflicts.

Consolidating the System through Imperial Gifts and Extra Gifts

After Chosŏn's emissaries presented their tribute gifts to the emperor, the sovereign would bestow "routine gifts" (Ch., *lishang*) on them and the king. At least since the Shunzhi period, the Qing presented the tribute missions with gifts whose value exceeded that of the tribute, based on detailed calculations.[95] The gifts and their quantities varied according to the category of the mission, and when the Korean envoy was a member of the royal house, the amount and quality of the gifts would increase. The silk and satin among the gifts were taken from the Imperial Household Department, rather than the Ministry of Revenue, in order to show the emperor's personal favor toward the "king of the *fan*" (Ch., *fanwang*). To mark the imperial birthday and the lunar New Year, the Qing would give the king a second-class horse with bridle and each of the two envoys a third-class horse with bridle, highlighting the Manchu character of the Qing regime. The Qing would also give the envoys silver in the average amount of at least 680 taels (for annual tributary missions and winter solstice missions) or 850 taels (for imperial birthday missions and lunar New Year missions), along with other gifts.[96]

Some scholars have argued that the routine gifts were an institutionalized part of the overall Zongfan mechanism and hence afforded little flexibility.[97] Yet the emperor could break this routine at his discretion by awarding the emissaries extra gifts during audiences. For instance, in early 1795 Emperor Qianlong awarded the king a hundred copies of the Chinese character for "happiness" (Ch., *fu*) that he had written on small squares of red paper.[98] This sort of largesse was seemingly random,[99] but it did not simply represent imperial prerogative or a deviation from the flowcharts of ritual codes. Rather, the practice of giving supererogatory gifts highlighted the Qing policy of "giving more to the visitors and benefiting less from them" (Ch., *houwang bolai*), as Emperor Qianlong explained it to Chosŏn in 1736.[100] The emperor thus moderated the system by lending it flexibility and novelty. In the late eighteenth century, Emperor Qianlong disbursed an increasing quantity of extra gifts, while the amount of the tribute sent by Chosŏn remained remarkably stable. The extra imperial gifts reached their peak in the 1790s, a time when Emperor Qianlong was particularly keen to enhance the image of his dynasty as the Heavenly Dynasty. Given these priorities, the Qing court was not concerned about maintaining a balance between the value of the tributes and that of the imperial gifts. In 1793 a Korean emissary acknowledged that the Qing treated Chosŏn in such a favorable way that the Qing's spending on accommodations for the tributary emissaries and the value of the various imperial gifts far exceeded the value of the Korean "local products."[101]

Constructing a Positive Image of the Qing and Highlighting the Envoys' Manchu Identity

The Qing emperor sought to further burnish his dynasty's image in his contacts with Chosŏn by taking steps to prevent the Manchu envoys to Chosŏn and the bannermen who resided along the border in Manchuria from compromising the dignity of the Heavenly Dynasty through open degeneracy. Emperor Qianlong, for example, felt it necessary to extend the Qing's prolonged campaign to maintain Manchu traditions and identity to the field of the Sino-Korean communications by closely monitoring his envoys' behavior.

His first reform aimed to bolster the Manchu envoys' integrity by discouraging corruption during their trip to Chosŏn. In 1736, after reducing by half the amount of the gifts the Koreans were expected to provide to the imperial envoys, the emperor punished two envoys who violated the new rules. He decreed that in the future the garrison generals at Mukden and Shanhai Pass should check the envoys' luggage when they returned from Hansŏng to make sure they had not received unauthorized gifts.[102] Until the last imperial mission in 1890, subsequent emperors continued to admonish their envoys to Chosŏn to remain upright and honest. Compared with their pre-1637 Ming counterparts, who had exploited Chosŏn for maximum profit, the Manchu envoys, in particular after the Kangxi period, behaved well on their visits to Chosŏn, which helped reduce the tension between the two countries caused by the Qing invasions in the 1630s. The Korean scholar Hong Tae-yong acknowledged in 1766 that the Qing was much more generous and kind to Chosŏn than the Ming had been.[103]

The Qianlong emperor also believed that the Manchu officers and soldiers in Manchuria should focus on border security. In 1737, under the claim of "giving kindness to the people from afar," he decided to prohibit the Manchus from trading with Koreans in the Middle River area of the Yalu River and to ask "merchants and commoners of inner China" (Ch., *neidi shangmin*) to undertake this trade instead. The Middle River market had been established in 1592 between Chosŏn and the Ming; it had barely opened during the Ming-Qing war but was restored as a major trading center between the Qing and Chosŏn after 1646. Manchu bannermen and merchants near Fenghuang City had thereafter constituted the Qing's traders in the market. Now the Qianlong emperor abruptly concluded that the bannermen were "not good at doing business" and sought to direct his Manchu warriors back to the military realm. The king, however, was deeply concerned about the potential arrival of the people of "inner China," so he petitioned the emperor to maintain the trade with the bannermen. The emperor granted the petition but explained that by people of "inner China" he meant only those living near the banner garrisons in Manchuria, not those south of the Great Wall or in Beijing.[104] This episode shows that in the border area the Manchu court was concerned more about political consequences and border security than about the economic interests of the local bannermen. It also suggests that at least by the 1730s the Qing had come to integrate Manchuria into its concept of "inner China" (Ch., *neidi*), further nullifying the border function of the Great Wall within the multiethnic empire.

Emperor Qianlong's more dramatic reform took place in 1763, when he dictated that all Manchu envoys to Chosŏn from that moment onward should ride horses instead of taking sedan chairs in Chosŏn. The emperor explained that although Chosŏn had provided sedan chairs for the missions to show its obedience to and respect for the "imperial envoys of the Heavenly Dynasty," the Manchu officials were expert horsemen and should not ride in sedan chairs. The emperor instructed the king to end permanently the convention of welcoming the imperial envoys with sedan chairs and to provide only horses instead. The Qing documents do not explain why the emperor suddenly changed this longstanding convention. But according to the first-rank translator of the mission led by Hongying (1707–71), Xu Zongmen, who was a Beijing resident of Korean background, the emperor had originally picked another Manchu official as the envoy but, realizing how obese the chosen official was, asked him how he would make the long trip to Chosŏn. The envoy replied that since he would ride in a sedan chair, his weight would not be a problem. The emperor became angry, and to underline the Manchu martial spirit, he immediately replaced the envoy with Hongying, who was an excellent horseman. The emperor admonished Hongying to display "righteousness" (Ch., *zhengda*) in the outer *fan* and to avoid any "wretchedness" (Ch., *weisuo*). Meanwhile, the Korean emissaries, the emperor said, were exempt from the new rules and could maintain their custom of taking carriages to Beijing.[105] The Qianlong emperor's quest to maintain and strengthen the Manchuness of the Manchus under his supervision thus helped the Qing improve its image in the eyes of its subordinate and to showcase its virtues in practice.

Arbitrating Border Disputes

The Qing emperor also served as the highest arbitrator in border conflicts and border-crossing disputes. In each case of border conflict with Chosŏn, it was the emperor—rather than the king, a historical precedent, or a border rule—who made the final decision. The geographical connection between the two countries occasioned a considerable number of illegal border crossings from the early seventeenth to the late nineteenth century. These thorny cases posed a challenge to the Qing, in particular to the emperors, in terms of balancing the Qing's lofty Zongfan discourse and its practical concerns. This aspect of the Qing's policy underwent a major change from the Kangxi to the Qianlong period.

In the Shunzhi and early Kangxi periods, the Manchu monarchs often doled out severe punishments to the king or his officials over border disputes and often sent special envoys to Chosŏn for in-person investigation. The emperors embraced this approach primarily because the Qing had not yet consolidated its rule in the wake of the Southern Ming (1644–62) and its influences and was worried about the possibility of a Chosŏn rebellion against the Qing. But after the Kangxi emperor suppressed the revolt of the Three Feudatories in the 1680s, the Qing praised Chosŏn for its loyalty and adopted a more relaxed policy on border conflicts with the country, eventually ceasing to send special investigative envoys.

The Qing court in the Yongzheng and Qianlong periods following Kangxi governed a country that had been unified to an unprecedented degree since 1644. The court consequently focused on reinforcing the cosmopolitan ideology of all-under-Heaven in the Qing's foreign relations. Although the emperors had clear views on the Qing's geographical borders, they preferred to rely on traditional Zongfan norms in settling border disputes with Chosŏn. The Qing's border policy toward Chosŏn thus became more conservative than aggressive, forming a sharp contrast with the Qing's contemporary policy in the southwest and northwest, where the new empire continued to expand its territory. On the Chosŏn side, the savvy king and local officials applied the same Zongfan norms in their sophisticated negotiations with their Qing counterparts, leaving the emperor in Beijing with no option but to endorse one Korean proposal after another.

The Mangniushao case provides a good example. In 1745 the Manchu general of Mukden, Daldangga (?–1760), suggested to Emperor Qianlong that the Qing set up a border outpost at Mangniushao near the Yalu River in order to prevent Koreans from illegally crossing the border river to sell or buy grains or to search for ginseng in Manchuria. Although in 1731 Daldangga's predecessor, Nasutu (?–1749), had likewise proposed an outpost at Mangniushao, Emperor Yongzheng had rejected the proposal because of the king's opposition and upheld his father's policy, in place since 1715, of prohibiting all construction in this area.[106] Prompted by an increase in illegal border crossings, Daldangga resurrected Nasutu's plan and proposed to repair the broken parts of the Willow Palisade and to open lands outside the palisade for cultivation. Emperor Qianlong initially supported Daldangga's plan and sent a Mongol minister, Bandi (?–1755), to visit the area to confirm that Mangniushao was indeed inside China's borders and that it would be appropriate for China to establish an outpost there. At the last moment, however, the emperor reversed his stance, invoking the precedents set by the decisions of his grandfather in 1715 and his father in 1731, as well as a decision he himself had made in another case in 1737. To justify his rejection of the proposal, he cited the imperative of "cherishing the small." Furthermore, the emperor told Daldangga that no further such proposals should be made to the court and that Daldangga and his successors in Mukden should follow established rules in managing border affairs with Chosŏn.[107] In this way, the emperor reduced the possibility of further conflicts in this border area and helped stabilize the two countries' relationship from the top down.

Barbarianizing the Periphery: The Qing's Institutional Zongfan Discourse

The Changing Meaning of Barbarians from Yongzheng to Qianlong

The Qing interpretation of the civilized–barbarian distinction underwent a sharp change in the transitional days between the reigns of Yongzheng and Qianlong. In the late 1720s, Emperor Yongzheng had made the putative barbarity of the Qing a public issue among Qing scholars because of his response to the case of Zeng Jing (1679–1735). Encouraged by the civilized–barbarian discourse, Zeng had plotted to rebel against the Manchu "barbarians," but after he was prosecuted, he reversed his stance and endorsed the Qing, whereupon the emperor released him from prison. In June 1733, while Zeng was in the provinces giving lectures on the dynasty's virtues, the emperor issued an edict to prohibit the practice of changing Chinese characters with the meaning of "barbarian" (Ch., *hu, lu, yi, di*) in books. The Manchu monarch defined the term "barbarian" geographically and confessed that the ancestors of the current dynasty could be called "eastern barbarians," like ancient Chinese saints. This tone had been set by his great-grandfather Hongtaiji in 1636 in his letter to the king of Chosŏn, and Yongzheng himself had repeated the same points in his book responding to Zeng, *Great Righteousness Resolving Confusion* (Ch., *Dayi juemi lu*) in 1729.[108] By proclaiming that "people living both within and outside China belong to the same family" (Ch., *Zhong Wai yijia*), Yongzheng insisted that the civilized–barbarian distinction should not be understood in a cultural sense, and even if it were, only those who were "beyond civilization" (Ch., *wanghua zhi wai*), like the Zunghar, might truly be called "barbarians."[109] Under this definition, the outer *fan* of the Qing also seemed to be excluded from the category of barbarians.

Yongzheng's statements suggest that the Manchu rulers embraced cultural egalitarianism in order to redistribute cultural resources within the multiethnic empire.[110] It is safe to say that the Manchu emperor was trying to overcome the prejudice inherent in the stereotypical civilized–barbarian distinction among

Han Chinese intellectuals in the process of consolidating the Manchu regime's orthodox legitimacy. This sustained effort can also be seen in the move by Yong-zheng's father and grandfather to expand considerably the list of Chinese monarchs who were enshrined in the Temple of Ancient Monarchs (Ch., Lidai diwang miao), with the goal of establishing the Qing as the legitimate successor to previous dynasties that had likewise been identified as "China."[111] With Yongzheng's policy, the yardstick for judging "barbarians" suddenly snapped, as the ruling dynasty now identified itself both with the ancient rulers and with the eastern barbarians.

After assuming the throne in 1735, the Qianlong emperor not only quickly revoked his father's pardon and executed Zeng but also reversed Yongzheng's approach by clearly differentiating the "civilized" Qing from the "barbarian" countries surrounding it. Qianlong thus brought the civilized–barbarian discourse back to its pre-Yongzheng meaning, in which cultural factors played a pivotal role. He exploited his father's heritage by turning the latter's policy of permitting the free and public use of all Chinese characters for "barbarian" into a tool for propagating the opposite message in the context of the civilized–barbarian discourse—namely, one that excluded the Qing from this category. No longer would the Great Qing downgrade itself to the rank of barbarian.[112] Consequently, in the Qianlong period the use of the term "foreign barbarians" in official documents reached its historical zenith.[113] Through this terminology, the Qing combined its civilized centrality with cultural superiority. Qianlong achieved this symbolic goal by formally designating all other countries as barbarians, along with the majority of the ethnic groups under his rule, and one of the most important targets of this barbarization at the normative level was Chosŏn.

At the time when Yongzheng published his book on the definition of "barbarian," some Manchu envoys to Chosŏn had taken to visiting Jizi Shrine in P'yŏngyang on their way back from Hansŏng.[114] As mentioned in the introduction, Jizi was said to be the founding father of the ancient Korean regime, invested by the Chinese monarch of the Zhou Dynasty with the lands of Chosŏn, where he maintained a familistic and tributary relationship with the central court of China. Given the intense debate around ethnicity and the civilized–barbarian dichotomy in the late years of Yongzheng's reign, the Manchu envoys' visits to Jizi Shrine could help the Manchu regime bolster its Chineseness and its claims to legitimacy beyond its borders. When the Qing overcame the challenge of the civilized–barbarian distinction within China in the first half of the Qianlong period, visits to Jizi Shrine ceased, although Chinese historical records continued to celebrate the familial relationship between the Chinese and the Koreans.

The Qing's Systematic, Institutional Barbarianization of Chosŏn and Others

In June 1751 the Qianlong emperor instructed the governors-general and governors of border provinces to draw and submit pictures of "domestic and foreign barbarians" (Ch., *neiwai miaoyi, waiyi fanzhong*) in order to demonstrate the flourishing of the Qing.[115] The emperor was following a precedent set by Emperor Taizong (r. 627–49) of the Tang Dynasty, who was believed to have brought China its most prosperous days in the pre-Qing era. Since Tang Taizong had commissioned paintings of the barbarians to celebrate the great moment in which "ten thousand countries came to revere the emperor" (Ch., *wanguo laichao*),[116] Qianlong had every reason to commemorate his dynasty's accomplishments in the same way. Even during the Qing expansion into Central Asia, Qianlong identified "the efforts of the Han and Tang dynasties to extend Chinese power into Central Asia" as "historical milestones" by which to measure his own progress.[117]

Beyond the obvious political factors, contemporary popular culture may also have motivated Qianlong's desire for an illustrated record of the Qing's imperial expansion. As a big fan of Chinese opera who contributed to the birth of Peking opera, Qianlong may have been influenced by popular operas that extolled the virtues of the civilized center of the world. These operas can be dated at least to the Yuan, but in the Ming and early Qing they were still being performed in cities such as Beijing. Their scripts described the Ming as the "Heavenly Dynasty," the "upper country," or the "central civilized country," bordered by "barbarians in four directions" (primarily represented as Chosŏn, Annam, and political units in Inner Asia) who paid tribute and presented palace memorials to the great emperor of China.[118]

In 1761, ten years after Qianlong ordered the drawings, the first edition of the *Illustrations of Subordinate Peoples of the Imperial Qing* (Ch., *Huang Qing zhigong tu*) was published in four volumes, featuring six hundred pictures of people from the Qing's outer *fan* and from "barbarian places" within Qing territory or on its periphery. The first picture in the collection was of a Korean official who wore a Ming-style official robe but was labeled "a barbarian official of the country of Chosŏn" (Ch., *Chaoxian guo yiguan*) (see figure 2.3). Once again, Chosŏn served as the model for others in the collection, and its prototypical role was made clear by Qing scholars in the *Essentials of Complete Books of the Four Storehouses Catalog* (Ch., *Siku quanshu zongmu tiyao*).[119] Chosŏn, "Little China," was thus institutionally converted into a country of barbarians by the Qing's political discourse and imperial documentary mechanism.

Following Chosŏn, other countries, including Ryukyu, Annam, Siam, Sulu, Lanchang, Burma, Britain, France, Japan, the Netherlands, and Russia, likewise

朝
鮮
國
夷
官

FIGURE 2.3. A Chosŏn official in the *Illustrations of Subordinate Peoples of the Imperial Qing* (*Huang Qing zhigong tu*, 33).

became barbarians in the Qing nomenclature, as did many of the diverse peoples within Qing territory. In nearly every case, the Qing narrative constructed an imperial pedigree by reviewing a long history of Zongfan relations with the foreign "country" (Ch., *guo*; Ma., *gurun*) or domestic "tribe" (Ch., *buluo*; Ma., *aiman*) from the Zhou to the Ming Dynasties and emphasized that it was the Qing's merits that prompted the "barbarians" to "send emissaries to come and pay tribute" (Ch., *qianshi rugong*; Ma., *elcin takūrafi albabun jafanjimbi*) or "come to kowtow with tribute" (Ch., *chaogong*; Ma., *albabun jafame hengkilenjimbi*).[120] In this way, the Qing systematically assimilated the historical legacies of previous dynasties into its own Zongfan relations with these countries and tribes and consolidated its legitimacy as the civilized center, or Zhongguo (Ma., *Dulimbai gurun*).[121] Also in 1761, in order to celebrate the empress dowager's seventieth birthday, the Qing published another magnificent collection, *Illustrations of the*

Great Celebration (Ch., *Luhuan huijing tu*). The first illustration carried the title "Ten thousand countries came to revere the emperor," the precise phrase the Tang Dynasty had used, and Chosŏn's emissaries occupied a distinguished position within it.[122] If there was a "documentary institutionalization" for the Qing,[123] in terms of the Qing's construction of its civilized identity, this process was substantially accomplished in 1761.

Behind the cheerful facade of the great multiethnic empire lay the axiom of the Qing's centrality in the world. And that world, of course, often found its way to the Qing threshold. Britain, which the Qing knew as "the country of Ying ji li" ("Ying ji li" is a transliteration of "England"; Ch., *Yingjili guo*; Ma., *Ing gi lii gurun*), was one of the countries portrayed as barbarian in the collection of 1761. At the end of that year, the Qianlong emperor instructed his representatives in Guangzhou to notify the "men from afar" and "foreign barbarians" there—the British merchants—that "the Heavenly Dynasty has everything it needs, so it does not need foreign barbarians to bring trivial goods for trade."[124] The edict was a response to petitions from James Flint in 1759 and Nicholas Skottowe in 1761. The two were representatives of the British merchants who wanted to change the Canton system of trade, which channeled all trade with the West through that southern port. Their efforts not only were futile but in fact led to stricter regulations on Western traders in China.[125] In this sense, the rebuff that George Macartney's mission later received from the emperor in 1793 was merely a repetition of the institutionalized rhetoric that had been directed at the British in China more than three decades earlier.

Popularizing Chosŏn's Status as Foreign Barbarians in Imperial Discourse

The prolonged construction of the Qing's new identity and the reorientation of its political discourse vis-à-vis other countries was not just the result of the emperor's personal activities or political motivations, imposed on the administration from the top down. Nor should they be understood purely as the outcome of implementing the political will of the Manchu court. Rather, Qing officials at the local level, from counties to prefectures to provinces, also contributed to this construction from the bottom up. As a result, in the eighteenth century, Chosŏn's status as foreign barbarians was popularized within the norms of Qing foreign relations.

This point is illustrated by the Qing policy toward shipwrecked fishermen from Chosŏn, Ryukyu, Annam, and other countries who were rescued by local Chinese officials along the coast. At least from the early Qianlong period, Qing officials called these victims "barbarians who suffered from storms" (Ch., *zaofeng nanyi*; Ma., *edun de lasihibufi jobolon de tušaha i niyalma*) and sent them to Beijing or to the nearest provincial capital, from whence they could return home with embassies from their countries. From the 1730s to the 1880s, the Qing archives were full of such reports of local officials looking after shipwrecked fishermen; reports concerning fishermen from Chosŏn were particularly prominent.[126] By accommodating these victims on humanitarian grounds, the Qing sought to highlight its policy of "cherishing men from afar" and to "display the deep and outstanding merits of the Heavenly Dynasty" (Ch., *zhao tianchao rouyuan shenren*; Ma., *abkai gurun i goroki urse be gosire šumin gosin be iletulembi*). This sort of rhetoric, aimed at justifying and consolidating the "way of the Heavenly Dynasty" (Ch., *tianchao tizhi*; Ma., *abkai gurun i doro yoso*), reached its peak in the Qianlong period.[127]

Chosŏn again represented the best example of the "way of the Heavenly Dynasty," a fact that permeated many aspects of Qing-Chosŏn contacts. For instance, in 1776, one thousand taels of silver belonging to a Korean mission were stolen by Chinese thieves near Mukden. Emperor Qianlong instructed the Manchu general of Mukden, Hūngšang (1718–81), to compensate the mission for its losses in order to "uphold the way of our Heavenly Dynasty" (Ch., *he wo tianchao tizhi*; Ma. *musei amba gurun i doro de acanambi*). The emperor emphasized in his Chinese edict that "the Chosŏn are a people of foreign barbarians" (Ch., *Chaoxian nai waiyi zhi ren*), further elucidating in the Manchu version of the edict that "the people of the country of Chosŏn are a people of foreign barbarians" (Ma., *Coohiyan gurun i niyalma serengge, tulergi aiman i niyalma*).[128] This case was not exceptional, and the wealth of similar cases indicates the maturation of the Qing's Zongfan discourse.[129]

Despite the harmonious imperial picture the Qing painted, its model *fan* was simultaneously creating an alternate vision. While Chosŏn continued publicly to display its obedience to the Qing, sending tributary missions to Beijing over and above what imperial edicts demanded, in private the Chosŏn king and his officials, along with Chosŏn intellectuals, were reluctant to identify the Qing as the supreme representative of Chinese culture. This story is explored in the next chapter.

3

JUSTIFYING THE CIVILIZED

The Qing's Contacts with Chosŏn,
Annam, and Britain, 1762–1861

As Chosŏn carefully maintained its political subordination to the Qing on the surface, and the Manchu ruling house used this submission to reinforce the Qing's centrality and Chineseness, Chosŏn simultaneously constructed its own Chineseness within its borders by depicting the Qing as barbarians in particular moments. The civilized–barbarian discourse pervaded Chosŏn, nourishing a strong pro-Ming and anti-Qing attitude among the educated in the late seventeenth and the eighteenth century. Chosŏn entered the contest for civilized status in a cultural sense, and its perennial missions to the Qing served this domestic construction of identity. As the Qing was proclaiming Chineseness in the post-Ming era, Chosŏn, too, sought to establish itself as the exclusive legitimate successor to the Ming. In the second half of the eighteenth century, however, a group of Korean scholars who observed the Qing's prosperity and the economic gap between the Qing and Chosŏn dared to voice their support for the Qing's claim to civilized status. Their arguments counterbalanced the prevalent anti-Qing attitude among Korean scholars and helped Chosŏn cope with the paradox of the civilized–barbarian discourse in a practical sense.

This chapter examines the interior aspects and function of the Zongfan order by showing how the Qing's rule of "cherishing the men from afar" operated in the ritual protocol and presentations of diplomatic missions between the Qing, Chosŏn, and other countries from 1762 to 1861. The chapter discusses several cases of emissary exchanges between the Qing and Chosŏn against the background of the sharp reversal of the civilized–barbarian discourse that both sides exploited intensively for their own domestic politico-cultural legiti-macy. It suggests that the Qing eventually prevailed over Chosŏn. By introducing Annam's and Britain's missions to China as a point of comparison for those from Chosŏn, the chapter further explores how the Manchu ruling house navigated the balance between the Chinese rhetoric commensurate with China's claimed preeminence in the cosmopolitan world and the practical consequences of this superiority in bilateral communications. This balance illustrates the Qing state-craft and helps explain why, in the second half of the nineteenth century, both the Qing and Chosŏn, along with Vietnam and Ryukyu, encountered such tremen-dous difficulty in defining the nature of their relationship in accordance with the newly imported international law, a topic examined in part 2 of this book.

Historical Memory of the Civilized: Chosŏn's Anti-Manchu Mentality

The Perception of a Barbarous Qing within Little China after 1644

With the irreversible downfall of the Ming in 1644, Chosŏn intensified its efforts to identify itself as the exclusive and genuine heir to Chinese civilization. In their daily training and practices, Korean intellectuals who were followers of Neo-Confucianism shared a consensus that the Manchu conquest of China proper in 1644 marked the "fall of the central civilized country" (K., *Chunghwa ham-nak*).[1] In Chosŏn, numerous scholars used the regnal title of the last emperor of the Ming, Chongzhen, to date their personal letters and domestic documents. Their attitude was consolidated in the "Little China" discourse that emphasized the succession of Confucian orthodox legitimacy (K., *tot'ong*) instead of denying explicitly that the Qing possessed political orthodox legitimacy as the Middle Kingdom. Thus, within its borders Chosŏn presented itself as the successor to Confucius, Mencius, and Zhu Xi after the demise of the Ming.

On the Qing side, Chosŏn's status as Little China was widely accepted by both ethnic Han and Manchu scholars. The Chinese officials and intelligentsia did not treat their Korean counterparts as barbarians, as they did many Europeans. On occasion, the Qing court explicitly appraised Chosŏn as "a country of rituals and literature" (Ch., *wenwu zhi bang*; Ma., *doro yoso i gurun*), a statement also endorsed by many Chinese scholars of the Qing.[2] Yet when it came to locating Chosŏn within the multilevel structure of all-under-Heaven in the Qing's politi-cal and cultural discourse, Chosŏn was inevitably designated a country of bar-barians on China's periphery. As this chapter shows, Korean scholars who visited

Beijing had to face the challenge of reconciling their country's putative barbarity with their conviction in its superior cultural pedigree.

In late seventeenth-century Chosŏn, in particular during the reigns of King Hyojong and King Hyŏngjong, anti-Qing sentiment was widespread among intellectuals. Song Si-yŏl (1607–89), a leading scholar and King Hyojong's mentor, zealously proposed a northern expedition (K., bukpŏl) against the Manchus in order to "recover the central plain" on behalf of the Ming.[3] Song's plan was never put into practice, but it won strong moral support from the court and from Confucian scholars and contributed to the rise of a Korean national identity in the post-Ming period when the country was struggling for a new episteme.[4] Another scholar, Sin Yu-han (1681–1752), in a letter to a friend who was about to visit Beijing as a member of a tributary mission, claimed that "we are also Chinese" (K., uri yŏk Chunggukin) and that Chosŏn was "China"—a "China with Classic of Poetry and Book of Documents" (K., sisŏ Chungguk) and a "China with [Chinese-style] clothes and belts" (K., ŭidae Chungguk). Sin went on to claim that since the fall of the Ming in 1644 China had not had a Son of Heaven, implying that political orthodox legitimacy also lay in Chosŏn, the successor to Kija (Jizi).[5]

The cases of Song and Sin reveal a pronounced victim mentality within the Korean ruling house and intellectual stratum after the humiliating Manchu invasions and the fall of the Ming. Highlighting Korea's filial duty to the deposed Ming became an ideological tool to maintain Chosŏn's domestic order and raise the morale of the learned class. On the one hand, the king presented himself as a loyal subordinate of the Qing for the sake of the political orthodox legitimacy granted by the Qing; but on the other hand, he was the moral sponsor of the anti-Qing movement inside Chosŏn, seeking to capture the political orthodox legitimacy embedded in the connection between his rulership and his subjects. Like the Qing emperors, the Korean kings had to deal with grave challenges arising from the framework of the civilized–barbarian discourse.

Against the background of this volatile balance, Chosŏn entered a more radical period of actively commemorating the "imperial Ming" during the reign of King Sukchong, when the Qing's control over Chosŏn was loosened as the Kangxi emperor was preoccupied with suppressing the revolt of the Three Feudatories in the 1680s. In April 1704, on the sixtieth anniversary of Emperor Chongzhen's suicide, the king established an altar near the palace in Hansŏng and performed a new ceremony to commemorate Chongzhen. Although it was the forty-third year of Kangxi, the king called the moment the "seventy-seventh year of Chongzhen," setting the starting year to 1628, when Chongzhen ascended the throne. The king declared that the "imperial Ming" was the "owner of the civilized and the barbarians" (K., Hwa–I ju) but that the "northern barbarians"—that is, the Manchus—had taken the opportunity to "occupy our central plain" (K., kŏ a *chungwŏn*), with the result that the "rituals and clothes" (K., *yeak ŭigwan*)—the traditional metaphor for civilization—had become barbarous. Chosŏn, the king claimed, was the only place that still loyally worshipped the "old motherland" (K., *koguk*). Reciting these words at the ceremony, the king burst into tears. All of the officials around him wept too.

Soon thereafter, in October of the same year, the king had a long discussion with several ministers about building a temple to Wanli, the Ming emperor who saved Chosŏn from the Japanese invasion in the 1590s. The ministers endorsed the king's pro-Ming attitude but pointed out that it was inappropriate for a "vassal" to offer sacrifices to the "Son of Heaven," so the king instead constructed a nine-floor altar and named it the Great Altar for Gratitude (K., Taebodan), where a state ceremony would be performed twice a year, in spring and autumn. The altar was completed in January 1705.[6] Thereafter, Chosŏn continued to commemorate the Ming for another 190 years until 1895, when it declared independence from the Qing. The altar was permanently closed in 1908, three years after Chosŏn became a protectorate of Japan and two years before it was annexed by Japan.

Korean emissaries to Beijing continuously fed the popular antipathy toward the Qing in Chosŏn by providing firsthand accounts of their dealings with the barbarous usurpers of the Ming. For these emissaries, the trip to Beijing was a journey for mourning the Ming, deprecating the Qing, and strengthening Chosŏn's identity as Little China. As they reached various landmarks—the Yalu River, Fenghuang Gate, Liaoyang, the Korean compound in Mukden where Crown Prince Sohyŏn had been detained between 1637 and 1644, Shanhai Pass, and the Forbidden City in Beijing, where the Ming emperors had resided for centuries—the emissaries often wrote poems lamenting the fall of the Ming. These poems became part of their journals, which were widely circulated in Chosŏn and were generically known as *Yŏnhaengnok* (The records of the journey to Beijing).[7]

From the second half of the eighteenth century, however, some Korean intellectuals, having witnessed the Qing's prosperity on their journeys to Beijing and having engaged in extensive conversations with Han Chinese and Manchu scholars in Beijing, started to reconsider their entrenched view of the barbarous Qing. Disillusioned with Chosŏn's self-proclaimed cultural superiority, these pundits recognized the Qing as a civilized country and called for Chosŏn to learn from Qing China for its own good, beyond the popular doctrine of "revering China and expelling the barbarians." These scholars constituted the School of Northern Learning (K., Pukhak p'ae), focusing on "practical knowledge" (K., *Sirhak*). They successfully resumed contacts between the literati of Korea and those of China that had been suspended for more than 120 years since 1644. Among these scholars, three in particular stood out: Hong Tae-yong, Pak Che-ka (1750–1805), and Pak Chi-wŏn (1737–1805).

Honoring the Great Ming: Hong Tae-yong's Perception of the Qing

Hong Tae-yong was born in Hansŏng in 1731 into Chosŏn's ruling gentry and the hereditary class of *yangban* (lit. "two branches [of the ruling class]"), and he studied with Kim Wŏn-haeng (1702–72), a leading scholar of the time. In late 1765, when his uncle was appointed the secretary of the annual tributary mission to Beijing, Hong became affiliated with the mission as an officer of the emissaries' junior relatives (K., *chaje gungwan*).[8] Although Hong regarded the Qing as a barbarous country, he was excited about the trip and was eager to exchange ideas with his Chinese counterparts. After arriving in Beijing in early 1766, Hong put almost all his time and energy into getting to know Chinese scholars, mainly through written conversations (K., *p'iltam*, "conversing by writing Chinese characters"). These dialogues led him to conclude that the Qing, no matter how barbarous in Chosŏn's eyes, was indeed the civilized Middle Kingdom, whereas Chosŏn, no matter how superior in its own mind, nonetheless fell into the category of barbarians.

Hong, like other Koreans, was extremely proud of Chosŏn's fashion of Ming-style clothes and hats and disparaged the Manchu hairstyle and robes. His choice of dress signaled that he maintained the true way of Chinese culture. In his conversations with Chinese intellectuals in the first weeks of his stay in Beijing, Hong frequently used his clothing to highlight Chosŏn's cultural superiority over the Qing.[9] Shortly thereafter, however, Hong entered into dialogue with other Chinese intellectuals, in particular Yan Cheng and Pan Tingyun (1743–?), and these highly trained scholars dramatically changed his view of the Qing.

Yan and Pan, both Han Chinese, were from Hangzhou in Zhejiang Province, where they had successfully passed the imperial civil-service examinations and won the title of *Juren* (a qualified graduate at the provincial level). They were determined to pass the last round of imperial exams in Beijing to realize their dream of serving their country as officials. To enhance their communications with Hong, they shared with him their provincial exam essays. In the first conversation among Hong, Yan, Pan, and their Korean and Chinese peers, another Korean, Kim P'yŏng-jung, asked Pan why he had said in his exam essay that people should worship only the Zhou Dynasty—a statement that, Kim felt, could be seen as an expression of nostalgia for the deposed Ming and as an act of defiance against the Manchus. Pan explained that his words referred to the "central civilized country," which was the "patriarch for myriad countries" (Ch., *wanguo suozong*), and he emphasized that the current Son of Heaven, the Qianlong emperor, was so great that all subjects should show him obedience and respect. Worshipping the Zhou, Pan concluded, was akin to worshipping the current dynasty. Hong, for the first time in his life, heard the Qing called the central civilized country. Seeing Pan's response as a consequence of the sensitive Manchu–Han Chinese ethnic relationship, Hong disregarded his claim and instead responded by highlighting Chosŏn's identity as Little China. But by the end of the conversation, the two sides had found common ground in celebrating the Qing conceit that "all-under-Heaven is one unified family" (Ch., *tianxia yijia*).[10]

Hong did not reveal his sense of cultural superiority until his second conversation with Yan and Pan at the Korean residence. The conversation included a long discussion about clothes and hats, in which the Korean hosts and the Chinese guests articulated their respective understandings of the Ming-Qing transition and the Qing's position in Chinese history. Hong emphasized several times that Koreans wore Ming-style garments, which in China by this time were worn only on the opera stage. Hong indicated that the garments served as a visible reminder of the "dignified manner of Han Chinese officials" (Ch., *hanguan weiyi*). The Korean hosts asked Pan and Yan critical questions regarding the Manchu hairstyle, clothes, and hats, and about the Ming's stories. Pan, who was in charge of recording the conversation, answered their questions carefully and praised the Qing volubly.[11] Pan later became an official in Beijing and never gave Hong the copies of their correspondence that Hong had requested after returning to Hansŏng, although the two maintained a good relationship.[12]

In another long conversation with Yan, Hong again used Chosŏn's style of dress to criticize the Qing and mourn the Ming. Hong told Yan he felt extremely sad that China had lost itself with its adoption of Manchu fashions in hair and clothes and that China's situation was in his view even worse than it had been under the Jin and Yuan Dynasties. In comparison, Hong proudly noted Chosŏn's loyalty to the Ming, which he called the "parent nation." Yan, however, argued that in 1644 the Qing had legitimately become the ruler of the country by defeating the rebels and defending and enacting justice. At the end of the conversation, Hong acknowledged that whereas the Ming had exploited his country, the Qing was much more generous toward Chosŏn.[13] Hong realized that Han Chinese scholars identified the Qing both as a legitimate successor to the Ming in the political sense and as a legitimate heir to Confucianism in the cultural sense. Although the Han Chinese had adopted the Manchu queue and clothes, Hong concluded, they were still the "offspring of the old home of the central civilized country" (K., *Chunghwa koga chi ye*). By contrast, Hong conceded that although Koreans took pride in their Ming-style dress, on a fundamental level they still belonged to the "barbarians by the sea." By arguing that "the civilized and the barbarians are the same," he acknowledged the Qing's civilized status.[14] Hong returned to Chosŏn with a new perception of Qing China, and he made an immense contribution to the School of Northern Learning.

Learning from the North: The Korean Visitors' New Tone toward the Qing

Revisiting the Civilized–Barbarian Discourse: Pak Che-ka's Visit to Beijing

After Hong returned to Hansŏng in 1766, his strong relationships with Pan, Yan, and other Chinese friends, and his continuous correspondence with them, swiftly became legend among his fellow scholars in Chosŏn. One of them was Pak Che-ka, born in 1750 in Hansŏng, where his father served as a minister at the court. Because his mother was a concubine, Pak was not allowed to take the civil-service examinations, but he won fame as a poet when he was young and joined a wide aristocratic and intellectual social network, through which he became acquainted with Hong. Pak was fascinated by the contacts between Hong and Chinese scholars and hoped to visit Beijing himself. His opportunity came in the spring of 1778, when the emissary Ch'ae Che-gong (1720–99) invited Pak and another famous young scholar, Yi Tŏng-mu (1741–93), to join him on a tributary mission to Beijing. This trip helped transform Pak into a leading proponent of *Sirhak*—"practical knowledge."

In Beijing Pak exchanged poems or conducted written conversations with more than fifty famous Han Chinese and Manchu scholars, almost all of them high-ranking officials at court, including Ji Yun (1724–1805), Pan Tingyun, Tiyeboo (1752–1824), and Fengšen Yendehe (1775–1810). He also conversed with a Muslim prince from Central Asia. After returning to Chosŏn, he spent three months composing a treatise entitled "Discussions on Northern Learning" (K., Pukhak ŭi), in which he discussed what Chosŏn could learn from the Qing in matters ranging from the construction of bridges, roads, ships, and cities to the production of porcelain, paper, bows, and brushes, as well as language and medicine.[15] On each of these matters and many others, Pak described how advanced the Qing was, then compared it to Chosŏn. He suggested that it was Chosŏn's self-imposed isolation, informed by the civilized–barbarian discourse, that prevented the country from perceiving the Qing's accomplishments and embracing the Qing's sophisticated practical skills. For example, he pointed out that Korean emissaries to Beijing did not directly contact local Chinese officials on their journey from Fenghuang Gate to Beijing but rather commissioned Korean interpreters to do so, which caused much inconvenience. Pak passionately urged his fellow scholars to study the Chinese, Manchu, Mongolian, and Japanese languages. Proposals such as this one came very close to calling for a comprehensive reform of Chosŏn's daily practices and statecraft.

At the end of his treatise, Pak wrote a short piece under the title "On Worshipping the Zhou" (K., Chonju non), addressing Chosŏn's understanding of the Qing based on the civilized–barbarian discourse. Pak followed the popular anti-Qing trend in acknowledging that the Qing were among the barbarians, but he critically pointed out that Chosŏn could nonetheless learn from the Qing in many aspects. Otherwise, Pak warned, Chosŏn could neither expel "China's barbarians" nor transform the "eastern country's barbarians." "If we want to expel the barbarians," Pak stated, "we had better know who the barbarians are first." Pak stressed that it would not be too late for Chosŏn to seek revenge for the Ming's demise after first carefully learning from the Qing for twenty years. Pak followed this piece with "Debate on Northern Learning" (K., Pukhak pyŏl), in which he justified his call to learn from the Qing on the basis of Neo-Confucian principles. He divided those Korean scholars who denigrated the Qing while acclaiming Chosŏn into three groups: the "lower savants" (K., hasa), focused on grains and foods; the "middle savants" (K., chongsa), who were concerned with literature; and the "upper savants" (K., sangsa), who concentrated on Neo-Confucian principles. Pak argued that Chosŏn's perception of Qing China was based on woefully incomplete knowledge of it and that Chosŏn was in fact underdeveloped compared to the prosperous Qing. Citing Zhu Xi, Pak expressed a wish that Chosŏn had more people who truly understood the principles as he did.[16] Pak's proposal that Chosŏn learn from the Qing before it fought against the Qing bore a striking resemblance to the strategy of "learning the superior techniques of the barbarians to constrain the barbarians" (Ch., shiyi changji yi zhiyi) put forward by the Chinese scholar Wei Yuan (1794–1857) in the 1840s, although Wei's "barbarians" referred to Europeans.

Pak's acknowledgment that the Qing was the civilized country disillusioned many of his fellow scholars. For those who had never seen the Qing, Pak described a society prosperous beyond their imaginations. Following Hong, Pak constructed a new image of the Qing, one the upper savants were reluctant to accept. Ch'ae Che-gong, the emissary who had invited Pak to Beijing, was one such upper savant. Ch'ae mourned the fall of the Ming and called the Manchu general of Fenghuang Gate "barbarous." When he arrived in Beijing and saw the artificial hill next to the Forbidden City on which Chongzhen had committed suicide in 1644, Ch'ae composed a poem commemorating the Ming. He lamented that Chinese children on the street jeered at his Ming-style clothing. After the summer solstice rituals at the Temple of Earth, the Qianlong emperor praised the Korean mission for the best ritual performance among the outer *fan*. Ch'ae interpreted this as evidence that the Manchu emperor, whom he sometimes referred to as "khan," tacitly approved of the "Han Chinese clothes and hats" that he and the other Korean visitors wore.[17] When he returned to Chosŏn, Ch'ae collected the poems he had written on the trip into an anthology entitled *Records of Enduring Contempt and Insults* (K., *Ham'in nok*). In stark contrast, Korean scholars at the middle and lower levels found Pak's proposal to "use techniques to benefit people's livelihoods" (K., *iyong husaeng*) very attractive. Seeking to avoid pedanticism, these scholars contributed to the remarkable rise and dissemination of northern learning. One of them was Pak Chi-wŏn.

Reenvisioning the Barbarous Qing: Pak Chi-wŏn's Trip to Beijing

Pak Chi-wŏn was also of an aristocratic *yangban* background. In 1780, his cousin Pak Myŏng-wŏn (1725–90) was appointed the emissary to Beijing for Emperor Qianlong's seventieth birthday, providing Pak Chi-wŏn an opportunity for "tourism in the upper country." Shocked by the Qing's wealth, evident everywhere from small towns on the Sino-Korean border to the metropolitan areas of Mukden and Beijing, Pak realized that the stereotypical perception of the Qing among the meritocracy of Chosŏn had become an obstacle to progress. Pak found it difficult to overcome the prejudices rooted in the hegemonic assumption of the Qing's barbarity, although he was deeply influenced by Hong and had an open mind. In his *Rehe Diary* (K., *Yŏlha ilgi*), Pak frequently struggled with the moral correctness of the pro-Ming, anti-Qing principles, on the one hand, and his desire to learn from the Qing, on the other. He was uncomfortable, even pained, by any admission of the achievements of the Qing, which implied that the Qing was civilized but Chosŏn was not, just as Pak Che-ka had painfully suggested.

Pak Chi-wŏn's astonishment began on the first day of his journey, when he reached Fenghuang Gate and saw the small town inside the fence. Pak noticed that the houses, walls, doors, and streets of the town were well designed and maintained, and that the town bore no "indication of inferior rural style." He realized that a scene like this at the "eastern end" of the Qing's territory could only portend still more prosperous vistas in the inner reaches of the empire. How could the Manchu barbarians manage the land so efficiently, in such an impressive way, and to such a significant degree of control? Pak felt so unsettled that he wanted to return to Hansŏng. He asked his private servant, Chang Bok, "How would it be if you were born in China?" Chang, an illiterate boy, immediately answered, "China is barbarian [K., *Chungguk ho ya*], so I would not want to be born in China."[18] The boy's answer was exactly the reassurance his master needed. It also reflects the prevalence among Koreans of the perception of the Qing as barbarians. Nevertheless, Pak realized that his journey would not be as peaceful as he had wished.

Indeed, after he entered Fenghuang Gate, Pak's preconceptions about the barbarous Qing crumbled a little more each day. As he passed by Liaoyang, Mukden, and many small towns and villages, Pak was confronted by beautiful buildings, thriving markets, and flourishing urban and rural communities where local civilians and officials treated him in a friendly manner. He enjoyed written conversations with Han Chinese and Manchu scholars and officials and appreciated local scenery and historical sites. In the course of these experiences, the charge that the Qing was barbarous completely vanished from Pak's diary. Rather, Pak began to discern a gap between himself and his Chinese counterparts in practical terms that had been caused by Chosŏn's cultural isolation from the Qing after 1644. His experience in two villages illustrates this point vividly.

When Pak visited a pawnshop in a village called Xinmin, he was invited by the owner to write some Chinese characters as an honorable gift. Pak recalled that he had seen four big characters denoting "exceeding frost, surpassing snow" (Ch., *qishuang saixue*) on the front doors of some shops in Mukden and Liaoyang, so he wrote these down, assuming that they must mean that a businessman's heart should be as pure as frost and snow. However, the four characters were actually a metaphor for the high quality of flour. The confused shop owner shook his head and murmured that the characters were not at all related to his business. Pak left the store in anger. The next day, when he camped at Xiaoheishan Village, he wrote the same four characters for a jewelry shop owner. Just as puzzled as the Xinmin merchant had been, the jeweler said, "I am selling women's jewelry, not flour, so why did you write these characters for me?" Pak, suddenly aware of the characters' actual meaning, overcame his embarrassment and calmly wrote other characters that won him high praise from the shop owner.[19]

Frustrated by this episode, Pak took a critical look at Chosŏn's perception of the Qing and put forward the idea of "using techniques to benefit people's livelihoods" by comparing different attitudes toward the Qing among his fellow Korean intellectuals. Like Pak Che-ka, he divided Korean scholars into upper savants, middle savants, and lower savants. He began with a scenario in which Korean people who had never visited the Qing would ask those returning from Beijing about the impressive things they had observed on their journey. According to Pak, whereas many visitors would list without hesitation such things as the White Pagoda in Liaodong, Chinese markets, and Shanhai Pass, the upper savants would instead insist that "nothing is impressive" because the people in China, from the Son of Heaven to the common subjects, were "barbarians as long as they shaved their foreheads." Since "barbarians are dogs and sheep," nothing of theirs was worth praising. The middle savants would also argue that "the mountains and lands became barbarous and nothing over there is impressive until we lead a hundred thousand troops to cross Shanhai Pass to recover China." Identifying himself as one of the lower savants who shared with the upper and middle savants the belief in "revering China and expelling the barbarians," Pak nevertheless passionately called on his colleagues to "learn the good ways and useful systems [of the Qing] as long as they benefit our people and country, even if they are created by barbarians." He argued, "If we want to expel the barbarians, we should learn all the good Chinese systems to change ours, after which we might be able to say that China has nothing impressive."[20] Pak tried to separate recognition of the Qing's superior practical techniques from the cultural and moral charges against the Qing. Yet this approach, which meant blurring the boundaries between civilized and barbarian, was a double-edged sword not only for himself but also for the general moral foundation of his country.

On August 30, 1780, when Pak arrived in Beijing, he was stunned by the grandness of the splendid metropolis. In his diary, for the first time, he embraced the Qing regnal title to express the date—"the first day of the eighth month of the forty-fifth year of Qianlong"—thus incorporating himself into the Zongfan mindset by identifying the Qing as the center of the world. On that day, Pak completely overlooked the fact that he was in a country of "barbarians."[21]

Identifying Chosŏn as a Loyal Subordinate of the Qing: Pak Chi-wŏn at Rehe

When Pak Chi-wŏn and his fellow Koreans arrived in Beijing, they learned that the emperor had moved to the summer palace at Rehe, where the sixth Panchen Erdeni (1738–80) and Mongol princes would convene to celebrate the imperial birthday on September 11. On September 2, the emperor instructed the Ministry of Rites to ask the Korean emissaries to visit Rehe and ordered a minister of the Grand Council (Ch., Junjichu) to Beijing to welcome them, an act of "extraordinary imperial benevolence." The Koreans immediately organized a special ad hoc team to travel to Rehe, to which Pak Chi-wŏn was attached. Five days later, the group arrived at Rehe, where it quickly became involved in subtle conflicts with the Chinese side. The emperor and his officials were keen to showcase Chosŏn's subservience as a model outer *fan*, but the Koreans were equally keen to avoid this role, given their ambivalence about the Qing. However, Chosŏn's subordinate position in the bilateral framework meant that the emissaries had few alternatives.

The first incident that revealed this tension took place upon the emissaries' arrival, when the emperor informed the emissaries that they would stand at the end of the right wing of China's second-rank civil officials during the grand ceremony on the celebration day. This was a "special and unprecedented grace" from the emperor, because the ritual code generally required the emissaries to stand at the end of the left wing of civil officials. The ministers of the Ministry of Rites asked the emissaries to submit a memorial showing their sincere appreciation. The emissaries hesitated, as it would have been inappropriate to do so without the king's authorization, but the ministers pushed them to draft the memorial. Pak commented that as the aged emperor became more suspicious, the ministers had to work harder to meet his wishes.[22]

On a subsequent occasion, the emperor sent a minister of the Grand Council to inquire whether the two emissaries would like to visit "the saintly monk from the western area" (Ch., *xifan shengseng*), referring to the Panchen Erdeni. The Koreans replied that they never stopped communicating with "people of China" (K., *Chungguk insa*), but that they did not dare to communicate with "people of other countries" (K., *taguk in*). Undeterred, the emperor ordered the emissaries to visit the lama at his monastery. At the monastery, the communications between the Korean emissaries and the Panchen Erdeni followed a labyrinthine path: the Erdeni spoke to the Mongol prince next to him, who relayed the message to the minister of the Grand Council, who forwarded it to the Qing interpreter, who passed it to the interpreter from Chosŏn, who finally translated the words into Korean for the emissaries. The conversation involved Tibetan, Mongolian, Manchu, Chinese, and Korean, highlighting the multiethnic and multicultural nature of the unified empire, but the extent to which the Panchen Erdeni and the Korean emissaries could actually understand each other and grasp the political meanings behind the words used remains unclear. Acting on the guidance of the minister of the Grand Council, the emissaries, who were as stiff as "clay dolls and wooden puppets," presented the Panchen Erdeni with silk handkerchiefs, and the Panchen Erdeni gave the Koreans three small bronze figurines of the Buddha and some Hada, Pulu, and Tibetan incense in return. Since the figurines contravened Confucian beliefs, the emissaries traded them for silver that they then distributed among their servants instead of bringing the figurines back to Chosŏn.[23]

Behind the envoys' reluctance to visit the Panchen Erdeni was the problem of the ritual of kowtow: the Korean emissaries refused to perform the ceremony to the lama. Pak later defended their behavior in a written conversation with a Manchu official: "Our humble country is in the same family with the big country, and there is no difference between inside and outside between us. Yet the lama is a man of the western area, so how could our envoys dare go and visit him? There is a rule that 'subordinates have no right to conduct diplomacy' [K., *insin mu oegyo*]."[24] Chosŏn was demonstrating its loyalty as China's *fan* and subordinate. The principle that a subordinate country had no right to conduct diplomacy would be emphasized by the king of Chosŏn again and again when Western states tried to open direct lines of contact with Chosŏn between the 1830s and the 1870s. Their overtures created a tremendous and insurmountable dilemma for the scholars of Chosŏn. Although they viewed the Qing as a barbarous place and themselves as the civilized successors of the Ming within a Chosŏn-centric cultural world, as soon as another political entity approached Chosŏn, they would identify the Qing as China and hew to the Qing's Zongfan line to embrace their unique role as the representatives of the men from afar cherished by China.[25]

At a banquet held for representatives of the Qing's subordinates and attended by the Panchen Erdeni, Mongol princes from Mongolia, Muslim princes from Xinjiang, emissaries from Chosŏn, and indigenous chiefs from southwestern China, the emperor lauded Chosŏn's fealty, declaring to those gathered at the banquet that "Chosŏn has been serving as a *fan* for generations and has always been loyal. It pays its annual tribute on time, and that is truly worth praising." The emperor added, "We, the monarch and the subordinates, trust each other fully and belong to the same family inside and outside China, so we should not bother ourselves with these overelaborate rituals." He then issued an edict according to which Chosŏn needed to present only an annual tribute; all other tributes, along with humble memorials, would be permanently canceled, reflecting the Qing's policy of "cherishing men from afar with substantial measures rather than rhetoric" (Ch., *rouhui yuanren, yishi bu yiwen*).[26] Again, the Korean emissaries served as the typical men from afar for the purposes of imperial discourse extolling the Qing's civilization and centrality.

After returning home, Pak Chi-wŏn, like Pak Che-ka before him, called on his fellow scholars to learn from the Qing. In 1781 he wrote a foreword to Pak Che-ka's "Discussions on Northern Learning," in which he reiterated that Chosŏn should abandon its incorrect assumptions about the Qing.[27] As other Korean scholars followed in Pak's footsteps and made their own visits to Beijing, the Koreans' perceptions about the Ming and the Qing continued to evolve.

The Way of the Heavenly Dynasty: The Qing and the Tributary Missions of 1790 and 1793

The Imperial Grand Banquet and the Korean Mission of 1790

The Chosŏn meritocracy increasingly realized that it could not restore the Ming in China, and this recognition helped normalize its service to the Qing under the rubric of "serving the great." Compared to Pak Che-ka in 1778 and Pak Chi-wŏn in 1780, Sŏ Ho-su (1736–99), who visited Rehe as an associate envoy to celebrate

Emperor Qianlong's eightieth birthday in 1790, described Chosŏn's Zongfan contacts with the Qing in very moderate terms. The mission, led by envoy Hwang In-jŏm (?–1802), associate envoy Sŏ, and secretary Yi Paek-hyŏng (1737–?), left Hansŏng on July 9 and two weeks later arrived at Ŭiju, where it could not cross the Yalu River because of flooding. During his sojourn in Ŭiju, Sŏ commented in one of his poems that "the Yalu River is the boundary between the civilized and the barbarians" (K., *Hwa–I bungye*), but in his diary he used the Qing's regnal title for the date.[28]

The Qianlong emperor was concerned about the time it would take for the Koreans to reach the celebration at Rehe. As the representatives of the Qing's outer and inner *fan* convened again at Rehe, the emperor saw the attendance of Chosŏn's emissaries as an indispensable part of the "system," "way," or "fundamentals" (Ch., *tizhi*) of the big family. On August 1, the Korean emissaries, still in Ŭiju, received an official note from the Ministry of Rites in Beijing via the Manchu general of Mukden. The message had traveled 500 *li* (about 155 miles) per day, one of the fastest rates possible for the Qing mail system. The ministry instructed the Koreans to head directly to Rehe, as they needed to arrive by August 19, the same deadline that the emperor had set for the king of Annam and the emissaries of Lanchang and Burma. When the mission crossed the river the next day, a second note from Beijing arrived, urging the envoys to meet the deadline because Chosŏn's presence was "particularly crucial to the system" (Ch., *shu yu tizhi youguan*). They subsequently received a third note in a completely different tone, saying that it would be fine if the mission could not reach Rehe in time.

The emissaries, perceiving the reversal as a subtle way of cherishing the men from afar, immediately organized a special team that would head directly for Rehe with humble palace memorials and selected tributes, while the rest of the mission would go to Beijing as planned. Covering more than 260 miles after passing Mukden, the emissaries reached Rehe on August 24 and learned that the emperor had changed the date of the grand banquet to August 25 to accommodate Chosŏn's mission. The Mongol and Muslim princes, the emissaries of Burma and Lanchang, the indigenous chiefs of Taiwan, and the king of Annam had all arrived several days earlier.[29] The emperor's decision conveyed eloquently that Chosŏn's position was irreplaceable in the Qing-centric world.

The following day, the Ministry of Rites guided Chosŏn's emissaries to the imperial palace for an audience with the Qianlong emperor. After asking for the emissaries' names and ranks, the emperor instructed them to attend the grand banquet and to watch the Peking opera. In further illustration of Chosŏn's prominent status, the Korean emissaries were arranged in first position in the wing of the "emissaries of other countries," while those of Annam were in second position, those of Lanchang in third, those of Burma in fourth, and the indigenous chiefs in fifth. In addition, Chosŏn's well-written humble palace memorials were considered exemplary. Hešen (1750–99), the most influential Manchu minister in the Grand Council, showed one of the Korean memorials to the king of Annam, Nguyễn Huệ, and commented, "Chosŏn serves the great in such a good manner that it is the model for other *fan.*" The Vietnamese king inspected the memorial several times and praised it highly.[30]

With the move of the grand meeting from Rehe to Beijing in early September, the emissaries of Chosŏn retained their prominent role in all ritual performances in the palaces of Yuan-Ming-Yuan and the Forbidden City. The emperor frequently granted the emissaries audiences, invited them to watch operas, treated them to Manchu banquets, and gave them gifts. On October 11 the Korean mission finally left Beijing for their homeland after a successful stay.

Local Banquets and the Vietnamese Mission in 1790

The Qing expected the tributary emissaries from its other *fan* to accept and follow the imperial etiquette as readily as those from Chosŏn did. Any deviation from the prescribed practices would not only cause conflict between the Qing and the specific *fan* but also result in internal tension between the Qing monarch and his local officials. Such an instance occurred during the visit to Beijing of the king of Annam, Nguyễn Huệ, in 1790.

Annam experienced a turbulent period toward the end of the eighteenth century, and the Qing was drawn into the turmoil. In 1771, in what was called the Tây-so'n Rebellion, Nguyễn Huệ and his two brothers overthrew the Nguyễn family, which controlled the south of Vietnam, and restored the later Lê Dynasty (1428–1788). In 1788, worried about Nguyễn's growing power, the young king, Lê Duy Kỳ (1765–93), fled the capital. At Lê's request, Emperor Qianlong sent troops to Annam, which had been the Qing's "outer *fan* for more than one hundred years." Under the command of the governor-general of Liangguang, Sun Shiyi (1720–96), the Chinese army quickly occupied Hanoi and restored the government of Lê Duy Kỳ. But the Chinese forces were defeated in an unexpected attack by Nguyễn in January 1789, and Lê fled Hanoi again. Emperor Qianlong appointed his favorite Manchu general, Fuk'anggan (1753–96), who had just suppressed a rebellion in Taiwan, to replace Sun and organize a counterattack. However, the emperor was not interested in conquering Vietnam through a large-scale war, and he instructed Fuk'anggan and Sun to be receptive to any attempts by Nguyễn to sue for peace. The emperor reviewed China's frustrating experience with "converting Vietnam into China's prefectures and counties" (Ch., *junxian qi di*) in pre-Qing history and stressed that the Qing would not "integrate Annam into China's map and register" (Ch., *shouru bantu*) by imitating the case of Xinjiang, where the court had had to dispatch numerous officials to manage the land after the military conquest, in particular after the war with the Zunghar Mongols.[31] Qing policymakers thus clearly understood that policies were to be applied flexibly in different parts of the Qing frontier. As it turned out, Nguyễn was not ready for another fight with the Qing either, so in the same month he presented Sun with "a humble palace memorial" to express his willingness to become a subordinate of the "Heavenly Dynasty," marking the end of the conflict on the battlefield.

Recognizing the motivation behind Nguyễn's act of submission to the Qing, Qianlong issued an edict on May 15, declaring that he would not use force against the country for the sake of the "barbarian people of Annam." Believing that "Heaven has abandoned the Lê," the emperor settled the Lê family and its loyal followers in the city of Guilin in Guangxi, a Chinese province bordering Vietnam.[32] This arrangement signaled that the Qing was preparing to support a new Vietnamese regime. To that end, the emperor indicated that he might invest Nguyễn as king if Nguyễn visited Beijing in person. This, according to the emperor, was precisely how he managed foreign barbarians—with mercy and discipline. The emperor also confirmed that Lê and his followers would not be sent back to Annam for restoration, and to prove his intentions he ordered them to cut their hair according to the Qing style and to wear Qing clothes. In Guilin, Fuk'anggan and Sun Shiyi told the desperate young king, "You are in the land of the central civilized country [Ch., *Zhonghua zhi tu*], so you should follow China's system [Ch., *Zhongguo zhi zhi*] and change your hairstyle and clothes."[33]

As the manager of communications at the border, Fuk'anggan understood the mood of his aging and vainglorious master in Beijing, so he impressed on the emperor Nguyễn's willingness to visit Beijing. In August the emperor quickly invested Nguyễn as the new king in order to provide him with the necessary orthodox legitimacy to govern and stabilize Annam domestically. In the book of investiture, the emperor emphasized the importance of the principle of "serving the great" on the part of an outer *fan* and that of "cherishing the small" on the part of China, highlighting the same ideological reciprocity that existed between Chosŏn and the Qing. The emperor took four steps to welcome the new king to Beijing. First, he instructed the Grand Secretariat and the Ministry of Rites to create new "guest-host rituals" (Ch., *binzhu zhi li*) between the king and the Qing's governors-general and governors. He also endowed the king with a golden belt that was reserved for the Qing's "royal vassals" (Ch., *Zongfan*).[34] Second, he moved the dethroned Lê to Beijing and appointed him a hereditary major in the Han Eight Banners. The 376 followers who had accompanied Lê were registered with the banner household system, and many were moved to Jiangnan, Zhejiang, Sichuan, and other provinces. Third, the emperor allowed the new Nguyễn regime to pick up their Chinese calendar books every year from the governor of Guangxi instead of traveling to Beijing for them. And fourth, he promised to open a border market after Nguyễn had visited Beijing, in recognition of the idea that "the barbarian people of that country are all loyal children of the Heavenly Dynasty." All of these measures were aimed at encouraging Nguyễn's "sincerity in transforming into a subordinate of the civilized" (Ch., *xianghua zhi cheng*).[35]

On May 26, 1790, the king and his mission of 150 members reached the Qing border, where he performed the highest level of kowtow to the imperial edicts and gifts.[36] Fuk'anggan then accompanied Nguyễn to Rehe, passing through Guangxi, Guangdong, Hunan, Jiangxi, Hubei, Henan, and Zhili Provinces. In early June the mission arrived in the port of Guangzhou, and the "Western barbarians" of the Cohongs (referring to local factories through which the Western merchants traded with the Chinese side) gathered to witness the homage paid to the Qing by the king of an outer *fan*.[37] Two months later the Qing court invested Nguyễn's son as crown prince, and the emperor applauded the father-son relationship between the emperor and Nguyễn. Following the precedents set by his reception of the king of Chosŏn and the Mongol khan of Korcin, the emperor dispatched a minister from the Ministry of Rites to welcome the king to a tea ceremony at Liangxiang, a few miles south of Beijing.

The practice of the policy of cherishing the men from afar went smoothly until a report from Rehe in late July made the emperor uncomfortable. The officials there sent word that they had received an unofficial note (Ch., *chuandan*) saying that the daily cost of entertaining and accommodating the Vietnamese mission in Jiangxi was around four thousand taels of silver—an astounding sum. The officials were worried that it would be inappropriate for them to host the mission with less luxury once it reached Rehe, but they could only work with the funds they had available. The emperor, too, was shocked by the cost, as he had treated Mongol princes and emissaries of other countries to annual banquets for less than one thousand taels. An expense of 4,000 taels per day meant that the total amount spent on the king and his entourage would reach 0.8 million taels during their two-hundred-day sojourn in China.

Believing that this issue "deeply concerned the way of the Heavenly Dynasty," the emperor lectured his officials that "the great Heavenly Dynasty should not welcome one or two subordinates from the remote lands in a luxurious way." In addition, said the emperor, if the king were entertained too lavishly in the provinces, he would not sufficiently appreciate the imperial grace when treated with less opulence in Rehe. Chosŏn's missions illustrated the emperor's point. The Koreans prepared their own meals at each transfer station, but once they arrived in Beijing or Rehe, their daily logistics were entirely taken over by Qing personnel and the emissaries were hosted in a sumptuous manner. This substantial difference in hospitality between the provinces and Beijing created exactly the effect that the emperor sought. The danger posed by the luxurious treatment of Annam's emissaries along their route lay in its potential to undermine the spectacle of imperial generosity that the emperor, informed by the Chosŏn model, wished to present at the mission's final destination. Thus, the emperor instructed the provincial authorities in Jiangxi, Hubei, Henan, and Zhili to tone down the extravagance of their receptions, as this was the only way that "the mean between abundance and scarcity" (Ch., *fengjian shizhong*) could be realized. It was the first time in the Qianlong period that the emperor gave orders to temper the level of luxury in entertaining foreign dignitaries.[38]

The event created an opportunity for the emperor to discipline his officials. He listed two possible reasons for the astonishing costs: either local officials deliberately spent too much in order to seek profitable reimbursement from the imperial coffers in the future, or the Chinese escorts extorted too much money from the provinces they passed through. Either possibility could damage the "way of the Heavenly Dynasty." The emperor ordered governors in Guangdong, Jiangxi, Hubei, Anhui, and Zhili to investigate how the four-thousand-tael figure had come about. None of the officials claimed responsibility, but the emperor insisted that the origin of the unofficial note be identified and suggested it might have come from Zhili. Liang Kentang (1715–1802), the governor-general of Zhili, immediately reported that the note was wrongly printed in his province. The emperor condemned Liang and closed the case, but he did not punish Liang, who was apparently the scapegoat of the emperor's face-saving inquiry.[39]

When the mission from Annam arrived in Rehe on August 20, 1790, Nguyễn was granted an imperial audience together with the indigenous chiefs of southwestern China and Taiwan, the khan of Kazak, the princes of Mongolia and the Muslim tributaries, and the emissaries of Burma and Lanchang. The emperor bestowed official Qing robes on the king and his followers. On August 25, as described in the previous section, Chosŏn's bedraggled emissaries reached Rehe, and all the men from afar could finally convene at the imperial hall for the grand banquet. There and later in Beijing, the envoys from the Qing's periphery kowtowed to their shared Son of Heaven in China. What Qianlong saw and experienced was indeed a harmonious picture of the Heavenly Dynasty.

The Way of the Heavenly Dynasty: The British Mission in 1793

Three years later, the emperor would receive a very different group of men from afar. This mission came from England, known in China as Yingjili. In September 1792 Lord Macartney (1737–1806) left Portsmouth for China to seek greater commercial opportunities in the name of celebrating Qianlong's birthday. In July

1793 the mission reached Dagu Harbor in Tianjin and was welcomed by Liang Kentang and by Zhengrui, the salt tax commissioner of Changlu. On September 14 Macartney and his assistants, who were called "British tributary emissaries" (Ch., *Yingjili guo gongshi*), were granted an audience with Qianlong at Rehe, after which the mission was sent back to Guangzhou via the overland route. Scholars have described the visit as an epoch-making collision of two different cultural, social, and imperial systems and as the beginning of the East-West encounter that eventually led to the Opium War of 1839–42.[40] Rather than reviewing the entire event, which has been well examined, this section focuses on the connection between the British mission and the legacy of Annam's mission in 1790 against the historical backdrop of the Qing's institutional barbarianization of all other countries, including Britain.

Until 1793 the Qing did not have a clear sense of the British presence in India and failed to connect the British activities on the Tibetan frontier with those in India.[41] The Qing court saw the British embassy of 1793 as a tributary mission from an outer *fan*, so all bilateral contacts had to be conducted in accordance with imperial codes just like those that applied to Chosŏn, Annam, and Ryukyu. This time, the emperor made a point of instructing his local officials to treat the "foreign barbarians" of the British tributary mission appropriately "between abundance and scarcity." Such treatment, said the emperor, would befit "the way" of the "upper country" and ensure that the "men from afar" would not disdain China. Of the officials involved in hosting the mission, Liang Kentang, still smarting from the scandal of the overly extravagant hospitality shown to Annam in 1790, was perhaps the only one who thoroughly understood what the emperor meant. The emperor, too, might have taken the precedent of Annam as a standard for testing his officials. The game between the emperor and his officials was back on. In August, after learning that Zhejiang, Shandong, and Tianjin had lavished food on the British envoys, the emperor admonished his officials on the proper balance to be observed in welcoming the men from afar. Too little generosity, he explained, might "prevent them from transforming into the civilized," while too much might "result in their contempt for the way and dignity of the Heavenly Dynasty." The point was to show "neither inferiority nor superiority" in entertaining, but to "remain in accord with the way and highlight the act of cherishing." He reminded Liang several times of this "proper way."[42]

When the mission reached Rehe on September 8, Macartney and his assistants refused to prostrate themselves before the emperor. The next day the emperor issued an edict to Liang and his colleagues, expressing his disappointment in the British envoys. The edict attributed the envoys' shocking lack of respect to the extravagant treatment they had received in the provinces, which must have encouraged the barbarians' arrogance and overshadowed the impression that

Rehe ought to have made on them. To remedy the matter and punish the provinces, the emperor ordered that the mission return to Guangdong by the overland route and along interior rivers, and that all accommodations and meals at transfer stations be provided in strict conformity with tributary precedents for "such rude foreign barbarians." The emperor further stressed that the hospitality extended to the envoys in Beijing should be moderated in order to highlight the Chinese system through this punishment and to show the "[appropriate] way to manage an outer *fan*" (Ch., *jiayu waifan zhi dao*).[43] From the emperor's perspective, the accommodations and meals were meant to reflect the way of the dynasty, a point the British visitors and many local Chinese officials completely missed. For the emperor, an essential aspect of controlling the envoys of outer *fan* was the skillful deployment of the bureaucratic apparatus to cherish the men from afar appropriately.

After negotiations concerning the performance of rituals, the British group—consisting of Macartney; his deputy, George Staunton (1737–1801); Staunton's twelve-year-old son, George Thomas Staunton (1781–1859); and other members of the mission—was granted an imperial audience at the grand tent on September 14. Instead of kowtowing, the members of the mission knelt down on one knee and bowed their heads nine times. The British performed the same compromise ritual again on September 17, the imperial birthday, and days after that both in Rehe and in Beijing.[44] Simultaneously, the Manchu and Mongol princes and Burmese emissaries performed the rituals in strict observance of the imperial codes. After the ceremony, the emperor endowed the British mission with many gifts, including Korean clothing that had been piling up in Beijing as a result of Chosŏn's annual tributes.

For their part, the British submitted to the emperor their version of a "humble palace memorial," which, among other things, asked him to station a permanent representative in Beijing and to begin trading outside Guangzhou. In reply, the emperor issued a long edict to King George III, refusing all of their requests. He explained that no precedents beyond the "established rules" existed, so Britain could not hope to change China's "way of cherishing the men from afar and the barbarians in the four directions of the Heavenly Dynasty" (Ch., *tianchao jiahui yuanren fuyu siyi zhi dao*). The emperor explained that he understood that Yingjili was so far from China that it was unfamiliar with the magnificent "way of the Heavenly Dynasty" (Ch., *tianchao tizhi*), but he stressed that the British could not live and trade in Beijing because "the civilized–barbarian distinction is extremely strict" (Ch., *Hua–Yi zhi bian shenyan*). The Jesuit missionaries in Beijing, the emperor said, were not allowed to contact Chinese people either.[45] Macartney failed to obtain any trade concessions and thus shared the fate of his predecessors, James Flint in 1759 and Nicholas Skottowe in 1761. Instead the

British embassy's visit to China, which the Qing considered a tributary mission, strengthened the Qing's position as the civilized center and reinforced its institutionalized norms regarding its foreign relations. After all, it was Qing China that, as Li Chen observes, "maintained a dominant position in deciding the terms of the Sino-Western economic, cultural, and political relationships."[46]

The British thus had no effect on the Qing's worldview. On January 8, 1794, Macartney departed Guangzhou for Calcutta. The next day, three emissaries from Ryukyu were granted an audience with Qianlong in the Forbidden City, where they kowtowed to the emperor as usual. On January 22 the Mongol and Muslim princes and the chieftains of indigenous tribes from southwestern China were granted an imperial audience in which they too kowtowed to the Son of Heaven in the traditional manner. Three days later the Korean emissaries of the annual tributary mission prostrated themselves in front of the emperor. Then came New Year's Day, and all princes and tributary emissaries convened in the Forbidden City to attend the grand assembly and lavish banquets together with Chinese officials, all performing the highest level of kowtow again.[47] After the British mission left, then, the Zongfan mechanism between the Qing and its outer *fan* continued to operate in its accustomed seamless manner.

Rebellious Western and Loyal Eastern Barbarians in the 1840s

The First Opium War and the Diplomatic Paradox of Qing China

Britain did not give up. In 1816 Lord Amherst (1783–1857) visited China as an ambassador. George Thomas Staunton, who had met with Qianlong as part of the Macartney mission and later served as the director of the British East India Company in Guangzhou, acted as Amherst's deputy. By this time, China was ruled by Qianlong's son, Jiaqing. When the British mission arrived in Tianjin and contacted local officials, the deputy governor-general of Zhili, Tojin (1755–1835), adopted the tone of the provincial hosts during the Vietnamese mission in 1790 and the British mission in 1793, assuring Jiaqing that he would adhere to precedent and welcome the tributary mission in order to prevent the foreigners from disdaining China.

The crisis over kowtow, however, erupted again between the two sides. Because the dispute remained unsettled by the time the mission arrived in Beijing in late August, the British did not immediately visit the emperor. The emperor read their absence as a sign of British contempt that "China as the common leader under the Heaven" (Ch., *Zhongguo wei tianxia gongzhu*) could not tolerate. The emperor also did not trust Staunton, saying that the latter should remember what ceremonies he had performed to Qianlong in 1793. In the end, the emperor refused to accept Amherst's "humble palace memorial," returned the British "tributes," and ordered the envoys to be sent back to their homeland with token gifts from China.[48] The second British mission had also failed.

In 1821 Staunton published a translation of the travelogue of Tulišen, the official who had visited Russia as the Qing envoy in 1712. In the preface, Staunton pointed out that the Chinese government followed an "anti-social system" in their intercourse with other nations and that China would consequently "rank very low indeed in the scale of civilized nations."[49] Staunton's ranking of civilization from his Eurocentric point of view served well the British strategy in China at the time. As the British-dominated opium trade reached new heights, the large inflows of opium and the dramatic outflows of silver were creating a financial crisis in China, forcing Beijing to consider banning the opium trade. In April 1840 Staunton, by then a member of the British Parliament, urged his colleagues to use force against China.[50] The ensuing Opium War between the two countries ended with the conclusion of the Treaty of Nanjing in 1842, the twenty-second year of Daoguang, Qianlong's grandson. According to the Treaty of Nanjing and the Supplementary Treaty of Bogue, which was negotiated according to Western norms and signed in 1843, Britain gained the right of extraterritoriality and "most favored nation" status in China. The treaties thus planted the seeds of European imperialism in the Chinese world through the emerging treaty port framework.

In 1844 the Qing established the position of superintendent of trade for the five ports (Ch., *Wukou tongshang dachen*) to manage contacts with Britain, France, the United States, and other Western countries. On the surface, the new post moved these treaty nations out of the orbit of the Ministry of Rites and the scope of the Zongfan framework. But the first official to hold the post was Qiying (1787–1858), a Manchu and a signatory of the Treaty of Nanjing who soon after became governor-general of Liangguang, where he was in charge of China's contacts not only with Western countries in Guangzhou but also with Annam, Siam, and several other outer *fan*. This new post was thus added to the established Zongfan system without changing the nature of the system per se. Likewise, nothing really changed in other parts of the Qing periphery after the war.

Keeping the West out of the Ritual: Qing Envoys to Chosŏn

After Queen Kim of Chosŏn passed away in late 1843, the Daoguang emperor appointed two Manchu officials, Baijun (?–1859) and Hengxing, as envoys to deliver his condolences to Hansŏng. In February 1844 the two envoys left Beijing for Chosŏn with the imperial book of condolences and other items. After crossing Fenghuang Gate and marching toward the Yalu River, they found that the Koreans had set up several shanties to welcome them. In Ŭiju more Korean officials, including one with the king's name card, greeted the envoys. On April 7 the envoys arrived in Hongjewŏn, in the suburbs of Hansŏng, where a high-ranking official with the king's name card and a minister of the Ŭijŏngbu, the Korean cabinet, welcomed them.

The grand ceremony was held the next day. In the morning the envoys were escorted to the Hall of Admiring the Central Civilized Country outside the West Gate of the capital. The king came out through the West Gate to receive the impe-rial edict and returned to his palace first. The envoys were then escorted through the South Gate and dismounted from their horses near a gate to the palace. Bai-jun was guided by an usher to the grand hall, where he placed the imperial book of condolences and the condolence money on a desk on the east side of the hall and stood next to the desk. The king, at the foot of the steps to the hall, kowtowed to the imperial items and then proceeded to the mourning hall. There the two envoys in turn made offerings to the spirit of the dead. The king led the royal family members into the hall and knelt down in front of the envoys to receive the emperor's condolences. Following ritual wailing, the last step of the ceremony, the imperial book of condolences was burned.[51]

The king then invited the envoys to the grand hall for a tea ceremony, after which the envoys went to their residence, the South Palace Annex. The next day the king visited the envoys to treat them to a tea banquet, and Korean officials visited the envoys to ask them to write Chinese characters, keeping the guests busy. The envoys also distributed 300 taels of silver and 490 felt caps among local servants. On April 12 the king sent off the envoys, giving each a gift of 2,500 taels of silver. After they returned to Beijing, the envoys reported on their mission to the emperor and suggested that the emperor preserve the 5,000 taels of silver in the Ministry of Rites, which could return the silver to Chosŏn through the country's next mission to Beijing to show the imperial kindness of cherishing the men from afar.[52] During their three-day sojourn in Hansŏng, the envoys did not talk with the king about any events in China related to the Opium War, the treaties signed with Western countries, or the changes in China's foreign policies in South China, nor did the king ask about these matters. Their interactions were confined to the performance of minutely prescribed rituals that undergirded the longstanding mutual dependence of their legitimacy as Zhongguo and its outer *fan*, respectively. This primacy of ritual was demonstrated again soon afterward, in 1845.

In April 1845 Emperor Daoguang appointed Huashana (1806–59), a Manchu minister of the Ministry of Revenue, and Deshun, an associate general of the Mon-gol Eight Banners, as envoys to Hansŏng to invest a new queen. The envoys arrived in Hansŏng in late May. The king went outside the city to welcome the envoys and the imperial books of investiture, after which the envoys were taken in sedan chairs to the palace, where they alighted in front of the grand hall and carried in the books of investiture. The king entered the hall to receive the imperial books by performing the kowtow. An usher read the books aloud to Chosŏn's officials outside the hall, and then the king led his officials in three cheers of "Long live the emperor" (Ch., *shanhu wansui*). After a stay of three days, the envoys left the capital.[53] When the envoys reported to Beijing, the emperor asked them about the distance they had traveled, the king's clothes, and the gifts sent by the king, but no mention was made of Chosŏn's politics or other domestic Korean issues. For the emperor, the crises and challenges imposed by the war with Britain and the opening of treaty ports in Southeast China were entirely outside the purview of Qing-Chosŏn relations. At the top of the Qing administration, the Sinocentric cosmopolitan order and the Qing's identity as the Heavenly Dynasty remained untouched. Chosŏn, the prototypical outer *fan*, still maintained its loyalty to the Great Qing.

Ministers and Emissaries: The British and Korean Missions to Beijing, 1860 and 1861

The Permanent Residence of Western Representatives in Beijing

In 1856 the Second Opium War erupted in Guangzhou. The Chinese governor-general and imperial commissioner, Ye Mingchen (1807–59), who was in charge of foreign affairs, was captured in his office in the city in January 1858 by the Anglo-French forces under the leadership of Lord Elgin (1811–63). Part of a family that had enjoyed close contacts with Korean visitors in Beijing, Ye shared with Koreans the discourse of the civilized–barbarian distinction.[54] He had served in Guangzhou for more than a decade as one of the strongest opponents of allowing British representatives and merchants to move into the walled city. In his last memorial to the Xianfeng emperor before he was captured, Ye analyzed his negotiations with the British, French, and American ministers in Guangzhou and underlined his strategy of "secretly preparing for crises and publicly cherishing the barbarians."[55] The Western colonial states' expansion to East Asia remained incomprehensible to Ye, who still conceptualized all international contacts, including conflicts, skirmishes, and even the ongoing war, within the Zongfan framework. The emperor, with no better understanding than Ye, regarded the behavior of the British and French as "rebellion" and emphasized that China's first imperative was to "cherish" these wayward subordinates to "preserve the national polity and refuse their requests." The rationale was the same as that behind Qianlong's instructions regarding the Macartney embassy in 1793. Neither the emperor nor his ministers at court nor his governors at the border realized that they were dealing with several global powers engaging in gunboat diplomacy from Africa to East Asia.

The war situation continued to escalate. In April 1858 the British, French, American, and Russian ministers convened in Tianjin and dispatched an ultimatum to Beijing, demanding negotiations with Chinese "plenipotentiaries" (Ch., *bianyi xingshi*). Among the requests made by these states, such as expanding trade to the Chinese interior and opening more ports, the most offensive to the Qing was the demand to lodge permanent representatives in Beijing, precisely as Macartney had proposed in 1793. The court instructed the governor-general of Zhili, Tan Tingxiang (?–1870), who was negotiating with the European ministers in Tianjin, to clarify that "all contacts between China and foreign countries have always been conducted at the borders, and only countries among China's subordinates [Ch., *shuguo*] can visit Beijing to pay tribute [Ch., *chaogong*]. No commissioner from those countries has ever been allowed to reside in Beijing permanently." The court also refused to appoint any plenipotentiaries. The emperor argued that his stance was not xenophobic because "China is not afraid of the visit of the barbarians to Beijing, however many people were to come; the problem is that such a visit does not fit the system." Along the same lines, he refused to allow the American minister, William Reed (1806–76), to visit Beijing because "the United States is a friendly country [Ch., *yuguo*], but the imperial collection of precedents does not record how we should treat a friendly country, so the practice of entertaining might be inappropriate."[56] The emperor asked that the ministers return to Guangzhou and discuss such issues as tariffs with the governor-general there, suggesting that the negotiations should be conducted with the superintendent of trade for the five ports at the border rather than in Beijing. The location of the negotiations was an integral aspect of the Sinocentric world order and thus mattered greatly in the eyes of the Qing rulers.

The Anglo-French Alliance ignored the emperor's instructions and occupied the Dagu Forts on May 20, after which they forwarded Tan Tingxiang a note requesting that the four nations be allowed entry into Tianjin for negotiations with the Chinese plenipotentiaries as well as entry into Beijing, where they would either pay a visit to the emperor or meet with grand secretaries. On May 28 the emperor appointed the Manchu grand secretary, Guiliang (1785–62), as minister extraordinary and the Manchu minister Huashana as plenipotentiary and sent them to Tianjin for negotiations. Huashana, who had served as the deputy of the Son of Heaven on the mission to Chosŏn in 1845, now became a diplomatic representative of the Chinese sovereign who was equal to the monarchs of

Britain and France. The emperor particularly instructed Tan to inform the foreign ministers that there was no need for them to visit Beijing. In the meantime, he ordered Prince Sengge Rinchen (1811–65) of the Korcin Mongols to use his Mongol warriors to reinforce the garrison between Tianjin and Beijing.

The Sino-British negotiations reached a deadlock over the issue of a permanent representative in Beijing. At court, many high-ranking officials, such as Prince Yi (Dzai Yūwan, 1816–61), firmly refused the Western request to place representatives in Beijing. They suggested instead that Britain could follow the established practice of the "Russian barbarians" (Ch., *E yi*) and station students rather than commissioners in Beijing. The students would dress in "the clothes and caps of China" (Ch., *Zhongguo yiguan*), abide by local rules, and refrain from involvement in official affairs. Britain could negotiate with Chinese governors-general and governors over trade affairs at treaty ports. If the British insisted on visiting Beijing, the emperor said that they would have to travel from Shanghai via the overland route, escorted by Chinese officials, with all accommodations and meals covered by China. They could visit Beijing once every three or five years, not annually.[57] Not coincidentally, this proposal fit precisely into the existing tributary ritual codes: Beijing was trying to draw Britain into the established Zongfan system. From 1761 to 1793, then to 1858, the Qing court's understanding of Britain remained the same because the Qing's institutionalized Zongfan norms never changed.

This ideal model was soon partly—if opaquely—realized in the treaty with the United States, concluded on June 18, 1858, in Tianjin. Article 5 of the treaty regulated the visit of the American minister to Beijing in accordance with the specific ritual codes for the Qing's outer *fan*.[58] The regulations specified the frequency of the Americans' visits to Beijing, the overland route they were to take from Tianjin to Beijing, their entertainment by local authorities, the requisite written notice to the Ministry of Rites, and especially the size of the mission—twenty members, which was the maximum head count of tributary missions allowed for Ryukyu, Lanchang, Burma, and the Netherlands. Although the treaty granted the United States the status of a most favored nation, Beijing saw this status simply as a special favor for foreign barbarians, unrelated to China's statehood and sovereignty. In this sense, the Qing court treated the United States as a tributary state, which the latter, of course, completely failed to realize.

Within the domestic Confucianism-centered intellectual framework, neither the Qing ruling house nor the majority of its officials who had passed the imperial civil-service examinations thought beyond the framework of the civilized–barbarian distinction. The new knowledge imported from the West by American and European missionaries who were active in Southeast Asia and South China had not yet had an impact on the Chinese intellectual forces behind the post-Qianlong institutionalized order. On June 23, 1858, the Chinese minister Zhou Zupei (1793–1867) and thirty of his colleagues submitted memorials against the permanent residence of "barbarous emissaries" in Beijing. Among the "eight evils" of such residence highlighted in Zhou's memorial was the preaching of the gospel by the foreigners, which would "turn our manner of clothes, caps, rituals, and music into something fit for beasts" (Ch., *yiguan liyue zhi zu, yi yu qinshou*). He also warned that "if countries such as Chosŏn and Ryukyu, which have been loyal to China for a long time and sincerely send emissaries and pay tribute to the court, saw the disobedience of these barbarians, they, too, would despise the Heavenly Dynasty." This argument was further underscored by Chen Rui, who emphasized the "fundamental divide between China and the others" (Ch., *Zhong Wai zhi dafang*).[59] In terms of their thinking, these officials were no different from Ye Mingchen, who at the time was detained by the British in Calcutta.

Despite such keen resistance, Guiliang and Huashana accepted the British-drafted treaty after they realized the situation was beyond China's control. The treaty with Britain, signed on June 26, allowed Britain to appoint diplomatic agents to the court in Beijing, where they would not kowtow to the emperor. According to article 3, the British ambassador, minister, or other diplomatic agent "shall not be called upon to perform any ceremony derogatory to him as representing the Sovereign of an independent nation, on a footing of equality with that of China. On the other hand, he shall use the same forms of ceremony and respect to His Majesty the Emperor as are employed by the Ambassadors, Ministers, or Diplomatic Agents of Her Majesty toward the Sovereigns of independent and equal European nations."[60] In retrospect, this article opened the gates of Beijing to the representatives of Britain and other treaty nations and marked the beginning of the collapse of the centuries-long ritual system and the erosion of the Zongfan infrastructure. Being forced to fundamentally change its time-honored ritual norms, even if only in part, the Great Qing moved toward its eventual transformation from a cosmopolitan empire to a state equal to Britain according to post-Westphalian political and diplomatic norms.

Historic though the change was, the Chinese may not have fully understood the treaty's importance because of linguistic discrepancies. The Chinese version of the treaty, for instance, states that "Britain is a nation of *zizhu* on a footing of equality with China" (Ch., *Yingguo zizhu zhi bang, yu Zhongguo pingdeng*). The term *zizhu*, which meant self-rule or autonomy, was usually used in a Zongfan context. China regarded its outer *fan* as possessing this right, so it was different from the British understanding of the term "independence." This divergence would become apparent in the following years, when China and the Western states as well as Japan tried to define the nature of the Sino-Korean relationship and Chosŏn's international position. The seeds of further conflicts between the norms of the Chinese Zongfan system and those of European international law were thus planted directly in these treaties.

What further shook the foundation of the civilized–barbarian discourse was article 51 of the Sino-British treaty of 1858, which decreed that the character *yi* ("barbarian") "shall not be applied to the Government or subjects of Her Britannic Majesty in any Chinese official document issued by the Chinese Authorities either in the Capital or in the Provinces."[61] Britain and other Western nations that were eligible to invoke the most-favored-nation clause thus broke away legally and institutionally from the category of barbarians in Chinese diplomatic discourse. From then on, in Chinese official narratives the character *yi* was increasingly replaced by *yang* ("overseas," "foreign") and the term "barbarians" (Ch., *yiren*) by "foreigners" (Ch., *yangren*).

This amendment, however, applied only to Western treaty nations that had never occupied an essential position in the Zongfan system. The Qing still considered its major outer *fan*, such as Chosŏn, Vietnam, and Ryukyu, countries of barbarians. In this sense, the treaty port system, although it was expanding rapidly at the end of the 1850s, merely complicated the Qing's view of the countries in the "Western Ocean." In other words, the disintegration of Sinocentrism as a result of the 1858 treaties occurred on the Qing's intellectual periphery, not at the core of its intellectual and ideological structure as informed and represented by the Qing's principal outer *fan*. The ministers of the treaty nations residing in Beijing would soon be confronted with the complexity and perplexity of this distinction.

Who Were the Barbarians Now? The British and Korean Missions to Beijing

Treaties in hand, the ministers of Britain, France, Russia, and the United States left Tianjin for Shanghai, where they and Chinese representatives signed additional treaties on tariffs. The war would have been over had the British and French ministers in the summer of 1859 followed the Qing's designated route to enter Beijing after they landed at Tianjin for the ratification of the treaties. But the ministers refused to follow Qing instructions, and their rash entry into the firth of the Beihe River near the Dagu Forts led to Chinese bombardment. The war resumed less than a year after the British Crown imposed direct control over India by nationalizing the British East India Company in August 1858. Under the leadership of Lord Elgin, who was determined to employ gunboat diplomacy against Beijing, the Anglo-French alliance returned to China in the summer of 1860 and reoccupied the Dagu Forts. There the alliance almost annihilated the Mongol cavalry of Prince Sengge Rinchen with the Armstrong gun, a weapon created by Britain and employed in combat for the first time. The Qing succumbed not only to the joint colonialism of the European states but also to revolutionary post–Crimean War European military technology.

The alliance occupied Tianjin and marched toward Beijing in late August. Although the Beijing court sent representatives to Tongzhou, near Beijing, for negotiations, on September 18 Prince Sengge Rinchen captured Harry Parkes (1828–85), the British commissioner in Guangzhou, as well as Henry Loch (1827–1900), Elgin's private secretary, and twenty-four British and thirteen French officers and soldiers. Only half of these prisoners of war—including Parkes and Loch—survived and were eventually released on October 8, when the alliance gained control of Beijing's suburbs and started looting the imperial palace of Yuan-Ming-Yuan. The frightened Son of Heaven, Emperor Xianfeng, had fled to Rehe on September 22 after appointing his younger brother Prince Gong (a.k.a. Prince Kung, 1833–98) as the envoy extraordinary and plenipotentiary to supervise the uncertain peace negotiations. On October 13 the Western forces took over the Anding Gate of the city. The Qing saw this as a more serious threat than it did the ongoing Taiping Rebellion in South China, as the court in Rehe and the caretaker administration in Beijing were extremely vulnerable to the aggressive European alliance and their powerful cannons positioned on the city's old walls.

From October 12 to 16, the survivors and bodies of the prisoners of war were returned to the alliance. The evident cruelty inflicted on the corpses, mutilated beyond recognition, shocked Elgin and his fellow commanders. Elgin "at once notified to Prince Kung that he was too horrified by what had occurred to hold further communication with a government guilty of such deeds of treachery and bloodshed, until by some great punishment inflicted upon the Emperor and the governing classes, he had made apparent . . . the detestation with which the Allies viewed such conduct." The "great punishment" turned out to be the immolation of Yuan-Ming-Yuan. On October 18, the second day after the alliance buried the former prisoners, flames engulfed the magnificent imperial garden that had been co-designed by European Jesuit missionaries. Loch recorded that "during the whole of Friday the 19th, Yuen-Ming-Yuen was still burning; the clouds of smoke driven by the wind, hung like a vast black pall over Pekin."[62] Numerous buildings in which the Qing emperors had given audience to emissaries of its outer *fan*—once including Britain and always including Chosŏn—were burned to the ground. On October 20 Prince Gong offered Elgin China's submission to the alliance's demands. The capital was fully opened to the alliance. Parkes and Loch entered the city the next day and ironically selected the grand hall of the Ministry of Rites as the site for the signing of the convention.

Elgin departed for the grand hall on October 24, carried in a sedan chair by sixteen Chinese footmen—an honor previously reserved for the emperor—and accompanied by an escort of more than six hundred men. When the procession reached the hall, according to Loch, Prince Gong "advanced to receive Lord Elgin with an anxious, hesitating salutation," while the latter "bowed, and at once walked forward to his seat, motioning Prince Kung to take the one on the right." After they signed the convention, exchanged treaties, and talked briefly about maintaining friendship, "Lord Elgin rose to take leave; Prince Kung accompanied him a short distance, and then stopped; but on Lord Elgin doing so likewise, the principal mandarins in attendance urgently beckoned Prince Kung to move forward, and after a few moments of hesitation he walked with Lord Elgin to the edge of the steps." Prince Gong was apparently adjusting to a new etiquette that he had never before performed. Witnessing the entire procedure, Loch enthusiastically claimed, "Thus was happily concluded an event which was the commencement of a new era, not only in the history of the Empire of China, but of the world, by the introduction of four hundred millions of the human race into the family of civilized nations."[63] Like George Thomas Staunton's, Loch's judgment on civilization was thoroughly Eurocentric.

Loch was correct in asserting that China had entered a new era. In January 1861 the Qing court established a temporary "office in charge of affairs concerning all countries" (Ch., Zongli geguo shiwu yamen, hereafter "the Zongli Yamen") under Prince Gong's supervision. The Yamen was responsible for China's foreign relations only with Britain, France, the United States, Russia, and other treaty nations, not with Chosŏn, Ryukyu, Vietnam, and other outer *fan*, whose contacts with Beijing were still under the auspices of the Ministry of Rites. The new institution was designed with the goal of expediency to meet challenges in a time of crisis, and it was modeled on the Grand Council.[64] The officials who served in the Yamen did so only on a part-time basis. The official tablet hanging at the main entrance of the institution read, "Goodness and happiness between the center and the outside" (Ch., *Zhong Wai tifu*), highlighting the key Confucian doctrine of the mean. More importantly, the Yamen was deemed an imitation of the Foreign Emissaries' Common Accommodations and was consequently categorized as part of the established Zongfan system. According to the court's plan, once the momentary crisis had passed, foreign affairs would revert to the management of the Ministry of Rites as usual, for the sake of "cherishing the outer *fan*."[65]

Yet like the Grand Council, the Zongli Yamen continued to serve the court after the crisis, and in 1901 it became the Ministry of Foreign Affairs (Ch., Waiwu bu). The Yamen survived primarily because China's treaty partners always treated it as a ministry of foreign affairs at which Western diplomats could apply the concepts of international law to their negotiations with the Chinese side; still, the diplomats were not blind to the fact that the Yamen was different from a ministry of foreign affairs in the Western sense.[66] Beijing also realized that it was impossible to disband the Zongli Yamen, in particular after March 1861, when the French,

British, Russian, and American ministers arrived in Beijing and established their offices next to the Forbidden City. In response, Beijing quickly organized a diplomatic network from the top down by appointing superintendents of trade for Tianjin and Shanghai. So began a new era.

As noted earlier, these institutional changes to the Zongfan framework affected only those parts that governed relations with treaty nations; beyond those, the Zongfan system stood unchanged. As ever, Chosŏn played an exemplary role in maintaining the Qing's superiority within this established system. After learning from the 1860 annual tributary mission to Beijing that the emperor had moved to Rehe, the king of Chosŏn immediately sent a special mission to China with the aim of visiting the emperor at Rehe and demonstrating to him Chosŏn's concern as a loyal subordinate of the imperial dynasty. In early 1861 the Korean emissaries reached postwar Beijing, bearing various tributes. The Ministry of Rites asked the emperor whether the emissaries should visit Rehe, following the precedents of Annam's mission in 1790, Lanchang's and Burma's missions in 1795, and Annam's mission in 1803. The emperor responded that there was no need for the Korean emissaries to travel to Rehe, but he instructed the ministry to follow convention by treating the emissaries to banquets and endowing them and the king with generous gifts in order to show his "ultimate kindness of cherishing the *fan* in a favored way."[67]

In fact, between November 1858 and May 1861, Chosŏn dispatched five tributary missions to Beijing in spite of the war in China. In the early 1790s, Chosŏn and British emissaries had convened in Rehe and Beijing as representatives of two outer *fan*—both of them nations of barbarians in the Qing's eyes. But whereas the British emissaries had violently changed their status in the Chinese world by the early 1860s by entering Beijing under the cover of cannons, their Korean counterparts continued to approach the imperial capital with humble palace memorials and tributes. Although the Korean emissaries also pursued the secret mission of obtaining intelligence in China in order to enable the Korean court to assess the situation there, their frequent presence in Beijing provided the Qing with a steady stream of resources to maintain its conventional ritual code, politico-cultural hierarchy, and imperial norms, which were under fire from the British and the French. However, the Korean emissaries never again saw the Xianfeng emperor, who died in Rehe in August and became the last emperor who refused to allow the Western barbarians to stand before him without kowtowing.[68]

It was not until 1873 that Xianfeng's son, Tongzhi, gave foreign ministers their first imperial audience at which the ministers did not kowtow. The audience took place at the Purple Light Pavilion (Ch., Ziguang ge) in the Forbidden City, the same venue at which the Qing emperor had met with emissaries of China's outer *fan* since 1761—the year in which the Qing institutionalized the status of all other countries within its own imperial norms, as described in chapter 2. In 1873 the pavilion no longer witnessed the ritual of kowtow, but the politico-cultural significance of the imperial audience in that location remained essentially the same. Interestingly, and ironically, since 1949 the state leaders of the People's Republic of China, who converted part of the Qing imperial palace into their living quarters and political headquarters, have used the pavilion to meet with foreign guests from other, equal states of the world—if no longer in the sense of all-under-Heaven.

Part II
SAVING OUR CHOSŎN

4

DEFINING CHOSŎN

Qing China's Depiction of Chosŏn's
Status, 1862–76

For the Qing ruling house and intelligentsia, "everyday familiarity" collapsed on
the very first day that the Westerners entered Beijing as permanent diplomatic
representatives.[1] As the self-strengthening movement unfolded in the 1860s, Beijing was increasingly intrigued by the possibility of employing European methods to enhance China's military and technical capabilities for the sake of China's
future. The innovations proposed by various reformers caught the attention of
more open-minded Chinese officials who were interested in statecraft outside
their ivory towers. This elite drew on knowledge from abroad and pioneered
Chinese modernization, aware that the entrenched politico-cultural concept
of all-under-Heaven embedded in a cosmopolitan, Confucian worldview was
ineluctably giving way to more realistic world politics born of sophisticated
foreign negotiations informed by Western norms. The elite realized that they
must first learn those norms from their Western counterparts. In 1864 the Zongli
Yamen published *Wanguo gongfa* (lit. "the common law among ten thousand
countries"), the Chinese edition of Henry Wheaton's *Elements of International
Law*, which had appeared in English in 1836.[2] Translated by an American Presbyterian missionary in Beijing, William A. P. Martin (1827–1916; known in Chinese
as Ding Weiliang), it was the first guide to international law in China and the
Chinese world. The Chinese edition pointedly added a map of the world that presented it in the conventional arrangement of eastern and western hemispheres,
which further eroded the Sinocentric view by portraying China as merely one
country among others.[3] The Great Qing began to transform its political and

diplomatic norms by integrating notions of international law into its own constitutional and institutional systems.

However, the disintegration of the Qing's old conceptualization of Western countries as barbarians did not lead to a similar breakdown in the Zongfan framework that bound together the Manchu and Korean courts. Their symbiotic legitimacy, which could not be redefined or circumscribed by international law, still strongly influenced their internal and external policies and behavior in the middle of the nineteenth century. In this sense, the two Opium Wars and the treaties from 1842 to 1860 did not simply mark "the twilight of the Old" and "the dawn of the New," as the East-West dichotomy would have it.[4] Rather, the treaty port network imposed from the outside and the time-honored Zongfan arrangement inside the Qing realm formed a dual system of two coexisting elements, and the former did not immediately begin to replace or incorporate the latter, as many scholars have retrospectively presumed. Since the 1860s, as contacts between Chosŏn and Western countries grew more frequent, both Beijing and Hansŏng found it increasingly difficult to define their Zongfan relationship and Chosŏn's international status and state sovereignty. While the two countries asserted unanimously that Chosŏn was China's *shuguo* or *shubang* ("subordinate country") possessing the right of *zizhu*, China's treaty counterparts treated Chosŏn as a state with independent sovereignty that maintained a merely ritual relationship to China. This chapter explores this diplomatic conundrum and its consequences.

Chosŏn as China's *Shuguo*: The Sino-French Conflict of 1866

The Beginning of the Puzzle: The French Invasion and China's Response

In 1866, France decided to launch an expedition against Chosŏn in response to the killing of French missionaries in anti-Catholic purges initiated by Yi Ha-ŭng (1820–98), better known by his title, Taewŏn'gun (Prince of the great court). The Taewŏn'gun had become the de facto regent after his twelve-year-old son, Yi Hŭi (King Kojong), assumed the throne in 1863 as the closest male relative and thus the legitimate successor of the late King Ikchong.[5] During the decade of his regency, the Taewŏn'gun carried out a series of domestic reforms, but as a follower of Confucianism he also regarded Western religions as heresies or "evil ideas" (K., *sahak*). In early 1866 he started to persecute converts to Christianity and Catholicism, leading to the execution of thirteen French missionaries and hundreds of native converts in a short time.[6]

When news of the purge reached Beijing, the French chargé d'affaires, Henri de Bellonet, decided to launch a punitive expedition against Chosŏn. On July 14, 1866, Bellonet sent the Zongli Yamen a letter threatening that France would invade and temporarily occupy Chosŏn and appoint a new king. He noted that the expedition would have nothing to do with China, as he had earlier been informed by the Yamen that Chosŏn managed its own affairs. Indeed, in 1865 Bellonet had asked the Yamen to issue a dispatch to Chosŏn to inform the king that French missionaries wanted to bring their teachings to the kingdom. The Yamen had declined to do so, explaining that "Chosŏn, as a *shuguo* of China, only uses the Chinese calendar, uses Chinese regnal titles, and pays annual tribute to China." Bellonet interpreted this response to mean that "the Chinese government has no authority or power over Corea."[7] From then on, both Western states and the Zongli Yamen had continuous difficulty pinning down Chosŏn's status as China's *shuguo* in terms that the other side could accurately understand.

The Zongli Yamen claimed both that Chosŏn was a *shuguo* of China and that because Chosŏn managed all its own affairs under the rubric of *zizhu*, China would not intervene in them. This statement was clear in Zongfan terms but came across as equivocal and paradoxical to Western ministers. While Bellonet acknowledged that Chosŏn had "formerly assumed the bonds of vassalage to the Chinese empire," he asserted that at the present moment, "we do not recognize any authority whatever of the Chinese government over the kingdom of Corea."[8] This statement recognized Chosŏn as an independent nation, but the Yamen's Chinese translation of it missed its political meaning. The *Wanguo gongfa* of 1864 did not provide the Yamen with a definition of *shuguo* that could be translated into appropriate Western terms.

What, then, caused this misunderstanding between France and China? This question is closely connected to the Western perception of the Sinocentric political arrangement. At least since the late eighteenth century, Western travelers, observers, and diplomats who witnessed the practice of Korea and other entities of sending emissaries with tribute to Beijing used the term "tributary" to describe the nature of the relationship between China and Korea, Vietnam, and other countries.[9] Their descriptions constituted the first step toward using the terms "tribute system" or "tributary system" to refer to the Zongfan system in Western literature on China and East Asia. In the first half of the nineteenth century, when Western diplomats brought international law to East Asia, the Western understanding of this tribute system became increasingly skewed. As the Western states gradually integrated China and Japan into the family of nations defined according to European norms, they found that Chosŏn maintained a special relationship with China that they could not explain adequately within the framework of these norms. Thus, according to M. Frederick Nelson, "searching back into the categories which their international system listed, they hit upon that of suzerain and vassal as most nearly fitting this East Asiatic relationship, and they then proceeded to apply the legal attributes of vassalage to the non-legal status of a *shupang* [*shubang*, subordinate country]."[10] The Sino-Korean relationship was thus depicted as a form of a suzerain-vassal relationship in order to fit it into a Western interpretive setting.[11] As this and the following chapters show, the special relationship between Egypt and the Ottoman Empire was seen as an instructive analogy, in part as a result of Japan's strategy of using European legal terminology to undermine the Sino-Korean relationship.[12]

As the misunderstanding between the French and China shows, this suzerain-vassal rendering of the Zongfan order risked a legal quagmire regarding Chosŏn. Both China and Chosŏn declared that Chosŏn was China's subordinate country with the right of autonomy; the Western countries and Japan interpreted this to mean that Korea was an independent sovereign state with all international rights. The confusion was exacerbated by the fact that *Wanguo gongfa* used Chinese Zongfan concepts to translate English legal terms. For example, the English term "colony" was rendered as *pingfan* (fence), *shubang*, or *shuguo*; "dependency" as *shubang*; "vassal state" as *fanshu* (subordinate country or dependent country); "sovereign states" as *zizhu zhi guo* (countries with the right of self-rule); and "right of sovereignty" as *zizhu zhi quan* (right of self-rule).[13] The discrepancies between the Chinese and European terms show that China's perspective remained essentially familistic, whereas the Europeans and the Americans operated in a primarily legal context.[14] Martin, the *Wanguo gongfa* translator, was not the first to adopt these Chinese terms in translation. As early as the 1830s, some Protestant missionaries, such as Karl Gützlaff (1803–51) from Prussia, rendered "colony" as *fanshu guo* in their Chinese-language magazines published in South China. For example, the September 1833 issue of *Dong Xi-yang kao meiyue tongji zhuan* (Eastern-Western monthly magazine) calls India *Da Yingguo zhi fanshu guo* (the subordinate country of Great Britain) and Siberia *Eluosi fanshu guo* (the subordinate country of Russia).[15] Since the 1860s, the terminological inconsistency led to great confusion over the nature of the Zongfan relationship and growing conflicts between China, Korea, and other countries.

As a result, Western diplomats in East Asia widely perceived the Sino-Korean relationship as a "nominal" one, with China exercising "no real authority" over Korea.[16] Misunderstandings persisted through the late 1880s and early 1890s, as William W. Rockhill (1854–1914) confessed in his study of Sino-Korean relations, which was aimed at clarifying what he described as "a puzzle for Western nations"—whether Korea was "an integral part of the Chinese empire" or "a sovereign state enjoying absolute international rights." Rockhill argued that the Chinese term *shuguo*, generally but misleadingly converted into English terms such as "vassal kingdom" or "fief," was "the key-note to the whole system of Korean dependency."[17] What led Rockhill to identify Korea's status as a puzzle seems to have been its contrast with the European colonial experience of his day: the relationship between a European colonial power and its overseas colonies—that of Britain and India, or of France and Algeria—was clear, since the colony was undoubtedly an integral part of the empire, fully subject to the imperial administration. The questions regarding Sino-Korean relations raised in the early 1890s by George N. Curzon, who later served as viceroy of India, similarly reflected this colonial discourse.[18] But although these Europeans could not reconcile Chosŏn's status with their Eurocentric understanding of colonial relationships, they nonetheless regarded the Sino-Korean relationship as a legitimate one, which may explain why their states never publicly denied that Chosŏn was a dependency of China before 1895. The Sino-French negotiation over Chosŏn's international position in 1866 was the beginning of the exposure of a range of conceptual, textual, ideological, and epistemological conflicts between China and its Western counterparts. Bellonet was thus among the first Westerners who encountered difficulties in dealing with the Zongfan order in practice.

On the Chinese side, the Zongli Yamen, as a temporary institution established on an ad hoc basis, had no right to communicate with Chosŏn, and until the end of the Zongfan relationship in 1895 it never gained that right. Rather, the Ministry of Rites continued to carry responsibility for Chosŏn's affairs. The Zongli Yamen simply sent any cases involving Chosŏn to the Ministry of Rites for processing. The ministry, for its part, could not make changes to established imperial codes, formalities, or precedents regarding Chosŏn, so it often forwarded the cases to the emperor and the Grand Council to receive further instructions. This convention-driven arrangement persisted until 1882, when Beijing endowed Li Hongzhang—the Beiyang superintendent under the supervision of the Zongli Yamen—with the right to communicate with the king. Contacts between Chosŏn and Western states in the 1860s thus exposed China's policy deficit in the uncharted territory between the Zongli Yamen and the Ministry of Rites, and this deficit endured for another three decades. Given this context, the Zongli Yamen pursued a policy of "mediation" (Ch., *paijie*) between Chosŏn and the West. It replied to Bellonet that the French should not rush to attack Chosŏn and that China would mediate between France and Chosŏn, but it did not claim responsibility for the killing of the French missionaries. In a memorial to the emperor and in a confidential letter to governors-general and governors of the coastal provinces and Manchu generals in Manchuria, the Yamen expressed serious concern over the French hostility toward Chosŏn and proclaimed that China could "in no way sit it out" if Chosŏn were to come under foreign attack.[19] It also notified Chosŏn, via the Ministry of Rites, of the possibility that French forces might invade the country.[20]

Undeterred, Bellonet instructed Admiral Pierre-Gustave Roze (1812–83), commander of the French Far Eastern Squadron, to launch the expedition. On September 20 Roze led three warships from Zhifu (Chefoo, now Yantai) on the Shandong Peninsula across the Bohai Sea. They arrived at a small island off the coast of Inch'ŏn, where they made navigational charts of the waters along the coastlines. Roze refused to contact local officials while conducting these activities. At court, the Taewŏn'gun learned of the arrival of the foreign "strange-shaped ships" (K., *iyang sŏn*), but he nonetheless continued his anti-Catholic campaign by arresting and executing more converts. Ten days before the French forces arrived, the young king, at his father's suggestion, had issued a "decree of antiheresy" (K., *ch'ŏksa yunŭm*) to further stoke anti-Catholic resentment.[21]

On October 1 the three primary members of the most recent tributary mission to Beijing—Yu Hu-bok, Sŏ Tang-po, and Hong Sun-hak—returned to Hansŏng and were granted an audience with the king. The mission had been charged with requesting the Qing to invest the daughter of the late official Min Ch'i-rok with the title of queen; she would later be known as Queen Min (1851–95). Yu made a point of informing the king and senior ministers that the foreigners in Beijing were beyond Chinese jurisdiction and were not afraid of the "big country."[22] Yu's account may have given the court the impression that China had become a victim of Western invaders, and that Chosŏn would be next. This news reinforced the Taewŏn'gun's anti-Catholic and xenophobic attitude, convincing him that Chosŏn's security could be guaranteed only by resisting the "barbarians of the ocean" (K., *yang'i*).[23]

Two weeks after Yu's audience with the king, the French squadron reached Inch'ŏn and blockaded all entrances to the Han River of Hansŏng. In spite of Korean resistance, French marines landed on Korean soil and proceeded to loot the capital of Kanghwa Prefecture and other nearby towns. With the arrival of cold weather in early November, they withdrew back to Zhifu. The Western ministers in Beijing had assumed that the expedition would bring Chosŏn into the modern world. The American chargé d'affaires Samuel Wells Williams (1812–84), for instance, exclaimed that "it is full time that Corea was introduced into the family of nations."[24] But Williams and his colleagues soon realized that the French had failed to conduct any negotiations with the Koreans, much less introduce into the country any ideas of the family of nations. Instead the military invasion provided the Taewŏn'gun with a further justification for his policy of "countering barbarians and protecting the nation" (K., *yang'i poguk*).[25]

Parallel Tracks: Continuing Sino-Korean Zongfan Contacts

On November 1, 1866, while the battle with the French marines was raging in Kanghwa, the king held a grand ceremony in Hansŏng to welcome two Manchu envoys, Kuiling and Xiyuan, who came to invest the new queen. Following the customary ritual codes, the king went to the Hall of Admiring the Central Civilized Country on the city's outskirts to welcome the envoys. Afterward, inside the capital, the king performed the requisite ceremonies to receive the book of investiture. The investiture emphasized that the queen should assist the king in bringing prosperity to the country, which had been a loyal "*fan* and fence" (Ch., *fanping*) of China for generations.[26] In a domestic decree that the king issued after the grand ceremony to celebrate the investiture, he emphasized that Chosŏn, the "lower country," appreciated the magnanimous favor of the "central dynasty" and the "big country."[27] During the envoys' three-day sojourn, all rituals were performed precisely according to precedent. In conversations between the king and the envoys, the ongoing war with the French, raging just twenty-five miles away, never came up. The boundary between Zongfan matters and diplomatic affairs was as clear as the two countries' court-to-court and country-to-country relationships.

The arrival of an imperial mission in Chosŏn at this critical moment raised serious concerns among the French. Prince Gong explained that the envoys "were on affairs of ceremonial, and in accordance with long-established usage, having no reference to the quarrel between France and Corea," but Bellonet was suspicious.[28] Prince Gong circulated his correspondence with Bellonet among the foreign ministers, which served to publicize in the diplomatic corps China's definition of the Sino-Korean relationship. While Prince Gong argued with Bellonet about the Korean issue, two Korean tributary missions arrived in Beijing in succession.

The first mission, headed by Han Mun-kyu, arrived on November 6 to receive the imperial calendar for the upcoming year. In the king's memorial to the emperor that Han brought to Beijing, the king stated that Chosŏn had no wish to do business with foreign countries and that Catholicism and other foreign religions were not welcome in Chosŏn. In addition, Han brought to Wan Qingli, a minister of the Qing Ministry of Rites, a personal letter from Yi Hŭng-min (1809–81), a former tributary emissary who had become acquainted with Wan the previous year. In his letter, Yi tried to legitimize the Taewŏn'gun's anti-Catholic policy and hoped Wan would take advantage of his position to discuss the issue with the emperor and the Zongli Yamen, in the hope that China would persuade foreigners not to visit Chosŏn. Realizing that the issue was beyond the jurisdiction of his ministry and personal correspondence, Wan forwarded the letter to the emperor, asking for instructions and suggesting that he relay the court's recommendations to Chosŏn through his personal response to Yi.[29] The court did not take Wan up on his offer. The emperor's decree to the king likewise skirted the issue, simply telling the king to secure Chosŏn without offering any specific strategy.

Two months after Han's arrival, a second Korean mission, this one bearing the annual tribute, reached Beijing on February 1, 1867, three days before the Spring Festival. In his memorials to the emperor on the occasion of the lunar New Year, the king declared again that it was impossible for Chosŏn to trade with "foreign barbarians" such as the French or to allow them to spread the Gospel in the country. The king also reported that Yi Hŭng-min had been punished because his personal letter to "high-ranking officials of the imperial dynasty" had violated regulations. The Chinese court had no further instructions for the king. Meanwhile, the French did not follow their brief expedition with further campaigns against Chosŏn. The issue of Chosŏn's status remained unsettled and soon proved confusing to the United States.

The *Shuguo* between *Zizhu* and Independence: American Views of Chosŏn's Status, 1866–71

Shipwrecks and Savages: China's Disavowal of Responsibility for Chosŏn

In July and September 1866, two American schooners, the *Surprise* and the *General Sherman*, were wrecked in Chosŏn, the former off the coast of the country and the latter in the Taedong River in P'yŏngyang. The crew of the *Surprise* was treated kindly and escorted safely to the Chinese side via Fenghuang Gate, but the members of the *General Sherman*'s crew were mercilessly killed right in P'yŏngyang. After learning about the *General Sherman* case, the American minister in Beijing, Anson Burlingame (1820–70), immediately brought the issue to the attention of Prince Gong because "Corea was formerly tributary to China." To Burlingame's surprise, Prince Gong "at once disavowed all responsibility for the Coreans, and stated that the only connection between the two countries was one of ceremonial." In a letter to Rear Admiral Henry H. Bell (1808–68), the acting commander of the US Asiatic Squadron, Burlingame affirmed that "the Chinese government disavows any responsibility for that of Corea, and all jurisdiction over its people."[30] The case was thus passed on to Bell, who, in a confidential dispatch to the Secretary of the Navy, Gideon Welles (1802–78), suggested that the United States launch punitive action against Chosŏn.[31] In fact, Secretary of State William H. Seward (1801–72) had proposed to the

French representative in Washington that the United States and France initiate a combined action against Chosŏn, but France had declined.[32] Bell's proposed expedition did not take place either. In early 1867 the navy dispatched the USS *Wachusett* to Chosŏn under the command of Robert W. Shufeldt (1822–95) to investigate the *General Sherman* incident. But the expedition yielded nothing, as severe weather forced Shufeldt out of Chosŏn before he could receive an official response to his queries. To the United States, Chosŏn remained what American scholars would call a "hermit nation."[33]

American diplomats found themselves involved in another shipwreck in East Asia in March 1867, this time involving the schooner *Rover* in Taiwan (Formosa). The *Rover* foundered on the southern coast of the island, and the crew members who came ashore were ambushed and killed by aborigines known as the Koaluts. Believing that the incident was within his jurisdiction, Charles W. Le Gendre (1830–99), the American consul at Xiamen (Amoy), brought the matter to the attention of the governor-general in Fuzhou, the local officials of Taiwan Prefecture, and the Zongli Yamen. The local officials informed Le Gendre that the crew had met with their deaths in "savage lands" (Ch., *shengfan jie*) "beyond the civilization of the sovereign" (Ch., *wanghua buji*), not "within the waters over which the Chinese government exercises jurisdiction," and that their murderers were "savages" rather than "Chinese civilians" (Ch., *huamin*). Therefore, articles 11 and 13 of the 1858 Sino-American Treaty regarding China's jurisdiction did not apply, and the Chinese government had no responsibility to take action against the Koaluts as the consul had requested. Le Gendre, believing to the contrary that the "savages" were within China's jurisdiction, warned his Chinese counterparts that other states could cite such a disavowal of responsibility as an excuse to occupy the "savage lands."[34] Finally, the Chinese authorities dispatched soldiers to accompany Le Gendre to southern Taiwan, but the minister alone entered the Koaluts' territory and concluded an agreement with the chieftain.[35] Le Gendre's experience of negotiating with the Chinese side was not notable at the time and seemed unrelated to Chosŏn. But it would prove significant in the 1870s, when Tokyo hired Le Gendre to help reframe Japanese policy toward Taiwan, Ryukyu, Chosŏn, and China.

A "Nominal" Connection: Low's Assessment of the Sino-Korean Relationship

Before Japan joined the Western states in challenging Chosŏn's status, Frederick F. Low (1828–94), the American minister in Beijing and the former governor of California, organized an expedition to Chosŏn in 1871 with the aim of negotiating a treaty for the protection of shipwrecked mariners. His action pushed Beijing to clarify China's definition of the Sino-Korean relationship. As Low saw it, "Corea is substantially an independent nation" and the Korean tribute to China "is sent rather as a *quid pro quo* for the privilege of trading with the Chinese than a governmental tribute."[36] Low nonetheless solicited the aid of the Zongli Yamen to obtain useful information about Chosŏn. In February 1871 Low delivered to the Yamen a letter that he hoped would be forwarded to the king of Chosŏn via the Ministry of Rites. After sending the letter to Chosŏn, the ministry noted, in a confidential memorial to the emperor, that "Chosŏn has used China's ruling titles and calendars for a long time and proved the most loyal. All affairs regarding its government, religion, prohibitions, and laws are subject to its own management by the rule of *zizhu*, and none of these affairs has China hitherto interfered in."[37] These same words were used by the Zongli Yamen in its dispatch to Low in March.

Low decided, first, to interpret China's position as affirming Chosŏn's independent sovereignty, stating that "although Corea is regarded as a country subordinate to China, yet she is wholly independent in everything that relates to her government, her religion, her prohibitions, and her laws; in none of these things has China hitherto interfered." In essence, he translated the Chinese term *zizhu* into full independence. Second, he concluded that the Chinese declaration aimed to "guard against complications that may possibly grow out of an attempt by foreign nations to open intercourse with Corea, and relieve this Government of all responsibility for the acts of the Coreans, whether hostile or otherwise." Low thus interpreted Beijing's declaration as a repudiation of responsibility for Chosŏn's behavior. It seemed that it was time for him to sail for Chosŏn, a place that was, for him, "more of a sealed book than Japan was before Commodore Perry's visit."[38] Low determined to become another Perry.

Yet Low failed to crack the book. After arriving in Chosŏn in May, he was unable to establish official contacts with the Korean side. The expedition only intensified Chosŏn's hostility toward Western countries. Chosŏn continued to identify itself as "a subject of China" that had no right to "communicate with foreign countries"—that is, to conduct diplomacy. This point was reiterated by the king in his memorial to the emperor in June 1871 in response to Low's letter, forwarded from Beijing.[39] After the frustrating failure of his expedition, Low still hoped to contact Chosŏn through Beijing, and his conversations with the Zongli Yamen provided him with further opportunities to reconceptualize the Sino-Korean relationship. He concluded that the relations between the two countries, "established during the reign of the Ming Emperors, nominally continued unchanged, although, practically, they have little force."[40] Despite a sharp refutation from Prince Gong, Low continued to hold this opinion.

Between 1866 and 1871, the Western ministers' perception of Chosŏn shifted: they no longer considered it a tributary of China but rather saw it as an independent state beyond Chinese jurisdiction. Several key terms of international law were now applied to the Sinocentric Zongfan order, even though nothing within this order had changed. In 1871 the Qing signed its first Western-style treaty with Japan that portrayed the two countries as equals. Over the next five years, Japan, in the midst of dramatic Westernizing reforms under Emperor Meiji (r. 1867–1912), became the vanguard of the challenge to the Sino-Korean relationship, aided by its position as an insider in the East Asian community. The participation of the rising Japanese empire opened a new chapter in modern East Asian history.

The *Shuguo* between Chinese Legitimacy and International Law: The First Sino-Japanese Debate

Japan's Contacts with Chosŏn and the Sino-Japanese Treaty of 1871

During the Japanese Tokugawa bakufu period (1603–1867), communications between Japan and Chosŏn were conducted through the Sō family in the domain of Tsushima. Chosŏn interacted with the Sō in a semi-Zongfan framework. The head of the Sō sent boats to Chosŏn for trade in accordance with Chosŏn's regulations, and he presented himself as a subordinate in letters to the king. In return, when necessary, Chosŏn followed the policy of *kyorin*, communicating with a neighboring country, by dispatching messengers to Japan to consolidate the two countries' friendly relations. All such messengers visited Kyoto and Edo (Tokyo) via Tsushima. Following the Meiji Restoration of 1868, Japan established the Gaimushō, the Ministry of Foreign Affairs, to manage foreign relations under newly adopted Western norms. While its relationships with other countries evolved steadily, Japan failed to modernize its relationship with Chosŏn. Chosŏn refused to accept Japan's sovereign letters, figuratively closing the country's door in Japan's face.

In the meantime, Japan was approaching China to pursue an international status equal to it. In September 1871 the Japanese minister plenipotentiary, Date Munenari (1818–92), signed a treaty, written in both the Chinese and Japanese languages, with Li Hongzhang in Tianjin. The first article stated, "Relations of amity shall henceforth be maintained in redoubled force between China and Japan, in measure as boundless as the heaven and the earth. In all that regards the territorial possessions of either country the two Governments shall treat each other with proper courtesy, without the slightest infringement or encroachment on either side, to the end that there may be for evermore peace between them undisturbed."[41] The term "territorial possessions" and its applicability to Chosŏn later became a source of disagreement between the two countries. The term is a rough English equivalent of the Chinese *suoshu bangtu*. *Suoshu* means "to belong to," but *bangtu* is too vague to be accurately defined in international law. Literally, *bang* means "country" and *tu* means "land," but *bangtu* could mean "country," "land," or "territorial possessions." Both China and Japan subsequently realized that the term failed to establish whether the countries serving as China's outer *fan*, in particular Chosŏn, counted among China's "territorial possessions." Both sides used the term's uncertain definition to their own advantage, resulting in fierce disputes when Japan began implementing an aggressive policy toward Ryukyu and Chosŏn in the 1870s.

An Ambush on the Chinese: Soejima's Embassy to Beijing in 1873

In December 1871 a ship from Ryukyu was shipwrecked on the southern coast of Taiwan, where the aborigines killed fifty-four members of its crew. Since Japan was in the process of annexing Ryukyu by converting it into a Japanese domain (J., *han*), Tokyo regarded the incident as a good opportunity to finalize the matter by cutting off Ryukyu's Zongfan relationship with China. In February 1873 Emperor Meiji appointed the minister of foreign affairs, Soejima Taneomi (1828–1905), as ambassador extraordinary to China to ratify the Treaty of Tianjin of 1871. The emperor instructed Soejima to discuss the killings of the Ryukyuese sailors to determine whether the whole of Taiwan was under China's jurisdiction.[42] A key proponent of the *Seikan ron* (expedition against Korea), Soejima eagerly availed himself of this chance to glean information on China's attitude toward Japanese-Korean contacts. Among the members of the Japanese mission was Japan's newly appointed adviser on foreign policy toward Taiwan, Charles Le Gendre, whose experience was invaluable to Tokyo's efforts to formulate and implement a new policy toward the Chinese Zongfan system.[43] It was through Western advisers such as Le Gendre who mastered modern Western norms regarding sovereignty and international law that Japan transformed itself into an outsider to the East Asian community in terms of its foreign policy.

Soejima arrived in Tianjin in April, and his visit marked the first time that a Japanese official showed up in China in a Western tailcoat. After ratifying the treaty, Soejima briefly discussed Japanese-Korean relations with Li Hongzhang. Li warned that Japan should be friendly to Chosŏn and that any Japanese expedition against it would violate the Sino-Japanese treaty.[44] In Beijing, with

Le Gendre's assistance, Soejima visited foreign legations in the city. The current British minister, Thomas F. Wade (1818–95), reported to London that "the Japanese are also suspected of a design on Corea" and that Soejima "is evidently anxious for an assurance from the Chinese that Corea is an independent Kingdom, so independent of China, that is to say, as to make what may befall Corea no concern of the Chinese." Wade inferred that Japan would apply gunboat diplomacy to Korea.[45] According to Frederick Low, Soejima had "only two questions of importance which he desires to discuss with the Chinese government." First, he wanted to know "whether China is responsible for the acts of the aborigines on the island of Formosa." According to Low, "If the answer is in the negative, notice will then be given that Japan proposed to send a military force to Formosa to chastise the savage and semi-civilized tribes that practically hold undisputed possession of the large part of the island." Second, Soejima wanted to "ascertain the precise relations between China and Corea; whether the former claims to exercise such control over her tributary as to render China responsible for the acts of the Coreans, or whether other nations must look to Corea alone for redress for wrongs and outrages which her people may commit."[46]

Soejima's view of the likely relationship between China and its periphery—Taiwan and Chosŏn—matched Western countries' conclusions regarding the limits of China's jurisdiction over these regions. When Soejima solicited Low's opinions on Chosŏn, Low showed him the Zongli Yamen's dispatch of March 1871, mentioned earlier, which affirmed China's noninterference in Chosŏn's affairs in accordance with the principle of *zizhu*. Upon Low's assertion that Chosŏn was "wholly independent," Soejima made the judgment that Chosŏn lay "beyond the Qing's sovereignty [J., *shuken*]."[47] The Japanese policy of challenging Chosŏn's status as China's *shuguo* thus began to converge with the policies pursued by the United States, France, Britain, and other Western states in China.

Soejima's conclusion found support in a meeting at the Zongli Yamen on June 21, 1873, that brought together a Japanese representative, Yanagiwara Sakimitsu (1850–94), and the Chinese ministers Mao Changxi (1817–82) and Dong Xun (1807–92). Yanagiwara asked how China could justify claiming Chosŏn as a *shuguo*, since the Yamen had asserted in its 1871 note to the American minister that "China never interfered with its internal politics, religion, prohibitions, and laws." Mao, drawing on an understanding of Sino-Korean contacts that he might have gained when working at the Ministry of Rites, explained that "the so-called *shuguo* referred only to investiture and tribute submission" and that China would not interfere with Chosŏn's right to conduct negotiations over war and peace.[48] Mao's response satisfied Soejima because it corroborated Low's argument.[49] Soejima, along with his Western counterparts, was granted an audience with the Tongzhi emperor on June 29. It was the first imperial audience for

Western ministers since the 1840s and it encouraged both sides to improve their understanding of each other.

Upon his return to Tokyo, Soejima stepped up his advocacy for an expedition to Korea, but the return of a Japanese mission to the United States and Europe halted his plan. The three key members of the mission, Iwakura Tomomi (1825–83), Ōkubo Toshimichi (1830–78), and Kido Takayoshi (1833–77), argued that Japan should focus on domestic reforms to "reorganize its national politics and make its people rich."[50] As this policy prevailed, the proponents of the *Seikan ron*, such as Soejima, Saigō Takamori (1827–77), Itagaki Taisuke (1837–1919), and Etō Shinpei (1834–74), were pushed out of the cabinet. In December 1873 the young king of Chosŏn assumed direct rule and ended the regency of Taewŏn'gun. Tokyo tried to take advantage of this occasion to pursue a new diplomatic relationship with Hansŏng, but its efforts failed in the face of sharp resistance by local officials in Pusan, where the Koreans still preferred to communicate with the Japanese through the *kyorin* framework. Japan, it seemed, could not make any substantial progress on opening a new channel of communication with the Korean court.

The Birth of Chosŏn's "Sovereignty": The Second Sino-Japanese Debate and the Treaty of Kanghwa

Defining China's Territory: Taiwan, Kanghwa, and Mori's Visit to Beijing

In the summer of 1874, while Tokyo was sending troops to South Taiwan to deal with "the territory in question beyond the jurisdiction of the Chinese government," it also sent Yanagiwara Sakimitsu and Ōkubo Toshimichi to Beijing for further negotiations about Taiwan.[51] The Zongli Yamen told the Japanese representatives, "Even if the aborigines are 'barbarians,' they are still China's barbarians, and only China has the right to punish them if they are guilty." The Chinese ministers pointed to relevant rules of international law and Chinese historical evidence, such as local gazetteers, to bolster their point. Without close advice from Western advisers such as Le Gendre, the Japanese failed to prove that the aborigines' area of residence in South Taiwan was beyond China's jurisdiction. Under the mediation of Thomas Wade, the doyen of the diplomatic corps in Beijing, the Chinese and Japanese sides reached a succinct agreement. Interestingly, the third article of the agreement stated that "all correspondence that this question has occasioned between the two governments shall be canceled, and the discussions dropped for evermore."[52] In this way, Japan not only invalidated any documents that could expose its inferior position in the talks on the reach of China's territory but also shifted future negotiations to the track of international law. To the Japanese, the negotiations indicated that only a Japan equipped with European norms could challenge the Chinese discourse, which helps explain why, over the following decade, Japan frequently solicited its Western advisers for suggestions regarding Japan's foreign policy toward its neighbors.

A skirmish between Japan and Chosŏn near Kanghwa Island in September 1875 led to the resurgence of support for the *Seikan ron* in Japan. This time Iwakura and his fellow politicians endorsed the expedition, because Japan's diplomatic situation was much improved. In addition to reaching an agreement with China about the Taiwan incident, Tokyo had resolved its territorial disputes with Russia over Sakhalin Island and the Kuril Islands by signing a treaty in St. Petersburg in May 1875, through which it obtained Russian acquiescence to its actions in Chosŏn. Meanwhile, in order to check Russia's southern advance in East Asia during the Russo-British rivalry in Central Asia, Britain planned to occupy Port Hamilton, a small Korean island known as Kŏmundo near the Tsushima Strait.[53] This plan provided Japan with an excuse to initiate an expedition against Korea without triggering an intervention from these Western powers. In October 1875 Kido Takayoshi suggested that Japan should press China for an explanation of its relationship with Chosŏn; once Beijing had disavowed responsibility for Chosŏn's foreign affairs, Japan could freely take action against Chosŏn.[54]

The Japanese government appointed Mori Arinori (1847–89) as the minister plenipotentiary to Beijing. Educated in Britain and having worked in the United States, Mori was familiar with Western diplomatic rules and had consulted with Erasmus Peshine Smith (1814–82), the American special adviser to the Gaimushō on international law, regarding the Kanghwa incident. Sanjō Sanetomi (1837–91), chancellor of the realm, issued instructions to Mori's embassy, and the most important among them was to "identify Chosŏn as an independent country [J., *dokuritsu koku*]" and persuade China to help establish Japanese-Korean relations for the sake of Japan's and China's common interests. In short, Mori's mission was "to cut off the Sino-Korean relationship."[55] The foreign minister, Terashima Munenori (1832–93), telegraphed the chargé d'affaires in Beijing, Tei Einei (1829–97), saying that since Soejima's visit in 1873 had not confirmed that Chosŏn was not a "*fan* and subordinate" (J., *hanzoku*) of the Qing, Tei should be cautious about all contacts between Japan and the Qing regarding Chosŏn.[56]

Another Ambush on the Chinese: Mori's Debate with the Zongli Yamen

On January 2, 1876, the Qing court dispatched two envoys, Jihe and Wulasiconga, to Chosŏn to invest the king's son, Yi Ch'ŏk, as the crown prince. Three Han Chinese grand secretaries—Mao Changxi, Li Hongzhang, and Zuo Zongtang (1812–85)—drafted the imperial edict of investiture in December 1875. Two days later Mori arrived in Beijing with the aim of denying this Sino-Korean relationship from the perspective of international law.

Mori paid his first visit to Thomas Wade, in the hope that the latter could mediate between Japan and China. Wade was impressed by Mori, but his situation made it impossible for him to assist Mori.[57] Wade's relations with Beijing were strained due to an incident in the previous year in which a young British interpreter handpicked by Wade, Augustus R. Margary, had been killed on an expedition to Burma from Yunnan. Wade had repeatedly telegraphed London to ask for more naval forces to pressure China into negotiating with him for another treaty. Prime Minister Benjamin Disraeli (1804–81) supported Wade and conceived a plan to ally with Japan against China, a scheme he called "one of the greatest secrets of State going."[58] But the secretary of state for foreign affairs, Edward Henry Stanley (1826–93), did not endorse this aggressive approach.[59] Under the circumstances, Wade had no desire to be involved in the Sino-Japanese negotiations on Korean affairs, but after his conversation with Mori he reported to London that "the minister's manner, rather than his language, made me mistrustful. I inferred that an expedition of Corea is determined on and that the object of his confidential communications to me was to ascertain whether objection to the expedition would be taken by English, or any other foreign action."[60] Wade could not have been more correct. On January 6, 1876, the Japanese ambassador plenipotentiary to Chosŏn, Kuroda Kiyotaka (1840–1900), sailed from Tokyo for the Korean Peninsula, leading a fleet of two gunboats and four schooners.[61]

Mori, accompanied by his interpreter, Tei Einei, and two secretaries, met with five Chinese ministers on January 10 at the Zongli Yamen to discuss Chosŏn's status. Zhou Jiamei (1835–86) served as the secretary for the Chinese side. Mori, the youngest man in the room, was also the only person who knew international law and had Western educational and diplomatic experience. Shortly after the talks started, the two sides realized that they were on diametrically opposed tracks. The conversation unfolded mainly between Mori and Shen Guifen (1818–81), who had previously worked at the Ministry of Rites. Mori asked why China, identifying Chosŏn as its *shuguo*, nonetheless claimed that Chosŏn's "politics, religion, prohibitions, and laws fall under the principle of *zizhu*." Shen explained, "The *shuguo* is not land under the governance of our country [Ch., *yuan bushi woguo guanxia zhi di*]. But it pays tribute on time, receives our investiture, and accepts our country's calendar, and this has made it our *shuguo*." Shen further informed Mori that Vietnam, Ryukyu, and Burma were also China's *shuguo*, with different schedules for the payment of tribute. When Mori asked whether a *shuguo* could negotiate with foreign countries on trade without informing China, Shen replied that the country in question would manage its affairs by itself and China would not get involved, but that it would legally respond to any disputes arising between the *shuguo* and China's treaty partners. Shen warned Mori that any invasion of a *shuguo* of China would not be defensible and would contravene the first article of the Sino-Japanese Treaty of 1871.[62]

At this point it became apparent that the disagreement between the two sides hinged on their different definitions of the term *shuguo*. For Mori, a *shuguo* could mean a colony, a dependency, or a nation with semisovereign rights. In particular, he used the relationship between the Muhammad Ali dynasty of Egypt and the Ottoman Empire, that between Hungary and the Austro-Hungarian Empire, and that between Canada and the British Empire as three examples of *shuguo* in the Western context. The three examples were, however, completely lost in the Chinese translation because of the vast gap in international knowledge between the two parties. The Chinese ministers retorted with convincing examples drawn from the Chinese context to prove that Chosŏn was in all senses a *shuguo* of China. The debate ended without agreement.

The meeting having fallen short of his expectations, Mori acknowledged the gulf between the two sides and expressed frustration with Chinese officialdom.[63] In the aftermath of the so-called Tongzhi Restoration—an attempt to strengthen the dynasty and traditional order in the 1860s—the Qing was facing increasingly serious challenges from within as well as from outside the country. On the same day that Mori was arguing with the Zongli Yamen, Empress Dowagers Cian (1837–81) and Cixi (1835–1908), in the Forbidden City about two miles west of the Yamen, were tearfully beseeching two officials, Weng Tonghe (1830–1904) and Xia Tongshan (1830–80), to serve as teachers for the young emperor, Guangxu, who was Dowager Cixi's nephew.[64] The political heart of the empire was vulnerable. It was not until 1898, three years after his empire was humiliated by Japan in the war that broke out in Chosŏn, that the emperor was able to launch a reform with the strong support of Weng.

After the meeting, Mori asked the Zongli Yamen to issue a passport to a Japanese assistant whom he wanted to send to Chosŏn via Mukden to inform the Japanese ambassador to Chosŏn about the Sino-Japanese meetings. He also expressed his own desire to visit Li Hongzhang at Baoding, Li's political headquarters, to show his gratitude for Li's greetings. The Yamen refused to issue the passport because of the absence of relevant precedent, reiterating its assertion that Chosŏn was China's *shuguo*. This response triggered another exchange of verbal jousts through diplomatic notes. Mori argued that "Chosŏn is an independent country, and the status of a so-called *shuguo* of China is only a nominal title [J., *kūmei*; Ch., *kongming*]. . . . Any Japanese-Korean contacts have nothing to do with the Sino-Japanese Treaty."[65] This statement, echoing Low's comments in 1871, marked the complete convergence of Japanese and Western policies challenging the nature of the Sino-Korean relationship. Perceiving this alignment, the Yamen wrote to the emperor, expressing severe concern over the likely prospect of problems caused by Japan, a country that "has recently adopted Western politics and customs and changed its own costumes and calendars."[66] Japan had become a major troublemaker in China's eyes.

In order to inform Chosŏn of the situation, the Zongli Yamen asked the Ministry of Rites to immediately dispatch a copy of Mori's note to Hansŏng. The note was sent from Beijing on January 19, 1876, four days after Japanese naval forces had arrived at Pusan. The Yamen, completely blind to the Japanese advance on Chosŏn, busied itself with arguing with Mori. Once the two sides had arrived at an utter impasse, two officers sent by Li Hongzhang arrived in Beijing to accompany Mori to Baoding. Both the Yamen and Mori were happy to hand the case to Li in hopes of winning a favorable ruling at Baoding.

Li's "Sincere Advice": The Baoding Negotiations

Thus began Li Hongzhang's deep involvement in Chosŏn's affairs as a provincial official. On January 10, while the Yamen squabbled with Mori, Li briefly explained "some diplomatic ideas" regarding Chosŏn's possible contacts with the West in his reply to a letter from Yi Yu-wŏn (1814–88), a Korean prime minister who had visited Beijing in 1875 as a tributary emissary.[67] Two weeks later, while his letter was on its way to Hansŏng, Li welcomed Mori at Baoding. The conversations that ensued were all the more complicated in that they were conducted not in Chinese or Japanese but in English. Moreover, in their reports to their respective governments, written in their own languages instead of in English, both sides claimed to be prevailing over the other. Neither Beijing nor Tokyo had an accurate picture of the actual progress of the talks.[68]

The first conversation, on January 24, lasted for more than six hours over a banquet at Li's office. Li had invited two officials, Huang Pengnian and Huang Huilian, to attend the meeting as guests and assistants. While Huang Pengnian was an erudite Confucian scholar, Huang Huilian was Cantonese and had been educated at an American missionary school in Shanghai; his first name, Huilian, was a Chinese transliteration of William, the name of the school's headmaster, William Jones Boone (1811–64; known in Chinese as Wen Huilian). William

Huang had visited British Guiana and been drafted by Beijing to serve as an interpreter during the Second Opium War in 1860. It seems that Mori decided to speak with Li in English after learning of William Huang's English proficiency, as he felt that English would better allow him to convey the principles of international law as he believed they applied to the Korean issue.[69]

To Mori's argument that Chosŏn was an independent country rather than China's *shuguo*, Li responded,

> Everyone knows that Chosŏn has been subordinate to China for thousands of years. In the phrase *suoshu bangtu* [territorial possessions] of the [Sino-Japanese] treaty, the *tu* means Chinese provinces, namely, China's inner land [Ch., *neidi*] and inner subordinates [Ch., *neishu*], on which the Chinese government levies taxes and whose political affairs it manages. The *bang* refers to countries such as Chosŏn that are China's outer *fan* and outer subordinates [Ch., *waishu*], whose taxes and political affairs are always their own business. This is a convention, and it does not start with our dynasty. Chosŏn is indeed China's *shuguo*.[70]

This interpretation of *suoshu bangtu* implied that although Chosŏn did not lie within China's immediate orbit, it was nonetheless part of the broader Chinese empire. Mori realized that no agreement could be reached on this point, so he ended the argument with Li. In the subsequent discussion on the Kanghwa incident, whereas Li stressed several times that Japan should obey the Sino-Japanese Treaty of 1871 and international law, Mori, who had visited the prominent British philosopher and sociologist Herbert Spencer (1820–1903) before returning to Japan and had seen the dramatic expansion of the Western colonial enterprise, responded that state power was much more reliable than textual treaties. At the end, Mori asked Li what China would do if a war broke out between Japan and Chosŏn. Li replied that not only China but also Russia would send troops to defend Chosŏn. Li then wrote out for Mori, under the title "Sincere Advice" (Ch., Zhonggao), eight Chinese characters, which read, "Acting only to disturb harmony, brings no benefits at all" (Ch., Tushang heqi, haowu liyi). Mori did not mention Li's warning in his reports to Tokyo. The next day, New Year's Eve, Li visited Mori for a short conversation that did not touch on the Korean issue but included a discussion of Japan's reforms. Li did not inform the Zongli Yamen of the details of this conversation, but Mori kept a full record in English, which indicates the epistemological gulf that separated the two men and the worlds they represented and defended.[71] As Mori and Li closed their talks, the Japanese fleet dropped anchor at the offing of Kanghwa Island.

After Mori returned to Beijing, he resumed his debate with the Zongli Yamen. The Yamen emphasized to Mori that "solving its difficulties, resolving its disputes, and securing its safety and security [Ch., *shu qi nan, jie qi fen, qi qi anquan*] are the responsibilities to Chosŏn that China has taken upon itself, and they are how China treats its *shuguo*. It is the longstanding policy of China to refrain from forcing its *shuguo* to do what it is reluctant to do and to stand by when it runs into trouble."[72] Mori, however, continued to insist that "Chosŏn is indeed an independent country, so Japan will not take Chosŏn's relations with China into consideration in matters between Japan and Chosŏn. The so-called *shuguo* is no more than a nominal title. Nothing should be related to the treaty of 1871."[73] Thirty-four days of intensive negotiations had brought the two sides nowhere.

Old News and No News: The 1876 Imperial Mission to Chosŏn and the Limits of Zongfan Communications

The Sino-Korean Zongfan rituals that took place in Hansŏng in 1876 showed how untenable Mori's enthusiastic diplomatic rhetoric was. On February 16, two days after the end of the Sino-Japanese debate in Beijing, the king held a grand ceremony in Hansŏng for the two imperial envoys coming to invest the crown prince. All procedures followed the precedents of investiture, and the host and guests alike performed the rituals according to code. The king expressed to the envoys his sincere gratitude to the emperor and the Zongli Yamen for informing him of the Japanese activities in Beijing. The envoys, praising the stance that Chosŏn had taken against Japan's sovereign letters, said that Japan's forces had reportedly arrived in Kanghwa and wanted to establish a consulate there, and they voiced uneasiness about the situation.[74] In fact, the king had already dispatched two officials to negotiate with the Japanese at Kanghwa before receiving word from Beijing. He did not solicit advice from the envoys, nor did the envoys show any interest in obtaining details of the negotiations. Some historians have argued that Beijing used the imperial envoys to, among other things, persuade Chosŏn to conclude a treaty with Japan,[75] but records of the contact between the king and the envoys contradict this assertion.

On February 27 Chosŏn signed a treaty with Japan that ended their eight-year dispute. That same day, the Ministry of Rites in Beijing dispatched, at the top speed of five hundred *li* per day, a note to Chosŏn along with a copy of the Baoding conversations between Li and Mori. Handicapped by the sluggish speed of communications, the ministry, the Zongli Yamen, and Li Hongzhang could not follow the progress of the Japanese-Korean negotiations. Beijing did not receive a reply to its February note to Chosŏn about Japan's talks with China until May 31, three months after the conclusion of the Treaty of Kanghwa. By contrast, Mori could receive Tokyo's instructions by telegram within ten days, and Thomas Wade, who closely monitored the negotiations, was able to have his report delivered to London within eight days. Modern technology was changing international politics in an inconspicuous but concrete way, but no such improvements had yet reached the Sino-Korean channels of communication.

A week after the treaty was signed, the Manchu general at Mukden, Chongshi (1820–76), asked the Zongli Yamen whether the Ministry of Rites had received any response from the Koreans. Chongshi confessed that although Mukden bordered Chosŏn, the only information he had on Chosŏn consisted of rumors spread by Chinese and Korean merchants in the area. He hoped that the two imperial envoys could give him some reliable updates.[76] The general was, of course, disappointed in this hope. In the Forbidden City, meanwhile, the two empress dowagers discussed the Korean situation with Guo Songtao (1818–91), a minister of the Zongli Yamen who had been appointed the first minister to Britain. The dowagers disparaged Mori's and Wade's "cunning" personalities and called them "first-class bad men" (Ch., *diyi deng huairen*) whose mission was to "make trouble."[77] Like Chongshi, the dowagers and Guo were unaware that the Treaty of Kanghwa had already been signed.

At the time, China had no official channel for communications beyond the empire, although Western ministers had arrived in Beijing as early as 1861. Its first minister to Japan would not set foot on Japanese soil until December 1877, almost five years after the arrival of the first Japanese minister in Beijing. A week after Guo's conversation with the dowagers, it was from Mori, one of the "first-class bad men," that the Zongli Yamen and the Manchu court learned that Japan had signed a treaty with Chosŏn. And it was not for another month—and then through the German minister to Beijing, Max August von Brandt (1835–1920)—that the Yamen first heard about the contents of the treaty. Only on April 17, when Mori submitted a full copy of the treaty to the Zongli Yamen, did the Chinese side finally see what it entailed. China's passive position vis-à-vis Chosŏn and the treaty system with Japan was laid bare. In the two decades after 1876, it would become increasingly clear that this was China's normal state within the established framework.

On April 21 Beijing at last received a note from the king, who briefly reviewed the treaty negotiations. The king never submitted a copy of the treaty to the emperor, nor did the emperor ever request it or raise any questions about the agreement. The king reported that the mistrust between Chosŏn and Japan had evaporated thanks to the inauguration of the long-term friendship between them: "The bilateral contacts will be conducted by officials of the two countries on an equal footing. As it is not the first time that we have traded with Japan, we have allowed the Japanese to trade at our ports, where they must follow our rules."[78] Although the treaty endowed Japan with the right of consular jurisdiction and abolished all former trade conventions and junk trade (J., *saiken sen*), Chosŏn's perception of the treaty was still rooted in conventional *kyorin* norms, rather than in any understanding of international law. It is difficult, then, to define the treaty as a truly modern one.[79]

The Japanese Invention: The Birth of Chosŏn's "Sovereignty" as a Textual Derivative

On March 22, 1876, the Gaimushō released the contents of the Treaty of Kanghwa and distributed an English version among the foreign ministers in Tokyo. The English translation of article 1 reads,

> Chosŏn being an independent state enjoys the same sovereign rights as does Japan. In order to prove the sincerity of the friendship existing between the nations, their intercourse shall henceforward be carried on in terms of equality and courtesy, each avoiding the giving of offence by arrogance or manifestations of suspicion. In the first instance all rules and precedents that are apt to obstruct friendly intercourse shall be totally abrogated and, in their stead, rules, liberal and in general usage fit to secure a firm and perpetual peace, shall be established.[80]

Many diplomats at the time and scholars since then concluded that this article, and in particular the first sentence, explicitly defines Chosŏn as an independent state under the terms of international law, although some scholars have recognized that the English translation of the first sentence is not precise.[81] Given that the original text of the treaty used only Japanese and Chinese, a comparison of the Japanese and Chinese texts of the first article and the English version reveals critical discrepancies in several key terms.

The first sentence of the article in the Japanese version reads, "Chōsen koku wa jishu no kuni ni shite, Nihon koku to byōdō no ken o hoyū seri 朝鮮國ハ 自主ノ邦ニシテ日本國ト平等ノ權ヲ保有セリ" (lit., The country of Chosŏn is a nation with the right of self-rule, possessing rights equal to Japan's). The Chinese version of this sentence—"Chosŏn kug chaju ji bang, boyu yŏ Ilbon kug p'yŏngdŭng ji kwŏn 朝鮮國自主之邦保有與日本國平等之權"—has the same meaning.[82] It is clear that the Gaimushō made a deliberate choice to translate the term *jishu* (K., *chaju*; Ch., *zizhu*) as "independence" and the phrase *jishu no kuni* (K., *chaju ji bang*; Ch., *zizhu zhi bang*) as "independent state." More importantly, the English translation intentionally rendered the Chinese character *ken* (K., *kwŏn*; Ch., *quan*) not simply as "right" but as "sovereign right." The second half of the sentence, which literally says that Chosŏn "possesses rights equal to Japan's," thus ends up claiming that Chosŏn "enjoys the same sovereign rights as does Japan." Later in the article, the Gaimushō translated the phrase *dōtō no reigi*

(K., *tongdŭng ji ye*; Ch., *tongdeng zhi li*), which literally means "equal rituals" or "equal courtesy," as "equality and courtesy." By changing the term *dōtō* from an adjective to a noun, the Gaimushō reinforced the claim inherent in its translation of the first sentence.

Since the Western ministers in Tokyo could not read Chinese or Japanese texts, the Gaimushō may have hoped to mislead the English-speaking world by defining Chosŏn's sovereignty and independence in the English translation. Both the American minister, John Bingham (1815–1900), and the British minister, Harry Parkes, accepted the provided translation and helped disseminate it in the West.[83] Certainly, Chosŏn's sovereign right, or sovereignty, was not *created* by Japan's subtle English translation; rather, Chosŏn always enjoyed sovereignty on its own territory, but this sovereign was subject to China's emperorship in the Zongfan world.[84] It was not until 1882, when Chosŏn signed a treaty with the United States, that its "sovereign right" was explicitly defined for the first time in both Chinese and English. In 1876, neither Beijing nor Hansŏng foresaw the problems caused by the English translation of the treaty. Japan believed that it had successfully resolved the issue of Chosŏn's status through the treaty and that it had prevailed over Beijing in the debate on the topic. In his final report to the Gaimushō on his mission to Beijing, Mori was self-congratulatory: "Suffice it to say," he claimed, "that the Zongli Yamen has been convinced by my argument. . . . The only objective of the debate was to cut off the Sino-Korean relationship, which I have achieved."[85] Yet he would soon realize that he had been too optimistic.

Commodore Robert W. Shufeldt of the US Navy returned to East Asia in March 1880 in hopes of negotiating a treaty with Chosŏn. During the intervening four years, Chosŏn had dispatched only an envoy of amity (K., *Susin sa*) to Japan in 1876 in observance of conventions, whereas it continued to send annual tributary emissaries to Beijing. Chosŏn believed that it had restored the pre-1876 order that was maintained by the policy of serving the great in its relations with China and that of communicating with a neighboring country vis-à-vis Japan. The arrival of Shufeldt in the early 1880s created a stir in the hermit nation and became a test of the trilateral relations between Chosŏn, Japan, and China.

5

SUPERVISING CHOSŎN

Qing China's Patriarchal Role in Chosŏn,
1877–84

In the late 1870s and early 1880s, with China's vigorous encouragement, Chosŏn launched reforms to fortify itself domestically. However, the reform programs caused a backlash, prompting student petitions and eventually a bloody mutiny. China sent troops to Chosŏn in 1882 to help the Korean court suppress the mutiny, and it subsequently became deeply enmeshed in Chosŏn's domestic and foreign affairs. In the course of these events, China availed itself of its superior position to introduce Chosŏn into the family of nations, in particular through the negotiation of the Korean-American treaty in 1882. From the perspective of Japan and the Western states, China's involvement represented a fundamental change in China's traditional policy toward Korea, and it triggered a wave of intense political and diplomatic struggles between the various powers on the peninsula. To meet these new challenges, China and Chosŏn signed several commercial agreements to maintain and adjust their relations.

A pair of coexisting and correlated dual diplomatic networks developed between China and Chosŏn. The first dual network encompassed the Sino-Korean Zongfan system, on the one hand, and the newly imported treaty system that connected China, Chosŏn, and their treaty counterparts, on the other. This network, which I call the outer dual network, operated between the politico-cultural Chinese empire and the world beyond the empire, and both China and Chosŏn had to deal independently with the treaty aspects of this network. The second dual network, which I call the inner network, functioned within the Chinese empire and comprised, first, the conventional system of court-to-court interactions between the imperial court in Beijing and the royal court in Hansŏng, and, second, the newly founded state-to-state system between China and Chosŏn, in which the latter was theoretically equal to the former according to international law. Through the outer and inner dual networks, both China and Chosŏn modified and revised their policies toward each other.

Opening Chosŏn to the West: China and the Korean-American Negotiations

From Tokyo to Pusan and Tianjin: The Shufeldt-Li Agreement of 1880

By the late 1870s, China was aware of the grave challenges Chosŏn was facing from other countries, and it began to persuade Chosŏn to open its doors by negotiating treaties with Western states. Since Zongfan conventions prevented both the Zongli Yamen and the Ministry of Rites from making such a request of an outer *fan*, Li Hongzhang personally took on the task of cajoling Chosŏn. Li used his personal correspondence with the Korean minister Yi Yu-wŏn, mentioned in the previous chapter, for this purpose, but Yi was not enthusiastic about contacting the Western "barbarians."[1] In March 1880 the navy commander Robert Shufeldt arrived in Nagasaki with the USS *Ticonderoga*. The American minister John Bingham approached the Japanese foreign minister, Inoue Kaoru (1835–1915), to ask for Japan's good offices in introducing Shufeldt to Chosŏn.[2] Inoue was worried that Japan's acting as a go-between might harm its fragile relations with Chosŏn, but he decided to send a letter from Shufeldt to the Korean court through the Japanese consul at Pusan, Kondō Masuki (1840–92), and the chargé d'affaires at Hansŏng, Hanabusa Yoshimoto (1842–1917). Expecting to have further contact with the Koreans, Shufeldt went to Pusan, but he soon received his unopened letter back. Chosŏn's rebuff incurred Bingham's wrath and ended Japan's role as mediator.[3]

While Shufeldt was waiting in Nagasaki, the Chinese consul in the city, Yu Qiong, decided that it would be a good idea to grant the United States entrance into Chosŏn in order to check Russia, which was on the brink of war with China following the Ili incident on China's northwestern frontier in Xinjiang. Yu contacted the Chinese minister in Tokyo, He Ruzhang (1838–91), who immediately forwarded the news to the Zongli Yamen and Li Hongzhang. Li quickly decided to invite Shufeldt to Tianjin, and the latter happily accepted the invitation. After a meeting with Li in August, Shufeldt reported that Li had promised "he would use his influence with the Government of Corea to accede to the friendly request" made by Shufeldt "in behalf of the Government of the United States to open negotiations with a view to such a treaty [with Korea]."[4] Under the agreement, Shufeldt returned to the United States to secure more support from the Department of State, while Li turned his attention to coaxing Chosŏn to allow the United States in.

Behind a Cloak: Preparations for Chosŏn's Training Program in Tianjin

The ruling house of Chosŏn was not blind to the encroaching West. In 1879 the Korean emissary Yi Yong-suk (1818–?) informed the Chinese official You Zhikai (1816–99) at Yongping near Beijing that Chosŏn hoped to dispatch trainees to Tianjin to obtain advanced military and industrial skills, following the "precedent of foreign countries sending students to China for learning." Yi asked You to take the proposal to Li Hongzhang. Li heartily endorsed the plan. In a confidential letter to You, which was finally forwarded to the king via Yi, Li suggested that Chosŏn should submit a detailed proposal to the Ministry of Rites in Beijing.[5] Shortly thereafter the king sent Pyŏn Wŏn-kyu (1837–96) as an emissary to Beijing to discuss the plan, while the Chinese court put Li in charge of the training program that would encourage Chosŏn "to follow the mainstream of the world."[6]

In his summer office in Tianjin, Li underscored to Pyŏn that the best survival strategy for Chosŏn was "to trade with the Westerners." With Li's support, Pyŏn and several Chinese officials drafted an outline of the training program that broke several two-hundred-year-old Zongfan conventions. In addition to granting the Korean trainees, interpreters, and superintendents the special right to visit Tianjin via the maritime route, which had not happened since 1637, the outline required all program members to obtain passes from the office of the Beiyang superintendent, which would be filed at the Ministry of Rites. Given that this would be the first time Korean visitors had resided in a Chinese city outside Beijing since at least 1644, the outline prescribed that the trainees must "obey the Chinese rules and conventions" (Ch., *zunshou Zhongguo guiju*); otherwise they would be sent by the Chinese officials to their Korean superintendents for punishment according to Korean regulations. In this case, then, China endowed the Korean side with a right similar to the consular jurisdiction that it had conferred on its Western treaty partners.

The outline also required the king to send official correspondence on military training, weapon procurement, and other military affairs to both the Ministry of Rites and the Beiyang superintendent. The position of the Beiyang superintendent, as a subordinate official under the Zongli Yamen, was a secondary post held by the governor-general of Zhili, a post occupied almost exclusively by Li until 1894. According to Zongfan regulations, the superintendent should not be involved in Zongfan affairs with Chosŏn. However, since Li's meeting with

Mori in 1876, this rule had been eclipsed by the growth of Li's authority—itself a result of the Zongli Yamen's ambiguous definition of the Sino-Korean relationship, on the one hand, and the silence of the Ministry of Rites on affairs beyond the conventional court-to-court track, on the other. In a confidential memorial in February 1881 the Zongli Yamen pointed out that "it is extremely urgent for Chosŏn to conduct diplomacy [Ch., *waijiao*] with other countries" and requested that the Qing court make changes to old regulations in order to endow the Beiyang superintendent with greater privileges.[7] With the emperor's endorsement, the superintendent gained the right to communicate directly with—rather than simply receive notes from—the king on issues concerning not only the training program but also foreign affairs. The superintendent became the de jure mentor for Chosŏn's self-strengthening program. The king responded favorably, indicating to Li a strong intention of opening Chosŏn to Western countries and wanting to commission Li to make the first move toward initiating treaty negotiations with the United States.[8]

Modernity versus Heresy: China's Prescriptions and Korean Resistance

As the king was deciding to open up his country to foreigners, Chosŏn was caught in a series of dramatic political events that had strong ripple effects. The sequence of events was initiated by Chinese diplomats in Japan, who forwarded their advice regarding Chosŏn's policy to the king through the Korean envoy of amity to Japan, Kim Hong-jip (1842–96). When Kim visited Tokyo in late 1880, the Chinese minister, He Ruzhang, and the counselor of the Chinese legation, Huang Zunxian, had intensive talks with him. Their conversations took place in the Zongfan context, in which each party identified the other as a member of the "same family" (Ch., *yijia*) and saw Chosŏn as no different from an "inner subordinate" of China. The two Chinese diplomats tried to convince Kim that Chosŏn should abandon its parochialism and sign treaties with Western countries, beginning with the United States, in order to prevent a Russian onslaught. Kim agreed with the two officials, as did his Japanese counterparts at the Gaimushō.

Before Kim left Tokyo, Huang gave him a treatise entitled "A Strategy for Chosŏn" (Ch., *Chaoxian celue*), in which Huang argued that Chosŏn should check the Russian threat by "having intimate relations with China, associating with Japan, and allying with the United States" (Ch., *qin Zhongguo, jie Riben, lian Meiguo*). The treatise prescribed strategies aimed at ameliorating Chosŏn's perilous situation and encouraged it to launch a self-strengthening program. Chosŏn, Huang proposed, should ask China to allow its emissaries to stay in Beijing permanently, dispatch emissaries to reside in Tokyo and Washington, propose to expand trade at Fenghuang City, send trainees and students to China for training in military skills and Western languages, and invite Westerners to assist Chosŏn with educational reforms. In short, Chosŏn should immediately join the family of nations to bolster its diplomatic, military, and economic power. In order to present Chosŏn to the world as soon as possible, Huang even suggested that the Korean army and navy forces "use China's dragon flag as the national flag."[9]

Encouraged by Huang's passionate words, the king sent a secret commissioner to Tokyo to visit Huang and He Ruzhang with private letters that signaled his intention of negotiating a treaty with the United States. With Chosŏn's opening in sight, He composed a treatise, "On Managing Chosŏn's Diplomacy" (Ch., *Zhuchi Chaoxian waijiao yi*), for the consideration of Beijing and Li Hongzhang. The minister elaborated on his and Huang's ideas by laying out three policies in order of priority. The top-choice policy, which he admitted would be difficult to put into practice right away, was to follow the example of Mongolia and Tibet by dispatching an "imperial resident" (Ch., *banshi dachen*) to reside permanently in Chosŏn—a place that had been "almost no different from the inner prefectures and counties" (Ch., *ji wuyi neidi junxian*) during the Qianlong period—and to manage its "domestic politics and foreign treaties" (Ch., *neiguo zhi zhengzhi, waiguo zhi tiaoyue*). This proposal may have resembled the European concept of colonialism, but it represented He's understanding of the Zongfan system, and this perception obtained legitimacy from the Qing's management of Mongolia and Tibet. The second potential policy was to dispatch a skilled official to Chosŏn to assist it in negotiating treaties with other countries. This policy, He said, was the most practical one, as it could demonstrate Chosŏn's status as China's subordinate and avoid possible problems caused by Chosŏn's self-rule. Finally, the third-priority policy involved the Chinese court ordering the king to sign treaties with other countries and specifying in the first article of each treaty that Chosŏn was concluding the treaty on China's orders.[10] As history unfolded, Beijing would eventually endorse the second and third proposals.

The king was confident about the Chinese proposals and enthusiastically launched reforms after Pyŏn Wŏn-kyu returned home from Tianjin with the outline of the training program. On January 19, 1881, Chosŏn established the Office for Managing State Affairs (K., T'ongni kimu amun) in imitation of China's Zongli Yamen, laying the institutional cornerstone for the modernization of the country. This institution comprised twelve departments, the first among them being the Department of Serving the Great (K., Sadae sa).[11] At the same time, the king appointed twelve officials as inspectors of Dongnae Prefecture (K., Dongnaebu amhaeng ŏsa) to visit Japan and observe Japanese politics, society, foreign relations, and trade. The mission, later known as "the inspection mission of the court officials" (K., Chosa sich'al dan) or "the gentlemen's sighting group"

(K., *Sinsa yuram dan*) had a total of sixty-four members. It visited Nagasaki, Osaka, Kyoto, Kobe, Yokohama, and Tokyo between May and October 1881 and was granted audiences with senior Japanese officials. In October, when another mission headed by Cho Pyŏng-ho (1847–1910) and Yi Cho-yŏn (1843–84) as envoys of amity arrived in Japan for negotiations over duty tariffs, the inspection mission returned to Hansŏng, submitting to the king sixty-four reports and seventeen additional memorandums. The officials expressed their belief that bringing Chosŏn into the modern world and into alliances with other countries offered the best way for the country to survive the growing Japanese threat.[12] Their conclusions justified the king's policy of reforms and opening up.

The domestic situation, however, was not conducive to the realization of officials' strategic goals. Before the mission returned home, the king had arrested several officials headed by An Ki-yŏng (1819–81) of the Taewŏn'gun clan and charged them with planning a coup. Simultaneously, a nationwide protest among the literati against the king's reforms became more dramatic and provocative. In late 1880 some officials asked the king to reject Huang Zunxian's ideas, which they believed went against the doctrines of Confucianism.[13] In March 1881 a Confucian student from Kyŏngsang, Yi Man-son, submitted a petition cosigned by ten thousand fellow students, calling on the king to burn Huang's treatise and to reaffirm Confucianism. At court, the official Hwang Chae-hyŏn argued that the king should "reject heretical thought" by publicly burning not only Huang's treatise but all books and newspapers on international law and foreign history and geography. In order to sidestep the literati's moral charges, the king issued a "decree of antiheresy" that endorsed the defense of Confucianism and rejected heretical ideas.[14] Yet this action seemed only to encourage more students to travel to Hansŏng to submit petitions.

The literati protest reached its zenith in late August with the petitions of two students, Hong Chae-hak and Sin Sŏp. Besides appealing to the king to abolish the Office for Managing State Affairs and to restore old institutions, Hong accused the king of having taken no measures to "defend correct teaching and reject heterodoxy" (K., *wijŏng ch'ŏksa*). Sin, for his part, depicted Li Hongzhang's letters to Yi Yu-wŏn and Huang's treatise as elements of the same intrigue against Chosŏn.[15] In early September Hong was beheaded for "offending the sovereign," and Yi Yu-wŏn was exiled. The protests declined. The king and the Min clan, along with their program of reaching out, survived the turmoil and prevailed over other political cliques in fierce partisan struggles.

Amid the turbulence, in late July the king welcomed two imperial envoys from Beijing, who brought an edict about the death of Empress Dowager Cian. The monarch held a grand ceremony at the palace, where he performed rituals to the imperial documents. Afterward, he paid a visit to the envoys at their residence and then sent them off in person. The conversations between the king and the envoys did not touch on Chosŏn's domestic or foreign affairs.[16] The Zongfan mechanism continued to function smoothly, reaffirming its rituals, the autonomous right and dignity of the sovereign of Chosŏn, and the nature of the Zongfan relationship.

Secret Diplomacy: Chosŏn's Commissioning of China to Negotiate with the United States

On November 18, 1881, the emissary of superintending the selected trainees (K., *Yŏngsŏn sa*), Kim Yun-sik (1835–1922), left Hansŏng for China, bringing with him students who were to learn military skills and Western languages under the auspices of the new training program. Although the mission was unlike any that had gone to China before, it mostly acted like a conventional tributary one, with Kim treated as a standard tributary emissary in terms of his traveling expenses.[17] Not many young Koreans wanted to study in China: four days before his departure, Kim was still busy recruiting trainees. Of the more than thirty young men he interviewed, only six volunteered to go. Not until early December, when Kim reached Ŭiju, did he finally have the thirty-eight trainees China had suggested. Like the tributary missions in the eighteenth century, Kim's spent fifty days covering more than 950 miles from Hansŏng to Beijing via the overland route (the maritime route, which they had planned to take with Beijing's special approval, was not feasible in winter). The mission arrived in Beijing on January 6, 1882, and Kim submitted the king's notes to the Ministry of Rites after the group was lodged at the Foreign Emissaries' Common Accommodations.[18]

Leaving his mission in Beijing, Kim visited Li Hongzhang at Baoding with a confidential memorandum, which asked Li to assume, in secret, the task of negotiating Chosŏn's treaty with the United States; this treaty was then to serve as a prototype for subsequent treaties with other countries.[19] Emphasizing that what he did for Chosŏn was "legitimate and righteous" (Ch., *mingzheng yishun*), as Kim, too, believed, Li gave Kim a pamphlet about Chosŏn's potential treaties with Western countries that had been drafted by Ma Jianzhong (1845–1900), a protégé of Li's who had been educated in France.[20] Li further discussed with Kim key issues regarding Chosŏn's reforms, such as regulating tariffs, setting up a system of maritime customs and hiring Western staff to manage it, designing a national flag for Chosŏn for maritime identification, allowing the Japanese minister to reside in Hansŏng, and continuing to use the king's invested rank in his contacts with the Japanese sovereign. The most urgent goal of the two sides, then, was to negotiate and conclude a treaty with the United States rather than to teach the Korean trainees in China.

Within the Zongfan context, the Korean side abandoned its right of negotiation from the beginning. In late January, Beijing granted Li control over Chosŏn's treaty negotiations with the United States in order to "maintain the *fan* and *shuguo* and consolidate China's border."[21] Li also received a letter from Shufeldt, who had returned to China in June 1881 and waited in Tianjin for news from the Korean side. Shufeldt had been appointed by Washington as a special envoy to Chosŏn to pursue a treaty of amity aimed at addressing the issue of American shipwrecks on the Korean coast.[22] After the meeting with Kim, Li invited Shufeldt to Baoding to discuss the details of the forthcoming treaty negotiations, but Shufeldt decided first to visit the American legation in Beijing to solicit advice from the chargé d'affaires, Chester Holcombe (1842–1912).

Unlike Shufeldt, Holcombe was aware of the critical devolution of Beijing's negotiating power to Li and doubted it would be possible to persuade Chosŏn to conclude a treaty without the involvement of the central government in Beijing because Li was "only a provincial officer and not a member of the Central Government." To seek clarity on this question, Holcombe visited the Zongli Yamen, where he was informed that Prince Gong had transferred responsibility for Korean foreign affairs from the Ministry of Rites to the Zongli Yamen in 1881, which meant that Li as a subordinate of the Yamen was authorized to deal with Korean affairs. Holcombe also learned that China had advised Chosŏn to conclude a treaty with the United States because China believed that "sooner or later the autonomy of Corea would be threatened by the aggressions of Russia and/or Japan, and that this serious danger could be best met by bringing the peninsular Kingdom into the family of nations." Although the Yamen confirmed to him that China was ready "to aid the United States in any proper way to open friendly and commercial relations with Corea," Holcombe was worried that Beijing might "see fit to assume an entirely different attitude and policy in this business." His distrust seems to have affected Shufeldt, who replied to Li that he preferred to keep the prospective treaty negotiations secret by not visiting Baoding.[23]

For his part, after his meetings with Li at Baoding, Kim visited Tianjin for a week, sending five students to the Navy and Torpedo School for English-language training. China decided to cover the Korean students' meals and other costs because the students were also "loyal children of the Heavenly Dynasty." It was within this conventional politico-cultural context of the Chinese empire that Chinese officials enthusiastically engaged in Chosŏn's program of building its strength and reaching out to the West. Before he could place additional students in schools, Kim received confidential orders from the king to consult with Li over treaty negotiations with the United States. Kim immediately returned to Baoding, where he and Li discussed initiating negotiations with Shufeldt in order to prevent him from sailing directly for Chosŏn. This plan required a Korean envoy plenipotentiary. Given the limited time, Li proposed that Kim follow the king's secret instruction to adapt strategies for situations and serve as the plenipotentiary himself, but Kim declined. The only solution, then, was to quickly send a messenger to Hansŏng to ask the king to dispatch a plenipotentiary to Tianjin. Li cautioned that the plenipotentiary should come ostensibly to supervise the Korean trainees and keep his true mission secret.[24]

Opening Chosŏn's Doors: The Sino-American Treaty Negotiations

Li Hongzhang took up the task of composing a draft treaty primarily on the basis of a model proposed by Huang Zunxian. Li suggested that the treaty should define the Sino-Korean relationship by stating that "Chosŏn, being a *shuguo* of China, possesses the right of *zizhu* as to its diplomatic and domestic affairs, and this right shall not be challenged by other nations." Kim endorsed this "legitimate and justifiable" statement. In a confidential report to the king, Kim revealed the true reason for his approval: the statement meant that Chosŏn could use China's diplomatic relations with other countries for its own great benefit, and the affirmation of its right of *zizhu* would preserve Chosŏn's equality in its contacts with other countries.[25] Kim's comments indicate that the use of terms drawn from the Zongfan discourse—which in the end appeared not in the Korean-American treaty but in the Sino-Korean commercial regulations signed in the same year—were not unilaterally imposed on Chosŏn by China in order to strengthen China's "suzerainty" at the cost of Chosŏn's sovereignty and independence. Rather, each party to the Zongfan arrangement could exploit the relationship for its own benefit.

Another critical aspect of the discussion between Li and Kim focused on the prospect of granting an American right of consular jurisdiction. Huang, in his draft, suggested that Chosŏn temporarily allow American consuls to manage the affairs of American citizens in Chosŏn. Backing this idea, Li explained that "according to international conventions, foreigners living in treaty ports and hinterlands of a country are subject to the management of the officials of their own countries residing in the places of the said country. The local officials of the host country are not able to manage people of other nations due to the different laws, punishments, customs, and proprieties between the East and the West." For Li and Huang, consular jurisdiction was thus merely a way of managing foreigners rather than a clause undermining the sovereignty of a country. Kim agreed with this view, confirming that "our humble country is not familiar with foreign situations, so there will be many problems even if our country could manage foreigners by itself."[26] The two sides thus decided to grant the United States the right of consular jurisdiction, even though Shufeldt had not asked for this right.

Because the Korean-American treaty was a prototype for future treaties between Chosŏn and other countries, China gained this right too, through the commercial regulations examined later in this chapter. This episode calls into question the assumption that the Western powers always obtained extraterritoriality in East Asia by force. It further casts doubt on the notion that extraterritoriality can be uniformly regarded as a hallmark of imperialism, as historical narratives of East Asian countries have typically charged.[27]

After composing a draft treaty with Li, Kim returned to Tianjin, where a special envoy of the king, Yi Ŭng-jun, was waiting for him with a sovereign letter stating that the dispatch of a plenipotentiary was impossible and that it would be better for the Americans to travel to Chosŏn for further communication. When Kim asked the Chinese chief of the Tianjin Customs, Zhou Fu (1837–1921), to forward the message to Li, Zhou repeated the suggestion that Kim himself act as the plenipotentiary. Kim again refused, believing it would be better for China to negotiate on behalf of his country. Zhou also questioned the phrase "independence and half-autonomy" (Ch., *duli banzhu*) that appeared in a Korean note explaining the term *zizhu* in the Korean-Japanese Treaty of 1876. Zhou warned that the statement, which seemed to claim much greater independence than was foreseen by Kim and Li, was a "Japanese plot" and could only damage Chosŏn's interests. In response, Kim confirmed that Chosŏn would not claim to be "independent and autonomous" (K., *chajon t'ŭknip*) in its treaty with the United States.[28]

Soon thereafter, the treaty negotiations between Li Hongzhang and Shufeldt opened. Whether the treaty should include a clause defining Chosŏn as China's *shuguo* became the most controversial issue. The first article of Li's draft, as Li and Kim had discussed, stated that "Chosŏn is China's *shubang* and always enjoys the right of *zizhu* in its domestic and foreign affairs."[29] Shufeldt objected to this statement, so the two sides drew up a draft treaty with fifteen articles, leaving the first one blank. According to the Sino-Korean plan, if it proved impossible to include the statement in the final version of the treaty, Chosŏn would send a special note to the US government to articulate its status as China's *shuguo*. Kim did not hold any conversations with Shufeldt, nor did he participate in the negotiations. On April 21, 1882, Li gave Kim and Yi Ŭng-jun a copy of the draft treaty and instructed Yi to return to Chosŏn immediately from Tianjin by a Chinese steamer. At Kim's request, Li instructed Ma Jianzhong, who was "very skilled in international law," to accompany Shufeldt to Inch'ŏn to ensure that everything would go smoothly. In the meantime, two Korean officials, Ŏ Yun-jung (1848–96) and Yi Cho-yŏn, left Hansŏng for Tianjin as officials of examination and selection (K., *kosŏn kwan*), not as the plenipotentiaries that Li, Kim, and Shufeldt desperately wanted.

On May 8 Ma Jianzhong and the Chinese admiral Ding Ruchang (1836–95) arrived at Inch'ŏn, where Ma met with the Japanese minister, Hanabusa Yoshimoto, who had arrived a day earlier in the hope of influencing the negotiations. Four days later, Shufeldt arrived on the USS *Swatara* and negotiated with the Korean plenipotentiaries, Kim Hong-jip and Sin Hŏn (1810–84), the latter of whom had signed the Treaty of Kanghwa in 1876. The negotiations ended on May 22 with a treaty of fourteen articles, omitting the first article about Chosŏn's status that Li had proposed. For Chosŏn's national flag, Ma suggested Yi Ŭng-jun's design of the Taiji and eight trigrams as the basic model.[30] After Shufeldt left for Shanghai with a copy of the treaty, Ma remained in Inch'ŏn to help Chosŏn negotiate treaties with Britain and other states.[31] Following the middle course, as determined by Li, Ma, and Kim, the king sent a dispatch that Ma had drafted to the US president Chester Arthur on May 29, claiming that "Corea is a tributary of China, but in regard to both internal administration and foreign intercourse it enjoys complete independence."[32] The king sent the same announcement to the sovereigns of other treaty countries, including Britain (June 6, 1882), Germany (November 26, 1883), Italy (June 26, 1884), Russia (July 7, 1884), and France (June 4, 1886). As the hermit nation entered the family of nations, its de jure independent status as a sovereign state in terms of international law and its de facto *and* de jure dependent status as a subordinate of China in accordance with Zongfan principles became one of the most controversial and perplexing issues for Western states in East Asia. The new situation also complicated Sino-Korean relations as Chosŏn moved toward modifying its relations with China.

Protecting Chosŏn as the Patriarch: The Chinese Military Intervention in 1882

Challenges from Within: The King's Requests for Change

By the time Chosŏn concluded its treaty with the United States, more than one-third of the Korean trainees in Tianjin had returned home. The training program had provided cover for Korean-American treaty negotiations and a new channel of communication outside the Zongfan mechanism, but it was never independently a focus for either the Chinese or the Korean side. Ŏ Yun-jung and Yi Cho-yŏn, the two Korean officials who had nominally been sent to evaluate the trainees in Tianjin, also ignored the training program in order to focus on their true diplomatic mission. In May 1882 Ŏ and Yi submitted four detailed requests from the king to the acting Beiyang superintendent, Zhang Shusheng (1824–84), who had assumed Li Hongzhang's position when Li returned to his hometown in Anhui for one hundred days of mourning for his mother.

The first request proposed that the two countries negotiate a treaty in keeping with the new international situation. The second recommended that the two sides close the markets on the northeastern border of Manchuria in order to prevent Russian interference. The third request offered to replace Chosŏn's periodic dispatch of emissaries to Beijing with representatives who would reside in the capital permanently, receiving imperial edicts and calendars and making China's dispatch of imperial envoys to Chosŏn unnecessary. The fourth request further specified that the Korean emissaries residing in Beijing would be responsible for their own travel expenses and meals, effectively making them no different from the ministers of other countries.[33] These bold requests reflected Huang Zunxian's blueprint for Korea's reforms as laid out in his "A Strategy for Chosŏn" in late 1880, and they were aimed at replacing certain Zongfan conventions with Western diplomatic principles as practiced between sovereign states.

Concluding a treaty with China was Chosŏn's primary goal. For that purpose, Ŏ discussed with Zhou Fu key issues such as the posting of permanent emissaries in Beijing, the granting of most-favored-nation status to China, and the definition of Chosŏn's status as China's *shuguo* in the treaty. The two sides agreed that China's foreign affairs vis-à-vis Chosŏn would be managed by the Zongli Yamen and the Beiyang superintendent, whereas bilateral tributary affairs would remain under the jurisdiction of the Ministry of Rites. This discussion set the tone for the treaty. In June 1882 Ŏ arrived in Beijing, where he was lodged at the Foreign Emissaries' Common Accommodations by the Ministry of Rites. The ministry, following Zongfan conventions, presented Ŏ with silver, sheep, wine, and meals. In the meantime, Yi Ŭng-jun, another special emissary of the king, arrived in Beijing with a note expressing the king's sincere gratitude to the emperor and the "central dynasty" for protecting the "small country" and the *fan* in the negotiations with the United States. Yi was also lodged at the Common Accommodations and showered with silver, sheep, wine, and meals.

Although granting the king's requests would weaken the role of the Ministry of Rites, the cases of Ryukyu, Burma, and Vietnam—which by 1882 had been or were being separated from the Sinocentric realm and colonized by other states—had made the ministry realize that many issues lay beyond the capacity of the Zongfan mechanism to address effectively. The ministry passed the king's requests to the emperor and suggested that he instruct all officials familiar with foreign affairs, especially Li Hongzhang, to participate in a confidential discussion on the matter. Baoting (1840–90), a Manchu minister of the ministry, presented a memorial to the emperor to detail the ministry's preferences.

According to Baoting, Chosŏn, the first *shuguo* of "foreign barbarians" that had subordinated itself to the Great Qing during the Hongtaiji period, was far more important than the "countries in the South Sea" (Ch., *Nanyang zhuguo*, Southeast Asia). After Japan's invasion of Ryukyu, Britain's of Burma, and France's of Vietnam, all of which China failed to resist, Chosŏn's respect for China had diminished, but it had not betrayed China because of Chosŏn's weakness and still respected China's virtues.

Baoting argued that refusing to let the *shuguo* trade at China's treaty ports and pursue shared commercial interests with other "barbarians from afar" (Ch., *yuanyi*) would be unfair to Chosŏn and might push it to the Japanese side. But permitting Chosŏn's emissaries to reside in Beijing permanently would put Chosŏn on an equal footing with other countries with representatives in China and might make it as aggressive as the "British barbarians" had become. Baoting urged the Ministry of Rites to retain its right to administer Chosŏn but to continue to forward matters concerning trade to the Zongli Yamen. Even if Korean emissaries were permitted to reside permanently in Beijing, China should not allow Chosŏn to build a legation in the city. Instead, the emissaries should be lodged at the Common Accommodations to emphasize that China and Chosŏn remained members of the same family. Baoting also proposed that Beijing use Chosŏn's intention of exploiting China's power to check other countries as an opportunity to dispatch thousands of soldiers to Chosŏn to garrison its military forts in order to "protect it and place it under China's influence" (Ch., *yu hubi zhi zhong yu kongzhi zhi dao*).[34]

Baoting's opinions had a strong impact on the Qing court's decision. The court promptly issued an edict declining Chosŏn's request to place permanent emissaries in Beijing because of "various potential inconveniences" and the fact that "Chosŏn has been a *fan* for a long time, and all rituals have regulations." It also decided that the Zongli Yamen should be in charge of China's trade affairs with Chosŏn and the Ministry of Rites should continue to manage tributary affairs. Nevertheless, the court agreed to make changes to some conventions and instructed the Beiyang superintendent to negotiate a commercial treaty with Chosŏn.[35] This imperial order further augmented the superintendent's importance as the most powerful agent of Sino-Korean contacts beyond the court-to-court tributary track. Two weeks later, Baoting submitted another memorial to the emperor to argue that China should help Chosŏn strengthen its maritime defenses. To underline Chosŏn's critical position, Baoting went as far as to claim that China "would rather lose Yunnan and Guizhou than Chosŏn" (Ch., *jishi Yun Gui, buke shi Chaoxian*). The emperor commented that the comparison between Yunnan and Guizhou Provinces and Chosŏn was inappropriate, but he showed serious concern over the security of China's *shuguo*.[36]

Justifying China's Status as the Patriarch: The Dispatch of Chinese Troops to Chosŏn

While Chosŏn was successfully persuading China to sign a treaty with it, back home it was teetering on the brink of political upheaval. On July 23, 1882, a mutiny, known as the Imo incident, broke out in Hansŏng over the unfair distribution of rations of rice among troops after a severe drought. Hundreds of soldiers of a military unit called Muwiyŏng attacked the Japanese legation, killing several Japanese, including Lieutenant Horimoto Reizō, who had been teaching Chosŏn's Special Skills Army (K., Pyŏlgi gun) since 1881. After occupying the palace, the rebels held the king captive and killed several high-ranking officials who had been prominent pillars of Queen Min's clan in the partisan struggles at the court. The king's father, the Taewŏn'gun, seized the opportunity to restore his regency and retaliated against the queen's clan by announcing that the queen was dead. In fact, she had escaped the capital and had hidden in Ch'ungju Prefecture.[37] The Japanese chargé d'affaires, Hanabusa Yoshimoto, fled to Inch'ŏn, where he boarded a British steamer to Nagasaki and telegraphed news of the uprising to Tokyo.

Tokyo instructed Hanabusa to return to Inch'ŏn with navy forces to seek justice and compensation for the killings of the Japanese. The Chinese minister in Tokyo, Li Shuchang (1837–96), telegraphed Beijing, likewise to request the immediate dispatch of troops to Chosŏn. In Beijing the German minister, Max August von Brandt, and the inspector general of the imperial customs, Robert Hart (1835–1911), informed the Zongli Yamen about the mutiny on August 2 and 3, at the same time that copies of the German-Korean and British-Korean treaties, along with the Korean king's dispatches to the German and British sovereigns claiming Chosŏn's status as China's *shuguo*, reached the Zongli Yamen.[38] Within days, Beijing was in full alarm over the situation in Korea.

When Zhang Shusheng, who commanded the Beiyang Navy in Tianjin, instructed General Wu Changqing (1829–84) to be ready for military action, he was influenced in large part by the Korean officials Kim Yun-sik and Ŏ Yun-jung, who were in Tianjin at the time. As fervent proponents of the king's policy of opening up, Kim and Ŏ linked the mutiny with the aborted coup of the previous year, which had been linked to the Taewŏn'gun. They asked Zhang to send warships and soldiers to suppress the uprising and to check Japanese intrigue. Accusing the Taewŏn'gun of plotting against the king, Kim even secretly proposed to kill the Taewŏn'gun when the Chinese troops occupied Hansŏng in order to "erase the bane of the country."[39] Handicapped by the limited channels of communication and intelligence gathering, China was so unfamiliar with Chosŏn's domestic situation that Zhang and his Chinese colleagues became dependent on Kim's and Ŏ's biased information. The Chinese concluded that the Taewŏn'gun would dethrone the king if China failed to take action in time.

Beijing decided to exercise its patriarchal authority immediately. The Guangxu emperor instructed the Zongli Yamen and Zhang to send forces to Chosŏn under the leadership of Ma Jianzhong and Ding Ruchang to "cherish the small country," halt the "Japanese plot," and "protect the Japanese people along the same lines." The military action acquired legitimacy from the rationales of the Zong-fan arrangement. Zhang assembled thirteen warships and merchant ships under Admiral Ding's command and summoned four thousand soldiers, placing them under General Wu's command. Zhang also ordered Kim and Ŏ to return to Chosŏn together with the Chinese troops to serve as their guides. Meanwhile, Ma conducted a reconnaissance mission in Inch'ŏn that included several long conversations with Ŏ. Ŏ's personal resentment of the Taewŏn'gun deeply influenced Ma's judgment on the matter in his report to Zhang, confirming the Chinese side's earlier evaluation of the Korean situation. General Wu soon left Tianjin for Yantai, from where he would continue to Chosŏn with his fleet and officers, including the twenty-four-year-old Yuan Shikai. During the trip to Chosŏn, Yuan told Kim that he wanted to lead hundreds of warriors to seize Hansŏng, which impressed Kim considerably.[40] Yuan would later reside in Chosŏn for more than a decade and significantly shape the future of the country.

Japan, too, considered its action of sending troops to Chosŏn legal and legitimate. Inoue Kaoru informed the foreign ministers in Tokyo that Japan's operation was "completely based upon pacifism," and the aim of its warships and troops was to protect the Japanese embassy and citizens. The deputy foreign minister, Yoshida Kyonari (1845–91), declined Li Shuchang's offer of China's mediation. Very soon Inoue was giving Hanabusa detailed instructions on military operations and the terms of compensation, all of which were aimed at dealing with the situation unilaterally and by force, rather than through China or other countries.[41] As a result, the ideological conflict between China and Japan regarding Chosŏn's status evolved into a military rivalry on the peninsula.

For China, sending troops to its *shuguo* was legitimate and necessary. As the Zongli Yamen put it to Mori in 1876, China had long before assumed responsibility for helping Chosŏn "solve its difficulties, resolve its disputes, and secure its safety and security." Reviewing this point in his notes to Yoshida, Li Shuchang stated that China's actions followed "the rule of cherishing the small." China had to "suppress the rebellion for the sake of the *shubang*" and protect the Japanese legation in Hansŏng at the same time. The minister used a metaphor to explain the rationale behind China's operation, describing China as the "patriarch of a family" (Ch., *jiazhang*) who had the obligation to investigate why the belongings of "other people"—that is, Japan—left at the "houses of his sons or brothers" (Ch., *zidi jia*), namely, Chosŏn, had been stolen.[42] This metaphor crystallized China's role vis-à-vis Korea within the Zongfan world. It also clearly demonstrated that China's understanding of the mutiny and its decision to send troops to Chosŏn were not related to international law.

Japan had difficulty rebuffing China's statement and worried that the situation in Chosŏn might draw Japan into the abyss of a war with the powerful China. Having consulted with Charles Le Gendre about the Taiwan issue in 1872, the Gaimushō again resorted to its foreign intellectual resources, soliciting advice from the French jurist and legal adviser to the government, Gustave Boissonade (1825–1910). Boissonade suggested that Japan could insist that Chosŏn was an "independent country" and "only focus on negotiation with Chosŏn." He mentioned the relationship between the Ottoman Empire and Egypt as an analogy for the Sino-Korean relationship, as Mori had done in 1876. Since Britain and France had directly intervened in the mutiny of Egypt in January 1882, regardless of the Ottomans' attitude, Japan could directly intervene in the rebellion in Chosŏn without regard to China's response.[43] In Beijing, Inspector General Hart also believed that "China and Japan about Corea will just be in much the same position as Turkey and England about Egypt."[44] In this context, then, the trilateral relationship between China, Chosŏn, and Japan became analogous to the one between the Ottoman Empire, European powers represented by Britain and France, and African countries such as Egypt and Tunisia, reflecting the connection between the transformation of the East Asian community and the rise of new imperialism in world history.[45] The European colonial experience in Africa thus made a critical intellectual contribution to the development of the Japanese colonial enterprise in East Asia.

The Chinese side was not blind to the emergence of the new colonial model practiced by European states. Li Shuchang, from Tokyo, suggested to the Zongli Yamen that after suppressing the mutiny China should manage and supervise all of Chosŏn's affairs in order to ensure peace in its domestic situation as well as its foreign relations. He further proposed that China should "directly abolish the kingship and convert the country into prefectures and counties [of China]" (Ch., *zhi fei qiwang er junxian zhi*), imitating the approach of Britain in India, in order to resolve once and for all the thorny question of Chosŏn's status between China and other states.[46] China's possible provincialization of Korea was thus to some degree equated to and even justified by the colonialism practiced by European powers. Yet Li himself concluded that China would be unable to take the proposed action because it would violate China's self-imposed rule of humanity and virtue.[47] Until the outbreak of the Sino-Japanese War in 1894, China never initiated any plan to colonize Chosŏn; rather, it tried to protect and supervise the country along Zongfan lines.

Arriving in Chosŏn almost a month after the uprising, General Wu and his assistants were welcomed by the Korean officials.[48] The Chinese officials used China's uniquely favorable position and authority to quickly end the political turmoil by occupying the capital, capturing the Taewŏn'gun and sending him to Tianjin in China, restoring the king and the queen, and supporting Chosŏn in signing two conventions with Japan. Afterward, the king dispatched missions to Beijing and Tokyo along conventional lines to brief the two governments on the incident. At the end of September, the Zongli Yamen distributed a note to seven foreign ministers in Beijing, informing them about the Chinese intervention and reemphasizing that "Chosŏn, being a *shuguo* of our Great Qing, has maintained its status as *fan* for generations, and the court regards it as an inner subordinate [Ch., *neifu*] that shares solidarity with us."[49] The Yamen also announced that the Chinese troops would remain in Chosŏn to ensure the stability and security of the country.

A thornier issue for Beijing was how to deal with the Taewŏn'gun, who had been sent from Tianjin to Baoding. After reassuming the position of the Beiyang superintendent, Li Hongzhang endorsed Zhang Shusheng's proposal that Beijing should detain the Taewŏn'gun in China forever and allow the king to regularly send officials to visit him. Li cited a similar historical case from the early fourteenth century, when the Mongol court of the Yuan Dynasty exiled King Ch'unghye (r. 1330–32, 1339–43) of Koryŏ Korea to Guangdong Province in China.[50] In its contemporary reaction to the political turmoil of its outer *fan*, the Qing could point to historical precedent to argue that it retained the fully legal power to punish any official of the *fan* and even to depose the king, if necessary. The Qing's decision to dethrone the last king of the Lê Dynasty of Annam in 1789 was also a clear demonstration of this power. It was in this context that in 1886 Yuan Shikai enthusiastically proposed to Li Hongzhang that China should replace the king of Chosŏn with an able man from the Korean royal family.[51] In the end, after holding the Taewŏn'gun for three years, Beijing released him back to Chosŏn in October 1885, when Yuan Shikai was promoted to the position of an imperial resident in the country.

China's military intervention in 1882 was a turning point in Qing-Chosŏn relations, yet in a fundamental sense it was only a public presentation of the underlying nature of the supreme and patriarchal power the Qing had wielded over its subordinate country since 1637. The assertion that China's superiority was merely "titular" and its act of detaining the Taewŏn'gun "inconceivable" is a far cry from the truth.[52] So is the argument that through this particular intervention the Qing became a colonial power that inflicted Western-style imperialism on Chosŏn.

Defining Chosŏn through Treaties: The Sino-Korean Regulations and Their Consequences

Complicating the Zongfan Order: The First Sino-Korean Treaty

As Chosŏn's troubles seemed to continue, many Chinese officials advocated establishing stronger relations with the country. On February 28, 1882, Wu Dacheng (1835–1902), an assistant official of border affairs in Jilin in Manchuria, stressed in a memorial to the emperor that China's self-strengthening enterprise was also aimed at protecting Chosŏn and checking Japan and Russia. Wu argued that Beijing should dispatch imperial commissioners to Chosŏn to push the Koreans to determine whether such harbors as Wŏnsan (known in Russian as Lazarev), a port in northeastern Korea being surveyed by Russia, could become trade ports. Chosŏn, Wu proposed, should allow the China Merchants Steamship Navigation Company (Ch., Lunchuan zhaoshang ju) to survey the coastal conditions with the aim of establishing Chinese trade posts. In return, he suggested allowing Korean merchants to trade in Tianjin, Yantai, Shanghai, and other trade ports of China. Wu justified his proposal by invoking China's Zongfan relations with Chosŏn, the "outer *fan*" that "had been a subordinate to our dynasty for more than two hundred years."[53] International law was of no concern to him.

In order to help Chosŏn overcome the financial crisis triggered by the turmoil, China loaned the country 0.5 million taels of silver at the request of leading Korean officials Cho Yŏng-ha (1845–84) and Kim Hong-jip, who negotiated the loan with their Chinese counterparts Ma Jianzhong and Tang Tingshu (1832–92). Tang was the chief of the Kaiping Mining Administration (Ch., Kaiping kuangwu ju), a modern engineering and mining company founded by Li Hongzhang in Zhili Province in 1878. According to their agreement, 0.3 million of the loan would come from the China Merchants Steamship Navigation Company and 0.2 million from the Kaiping Mining Administration. Chosŏn's tariffs and taxes on red ginseng would serve as mortgage, and it would pay off the loan in twelve years at 0.8 percent interest. In return, the two Chinese creditors supervised by Li were granted economic privileges in Chosŏn. The Navigation Company gained the right to rent land at Chosŏn's treaty ports for its factories and offices, while Kaiping Mining could freely prospect for minerals in the hinterland of the country. Chinese commercial power thus quickly expanded into Chosŏn.

In addition, China agreed to provide Chosŏn with military supplies for its poorly equipped troops. In October 1882 Li Hongzhang gave Chosŏn ten twelve-pound cannons, three thousand cannonballs, 4,500 pounds of cannon powder, 1,500 pounds of bullet powder, one thousand British rifles, ten thousand pounds of rifle powder, and one million bullets from the Tianjin Arsenals.[54] A month later Chosŏn's military and industrial training program in Tianjin ended with the king's recall of the rest of the apprentices.[55] From that point on, Chosŏn had to invite foreign advisers to the country to train its forces, leaving the country more vulnerable to outside influences.[56]

After China quelled the mutiny in Chosŏn in the summer of 1882, the two countries resumed their negotiations for a commercial treaty in Tianjin, with Ŏ Yun-jung representing Chosŏn and Zhou Fu and Ma Jianzhong representing China. From the beginning of their meetings in May 1882, before the rebellion, the two sides agreed on clarifying in the treaty that Chosŏn was China's *shuguo* with the right of *zizhu*, not an independent country. After reviewing the Chinese draft, entitled "Regulations for Maritime and Overland Trade between Chinese and Chosŏn Subjects" (Ch., Zhongguo Chaoxian shangmin shuilu maoyi zhangcheng, hereafter "the Sino-Korean Regulations"), Ŏ questioned some of its elements, in particular the imbalance in consular jurisdiction enshrined in article 2 and the opening of Hansŏng as a trade city for Chinese merchants and the permission for Chinese merchants to trade in Chosŏn's hinterlands that were provided by article 4. Quoting Zongfan regulations, Zhou and Ma responded that this treaty was different from those signed between China and "friendly nations" (Ch., *yuguo*, such as Britain, France, and the United States); in this case, the two countries should uphold their "veritable orthodox legitimacy" (Ch., *shizai zhi mingfen*) in an established context. The Chinese response helps explain why the parties decided to call the document "regulations" (Ch., *zhangcheng*) rather than a "treaty" (Ch., *tiaoyue*). In the end, Zhou and Ma agreed to alter several terms but successfully added a preamble specifying that the regulations applied only to China's subordinate countries and were exempt from the most-favored-nation rule. The Korean side endorsed the revised text.[57]

In a memorial to Beijing, Li Hongzhang summarized the regulations and emphasized that the preamble would "clarify and define the orthodox legitimacy" (Ch., *zhengming dingfen*) between China and its *shuguo*.[58] Li did not mention that article 7 endowed Chinese warships with the right to cruise in Chosŏn's waters and to cast anchor at any of its ports in the interests of Chosŏn's security. This article impinged on Chosŏn's sovereignty, but Ŏ and his Korean colleagues, like Li and his Chinese colleagues, regarded it as part of the favorable protection that the upper country generously offered to the subordinate country. These scholar-officials, including the French-educated Ma Jianzhong, did not interpret the regulations' terms with reference to international law. In the aftermath of the mutiny, China was the only power that Chosŏn could trust as it wrestled with multiple crises. Yet not all Koreans applauded the treaty dictated by the Chinese. For example, Yun Ch'i-ho (1865–1945), who had served as the assistant to Ŏ Yun-jung in the "gentlemen's sighting group" to Japan to observe Japanese politics and society in 1881 and was visiting Tokyo when the Sino-Korean Regulations were signed, reported feeling "extremely sad" that the treaty placed Chosŏn in such an inferior position vis-à-vis China.[59] Having been exposed to Western and Japanese modernity and civilization, young Korean scholars such as Yun believed that such unequal arrangements between the two nations should be abandoned, signaling the rise of modern nationalism and national identity among these Korean intellectuals. Yun later became a leading figure in Korean modernization.

By concluding the regulations with Chosŏn, China fulfilled the majority of the requests that the king had made in the spring of 1882 (discussed earlier), changing or permanently abolishing certain conventions that had been in place for 245 years, since 1637. Scholars who embrace theories of power politics prefer to interpret the treaty as a tool by which China, the preponderant side in geopolitical terms, strengthened its control over Chosŏn, consolidating its suzerainty and even becoming another imperialist power pursuing its own commercial interests on the peninsula. From this perspective, China brought "multilateral imperialism" to Korea in exactly the same way in which China itself had been introduced to the concept by its Western counterparts.[60] However, the Manchu court of China in the 1880s still primarily followed conventional Zongfan rules and precedents in its policies toward Chosŏn, and these often contradicted international law and local Chinese officials' practical concerns over Sino-Korean contacts. For instance, on March 14, 1882, several months before the conclusion of the Sino-Korean Regulations, the Qing court learned from the Manchu general of Jilin, Ming'an (1828–1911), and his assistant Wu Dacheng that Chosŏn peasants kept crossing the border to cultivate wilderness areas in Jilin and that this trespassing was causing serious problems. The eleven-year-old Emperor Guangxu, under the tutelage of his mentors, responded, "Regarding these poor Chosŏn peasants, in the eyes of the local officials, there is certainly a line between them and us, but in the eyes of the court, there is originally no difference between the inside and the outside. Thus, these peasants should be managed well and not be punished by additional rules, as long as they have no intention of encroaching on our borders."[61]

This policy bears a striking similarity to Emperor Yongzheng's decision of 1727 to demarcate a new borderline with Annam on the basis of the idea that all lands of China's outer *fan* were under the emperor's jurisdiction. From 1727 to 1882, the politico-cultural ideology of all-under-Heaven as embraced by the Chinese court remained unchanged. Although the Kangxi emperor had established himself as a student of both Chinese and Western learning, in particular in the fields of mathematics and astronomy, in his active communications with the Jesuits, almost all emperors after him left such Sino-Western intellectual exchange to the Imperial Astronomical Bureau.[62] Until the late nineteenth century, the young emperors—Tongzhi and Guangxu—studied only Confucian classics and Chinese history in their daily lessons at court (Ch., *rijiang*). Even though European and American ministers started to reside in Beijing and China launched a self-strengthening movement in the 1860s, the Manchu court did not train emperors in international knowledge commensurate with China's needs and changing situation. The imperial civil-service examinations that selected officials for the Qing bureaucracy still tested the candidates only on the Confucian classics and showed no hint of change. The Guangxu emperor, along with his tutors, in particular Weng Tonghe, remained confined to this educational milieu. The first textbook on Western history and international law aimed at introducing Guangxu to European and American history since the Age of Discovery, titled *Lectures on Western History* (Ch., *Xishi jiangyi*), did not reach the emperor until November 1907, a year before he died.[63]

When the young Guangxu emperor approved the Sino-Korean Regulations in 1882, he adopted a typically Confucian tone to emphasize that "Chosŏn is our *shuguo* and exists as eastern barbarians far away" (Ch., Chaoxian wei wo shuguo, pizai dongyi).[64] The conventional discourse on the civilized–barbarian distinction was still firmly rooted at the court, at least in the minds of core leaders. For the Manchu ruling house of the Chinese empire, this discourse concerned not so much practical diplomatic negotiations at the provincial level as statecraft from the court's perspective. Qing China in the 1880s continued to act as the Middle Kingdom, the upper country, and the Heavenly Dynasty in the Sino-Korean Zongfan framework. As long as Chosŏn was a *shuguo*, China's centrality would persist and China's Western-oriented diplomacy would accordingly be circumscribed. In this sense, China's transformation into a modern state occurred with the involution of the universal politico-cultural Chinese empire, which revealed the discrepancy between provincial diplomatic practices and the court's ideological norms in the late nineteenth century and highlighted the significance of Chosŏn for the rise of a modern Chinese state.

Complementing the Zongfan Order: The Ritual Crisis and the Sino-Korean Border Treaties

By adopting the form, though not the name, of a Western-style treaty, the 1882 Sino-Korean Regulations helped lay out the inner dual network—introduced at the beginning of this chapter—of Sino-Korean contacts. In addition to maintaining the court-to-court system described in chapter 2, the two countries now had to adjust to the newly created state-to-state system, in which both countries were treated by their

Japanese and Western treaty counterparts as independent sovereign states that were theoretically equal to each other. This inner dual network introduced the two countries to a more complicated situation in the new setting of international politics, as the ritual crisis that unfolded in China in late 1882 demonstrates.

The crisis started with questions regarding the 1882 Sino-Korean Regulations raised by the Manchu general in Mukden, Chongqi (1830–1900). In three palace memorials in December 1882, Chongqi protested article 2, according to which the Chinese commissioners of trade at the treaty ports of Chosŏn "will, in their dealings with Chosŏn's officials, be on a footing of perfect equality, and are to be treated with the consideration due to the observance of etiquette," while the Chosŏn commissioners at Chinese ports "are likewise to be treated on a footing of equality in their dealings with the local authorities, namely, the *taotai* [*daotai*, circuit intendant], the prefect, and the magistrates of the place." Recalling that Chosŏn became a *fan* and subject of the Great Qing in 1637 and that the Korean officials were "ministers of ministers" and thus ranked below their Chinese counterparts, Chongqi pointed out that equality between Chosŏn commissioners and China's local authorities meant that the emperor himself would be on a footing of equality with the king. The assumption of equality thus severely undermined the established order, and "under no circumstances should such treatment be extended to Chosŏn." The term "equality" (Ch., *pingxing*) in the article should, argued Chongqi, be deleted for the sake of "moral principles" (Ch., *lunji*) and China's "national polity" (Ch., *guoti*). Mukden would treat the Chosŏn commissioners along conventional lines in order to defend "decorum" (Ch., *titong*).

The general also questioned article 5, which canceled the requirement of official supervision of trade at the border and allowed local people to trade freely at Zhamen and Ŭiju on the two sides of the Yalu River and at Hunchun and Hoeryŏng on the two sides of the Tumen River. Chongqi agreed that outdated rules ought to be rescinded, but he insisted that land border security should be strengthened by maintaining the existing patrols along the Chinese side. His concerns about unpredictable threats from Chosŏn itself and from the treaty powers present in Chosŏn were heightened by his perception of the uniqueness and importance of the Mukden area, the Qing's "ancestral territory."[65]

Chongqi's worries triggered a heated debate among the Ministry of Rites, the Zongli Yamen, and the Beiyang superintendent. Since the overland border trade regulations would soon be renegotiated at Mukden after a joint Sino-Korean investigation, the issue of the performance of equal rituals became the hottest topic in the discussion. Li Hongzhang argued that the imperial code did not regulate ritual performances between local Chinese officials and foreign tributary emissaries, but he noted that local officials treated the emissaries of Vietnam, Siam, and Ryukyu with "rituals of equality" (Ch., *pingli*), which should be applicable to Chosŏn too. Li also solicited theoretical support from the classics of the Zhou Dynasty and drew an analogy between the statuses of the authorities of the Qing and those of Chosŏn. According to this analogy, the king, as an "outer vassal" of the Son of Heaven, was equal to China's governors-general and governors who were "inner vassals"; meanwhile, Chosŏn's officials were equal to Chinese officials below the ranks of governor and governor-general. Accordingly, in China, the Chosŏn commissioners should perform "rituals of subordination" (Ch., shuli) to the Chinese governors-general, governors, and other officials with higher ranks, and rituals of equality to such local officials as taotai and prefects. They should also perform rituals of equality to Western ministers in Tianjin, where the commissioners would reside. In Chosŏn, on the other hand, the Chinese commissioners should perform rituals of equality to Korean officials whose rank was inferior to that of the cabinet, Ŭijŏngbu.

In his suggestions, Li Hongzhang tried to pursue a mean between Zongfan rituals embodying the "ancestral system" (Ch., zuzhi) and Western-style etiquette between foreign ministers and the host country. Agreeing that Chosŏn's commissioners could get favorable treatment since they were not tributary emissaries, the Ministry of Rites proposed that when Chinese commissioners at or below the rank of taotai visited the king, they should perform "guest-host rituals" (Ch., binzhu li), a proposal that involved a slight change to certain rules of the imperial code.[66] In February 1883 the court, via the Zongli Yamen, endorsed Li's and the ministry's solutions to the ritual crisis and set up a new framework for ritual performances between various officials of the two countries (see figure 5.1). As the diplomatic corps formed in Hansŏng, the new ritual arrangements would cause increasing conflicts between China, Chosŏn, Japan, and Western states in the following decade, demonstrating the strong influence of the dynamics of the inner dual network over the practices of the outer dual network between China and Chosŏn.

Chongqi found the new ritual code a good resolution to the problems he had noted. He went on to strengthen border security and maintain the "proper system" as he had wished by signing a convention with the Korean representative Ŏ Yun-jung in March 1883. The convention, "Regulations for Trade at the Border between Mukden and Chosŏn" (Ch., Fengtian yu Chaoxian bianmin jiaoyi zhangcheng), governed trade at the Zhongjiang (middle river) area of the Yalu River. Several articles were specifically aimed at upholding Zongfan conventions. Echoing the 1882 Sino-Korean Regulations, the preamble of the Mukden-Chosŏn Regulations stated that the border trade at Zhongjiang "is not on the same footing as the trade carried on at the treaty ports, inasmuch as it was originally established by the Heavenly Dynasty as a benefit to its shuguo with the distinct understanding that it should be a convenience to the population . . .

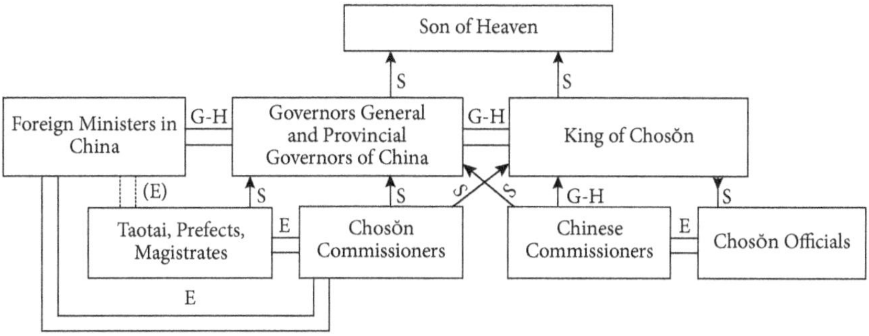

FIGURE 5.1. The rules of ritual performance between China and Chosŏn after 1883. S refers to rituals of subordination, E refers to rituals of equality, and G-H refers to guest-host rituals. Foreign ministers in China sometimes used the rituals of equality in their dealings with Chinese *taotai*, prefects, magistrates, and other local officials.

and that other nations are not concerned in these rules." According to articles 8 and 19, China would not impose taxes on Chosŏn's annual tributes and routine goods and would send soldiers to escort Chosŏn's tributary missions to Beijing from Fenghuang City, precisely as China had done for more than two centuries. Article 23 dictated that bilateral correspondence should be conducted in accordance with the established system, in which Chosŏn should call China the "upper country" or "Heavenly Dynasty" and avoid such abbreviated characters as *zhong* (for *Zhongguo*, the "Middle Kingdom," in reference to China) or *dong* (for *Dongguo*, the "eastern country," in reference to Chosŏn). For their part, Chinese officials would address Chosŏn as "the country of Chosŏn" or "your honorable country."[67]

Several months later, the two countries signed a third treaty, entitled "Regulations for Trade at the Border between Jilin and Chosŏn Whenever Necessary" (Ch., Jilin Chaoxian shangmin suishi maoyi zhangcheng). This treaty was a short version of the one governing trade between Mukden and Chosŏn and laid down the format of bilateral official correspondence in accordance with Zongfan hierarchy in the same way.

By the end of 1883, then, China and Chosŏn had signed three treaties, or regulations, that were firmly rooted in the Zongfan discourse. The sophisticated norms used in these texts continued to serve as a way of institutionalizing the hierarchical relationship, centering the Middle Kingdom, and articulating the parties' identities in the Chinese world, just as the Zongfan discourse had done in the 1630s, 1760s, and 1860s. Simultaneously, however, the new rules made adjustments to the traditional mechanism by introducing a new political and commercial network into the borderland between the two countries in Manchuria. This change extended China's modern diplomacy, which had been practiced primarily in inner China's coastal areas, into Manchuria, along with the considerable influence of its human agents such as Li Hongzhang. The three treaties therefore laid the legal foundation for state-to-state contacts between the two countries in the following, and final, decade of their longstanding Zongfan relationship. The border areas of Manchuria became a test field where the two countries negotiated the reach of their respective sovereignties between tradition and modernity, as discussed in chapter 6.

Joining Chosŏn's Foreign Network: The Chinese Commissioners and the Chinese Settlements

Struggling for Authority: The Chinese Commissioner of Trade in Chosŏn

After the mutiny of 1882, Chosŏn asked China to send specialists on diplomacy and trade to assist it in establishing a system of maritime customs. The request was made by the king, endorsed by China's court, and executed by both countries within the Zongfan framework. Consequently, Chosŏn's maritime customs system became a sub-branch of China's imperial customs, and its annual reports were affiliated with those of imperial customs until 1895. In November 1882 Li Hongzhang appointed Ma Jianchang (1840–1939), Ma Jianzhong's brother, and Paul Georg von Möllendorff (1847–1901), a German national who worked as an assistant in the Chinese Maritime Customs office in Beijing, as foreign advisers to the king.[68] Ma and Möllendorff took up their posts in early 1883, followed by the first group of representatives from Western treaty nations and China.

The first US envoy extraordinary and minister plenipotentiary, Lucius H. Foote (1826–1913), and the first Chinese commissioner of trade, Chen Shutang, were the two most important figures among the diplomats now arriving in Chosŏn, and they took diametrically different approaches to defining Chosŏn's status. Before he departed for Chosŏn in March 1883, Foote received instructions from Secretary of State Frederick Frelinghuysen (1817–85), emphasizing that the American treaty negotiations with Chosŏn "were conducted as between two independent and sovereign nations. . . . As far as we are concerned Corea is an independent sovereign power, with all the attendant rights, privileges, duties and responsibilities: in her relations to China we have no desire to interfere unless action should be taken prejudicial to the rights of the United States." The instructions reminded Foote that "for all purposes of intercourse between the United States and Corea the King is a sovereign, and that with sovereign states only do the United States treat. Further the representatives of the United States in China will treat the Corean representatives there as in the position assigned them by the Chinese government."[69] Other Western countries imitated this pragmatic policy.

Chen Shutang's appointment and authority derived from the 1882 Sino-Korean Regulations. Article 1 of the treaty endowed the Beiyang superintendent with the power to appoint commissioners of trade (Ch., *shangwu weiyuan*) to reside at Chosŏn's treaty ports and exercise jurisdiction over Chinese merchants, while Chosŏn would send similar commissioners of trade to Tianjin and other Chinese treaty ports for the sake of its own merchants. Chen was a Han Chinese official and had served as consul-general in San Francisco from January 1880 to April 1882. He arrived in Hansŏng in October 1883 and opened his office with ten thousand taels of silver that he had received from Shanghai Maritime Customs. His expenditures would be covered by Beijing's budget for overseas missions. As a second-rank *taotai*, Chen held the official title "commissioner of commercial affairs in Chosŏn" (Ch., *Zongban Chaoxian shangwu weiyuan*).[70] He was not an envoy of the imperial court, but his position carried imperial author-ity. As Beijing clarified to Chosŏn, Chen was "slightly different" from China's representatives to other countries, but the "rationale [for his dispatch] is gener-ally the same." Invoking again the notion that "Chosŏn is a subordinate coun-try of China," Beijing concluded that Chen should be the "center of the guests" and instructed Chosŏn's foreign office to give him favorable treatment whenever there was a banquet for foreign ministers.[71]

Chen himself was also a believer in China's superiority. He posted a notifica-tion on the wall of Hansŏng's southern gate, stating that "Chosŏn is a *shuguo* of China" and calling on all merchants intending to trade in Chosŏn to follow the established rituals and to report to him in case of any disputes with others in the country. The text sought to "highlight the friendship with the *shuguo* that uses the same language" (Ch., *zhao shuguo tongwen zhi yi*) and to "cherish the affec-tion within a family that respects a common patriarch" (Ch., *zhong yijia gongzhu zhi qing*).[72] Chen's stridency antagonized the American minister and Korean offi-cials, but he refused to change his tone. As in the case of Ma Jianzhong, who had studied in France, Chen's diplomatic experience in the United States seemed to have no effect on his line of reasoning in Chosŏn.

In practice, Chen acted as a Chinese consul and planned to build his official residence in the style of a "Chinese consulate" (Ch., *Zhongguo gongguan*).[73] Yet he was not a consul, and his official title did not put him in charge of foreign affairs. Instead of contacting Chen, then, the Japanese and Western ministers brought diplomatic matters concerning China directly to Chosŏn's Foreign Office, the T'ongni amun (K., T'ongni kyosŏp t'ongsang samu amun). Chosŏn also expressed a desire for independence from Chinese involvement by sending a special mission to the United States in the fall of 1883.[74] Chen felt so marginalized that in September 1884 he complained to Li Hongzhang that his awkward position was causing him to be snubbed by the Japanese and British ministers. Chen tried to justify his authority by invoking the 1882 Sino-Korean Regulations, but other ministers responded that the treaty, as its preamble stated, was effective only between China and Korea. After consulting with Li and Foote, Chen updated his title to "general commissioner of foreign and commercial affairs at Chosŏn's ports" (Ch., *Zongban Chaoxian gekou jiaoshe tongshang shiwu*) in November 1884.

According to Chen, this title perfectly fit the established "system," in accordance with which he, as an official of the "upper country," could discuss certain affairs of China's *shuguo* with his Japanese and Western counterparts. Unsurprisingly, by failing to draw a clear line between Chinese and Korean affairs at the ports, the new title aroused deep concern among Western ministers, including the first British minister to Chosŏn, Harry Parkes, who had been wondering about Chosŏn's international position for years. The Zongli Yamen clarified to Parkes that "Chosŏn is a *shuguo* of China, which means that the commissioner should not be understood as a minister to the country, but since Chen has been appointed by the emperor to be in charge of diplomatic affairs and he holds a second-rank *taotai*, his position is equal to that of the consuls-general of other countries."[75] This description thus strategically defined Chen as a consul-general.

Questionable Imperialism: Chinese Settlements in Chosŏn

Chen arrived in Hansŏng without a clear mission from Beijing or Tianjin, so he alone had to decide what to do. Beijing's original plan had been to place Chen in charge of Chinese business in Inch'ŏn too, but Chen realized that it was impossible for him to perform duties in both Hansŏng and Inch'ŏn. A series of commercial and diplomatic events involving Chinese merchants and citizens in Inch'ŏn and other treaty ports reached Chen's desk right after he opened his office, so he sent an assistant, Li Nairong, to Inch'ŏn as the first Chinese representative at that port. Due to his lack of an official status, Li Nairong found himself in the same uncomfortable situation as Chen had. Chen called Li a consul (Ch., *lingshi*) instead of a commissioner (Ch., *lishi*) in front of the Japanese consul and the commissioner of Inch'ŏn maritime customs, although Li was not, strictly speaking, a consul. Since the Chinese terms for "commissioner" and "consul" have very similar pronunciations, Chen may have planned to use the phonological likeness to tacitly confer on Li Nairong a clear status commensurate with international practice. Li Nairong later told Chen that it would be better to clarify his official rank as commissioner rather than consul to the Korean side.[76]

In February 1884 Chen informed Min Yŏng-muk (1826–84), Queen Min's nephew and the minister of Chosŏn's Foreign Office, that Li and other Chinese officials residing in Korean treaty ports held the title of "commissioner of Chinese merchants' affairs" (Ch., *huashang shiwu guan*). These commissioners, said Chen, were equal to Chosŏn officials and foreign consuls and were in charge of all affairs concerning Chinese merchants in Chosŏn.[77] Li Nairong was thus transformed from Chen's private assistant to a diplomatic representative of the Chinese state. As Kirk W. Larsen points out, "Chen was successful . . . in establishing and promoting an official Qing diplomatic and commercial presence in Korea."[78]

Li Nairong found his understaffed office in Inch'ŏn unable to handle the increase in Chinese business and Sino-Japanese conflicts at the port. Japan had opened more than one hundred stores in the city since 1876, and Japanese residents outnumbered the Koreans, Chinese, and Westerners. But now growing numbers of Chinese merchants, in particular from Shandong, Zhejiang, and Guangdong Provinces, were coming to seek their fortunes in the city, and these businessmen organized companies such as Tongshuntai hao (the Company of Union, Prosperity, and Peace) to challenge Japan's monopoly in local trade.[79] Within a single month, from October to November 1883, the number of Chinese stores in Inch'ŏn increased from two to seven and that of Chinese merchants from about ten to more than sixty. According to Chinese statistics, from 1883 to 1884 the number of Chinese in Inch'ŏn rose from 63 to 235 and that of Chinese in Hansŏng from 26 to 352.[80] Some Chinese merchants in Inch'ŏn had started to extend their businesses to Hansŏng. Chen Shutang and Li Nairong were thus facing a new Chinese presence in Chosŏn. In addition, hundreds of Chinese sailors working on Chinese and Japanese cargo ships frequently passed through Inch'ŏn, giving a major boost to local bars and brothels. These sailors were troublemakers not only in Korean and Japanese eyes but also from the perspective of the Chinese, because Chinese officials at the port did not have a full roster of these Chinese citizens and therefore did not know whom to prosecute if any of them were involved in local conflicts. In an attempt to control the sailors, Li followed international conventions by requesting that all Chinese citizens visiting Inch'ŏn, including civilians and soldiers, register with his office.[81]

Given the growing number of Chinese merchants in Inch'ŏn and the expansion of their businesses, Chen Shutang felt it was necessary to set up a Chinese settlement for trade purposes. He found legal support in article 4 of the 1882 Sino-Korean Regulations, which stated that "the merchants of either country who may proceed to the open ports of the other country for trade will be allowed to rent land or houses and erect buildings." In December 1883 Chen

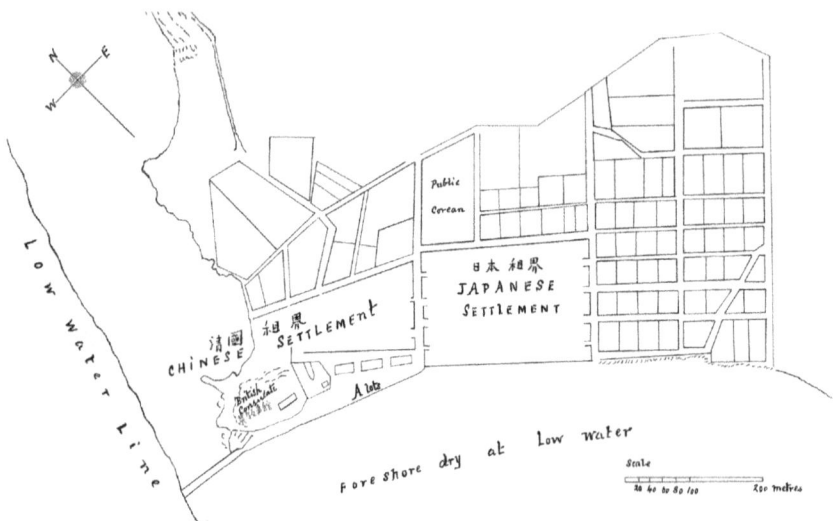

MAP 5.1. The Chinese settlement in Inch'ŏn in the early 1890s. 1 meter = 39.37 inches. *Plan of Settlements in Chemulpo* [Inch'ŏn], handwritten map, preserved at the Kyujanggak Institute for Korean Studies at Seoul National University. Copyright Kyujanggak Institute for Korean Studies.

and Möllendorff, the assistant minister of Chosŏn's Foreign Office, conducted a field investigation in Inch'ŏn and decided to secure a foundation for a Chinese settlement. Many parts of the area lay on hillsides or in marshland, so the project required land reclamation (see map 5.1). Li Nairong and the commissioner of Inch'ŏn maritime customs made a map of the Chinese settlement, and Li asked local Chinese merchants to provide financial support for the land reclamation project.[82]

Chen found the name of the settlement a challenge. In his notes to the Korean side, Chen—unlike his Chinese or Korean colleagues—avoided the term "settlement" (Ch., *zujie*), instead calling it "lands and boundary" (Ch., *dijie*, which generally means "land"). In a letter to Li Nairong in December 1883, Chen said he had been considering whether the settlement should be called "Lands of the Great Qing" (Ch., *Da Qing dijie*) or "Lands of the Chinese merchants" (Ch., *Huashang dijie*). Confessing that he thought the former was "not perfect," Chen decided on the latter, as it would not take advantage of Chosŏn and would maintain the "face of the upper country."[83] Chen's weighing of semantic options, like his maneuverings around the term "commissioner," betrayed the problems of the outer dual network between China and Chosŏn—that is, the overlapping operation of the Zongfan framework and the treaty system in the two countries' foreign relations.

Chosŏn, however, did not endorse Chen's plan to distinguish the Sino-Korean relationship in this particular case. When Min Yŏng-muk heard Chen's argument that the regulations governing the Chinese merchants' settlement should be different from those used for other countries in accordance with the "system," Min retorted that there was no difference between the two.[84] On April 2, 1884, Min and Chen signed the "Regulations for the Chinese Merchants Settlement in Inch'ŏn" (Ch., Renchuan kou huashang dijie zhangcheng), which was based on the draft Chen had presented to Min in February. The text was written only in Chinese and officially called the settlement "Lands of the Chinese Merchants," as Chen had proposed, but it omitted Chen's preamble, which imitated the preamble to the 1882 Sino-Korean Regulations by emphasizing that Sino-Korean trade was different from that between Chosŏn and other countries and that the regulations would apply only to the former.[85] Without the preamble, the two countries' state-to-state relations took center stage.

While Chen was opening the Chinese settlement in Inch'ŏn, an event occurred in Pusan that further legitimized his agenda of expanding this model to other treaty ports. In early November 1883 a Chinese grocery store in Kōbe, Japan, called Dexing hao (Store of Merit and Prosperity) had sent two agents to Pusan to open a branch in the Japanese settlement there, but the branch was suddenly shut down by the Japanese consul. As soon as he returned to Hansŏng, Chen raised the case with Min Yŏng-muk. Min explained that he would prefer to "select a settlement [K., *chogye*] for the Chinese merchants where they can quickly open their stores," rather than negotiate with the Japanese to allow the Chinese merchants to do business in the Japanese settlement in Pusan. Chen applauded this proposal and volunteered to visit Pusan together with a Korean official for a joint field investigation. Min again appointed Möllendorff to accompany Chen.[86] In the meantime, the Chinese minister to Japan, Li Shuchang, suggested to the Zongli Yamen that Beijing should "instruct Chosŏn's Foreign Office to establish Chinese settlements in Pusan and other ports."[87] Li's proposal fit Chen's agenda perfectly. As a result, China opened settlements in Pusan and Wŏnsan.

Observing that China became active in Chosŏn after a series of crises beginning in 1882, scholars have generally interpreted the phenomenon as a fundamental change in China's foreign policy toward Chosŏn and have described China as practicing imperialism under the cloak of suzerainty.[88] Two issues concerning the sovereignty of Chosŏn are worth discussing here: Chinese and Korean perceptions of the Chinese settlements and the extraterritoriality that Chinese citizens enjoyed in their settlements.

The negotiations between Chen and Min suggest that neither side perceived the settlements as a symbol of imperialist expansion that would damage Chosŏn's sovereignty or help China gain geopolitical hegemony on the peninsula. Min's proposal to open another Chinese settlement in Pusan in order to avoid cases like that of Dexing hao shows that he considered such settlements only pieces of rented land for whose use the Chinese, the Japanese, and other foreigners had to pay every year.[89] The term "sovereignty" never entered Min's and Chen's correspondence, and the term "settlement" carried a meaning that was very different from that which it would later convey in the strongly nationalist historical context of the twentieth century. The issue of establishing police forces in the Chinese settlement in Inch'ŏn, which involved Chinese, Korean, and British citizens, is another case that demonstrates the difference between China's understanding of settlement and that of scholars in an international law context.[90]

Furthermore, it is important to note that Chosŏn had the legal option of opening its own settlements at China's ports in accordance with article 4 of the 1882 Sino-Korean Regulations. Once the regulations went into effect, many Korean merchants traveled to Chinese ports, some even going as far as Gansu, Shaanxi, and Sichuan, to sell ginseng. In 1885 Chosŏn dispatched a commercial commissioner (K., *sangmu wiwŏn*) to Tianjin as a counterpart of Chen Shutang. Had the Korean merchants formed a strong and sizeable community in Tianjin, Shanghai, or other ports, as the Chinese did in Inch'ŏn and Pusan, Chosŏn could have established settlements at those Chinese ports through negotiations with Beijing. It was only Chosŏn's limited overseas commercial activity that made this scenario impracticable.

In terms of extraterritoriality, it is true that Chinese citizens held this right within Chinese settlements in Chosŏn, whereas Chosŏn merchants at Chinese treaty ports, according to article 2 of the 1882 Sino-Korean Regulations, were under local Chinese jurisdiction, a difference that highlighted the unequal nature of their terms. However, in addition to the connection between article 2 of the Sino-Korean Regulations and the extraterritoriality granted to American citizens in the Korean-American treaty discussed earlier in this chapter, we should keep in mind that Koreans who conducted illegal trade in Qing China outside of the treaty ports always enjoyed extraterritoriality. The case of Korean merchants illegally visiting Gansu and Sichuan Provinces illustrates this point.

After China opened its treaty ports to Koreans as required by the Sino-Korean Regulations, the number of Koreans traveling to Gansu and Sichuan to sell ginseng without passports issued by the Korean commissioners and local Chinese officials increased sharply. In June 1883 the officials of Langzhong County in Sichuan sent three such unauthorized Korean ginseng merchants to Nanbu County, from where they were sent further to Chengdu, the provincial capital.[91] At almost the same time, Gansu also sent a Korean merchant, Mun So-wun, who had sold ginseng illegally in the province, to the Ministry of Rites in Beijing; the ministry transferred him to Tianjin, from where he could board a ship for Chosŏn. The officials in Sichuan did not detain these "people of the *fan*" (Ch., *fanfu renmin*) who had traveled thousands of miles to make a profit, and they preferred to "follow the Western example" (Ch., *zhao Taixi yili*) by sending them to Beijing. Since article 4 of the 1882 Sino-Korean Regulations regarding trade licenses and passports did not address this scenario, the Ministry of Rites, the Zongli Yamen, and the Beiyang superintendent eventually instructed the local officials to send Korean violators to the Korean commercial commissioners at Chinese treaty ports, from where they would be deported to Chosŏn for punishment.

In these cases, the Chinese side regarded the Korean violators as guilty of a crime punishable by the laws of their own country, and therefore the Korean side had to take the necessary steps for extradition based on article 2 of the regulations.[92] These Korean citizens, or "criminals," were thus exempt from Chinese jurisdiction, which in the Zongfan context was seen as a manifestation of China's favor to the small country. Beijing particularly instructed local officials to treat the Korean violators well as a way of cherishing the subordinate country. For its part, Chosŏn also used Zongfan terminology to describe China's clemency as a demonstration of China's "extreme solicitude" to the "small country."[93] In their bilateral communications about such cases, no mention was made of Chosŏn's or China's sovereignty or international law. If extraterritoriality were to imply imperialism, one would have to conclude that the Qing and Chosŏn practiced imperialism on each other.

6

LOSING CHOSŎN

The Rise of a Modern Chinese State,
1885–1911

Since the 1860s, China had struggled to provide Western states with an unequivo-
cal definition of Chosŏn's status. Its difficulties were rooted in the institutional
discrepancies between the Zongfan mechanism and international law. The tacit
understanding among these states was that China's authority over Chosŏn was
valid and real. Yet in the wake of Japan's challenges in the 1880s and early 1890s,
at a time when the world was entering the age of empires as a consequence of
colonial powers' quest for territorial acquisition, China took steps to modify its
routine contacts with Chosŏn in an effort to save the fundamentals of the Zongfan
order, which were arousing concern among other empires present in the region.[1]
By the end of the 1880s, China found itself surrounded by Japanese and European
colonial forces. Japan, Britain, and France had colonized or annexed China's outer
fan in East and Southeast Asia, in particular Ryukyu, Burma, and Vietnam, while
Russia was encroaching on China's territory in Central Asia, forcing China to provincialize Xinjiang in 1884. As a result, the frontiers of the politico-cultural Chinese empire that had encompassed China's outer *fan* began to disappear, replaced
by clear national borders between the Chinese state and its former outer *fan*.

The threat posed to China by the presence of rival powers in Chosŏn was
not less than that which it faced at its other borders. China had two primary
options in terms of its policy toward the outer *fan*. It could either provincialize
Chosŏn by incorporating the country into its territory in the form of prefectures
and counties, or it could supervise and protect it by harnessing China's patriarchal authority. Both approaches won support from China's leading scholars

and officials. Beijing finally adopted an in-between policy: assisting Chosŏn with managing its diplomatic and commercial affairs and placing an imperial resident in Hansŏng. From the perspective of Western diplomats in East Asia, however, China was moving toward annexing Chosŏn under the guise of conventional Zongfan practices. This chapter shows that although China believed it was fulfilling its commitment to protect its *shuguo*, its policy turned out to cause increased tensions between Beijing and Hansŏng because of the rise of the Korean state in the international community and the impact of Korean nationalism within Chosŏn. After the termination of the Zongfan arrangement in 1895, both Qing China and Chosŏn Korea entered a new era as sovereign states. By withdrawing from its periphery in Chosŏn to its core in the Qing, the Chinese empire developed into a modern state and embarked on its own road to modernity.

Invoking the Zongfan Conventions: His Imperial Chinese Majesty's Resident in Chosŏn

Maintaining Zongfanism from Within: Yuan Shikai in Chosŏn and the Ritual Conundrum

As the imperial commissioner of commercial affairs in Chosŏn, Chen Shutang successfully augmented his power in the fall of 1884, as described in the previous chapter, but he barely had time to exercise his new authority before an attempted coup took place in Hansŏng. On December 4, 1884, a group of pro-Japanese members of the Kaehwadang (Enlightenment Party) occupied the palace, killed several pro-Chinese officials, and claimed they were terminating the country's hierarchical relations with China. These fervent nationalists, among them Hong Yŏng-sik (1855–84), Kim Ok-kyun (1851–94), and Pak Yŏng-hyo (1861–1939), won the strong support of the Japanese minister Takezoe Shinichirō (1842–1917), an assistant to Mori Arinori in the 1876 Sino-Japanese debate over Chosŏn's status.

The coup, known as *Kapsin jŏngbyŏn* (the coup of the year of Kapsin), was a result of increasing conflict between China, Japan, and Western states, along with Korean domestic political struggles and strong Korean nationalism cultivated primarily by Japan. The coup's leaders orchestrated the attack to coincide with China's dispatch of more troops to South China to fight the French in Vietnam. The dramatic and bloody nationalist revolution lasted only three days. Chinese troops led by Gen. Wu Zhaoyou successfully placed the king and members of the royal family under their protection and totally defeated the Kaehwadang and the Japanese forces in Hansŏng.[2]

Because there had been Chinese and Korean attacks on the Japanese legation and on Japanese citizens, and because the Korean court was in chaos, it was left to the Chinese and the Japanese to resolve the problems caused by the coup. The resulting Sino-Japanese talks again focused on Chosŏn's international status.[3] Tokyo sent Inoue Kaoru as the plenipotentiary to Hansŏng to conduct talks with the Chinese envoys Wu Dacheng and Xuchang. But Wu was not a plenipotentiary, so the negotiations were transferred to Tianjin and held between Li Hongzhang and Itō Hirobumi (1841–1909). The two sides signed a convention on April 18, 1885. Each agreed to pull its troops out of the peninsula within four months, to allow the king to hire officers from countries beyond China and Japan to train the Korean forces, and to notify the other of any decision to send troops to Chosŏn in the event of a serious disturbance.[4] Japan thus obtained the legal right to send troops to Chosŏn, which paved the way for its military involvement in the Korean rebellion in 1894.

The coup considerably alarmed China. Ma Jianchang, the Chinese adviser to the king, suggested to Li Hongzhang that "China should either allow Chosŏn to be independent from China and free from the current relationship or positively engage in its affairs by sending an able imperial resident to the country with Chinese forces so the resident can supervise certain affairs."[5] Li responded that China should focus on overcoming its own crises first, but he agreed that China should strengthen the authority of its representative in Chosŏn in order to check encroachment by Japan and other powers. The result was a considerable expansion in the powers enjoyed by Chen's successor, Yuan Shikai.

In November 1885, on Li's recommendation, Beijing appointed Yuan the "imperial resident in Chosŏn in charge of diplomatic and commercial intercourse" (Ch., *Qinming zhuzha Chaoxian zongli jiaoshe tongshang shiyi*) and bestowed on him a third-level rank with the title of backup candidate for a *taotai*. According to Li, this new title endowed Yuan with the right to "engage in diplomatic affairs in one way or another," which perfectly resolved the legal quagmire concerning the Chinese representative's status. Yuan promised both Li and Beijing that he would do his best to protect the "eastern fence that has been a *fan* of China for generations."[6] Over the following decade, Yuan put his words into practice along Zongfan lines, stirring up serious conflicts among diplomats in Chosŏn in the process.

The foreign diplomats in Hansŏng needed to establish whether Yuan's appointment marked the beginning of a Chinese absorption of the country, a colonial policy like those pursued by Britain, France, Italy, and Germany in Africa. The English translation of Yuan's title became a crucial issue in this regard. George C. Foulk (1856–93), the American chargé d'affaires ad interim, offered the translation "charge of diplomatic and commercial intercourse," but it was rejected by an unidentified young American-educated assistant of Yuan (possibly Tang Shaoyi, 1862–1938, a graduate of Columbia University who reached the country along with Ma Jianchang and Paul Georg von Möllendorff in 1883). The assistant then put forward the translation "his imperial Chinese majesty's resident, Seoul," perhaps inspired by the American minister's official title "minister resident and consul general."[7] When talks between Foulk, the British consul Edward C. Baber (1843–90), and the Japanese chargé d'affaires Takahira Kogorō (1854–1926) yielded no unanimous agreement on a translation, Yuan decided to use his assistant's suggestion, abbreviated as "H.I.C.M. Resident."[8] Although the resident's legitimacy and power derived from China's imperial might, the resident himself was not part of the Manchu court. Nor was the Beiyang superintendent. Figure 6.1 illustrates the various channels of communication between China and Korea.

Yuan may not have realized that the title "resident" possessed strong connotations of an imperialist regime's indirect rule over a region that would subsequently become a protectorate or colony of the empire. The British Empire, for instance, had accomplished its expansion into India by appointing a single British "resident" or "political agent" to each princely state, the resident virtually

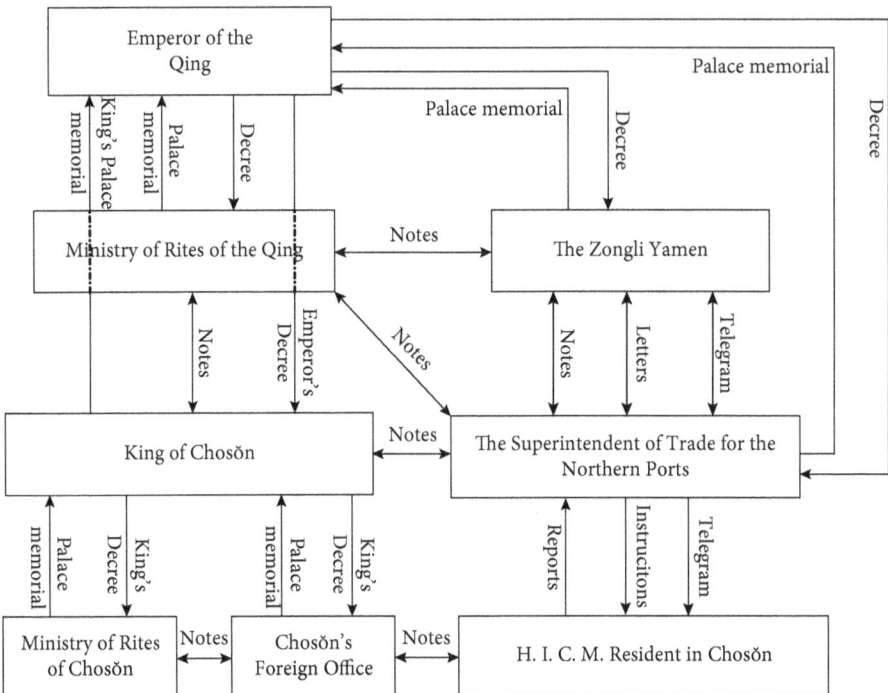

FIGURE 6.1. Channels of official Sino-Korean communications after 1883

controlling the state by offering advice to the local prince or chief. This type of indirect rule dated back to 1764 and was practiced until Queen Victoria's proclamation of 1858.[9] In the early 1880s, the title "resident" was still sensitive because of its connection to a colonial power's territorial expansion. For example, in the spring of 1881, after France signed the Treaty of Bardo with the Tunisian bey Muhammad al-Sadiq (1813–82), the French consul general in Tunisia assumed the new title "resident minister," or officially "the French resident and delegate [to the bey] for external affairs," which triggered the country's conversion into a French protectorate.[10] In 1883 the French also began to set up a resident at Huế in Vietnam; this resident was the representative of the French protectorate and thus was more powerful than the Vietnamese king. In this context, when Yuan claimed to be a resident of the Chinese empire in Chosŏn, he certainly puzzled his Western counterparts, who had tacitly defined him as China's "consul-general" or "consul-general with diplomatic functions," ignoring any potential roles based on Chinese imperial authority.[11]

Yuan was not a minister, but his status as an imperial resident endowed him with more power than a minister would have held. Unlike a British resident in India or a French resident in Tunisia, Yuan in Chosŏn could exploit the term "imperial" in his title, as it carried the authority of the Chinese emperor, to whom the Chosŏn sovereign was subordinate in Zongfan terms. When Korean officials expressed concern over the breadth of Yuan's power in the country, Yuan clarified that his aim was simply to "justify the orthodox legitimacy of Chosŏn's status as China's subordinate country" (Ch., *zheng shubang mingfen*).[12]

Yuan's handling of his relations with the Korean court demonstrates the authority he claimed for himself. In September 1886, for example, he spent hours in a face-to-face meeting with the king, lecturing him on how to deal with the Port Hamilton incident. The port in southern Chosŏn had been occupied by Britain in 1885 amid British-Russian rivalry, triggering an intense dispute between Britain, Russia, Chosŏn, China, and Japan. Following China's active intervention, the British fleet withdrew in 1887 on the agreement that no foreign power would occupy any part of Chosŏn's territory in the future.[13] Yuan's observation of Korean court politics persuaded him that the king was weak, and Yuan even secretly proposed to Li Hongzhang that China replace the king with an able man from the Korean royal family.[14] Not only did the king disapprove of Yuan's behavior, but Yuan's fellow diplomats also regarded his activities as violating diplomatic protocols and damaging Chosŏn's sovereignty, aggravating relations between Yuan and other diplomats in Hansŏng.

Illustrative of these tensions were the new rituals Yuan performed to the king. In a telegram soliciting Li Hongzhang's advice in 1886, Yuan mentioned that in past years, when Chinese officials had paid visits to the king, they had entered the palace gate in a sedan chair, bowed to the king three times with their hands folded in front (Ch., *sanyi*; *yi* means *zuoyi*, a ritual practiced between officials of equal rank), and then sat down at the king's side. In 1884, however, the Chinese envoys Wu Dacheng and Xuchang, Gen. Ding Ruchang, and Taotai Ma Jianzhong had sat down opposite the king, following guest-host rituals. Yuan also noted that the ministers of other countries had to dismount their sedan chairs outside the palace gate and pay visits to the king according to the etiquette for officials outside the capital. Quoting ritual codes applicable to relations between China and Chosŏn, Li advised Yuan that it would be "truly courteous" for Yuan to follow the rituals for Chinese provincial-level officials visiting first-degree princes. This category of ritual performance dictated that Yuan would dismount his sedan chair at the gate of the palace hall, bow to the king three times with his hands folded in front, and then sit down by the king's side. At grand ceremonies such as assemblies, Yuan would likewise bow three times with his hands folded in front, instead of performing a higher-level ritual of three bows (Ch., *san jugong*), in order to show that China was "neither haughty nor humble" and to harmonize his conduct with that of other ministers.[15] The new rituals eased Yuan's integration into the Korean court, but they created friction with other diplomats in the city.[16]

China's Two Options: Supervision versus Provincialization

In the turbulent 1880s, when Beijing dramatically changed its border policy in the northwest by converting Xinjiang into a province, the northeastern frontier, too, posed a major challenge to the Qing. Having lost Burma to Britain, Ryukyu to Japan, and Vietnam to France within three decades, China stood at a historical crossroads with regard to its future administration of Chosŏn, as it had to decide how best to avoid also losing its most exemplary outer *fan*: should it take a step back and adopt an indirect approach of sending high-ranking officials to supervise and protect Chosŏn, or would it be better to incorporate Chosŏn into Chinese territory as prefectures and counties of China? Both options had precedents in the Han and the Yuan Dynasties and so could be justified. Viewed from a modern perspective, however, both represented a colonial approach not unlike Japan's later annexation of Korea in 1910. It was on precisely this point that China fell into a dilemma that it was unable to overcome.

The Qing regarded Chosŏn as a loyal subordinate in its rhetoric, but as seen in the preceding chapters it never tried to incorporate Chosŏn into Chinese territory. The Chinese appraisal of Chosŏn as being "like prefectures and counties" merely acknowledged Korea's subordination to China's cultural superiority; it didn't express a practical political approach to annexing the country. For centuries, China, Chosŏn, and China's other outer *fan* shared the worldview of all-under-Heaven, according to which all their lands were subject to the authority of the Son of Heaven. There was also a rule, drawn up by the first emperor of the Ming in the fourteenth century, that China would not annex the fifteen outer *fan* whose contacts with China were supervised by the Ministry of Rites. The first of these outer *fan* was Korea.[17] This principle came under challenge in the 1880s, when the options of supervision and protection, on the one hand, and outright provincialization, on the other, were put forward by some Chinese officials and scholars.

In November 1880 the Chinese minister to Japan, He Ruzhang, argued that it would be the best policy for China to send an imperial commissioner to Chosŏn to manage the country's domestic and foreign affairs, as China had done in Mongolia and Tibet. However, realizing that such a move was almost impossible at the time, He Ruzhang suggested that Chosŏn sign treaties with other countries under China's supervision in order to pursue a balance of power. In August 1882, in the wake of Chosŏn's mutiny and Japan's provocative response, another Chinese minister to Japan, Li Shuchang, suggested that China "abolish the king and convert the country into prefectures and counties of China," imitating the relationship between Britain and India, in order to resolve all thorny issues related to Chosŏn once and for all. Li Shuchang was fully aware that such an action would undermine China's moral standards, but he nonetheless regarded it as the best available policy for China.[18] This was probably the first time that Chinese officials explicitly argued that China should provincialize Chosŏn during this period, but the proposal was confidential and strictly confined to a small group of policymakers.

In 1882 Zhang Jian (1853–1926), an assistant to Gen. Wu Changqing in Hansŏng, called for reforms in Chosŏn in his treatise "Six Strategies for Managing the Consequences of Chosŏn's Mutiny" (Ch., *Chaoxian shanhou liuce*).[19] This treatise, which was widely disseminated in Beijing through informal channels, encouraged officials of the so-called Pure Stream group (Ch., Qingliu)—who had seized the moral high ground in political struggles—to pursue a solution to the Chosŏn problem. In October 1882 Zhang Peilun (1848–1903), a pillar of the Pure Stream, urged Beijing to dispatch a commercial commissioner to manage Chosŏn's foreign and domestic affairs. Li Hongzhang did not endorse this plan because he was fearful of a scenario in which China would be drawn into an even more difficult situation and could not efficiently manage the country, but he noted that if Beijing decided to accept Zhang's proposal, he would recommend He Ruzhang for the position of imperial commissioner.[20]

At the same time, Li Hongzhang received a note from the king inviting Chinese specialists on foreign affairs to serve as his assistants. Li believed that China could exploit this opportunity to steer a middle course between supervising and protecting Chosŏn, on the one hand, and provincializing the country, on the other. The invited specialists would be under the king's command, guaranteeing Chosŏn the right of *zizhu* and underlining Chosŏn's status as China's *shuguo*. As described in the previous chapter, the specialists, Ma Jianchang and Paul Georg von Möllendorff, arrived in Hansŏng in 1883, followed by the Chinese commercial commissioner Chen Shutang. It was against this background of China's increasingly active role in Chosŏn that Yuan Shikai was appointed as an imperial resident a year and a half later.

In the wake of the bloody coup of 1884, a growing number of Chinese officials supported strengthening China's position in Chosŏn. In late 1885 the Manchu official Shengyu (1850–1900), then president of the Directorate of Education, declared that among China's *fan* Chosŏn was more important than Ryukyu and Vietnam had been. He suggested that the court send a competent man to "protect and cherish the country" by leading a powerful contingent of troops, and that it issue a decree to oust Queen Min and her followers with the aim of "mollifying the Korean people's resentment and proclaiming China's power and virtues."[21]

In the summer of 1890, hearing rumors that Russia was planning to invade Chosŏn, Kang Youwei (1858–1927), a Cantonese scholar who at the time was preparing for the civil-service examination, drafted a treatise entitled "Strategies for Saving Chosŏn" (Ch., *Bao Chaoxian ce*) that proposed "middle, upper, and lower" strategies. According to his middle strategy, China would "incorporate Chosŏn into the Chinese inner land and manage its administration" (Ch., *shouwei neidi er zhi qizheng*). Kang argued that in 1882 China should have appointed officials and officers to manage Chosŏn's politics and that it should have taken control of Chosŏn's taxes, trained its soldiers, and converted Chosŏn into an integral part of China's inner territory. Kang's upper strategy was to make Chosŏn into an international protectorate. By contrast, the lower strategy was to maintain Chosŏn's "nominal title as China's *fan* and *shuguo*" inwardly and to allow it to "conduct foreign affairs freely under *zizhu*" outwardly, which amounted to "no policy per se."[22] Kang castigated China for its inability to solve the Korean problem in the international political arena. Eight years later, Kang served as a mentor to Emperor Guangxu when the latter launched dramatic reforms after China's humiliating defeat in its war with Japan, which broke out in Chosŏn.

From Huang Zunxian and He Ruzhang in 1880 to Li Shuchang and Zhang Peilun in 1882 and then to Ma Jianchang in 1884, Shengyu in 1885, and Kang Youwei in 1890, Beijing was barraged with proposals to either supervise and protect Chosŏn or provincialize it. The advocates of these proposals frequently traced the point of departure for their suggested policies back to the early Qing and even earlier dynasties. They pointed out that Qing China had to take responsibility for saving Chosŏn from crises, as Ming China had done in the 1590s. In this sense, they saw China's policy in Chosŏn in the 1880s as a resurgence of the intrinsic power exerted by the patriarch of the Zongfan family over its outer *fan*. For scholars who prefer to interpret China's policy through the lens of international politics, this statement seems clichéd, but one should bear in mind that political rules informed by the Westphalian system cannot easily be applied to the Qing's rationale for its foreign relations with its outer *fan* as embodied in Qing-Chosŏn relations. Otherwise, Western diplomats in Hansŏng, Beijing, and Tokyo would not have suffered such confusion for more than two decades, and the Western consultants hired by the Japanese Ministry of Foreign Affairs would not have had to resort to the Ottoman-Egyptian example for lack of a model for the Qing-Chosŏn relationship in European history.

Although China believed it had the theoretical authority to carry out an annexation of Chosŏn and could justify to itself the political legitimacy of such a move, the Manchu imperial court never put this option on its agenda; rather, it continued to adhere firmly to Zongfan principles in its contacts with Chosŏn. Whereas the Yuan and Ming Dynasties had officially discussed plans to provincialize Korea, no textual evidence suggests that the Qing court entertained any court-level discussion on this subject. The Zongli Yamen and other central institutions and high-ranking officials did forward proposals for provincialization to Empress Dowager Cixi and Emperor Guangxu from the early 1880s to the peak of the war in 1894 and 1895, but the central court always remained silent on these proposals. The pleas for provincialization thus did not change the imperial court's established perception of Chosŏn. This perception may explain why, even after Chosŏn obtained its independence in 1895, the Qing's imperial calendars continued to include the country in the list of China's inner provinces until as late as 1909, a year before Chosŏn was colonized by Japan. In this regard, Zong-fanism manifested itself in a fundamentally different way from colonialism.

This interpretation does not imply that international politics had no influence on China's policy and behavior. In fact, China's provincialization of Chosŏn could have led to a domino effect in China's borderland in Manchuria, Xinjiang, Tibet, and Yunnan, where China was contending with Japan, Russia, Britain, and France. Chosŏn was a politico-cultural frontier of the Chinese empire, but this frontier was invisible and existed only in an intellectual sense within the Chinese world. Nor could this frontier be defined by international law. On the borders of its territorial empire, China did embrace the policy of provincialization at that time. In 1884 Beijing accepted the proposals of Zuo Zongtang and Liu Jintang (1844–94) and converted Xinjiang into a province; this multiethnic region in Inner Asia remains part of the Chinese state's territory today. The same policy was applied to Taiwan in 1885, turning the island into another province. Although Taiwan was ceded to Japan in 1895 as a result of the Sino-Japanese War, the Qing's earlier provincialization of Taiwan provided the Chinese state in the twentieth century with legitimate and legal resources to claim sovereignty over the island.

Reading Zongfanism from the Outside: Western Diplomats' Perceptions of Chosŏn's Sovereignty and Independence

Chosŏn's sovereignty became a heated topic in the late 1880s when Chosŏn stepped onto the world stage. In order to meet various diplomatic challenges, Chosŏn established new institutions and developed a pattern of dual diplomacy in the 1880s, just as China had done in the 1860s. Within this dual pattern, the royal court maintained its Zongfan relations with China's imperial court, while the new institutions, predominantly the Foreign Office, presented Chosŏn as an independent state in its contacts with Western countries. The agencies of China's state diplomacy, in particular the Beiyang superintendent and the H.I.C.M. Resident, sought to use China's authority to influence Chosŏn's state diplomacy. In the eyes of Western ministers, including the Western advisers appointed by China to Chosŏn, China was impinging on Chosŏn's independent sovereignty through calculated schemes. China's image suffered, not only in the estimation of Japan and the Western states that had interests in the peninsula, but also in Chosŏn itself.

The Western advisers recommended by Li Hongzhang to the king of Chosŏn serve as good examples in this regard. As the first Western adviser to the king on maritime customs, Möllendorff also assumed the vice presidency of Chosŏn's newly founded Foreign Office. But as he became eager to develop Chosŏn's military forces to counterbalance the country's weakness, his activities progressively deviated from Li's wishes. In 1884 Möllendorff asked Li to send officers to train the Korean army. When this request yielded no response, he persuaded the king to negotiate a convention with Russia whereby Russian officers would train the army in exchange for the use of Wŏnsan, the ice-free port on the eastern coast of the country. Under pressure from Li, the king dismissed Möllendorff in November 1885. At the recommendation of China's inspector general, Robert Hart, Henry F. Merrill, an American national, replaced Möllendorff as chief commissioner of the Korean Maritime Customs, and Owen N. Denny (1838–1900), a former US consul in Tianjin, assumed the post of vice president of the Foreign Office and adviser to the king. Whereas Merrill rarely commented on Chosŏn's affairs, Denny was very enthusiastic about assisting Chosŏn in pursuing independence from China.

In January 1887 a veteran Chinese diplomat, Zeng Jize (known as Marquis Tseng, 1839–90), the eldest son of the distinguished late official Zeng Guofan (1811–72), published an English-language article entitled "China: The Sleep and the Awakening" in the British journal *Asiatic Quarterly Review*. Making an ambitious argument that China would become "a great Asiatic Power" as awakened in the process of modernization, Zeng also commented on China's foreign policy toward its subordinate countries, noting that China "has decided on exercising a more effective supervision on the acts of her vassal Princes, and of accepting a larger responsibility for them than heretofore." The marquis further claimed that "the Warden of the Marches is now abroad, looking to the security of China's outlying provinces—of Corea, Thibet, and Chinese Turkestan. Henceforth, any hostile movements against these countries, or any interference with their affairs, will be viewed at Peking as a declaration, on the part of the Power committing it, of a desire to discontinue its friendly relations with the Chinese Government."[23] The reality, however, unfolded in a way that differed dramatically from what the marquis envisioned. In this regard, Denny was more prescient. A lawyer by profession, Denny found his legal training useful in Chosŏn. In February 1888 he published a booklet entitled *China and Korea*, in which he asserted that China was destroying Korea—an independent state with independent sovereignty—"by absorbing the country."[24]

Denny's pamphlet was emotional and exposed his limited knowledge of Sino-Korean relations, but it was welcomed by his fellow Western diplomats who desperately hoped to grasp the nature of China's presence in Chosŏn. The first two American ministers in Chosŏn, Lucius H. Foote and George C. Foulk, were very enthusiastic about China's influences in the country, and the United States was deeply involved in the issue of Chosŏn's international status.[25] In the summer of 1887, Yuan, Li, Foulk, the American chargé d'affaires William W. Rockhill, and the new American minister Hugh A. Dinsmore (1850–1930) became embroiled in an intense dispute resulting from a widely circulated rumor that Foulk had encouraged the king to seek independence from China. Dinsmore complained that "China is slowly but surely tightening her grasp upon this government and its King," and he blamed Yuan for his "declaration that Korea is a vassal state and altogether incapable of self-government."[26]

The United States also became entangled in another fierce dispute between China and Korea in 1887, when the king decided to send Pak Chŏng-yang (1842–1905) as an envoy to the United States, followed by another envoy to Britain, Germany, Russia, Italy, and France.[27] China endorsed the king's plan but urged the king not to endow the envoys with the title of plenipotentiary, and reminded the monarch that all Korean envoys overseas had to obey three rules outlined by Li Hongzhang: first, a Korean envoy arriving in a new posting should first report to the Chinese consulate and be accompanied by the Chinese minister to the host country's ministry of foreign affairs; second, the Korean envoy should always sit behind the Chinese minister at meetings and banquets in the host country; and third, the Korean envoy should consult with the Chinese minister about major events before contacting the institutions of the host country. These three rules were aimed at maintaining the established "system of *shuguo*" by emphasizing the hierarchy between the Chinese minister and the Korean envoy in the host country as well as that between China and Korea in general.[28]

The king did not follow Beijing's instructions: in the letter of credence to the United States he called himself "I, the emperor" and appointed Pak "envoy plenipotentiary" (K., *chŏngwŏn taesin*), although in his memorial to the Guangxu emperor he called Pak a "minister's minister."[29] Accordingly, the American side treated Pak as minister plenipotentiary when he arrived in Washington in January 1888. Under the strong influence of his American secretary Horace N. Allen (1858–1932),[30] Pak continued to flout the three rules: he did not subordinate himself to the Chinese minister in Washington, Zhang Yinhuan (1837–1900), which led to an awkward and even hostile relationship between the two representatives. Some American news reports also stated that Korea dispatched its minister to the United States independently and did not need to obtain China's permission.[31] In order to reassert Chosŏn's position as China's *shuguo*, Zhang delivered to Pak a Chinese imperial calendar for 1888 that he had received from Shanghai.[32] Finally, under pressure from China, the king of Chosŏn recalled Pak, turning this brief episode showcasing Chosŏn's apparent sovereignty and international status into a highly unpleasant footnote in Sino-Korean relations.

It was at this time that Denny's pamphlet was circulating among Westerners in Korea and, soon, further afield. For China, the Korean situation was becoming increasingly complicated, and in June 1888 Li Hongzhang secretly sent Möllendorff back to Hansŏng to "checkmate Denny who is urging the King to assert independence."[33] Denny's take on the issue of Korea's independence and its relationship to China quickly reached the United States. On August 31, 1888, with Pak still in Washington, Senator John H. Mitchell (1835–1905) of Oregon, Denny's home state, called on the Senate, and particularly the Committee on Foreign Relations, to pay attention to the Sino-Korean relationship. Mitchell, holding in his hand a copy of Denny's "very able and highly interesting brief," stated that "for some time past the Imperial Government of China has, through its chief officers and representatives, and especially and particularly its representative at the city of Seoul, been contemplating the subjugation and entire absorption of Corea." He emphasized that Korea's relationship with China was "that of a mere *tributary* state, in which none of the rights of *sovereignty* or *independence* are eliminated or destroyed, and not that of a *dependent* or *vassal* government without any of the prerogatives of sovereignty attaching."[34]

All of these episodes contributed to the deterioration of the Sino-Korean relationship by the end of the 1880s. Many a Western diplomat, sympathetic toward the king and his government, believed that China was controlling Chosŏn in dramatic or even colonialist ways, while Chosŏn was desperately distancing itself from the Sinocentric system by adopting Western political and diplomatic terms. As Dinsmore observed in the summer of 1887, "The Koreans do not impress me as having any affection or strong attachment for the Chinese. On the contrary there is among the common people a well-defined dislike for them, but they fear them and it is under the influence of this fear that they are gradually yielding to Chinese supremacy."[35] In this context, Chosŏn used its state-to-state contacts with China and other countries to propel itself out of China's orbit.

Perplexing issues such as Yuan Shikai's status as resident and Pak's mission to the United States led Western scholar-diplomats to study the history of Sino-Korean relations with the aim of exploring the origin of China's authority over Chosŏn. During a journey in the capital district of Chosŏn in 1884, George Foulk saw the Samjŏndo stele that had been erected in 1639, which he described as "a great marble tablet fully twelve feet high and a foot thick, mounted upon the back of a gigantic granite turtle." He added, "Historically, this monument presents much interest, and a thorough examination may develop information on the status of Corea with regard to China of more directly practical use."[36] Indeed, Rockhill soon tried to interpret Sino-Korean relations by using the inscriptions of the Samjŏndo stele and other Chinese materials; his efforts were published as a long article in 1889 under the title "Korea in Its Relations with China." In the article, Rockhill attempted to answer the "puzzle for Western nations" of whether Korea was "an integral part of the Chinese empire" or "a sovereign state enjoying absolute international rights."[37]

Rockhill noted that the British government considered the Burmese "tribute" to China within the Sino-Burmese framework to be of a "purely ceremonial nature," so in the Sino-British convention of 1886 the British side guaranteed the continuance of the Burmese decennial tribute mission to Beijing. The Sino-Korean relationship was much more complicated. After examining Sino-Korean relations from 1392 and reviewing Qing-Chosŏn contacts since the early seventeenth century, Rockhill determined that Chosŏn's conclusion of treaties with Japan and the United States "has not materially altered the nature of the relations existing for the last four centuries at least between China and its so-called vassal."[38] Rockhill's conclusion seriously challenged the popular perception among Western diplomats in East Asia that Chosŏn was independent from China. The puzzle, therefore, remained unsolved and in fact became even more vexing.

The Grand Performance of the Zongfan Order: China's Last Imperial Mission to Chosŏn

Rituals and Authority: Yuan's Efforts to Assert China's Superiority in Chosŏn

As its awareness of its own independent sovereignty (or the possibility thereof) deepened in the late 1880s, Chosŏn cautiously maintained its court-to-court contacts with China and conducted its own state diplomacy beyond China. Because of this dual diplomacy, whereas China wanted to preserve and highlight its superiority in Chosŏn, Hansŏng tried to compromise the hierarchical arrangement in practice. Along the way, in 1890, the two sides entered into intense negotiations over the Zongfan rituals.

On June 4, 1890, Korean Queen Dowager Cho died. A series of ritual practices between Hansŏng and Beijing had to be carried out. Aware that ritual matters were under the management of the Manchu court, Yuan responded to the Korean Foreign Office's announcement of the dowager's death with a short note expressing his condolences.[39] At a time when international intrigues and rivalries exerted such a strong influence on the peninsula, Sino-Korean court-to-court contacts through the exchange of emissaries seemed dwarfed by the two countries' state-to-state contacts over political and diplomatic issues. While the Korean court continued to send tributary missions to Beijing through the 1880s, Beijing did not dispatch envoys to Hansŏng for tributary affairs after Chosŏn opened its doors to the West in 1882. Although court diplomacy still played a key role in regulating and modifying the bilateral relationship, the decade-long absence of imperial envoys from Korean soil left Yuan Shikai in Hansŏng without any recent precedents to consult. The absence of such envoys also reinforced the impression of Western diplomats that China had little authority over Chosŏn. Yuan believed that the expression of China's condolences on the death of the dowager provided the perfect opportunity to counteract the Western perception of Sino-Korean relations.[40]

When the American minister Augustine Heard (1827–1905) invited Yuan to join a discussion with other ministers over an appropriate expression of their joint condolences to the Korean court, Yuan declined on the grounds that "China and Chosŏn have longtime established regulations on ritual exchanges that are different from other countries."[41] In a report to Li Hongzhang, in which he identified Chosŏn as "a friendly nation" (Ch., *youbang*) of other treaty nations, Yuan said that the other ministers would follow common diplomatic etiquette in expressing condolences to the Korean government on the occasion of a national funeral, but those countries would not send special representatives for this purpose. By contrast, Yuan argued, because Chosŏn was China's *shuguo* and always received China's special favors, when the country was in grand mourning, China should send an imperial mission in accordance with the established system (Ch., *tizhi*).[42] Yuan became the first Han Chinese official in Chosŏn's territory since 1637 to try to maintain China's superiority through appropriate rituals, including by proposing new ones.

On learning that other ministers would visit and bow to the king or visit the regent official and shake hands with him to show their sympathy, Yuan refused to follow their example. Instead he proposed a new ritual procedure endorsed by Li Hongzhang: after the first five days, during which the body of the dowager would lie in repose and the Korean people wore mourning clothes, Yuan would make an appointment with the Korean court to express his condolences based on "personal friendship" (Ch., *siqing*), which was considered equivalent to friendship among colleagues (Ch., *liaoyin jiaoqing*), rather than extending China's "national public condolences" (Ch., *guojia gongdiao*).[43] In early June, when other countries flew their legations' flags at half-mast for three days to express their condolences, Yuan and Li instructed Chinese warships and institutions in Inch'ŏn and at other Korean treaty ports to do so for only two days.[44] Their efforts to assert China's superiority through unique as well as unequal rituals simply magnified China's isolation from other countries.

Despite his efforts, Yuan found himself stuck in a ritual dilemma. When he notified Min Chong-muk (1835–1916), the resident of the Foreign Office, that he would like to visit the funeral hall in the inner palace, Min declined the offer because only royal family members could do so.[45] When the American minister, for his part, consulted with Min about how foreign ministers should perform funerary rituals, Min said that it would be inappropriate for the Korean court to invite foreign ministers to attend the funeral procession, but his office could provide a place near the East Gate of the city for the ministers to perform ceremonies as the hearse passed through the gate. Heard complied; Yuan did not. Yuan then told the Home Office and the Foreign Office that he would like to accompany the funeral team from the palace gate outside the city and hold the cord guiding the hearse, a Chinese funeral custom showing deep respect for the deceased. But the Home Office did not endorse this proposal and suggested that Yuan go directly to the East Gate, where other ministers would convene; when the hearse passed through the gate, the procession would stop for a moment, during which Yuan could perform a farewell ceremony. Disappointed by this response, Yuan decided to set himself apart from the other ministers with his own ritual: he would set an incense burner on a table and hold a memorial ceremony for the late dowager by the side of the road on the procession day.[46]

Soon thereafter, another event made Yuan reconsider his plans yet again. On October 11, 1890, seven American officers led fifty armed marines on a march from Inch'ŏn toward Hansŏng. Heard explained to Yuan that the United States, as a friend of Chosŏn, had sent naval troops to accompany the funeral procession "as a mark of respect and sympathy."[47] Yuan doubted his explanation. It was the second time in several months that Heard had summoned troops to the capital. The first time had been right after the death of the dowager in June, when the king had sent an agent to ask Heard to send forces to the palace at once to provide protection. Heard hesitated, but after considering the potential for disturbance and the jeopardy in which it might place American citizens, he ordered marines from the USS *Swatara* in Inch'ŏn to Hansŏng. Heard specified to the king that the troops were there to protect the legation, but the king, he said, "would benefit by the moral effect which their presence would produce."[48] The presence of American forces in Hansŏng sparked a rumor in Beijing that Chosŏn was planning to rent Port Hamilton to the United States as a coaling station in exchange for protection. Under these circumstances, to monitor the Americans, Yuan set up his memorial table at the East Gate, where Heard and the American soldiers stood in line on the side of the road. The hearse did not stop as promised, but Yuan still bowed three times with his hands folded in front.[49] The American soldiers returned to Inch'ŏn on October 15, defusing the tensions and allaying Yuan's suspicions.

Rituals and Sovereignty: Chosŏn's Bargaining with China about the Imperial Mission

While Yuan Shikai was tackling ritual dilemmas in Hansŏng, the Korean court was negotiating ritual conventions with Beijing.[50] On June 5, 1890, the king instructed the prefect of Ŭiju to inform the garrison major of the Manchu bannermen at Fenghuang City of the dowager's death. The monarch also appointed Hong Chong-yŏng as envoy and Cho Pyŏng-sŏng as attendant secretary of a mission to carry the news to Beijing. According to convention, Beijing in turn needed to dispatch a mission of condolence to Hansŏng. Two weeks later, through Yuan Shikai and Li Hongzhang, the king asked Beijing not to send envoys to Hansŏng but to allow Chosŏn's tributary emissaries to bring back the imperial condolence messages. The king explained that if China sent a mission, the United States, Britain, Germany, France, and Japan would send missions too, creating a situation that Chosŏn could not afford. What the king was requesting was known as "handing over for convenience" (Ch., shunfu), but Li was not sure whether this convention had ever been applied to condolence messages. He instructed Yuan to secretly consult precedents and warned him not to be rash, because Li felt that Hansŏng was forcing Beijing to do its bidding, despite the petition's beseeching tone.

After examining imperial missions of condolence to Chosŏn upon queen dowagers' deaths since the Qianlong period and enumerating six cases in 1757, 1805, 1821, 1844, 1858, and 1878, Yuan concluded that in the case of conferring noble rank on deceased royalty, Beijing always dispatched envoys and never used "handing over for convenience." In view of his findings, Yuan saw the king's request as a conspiracy. He reported to Li that Queen Min was dominating the king through her fear that the ceremonies performed to China's envoys in front of Westerners would damage Chosŏn's image as a country of zizhu. Yuan further asserted that Denny was inciting the king to urge Beijing not to send a mission because the rituals would damage Chosŏn's "national polity."[51] When the king discussed this issue with Yuan, Yuan insisted that the imperial mission would travel to Chosŏn and that all procedures to welcome the mission had to be conducted in conformity with precedent. However, the two Korean emissaries were already on their way to Beijing, carrying the king's special request.

Upon their arrival in Beijing, Hong Chong-yŏng and Cho Pyŏng-sŏng presented the king's memorial to the emperor via the Ministry of Rites. In the memorial, the king strictly followed the prescribed textual format by using China's regnal title and referring to himself as "subordinate" and to Chosŏn as "small country."[52] In a special note to the Ministry of Rites, Hong explained that as Chosŏn was facing a difficult situation because of political troubles, famine, and financial crisis, he preferred to convey the imperial message of condolence back to his country without the need for Beijing to send envoys for the purpose.

Neither the ministry nor the Guangxu emperor granted this request. The Grand Council forwarded a decree to Hong that declared that an imperial mission had to be sent because the Heavenly Dynasty would "cherish sympathy for its *shuguo* and *fan* on such occasions." The mission had "a fundamental relationship to the system" (Ch., *tizhi youguan*), and the rituals that Chosŏn should perform to it based on the established codes should not be curtailed in the least. Still, the emperor compromised by instructing the mission to take the maritime route between Tianjin and Inch'ŏn on warships of the Beiyang Navy. This was the first time since 1637 that an imperial mission had taken to the seas. Of the thirty-nine Manchu candidates recommended by the Ministry of Rites, the emperor selected Xuchang and Chongli (1834–1907) to serve as envoys. Given the possible international responses to the imperial mission's presence in Chosŏn, the emperor ordered all members of the mission to refuse gifts from Chosŏn for the sake of China's upright image.[53]

The emperor's decision to send the mission points to an established regulation of the Zongfan system: had Yuan Shikai, Li Hongzhang, or the Ministry of Rites been able to find any historical precedent for the omission of an imperial mission of condolence, Beijing would likely have consented to the king's request and refrained from dispatching the mission. The Zongfan regulations thus served both China and Korea as a double-edged sword. The Chinese side further confirmed that the mission would land in Inch'ŏn as scheduled, not in Masanpu, as Chosŏn proposed. According to Yuan, the king was hesitant about whether to go out of Hansŏng to welcome the envoys in the suburbs and perform ceremonies in person, for Denny was urging the king to receive the envoys in the palace. The envoys stressed that all ceremonies had to be performed as recorded in the ritual codes, and during their sojourn in Hansŏng they would not meet with any Westerners.[54]

Rituals and Dignity: The Imperial Mission to Chosŏn and the Grand Ceremony

On October 28, 1890, the two envoys picked up gifts for the king from the Ministry of Rites, including sandalwood incense, white and blue silk, and three hundred taels of silver. All of these items were in accordance with imperial codes determined in the eighteenth century.[55] Two days later they arrived in Tianjin, the headquarters of the Beiyang Navy commanded by Li Hongzhang, who had summoned three warships—the *Jiyuan*, the *Laiyuan*, and the *Jingyuan*—to harbor for the mission. Li first sent the *Jiyuan* to Chosŏn with a note in which the envoys again expressed their insistence that all prescribed ceremonies be carried out in full on their arrival in Chosŏn. The envoys also stated that the members of the mission would not accept any money or articles as routine gifts in order to show the emperor's concern for his *shuguo* and *fan*.[56]

Chosŏn was busy preparing to welcome the envoys according to precedent. To receive the mission, the king appointed several high-ranking officials, including Nam Chŏng-ch'ŏl, president of the Ministry of Punishment, and Sŏng Ki-un (1847–1924), grand chamberlain and superintendent of trade in the Inch'ŏn district. Both Nam and Sŏng had served as commissioners in Tianjin in 1884, where they had possessed a status equal to that of Western ministers, but now they were fully integrated into the Zongfan system as subordinates of both the king and the Chinese emperor. In addition to refurnishing a pavilion between Inch'ŏn and Hansŏng as the envoys' accommodations, the Koreans sent 130 foreign-drilled soldiers to the area for security. In Hansŏng the court had deployed around 590 soldiers to maintain local order.[57]

The king was still reluctant to leave the city to welcome the envoys, as he was worried that Japanese and Western diplomats and citizens would witness the hierarchical rituals, in particular his kowtowing to the envoys, which would undermine his dignity as a sovereign. But he nonetheless eventually decided to receive the envoys near the West Gate according to precedent.[58] After all, the king had been invested by the Chinese emperor, and at this particular moment the emperor's authority exerted a demand that the monarch could not ignore.

Once all the rituals had been blueprinted, the envoys sailed from Tianjin and reached the outer harbor of Inch'ŏn on November 6. After two high-ranking Korean officials boarded the cruisers to welcome the mission, the envoys landed by a small steamship with the imperial decree. The Korean officials, headed by the receivers of the mission, bowed to the imperial envoys and items. After the envoys had placed the decree in the dragon shrine customarily used for this purpose, the procession headed for the envoys' lodgings in Inch'ŏn. It was a long and magnificent procession. First came the Korean receivers and officials in columns, one on each side of the road, with the Hansŏng magnate and the metropolitan governor on the east side and the prefects and the magistrates on the west side. Next were the Korean escorts, flags, yellow umbrellas, drums, gongs, and bands. They were followed by the incense shrine and the dragon shrine and then by the Chinese attendants, all of whom were mounted. The two envoys followed in their sedan chairs, side by side, and behind them marched the high and low deputies with the supervisors and their attendants.

The colorful procession passed through the General Foreign Settlement and the Chinese Settlement (Ch., *Hua Yang zujie*), which the Chinese merchants had decorated with lanterns and streamers, undoubtedly feeling superior to their counterparts given the occasion. From the perspective of the envoys, the extraordinary procession and the elaborate ceremony that numerous Koreans and foreigners gathered to appreciate perfectly highlighted the Great Qing's superior authority in its subordinate country.[59] J. C. Johnston, the acting commissioner of customs in Inch'ŏn, was indeed impressed and commented that the arrival of the mission was "the most noteworthy event since the opening of Chemulpo [Inch'ŏn]."[60] When the envoys reached their residence at the Office of the Superintendent of Trade (K., Kamni amun), the Korean officials kowtowed toward the imperial envoys and decree, while the envoys replied by bowing with their hands folded in front. In the office the envoys reviewed the four ritual programs prepared by the Korean side and confirmed that all procedures would be performed the next day in Hansŏng. They declined to accept any gifts from the Korean officials.

The grand ceremony took place in the palace on November 8, and it included the reading of the imperial message of condolence and the ceremonial wailing by the king and the envoys.[61] When the ceremonies drew to a close, the king and the envoys had a short conversation in which the king expressed his gratitude for the "great honor" that China had given to the "small country."[62] Their conversation contained no mention of political or diplomatic issues. After drinking tea, the host and the guests bowed toward each other with hands folded in front. All of the rituals strictly followed the precedents of the eighteenth century. In addition, the king visited the envoys at their residence on November 10 and treated them to a tea ceremony. This would traditionally have been the time when the Korean side gave gifts to the envoys, but the envoys emphasized again that they could not accept even so much as a piece of paper. The next day the king sent off the envoys at the West Gate by performing the prescribed rituals. After a rest in Inch'ŏn, the envoys sailed back to Tianjin. Their departure marked the end of China's imperial missions to Chosŏn within the Zongfan framework and thus the conclusion to a tradition that had operated at least since 1401, when Ming China had officially invested the king of Chosŏn.

Already at the time of the event, and ever since, the dominant interpretation of this imperial mission has regarded it as a Chinese conspiracy conducted under the foil of tributary routines, aiming to strengthen China's control over Chosŏn at the cost of the latter's independent sovereignty.[63] Without knowing what occurred inside the palace between the king and the envoys, the Western ministers assumed that the envoys had persuaded the king to act in accordance with Beijing's interests in the name of conventional rituals.[64] These diplomats viewed the event in the context of modern diplomatic circumstances and saw ritual contacts as a tool that China used to influence or manipulate Chosŏn. Scholars in the twentieth century tended to juxtapose Chosŏn's vassalage vis-à-vis China with its independent sovereignty vis-à-vis its treaty counterparts, interpreting the mission as an application of China's new policy, which might be called the "Li-Yuan policy," after Li Hongzhang and Yuan Shikai.[65] This policy is said to have combined China's supremacy as the suzerain over Korea within the old tributary framework with China's hegemonic position in the new treaty port system in Chosŏn.

But Yuan's role may have been exaggerated by his counterparts in Hansŏng at the time and by scholars afterward. Their narratives have portrayed Yuan as an arrogant, overbearing, and peremptory person who acted as a "Chinese proconsul" and aggressively dominated the Chosŏn government for a decade.[66] The events surrounding the death of the dowager in 1890, however, cast doubt on this description. Yuan's efforts to negotiate his ritual performance in Hansŏng with the Korean side yielded nothing, which lays bare his unprivileged position as a foreign minister. Yuan did not go to Inch'ŏn to highlight China's superior position or attend the grand ceremony in the palace, nor did he meet or talk with the two imperial envoys. The envoys did not contact Yuan either, aside from sending him several routine notes about the ritual performance before they left Hansŏng. What Yuan's experience reflected was Chosŏn's independent power to manage its own affairs.

This interpretation does not deny the fact that Beijing did use the mission to demonstrate its superiority. After their return, the two envoys reported to the emperor, "All foreigners have seen the solemn and majestic rituals and learned that Chosŏn is subordinate to the Heavenly Dynasty. Chosŏn could not deny it either. If we can take advantage of the situation to pacify the country in an appropriate way, Chosŏn will serve as our fence and enjoy our great benevolence forever."[67] Johnston also observed that the mission "derived special political importance from the revival of the old-time ceremonies which mark the suzerain-tributary relations between China and Corea."[68] As a result, according to M. Frederick Nelson, this event "imparted, for the Western observers, a *de jure* status to China's *de facto* position in Korea. . . . The Western powers were beginning to attribute more force to the familial relationship which for two decades they had rejected as purely ceremonial."[69] Behind the rituals, it was evident, stood a vibrant politico-cultural Chinese empire. Rituals, therefore, were deeply involved in the tortuous transformation of both China and Korea from parts of the empire to modern sovereign states.

Beijing was not blind to the complex international situation as it considered modifying old conventions. Under the rubric of cherishing the subordinate country, the two envoys made the constructive suggestion that China treat the expenses of the envoys to Chosŏn as it did the outlays of ministers to other countries. The aim was to prevent Chosŏn from imposing exorbitant taxes and levies on its people in the name of welcoming the envoys. After consulting Emperor Yongzheng's edict of 1735, in which the emperor reduced by half the amount of silver the king was expected to give the imperial envoys as gifts, the Ministry of Rites endorsed the abolition of the custom of envoys' receiving silver from Chosŏn. The ministry and the Zongli Yamen decided that in the future each imperial envoy would receive two thousand taels of silver and each interpreter five hundred taels from the Zongli Yamen to cover expenses during the trip to Chosŏn. This reform blurred the line between imperial envoys to China's outer *fan* and ministers sent to other countries. Emperor Guangxu approved the change. The Beiyang superintendent, the Manchu general and the Ministry of Rites in Mukden, the king of Chosŏn, and the imperial resident in Hansŏng were all informed of the decision.[70] No imperial envoys, however, would ever have the chance to claim financial support from the Zongli Yamen before the Sino-Japanese War broke out in 1894 in Chosŏn.

Saving "Our Chosŏn": The Chinese Intelligentsia's Responses to the Sino-Japanese War

Assisting the Loyal *Fan*: The Prewar View

In May 1894 the Chinese general Nie Shicheng (1836–1900) returned to Tianjin from a ten-month trip to northern Manchuria, the Russian Far East, and Chosŏn. In Chosŏn he had met with the king and visited treaty ports in order to get a general picture of the situation in the country. According to Nie, "The king is weak, the officials are addicted to alcohol and women, and no one is considering self-strengthening programs. . . . There are no talented generals at the top and no able warriors at the bottom. Were the country to encounter trouble, it would need China to send troops to protect it. The situation is very dangerous." The general believed that "compared with Russia, which is powerful but only a superficial threat, Japan is a truly mortal danger." He argued that China should prepare to resist Japan's potential invasion of Chosŏn in order to "consolidate the *fan* and *shuguo* and protect China's frontier" (Ch., *gu fanshu, bao bianjiang*).[71]

Nie's predictions were proved true by the deterioration of Chosŏn's situation in the Tonghak Rebellion, an armed peasant uprising that broke out in January 1894 against corrupt aristocrats and against the Japanese and Western invasion of Chosŏn (Tonghak, an intellectual school founded in 1860, refers to "Eastern learning," indicating its anti-Western approach). Nie himself was dispatched to Chosŏn to assist the country in suppressing the rebellion; there he would witness China lose Chosŏn to Japan on the battlefield.

Many Chinese officials shared Nie's concerns. In July, when China was clashing with Japan over sending troops to Chosŏn, a group of officials in Beijing outlined in their memorials or position papers to the emperor what they believed would be the best policy to strengthen Chinese forces, protect Chosŏn, and defeat Japan. Zeng Guangjun (1866–1929) of the Imperial Academy suggested that China publicize its rationale for an expedition against Japan. Defining Chosŏn as the country that "was the first to subordinate itself to our dynasty and has conscientiously paid tributary visits for hundreds of years without interruption," Zeng proclaimed that "Japan has fabricated excuses and tried to make the country subordinate to two countries."[72] Pang Hongshu (1848–1915) of the Grand Censorate (Ch., Ducha yuan) alluded to the case of China's loss of Ryukyu and argued that China should not abandon Chosŏn because it was critical for China's overall situation. Pang emphasized that Chosŏn had been a *fan* of the Great Qing for a long time, "to the point that it is no different from the Mongols and the tribes in the western areas" (Ch., *Xiyu*, referring to Inner Asian areas). Therefore, China should stop the intervention of other countries in Chosŏn to protect the security of its territory, including the three provinces in Manchuria, the ancestral home of the current dynasty. Conceiving a Chinese strategy in the context of international politics, Pang exhorted China to protect Chosŏn by defeating Japan, so that China could focus on resolving its disputes with Russia over the borderline in the Pamir Mountains and with Britain over trade negotiations in Tibet.[73]

Other officials preferred to emphasize the internal connections between the Qing and Chosŏn since the early seventeenth century. After reviewing Hongtaiji's conquest of Chosŏn in 1637 and the erection of the Samjŏndo stele, Duanfang (1861–1911), a Manchu official who later became governor-general of Sichuan, argued that China should support Chosŏn because the country had loyally served the Great Qing for more than two hundred years without treachery.[74] On the day Duanfang submitted his position paper, the Japanese and the Chinese navies engaged in a battle at P'ungdo in Chosŏn. Thus began the war between the two countries.

Defending China Itself: The Link between "Our Chosŏn" and Manchuria, Mongolia, Xinjiang, Tibet, and Taiwan

Emperor Guangxu issued an edict to declare war on Japan on August 1, 1894. The edict reiterated that Chosŏn had been a *fan* and *shuguo* of the Great Qing and had paid tribute to China every year for more than two hundred years, so it was China's duty to send troops to Chosŏn to protect the Korean people from great suffering.[75] The edict justified China's action as "cherishing the small" within the Zongfan system and defending international law within the treaty port system. A growing number of Chinese officials identified China's move as a typical embodiment of the convention of cherishing men from afar.[76] These officials pointed passionately to all of China's outer and inner *fan* and other frontier areas, including Vietnam, Burma, Ryukyu, Outer Mongolia, Xinjiang, Tibet, Manchuria, and Taiwan, which were already being eyed covetously by Western powers, and declared that for its own good China should not lose Chosŏn. The growing crisis in Chosŏn thus became an issue related to Qing China's own fate. The Great Qing had to defend its territorial borderland and the politico-cultural frontier of the Chinese empire.

According to Changlin, the Manchu minister at the Ministry of Revenue, if Japan annexed Chosŏn, "all the *fan* of our dynasty would be subordinate to foreign barbarians, so other countries would encroach on China's inner land, and consequently Xinjiang, Taiwan, Tibet, and Manchuria would be in grave danger." Ding Lijun (1854–1903), a Han Chinese official at the Imperial Academy, further criticized Japan for "usurping our Chosŏn" (Ch., *duo wo Chaoxian*). He remarked, "If the fence collapsed, Mukden would be in great danger. Chosŏn, which is different from Vietnam and Burma, which are thousands of miles away from China, is mutually dependent with China, like the lips and the teeth, and like bones and flesh." Ding argued that Beijing should refuse British and Russian mediation between China and Japan, for if China ceded Chosŏn or Taiwan to Japan, as the Western mediators were suggesting, Britain would encroach on Tibet and Russia would seek to take Outer Mongolia.[77]

Changlin's and Ding's concerns about China's territorial integrity were widely shared by their fellow scholars and scholar-officials, who saw Chosŏn as the fence that protected Manchuria. As one of these officials, Kuai Guangdian, put it, "After we abandon Chosŏn, Russia will invade Mongolia and Britain will do the same to Tibet, so shall we let these countries alone or argue with them? If we opt to argue with them, we had better keep Chosŏn safe now."[78] All of these officials regarded

Chosŏn as an indispensable element of China's strategy to safeguard its territorial integrity. Saving "our Chosŏn" was equal to saving China itself.

The officials' ardent belief that Beijing should exercise its patriarchal authority reflected the revitalization of the potential policy of provincializing Chosŏn. Assuming that the king had been co-opted by Japan, Ding Lijun proposed that China invest the crown prince as the new king and keep him in the Chinese army for his own safety. Hong Liangpin (1826–96) similarly suggested that China select a member of the royal house of Chosŏn to guide the Chinese forces and invest him as the new king once the crisis was resolved. Yu Lianyuan (1844–1901) endorsed this proposal and suggested that the new investiture should be conducted in P'yŏngyang. Yan Youzhang further argued that China should immediately transform Chosŏn into a province (Ch., *gaijian xingsheng*) and should appoint officials and officers to govern it, yet treat the king and his officials generously and allow them to maintain their Korean titles. While Ding regarded this policy as a way of "publicizing our great justice to all people under Heaven," Yan saw it as legitimate and justifiable because Chosŏn was China's *fan* and had constituted two Chinese counties—Fuyu and Lelang—under the Han Dynasty.[79]

The storm of officials' opinions was triggered by the declaration of war against Japan on August 1, but it was also a result of political struggles between bureaucratic factions in Beijing. The majority of these officials were low-ranking members of the Pure Stream group, which drew on the thinking of the minister of the Grand Council, Li Hongzao (1820–97), and Emperor Guangxu's instructor Weng Tonghe. Embracing a hawkish approach, both men saw Li Hongzhang as their political adversary and accused him and his protégés, such as Ma Jianzhong, Liu Mingchuan (1836–96), and Ding Ruchang, of being afraid to fight the Japanese. With the rise of Weng and Li Hongzao in October, their followers became more active with more dramatic proposals during the second half of the war.

The core argument of these officials was that China could not lose Chosŏn, for it would mean the disintegration of the Great Qing itself. In fighting for Chosŏn, the Great Qing would fight not only for its territorial integrity but also for its own dignity and legitimacy as the Middle Kingdom and the Heavenly Dynasty. In the context of war, the ideology of all-under-Heaven became central for these scholar-officials, who saw the fate of the Great Qing at stake. Pragmatists dealing with the Japanese, Russians, and British on China's frontiers regarded the Pure Stream officials as armchair strategists with unrealistic plans, but the latter were undeniably accurate in their assessment of China's frontier security. The nightmare scenario they had sketched out in late 1894, in which China would encounter serious challenges in Manchuria, Outer Mongolia, Xinjiang, Tibet, and Taiwan from colonial powers such as Russia and Britain, became true in the postwar period. China's loss of territory halted only once the

People's Republic of China clearly claimed its territorial domain and defined China's borders. In this sense, China did not become a nation-state until the 1950s, when Korea—represented by two sovereign states because of the Cold War—became completely independent from the Chinese empire.

Losing the Eastern Fence: The Conclusion of the Treaty of Shimonoseki

While the war was escalating on China's eastern frontier, people on the western frontier in Tibet looked on with concern. On February 22, 1895, the imperial commissioner to Tibet, Kuihuan (1850–?), submitted a memorial to Emperor Guangxu, reporting that the thirteenth Dalai Lama (1876–1933) had led lamas and Tibetan Buddhists in reading sutras at primary monasteries after hearing that Japan had broken international law to invade Chosŏn. The Dalai Lama hoped their prayers before Buddha Sakyamuni would bring blessings to the "great emperor" and his "great forces," by which China would defeat the Japanese "clowns" in Chosŏn.[80] On April 17, ten days after the emperor learned about the Dalai Lama's prayers through Kuihuan's memorial, the Chinese representative Li Hongzhang, after painful negotiations with his Japanese counterparts, Itō Hirobumi and Mutsu Munemitsu (1844–97), signed a peace treaty at Shimonoseki in Japan.

The text of the treaty was written in Chinese, Japanese, and English. The first article, which was drafted by Japan, stated that "China recognizes definitively the full and complete independence and autonomy [Ch., *wanquan wuque zhi duli zizhu*] of Corea, and in consequence, the payment of tribute and the performance of ceremonies and formalities by Corea to China in derogation of such independence and autonomy, shall wholly cease for the future."[81] Unlike the Treaty of Kanghwa of 1876, which was written only in Chinese and Japanese, the English version of the Treaty of Shimonoseki explicitly defined Chosŏn's "full and complete independence and autonomy," erasing any ambiguity about the status of the country in the Chinese or Japanese versions. In addition, the terminology of the treaty reflected Qing China's transformation over the previous two centuries. In the treaty, the "Great Qing" was fully equal to "China" and "Zhongguo," although the preface and the end of the Japanese and Chinese versions of the treaty addressed the Qing as the "Great Qing Empire" in Chinese characters as a counterpart to the "Great Japanese Empire." Whereas the Japanese text called the Qing the "country of the Qing" (J., *Shinkoku*), the Chinese text referred to it as "Zhongguo" and the English version as "China." In this sense, what the treaty terminated was not only the Qing-Chosŏn Zongfan relationship that had existed since 1637 but also the general Sino-Korean Zongfan arrangement that had arguably started with Jizi.

When the news that Li Hongzhang had signed the treaty reached Beijing, the thousands of scholars attending the triennial imperial civil-service examination were dismayed at the humiliating terms. They began to submit long and passionate petitions to the emperor via the Grand Censorate. The majority of these petitions were signed by more than fifty scholars from different provinces, and they called for the annulment of the treaty and a continuation of the war with Japan. The scholars emphasized Chosŏn's strategic position as China's "eastern fence" and its historical significance for the rise of the Great Qing. The petitions echoed the fervent tone of the Pure Stream bureaucrats.

On May 1, Wang Rongxian, Hong Jiayu, and Bao Xinzeng, three candidate officials from the Ministry of Personnel, submitted a long petition in which they outlined the grave dangers that each article of the Treaty of Shimonoseki posed for China. Observing that the treaty made Chosŏn equal to China but subordinate to Japan, the three officials expressed their frustration that "a simple sentence of a treaty" could terminate China's long-term relationship with Chosŏn, "a *fan* for almost three hundred years that has embodied the superb achievements of Emperors Taizu [Nurhaci] and Taizong [Hongtaiji] and received kindness from other emperors for generations."[82] Two days later, ten low-ranking officials from the Directorate of Education submitted a joint petition via Weng Tonghe. They bitterly reviewed China's recent history of losing "our Burma" to Britain, "our Annam" to France, "our northern Heilong River" (the Amur River) to Russia, and "our Ryukyu" and Chosŏn to Japan, concluding that "we once had many *fan* in the four quarters of the world, but we have lost all of them within the past decades."[83] They further argued that China's cession of Taiwan and Liaodong to Japan would be a prologue to further surrenders of China's territory to foreign states, surrenders that would be much worse than the loss of outer *fan* on China's periphery. As these officials saw it, the Great Qing was collapsing along its frontiers. But even as petitions such as these were flooding Beijing, the exchange of ratifications of the Sino-Japanese treaty took place at Yantai in Shandong Province on May 8, 1895.

Redefining Chosŏn and China: The Qing-Korean Treaty of 1899 and Its Aftermath

A Ritual Dilemma: Chosŏn's Proposal to Negotiate a Treaty with China

The Treaty of Shimonoseki terminated the Sino-Korean court-to-court hierarchy, but it did not change the countries' state-to-state relationship. The post-1895 political framework between the two countries, therefore, was not a completely new arrangement; rather, it represented the institutionalization of the surviving section of the dual network. The two sides accomplished this institutionalization by negotiating a new and equal treaty. The original proposal for the treaty came from the Korean monarch, who was increasingly losing power to his Japanese advisers after the war. On January 7, 1895, as Japan approached victory in the war, the king of Chosŏn performed ceremonies at Chongmyo, the royal ancestral shrine in Hansŏng. The monarch announced "Great Laws" (K., Hongbŏm), calling himself "emperor" (K., chim; Ch., zhen) and explaining that he had decided to "cut off the thought of being dependent upon the country of the Qing in order to lay the foundation for autonomy and independence." In addition to ending the Qing's authority—or suzerainty, as many scholars prefer to call it—over Chosŏn, the king's fourteen items initiated a self-strengthening reform designed by Japan and carried out under Japanese supervision.[84]

In the postwar period, Japan's increasing domination of Chosŏn progressively curtailed the country's autonomy and independence, leading to serious political tensions between the king and his Japanese advisers. In October 1895 a mob of Japanese rioters entered the palace, killing Queen Min, the king's closest adviser for decades, and mercilessly burning her body. The Japanese atrocities frightened the king, who could foresee his fate as a puppet under draconian Japanese control. Adhering to the Japanese schedule, on January 1, 1896, Chosŏn adopted the solar calendar and the new regnal title Kŏnyang, the first independent regnal title of the dynasty since its establishment in 1392. However, realizing that these reforms could not ensure his personal safety, the king and the crown prince escaped to the Russian legation in February and sought asylum, leaving the fate of the Korean court uncertain and intensifying the competition between Russia and Japan on the peninsula.

Chosŏn had won its independence with the Sino-Japanese Treaty of Shimonoseki, but at that point it had not yet signed a treaty with China that would have identified its independent status. In June 1896 the Korean interpreter Pak T'ae-yŏng visited Tang Shaoyi, the manager of Chinese commercial affairs and de facto Chinese representative in Hansŏng, to convey the king's wish to negotiate a treaty with China. Tang did not refuse the proposal but suggested that the talks should be conducted later, as Chosŏn could not be regarded as an autonomous and independent country as long as the king was under Russian protection.[85]

The king's overtures posed a challenge to Beijing, which believed that "Chosŏn, as our dynasty's longtime *fan*, should not be regarded as equal to Western countries." According to the Zongli Yamen, China would agree to negotiate new "trade regulations" with Chosŏn, which would allow the country to maintain consuls in China, but China would not permit its former *fan* to sign treaties with it, send ministers to Beijing, or present letters of credence to the Chinese emperor.

Instead, China would send a consul-general to Hansŏng to manage Chinese affairs. In this way, China could "preserve the system of shuguo" (Ch., cun shu-guo zhi ti). The Yamen telegraphed Li Hongzhang for advice. Li, who was on a postwar trip to Europe and the United States, endorsed the plan but suggested that, to maintain China's dignity, the Chinese consul-general (a post for which Li recommended Tang Shaoyi) should not present his credentials to the king.[86] This attempt to preserve the prewar hierarchical system characterized Beijing's policy toward Chosŏn in the immediate postwar period.

Similarly, Korean policymakers generally continued to make use of traditional discourse as they adjusted their country's relations with China. In a conversation between the senior official Cho Pyŏng-chik (1833–1901) and Tang Shaoyi in July 1896, Cho stated that Chosŏn had been a "fan and shuguo of the central dynasty for a long time," and that it was not the king who had originally sought the auton-omous status outlined for Chosŏn in the Treaty of Shimonoseki. Chosŏn, Cho emphasized, had been coerced by its powerful neighbor (namely, Japan) into dis-claiming the status of China's shuguo, but the king "appreciated the deep favors of the imperial dynasty and would like to negotiate a new treaty to resume the con-cord." Cho expressed concern that by refusing to negotiate a treaty with Chosŏn, China might be signaling its refusal to acknowledge Chosŏn's autonomy. Tang responded that negotiating a treaty and recognizing Chosŏn's autonomy were two different matters, because the former "means only not following the old reg-ulations," but the latter "means that the two countries are equal to each other."[87] Their conversation yielded nothing.

In November 1896 Tang informed the Zongli Yamen that the king—Tang refused to acknowledge the monarch's claim to emperorship—would send rep-resentatives to Beijing for treaty negotiations. This prospect forced China to con-front the sensitive question of ritual procedures between Korean representatives and the imperial court in the postwar transitional context. If the self-declared emperor of Chosŏn dispatched a representative to Beijing for treaty negotiations, the representative, unlike a prewar tributary emissary, would no longer need to perform the ceremony of kowtow to the emperor, which would compromise Chi-na's dignity. Given this ritual conundrum, Tang argued that it would be prudent for Beijing to appoint a consul-general to Hansŏng who could negotiate a treaty with Chosŏn and protect the Chinese merchants and civilians; the affairs of Chi-nese subjects in Korea had been temporarily supervised by the British consul-general, John N. Jordan (1852–1925), on China's commission. Endorsing Tang's proposal, Beijing appointed Tang himself as "Chinese consul-general in Chosŏn" (Ch., Zhongguo zhuzha Chaoxian zonglingshi).

Tang's prewar view of Sino-Korean relations made it enormously difficult for him to adjust to the postwar arrangement. As he put it, "Although the system is now different, it is inconvenient for us to sign an equal treaty with Chosŏn given that it was a *fan* of our dynasty for centuries."[88] In the following years, Tang did his best to preserve a hierarchy between the two countries.[89]

Reluctance and Nostalgia: China's First Minister to Korea

In January 1897 Tang Shaoyi learned that the king had appointed Sŏng Ki-un as Chosŏn's representative for the treaty negotiations but had canceled the plan to send Sŏng to Beijing once he heard of Tang's appointment. Tang visited Sŏng and informed him that Chinese officials would not talk with him if he went directly to Beijing. In a conversation with Jordan, the British consul-general, Tang declared that he intended to focus solely on preventing the Korean representative from visiting Beijing, and to that end he wanted to commission Jordan to continue to manage Chinese commercial affairs.[90]

The dramatic changes in Chosŏn's political situation in 1897 prompted the Korean Foreign Office to pursue a more active agenda toward the goal of making a treaty with China. In the two years after the war, Chosŏn had begun to construct an image of itself as an independent country by removing or refashioning the icons of China's supremacy in the Zongfan era. The Korean government converted the Gate of Receiving Imperial Favors into the Gate of Independence (K., Tongnim mun), buried the Samjŏndo stele, changed the South Palace Annex into the Temple of Heaven (K., Ch'ŏndan), and replaced the Chinese managers of Chosŏn's customs with Russians. These efforts constituted a process of "decentering the Middle Kingdom," as Andre Schmid has described it.[91]

In August 1897, six months after returning to his palace from the refuge of the Russian legation, the Korean emperor adopted the new regnal title Kwangmu. On October 12 the sovereign called his country the "Great Korea" (K., Taehan) after performing ceremonies of sacrifice toward Heaven and Earth. Western diplomats soon formally recognized the new name of the country.[92] From Tang Shaoyi's perspective, the Korean sovereign was arrogating to himself an illegitimate emperorship, and his attitude toward treaty negotiations with Chosŏn became even more conservative. But the new Korean empire did not pin its hopes entirely on Tang.

In March 1898 the Russian minister in Beijing forwarded to the Zongli Yamen Korea's expression of willingness to send a representative to Beijing and to receive a Chinese counterpart in Hansŏng. The Yamen instructed Tang to block the dispatch of a Korean representative and decided to send a representative to Hansŏng first. Tang suggested that China send an official with a fourth-level rank, as opposed to the third-level representatives of other countries in Korea, in order to show the "difference between the owner and the servant in the past days" and to ensure that the "system" would not be violated. In the meantime, the Japanese minister in Beijing, Yano Fumio (1851–1931), contacted the Zongli Yamen as a mediator for Sino-Korean contacts. The Yamen informed Yano that Chosŏn could negotiate with Tang in Hansŏng for trade regulations and that China did not want to receive representatives of its former *shuguo* in Beijing.[93] Tang quickly contacted the Korean Foreign Office to discuss trade regulations, but the office refused on the grounds that a regulation was not a treaty—a retroactive protest against the 1882 Sino-Korean Regulations, which fell far short of a treaty and had been dictated by the Chinese side.

In July, Beijing realized that the situation was slipping out of its hands, when Tang reported that the Foreign Office of Korea had invited Jordan to ask the British minister in Beijing, Claude M. MacDonald (1852–1915), to serve as a broker. The Zongli Yamen told Tang that if Chosŏn insisted on sending a representative to Beijing, the representative should be a fourth-rank minister, and his credentials should be forwarded to the emperor by the Yamen; no audience with the emperor would be arranged, as the Yamen would negotiate potential trade regulations with the representative.[94] Three years after the Sino-Japanese War, the humiliating end of China's patriarchal superiority over Korea was still much on Chinese politicians' minds, and the Zongli Yamen was still reluctant to treat Korea as a state equal to China. As Tang saw it, allowing Hansŏng to send a minister to Beijing first would have "a detrimental effect on the relationship" given China's status as a "big country." To justify his concern, he pointed out that Britain and Spain, which were likewise "big countries," had also preemptively dispatched their own representatives to their former subordinates—the United States and South American countries, respectively—once these subordinates had become autonomous (Ch., *zizhu*).[95]

In China, the ambitious reform initiated by the Guangxu emperor in June 1898 reached its acme. Stimulated by the fiasco of the war, the reform aimed to modernize China by changing outdated conventions. The young emperor believed that China's relations with Chosŏn should change too. On August 5, at the emperor's instructions, the Grand Council telegraphed Tang that the emperor would allow Korea to send a minister to Beijing and would grant the minister an audience. The Zongli Yamen accordingly instructed Tang to inform Hansŏng that Korea could send its minister to China first, and that China would treat him with the ceremonies appropriate to "friendly nations" (Ch., *youbang*). China would dispatch its own minister to Korea for the sake of reciprocity.[96] Tang, however, chose not to inform the Koreans of Beijing's decision.[97]

In Beijing the emperor appointed Xu Shoupeng (?–1901) as the minister for Korea with a third-level rank and the title "imperial commissioner in the country of Chosŏn" (Ch., *Zhuzha Chaoxian guo qinchai dachen*). This title aroused concern among foreign ministers in Hansŏng because it carried strong Zongfan connotations and smacked of colonialism. In a conversation with Tang, the British inspector general of Korean customs, John M. Brown (1835–1926), expressed his suspicion that China still regarded Korea as its *shuguo*, because Beijing's imperial commissioners in Tibet and Mongolia held similar titles. The Russian minister to Korea, Nikolai Matyunin (1849–1907), regarded Xu's position as that of a second-rank minister, which was the highest rank among his counterparts in the diplomatic corps in Hansŏng. The Japanese, French, and German ministers were also disturbed by Xu's title and the format of the Chinese credentials, which used the old term "Chosŏn" rather than the newly adopted "Han" for Korea.[98] The diplomats saw such language as a sign that China might not endorse the new postwar political arrangement in the peninsula.

Indeed, what to call Korea and its monarch presented a challenge to the Chinese side. In the end, it was Zhang Yinhuan, the former minister to the United States, who drafted Xu's letter of credence on the basis of the first article of the Treaty of Shimonoseki, as instructed by Emperor Guangxu. Ma Jianzhong, the man who had been heavily involved in Korean affairs in the 1880s, offered some revisions to the draft.[99] The opening sentence of the letter read, "The Great Emperor of the country of the Great Qing respectfully gives his greetings to the Great Monarch of the country of the Great Korea."[100] The term "Great Monarch" (Ch., *da junzhu*) indicated the king's inferior position vis-à-vis the "Great Emperor" (Ch., *da huangdi*) of China, and the draft credential also used a modified format for the conventional honorific elevation that still elevated the Qing above Korea.

Emperor Guangxu disliked Zhang's proposed format but himself was at a loss as to how to refer to Korea and its sovereign.[101] When the emperor expressed his concerns to Zhang, Zhang explained that Chosŏn had renamed itself "Great Korea" without informing China, so the draft credential was simply based on the Treaty of Shimonoseki rather than on the domestic changes in Korea.[102] Subsequently the emperor instructed Tang Shaoyi to investigate which term—"Great Monarch" or "Great Emperor"—Britain, Japan, and Russia used in their letters of credence to Korea, for he wanted the Chinese letter to follow whatever practice other countries had adopted.[103] Because of the emperor's open-mindedness, the final version of the letter addressed the Korean monarch as the "Great Emperor" and placed "Great Qing" and "Great Korea" on the same line. The Korean letter of credence to China, which the first Korean minister to China presented to Emperor Guangxu in 1902, adopted the same equal format. This change in honorifics was the first since 1637 and represented a watershed moment in Qing-Chosŏn relations.

As the diplomatic changes were inching forward, Empress Dowager Cixi suddenly staged a coup on September 21, 1898, placing the emperor under house arrest and suspending his reforms. Despite the political chaos, Xu Shoupeng was allowed to carry on with his work. His title changed from "imperial commissioner" to "envoy plenipotentiary," and his explicit mission was to negotiate a treaty with the Korean Foreign Office.[104] This change entirely erased the ambiguity of Xu's former title and the worries of his Japanese and Western counterparts in Hansŏng. The Manchu ruling house eventually, if reluctantly, accepted the fact that Chosŏn was a country equal to the Great Qing.

Before he departed for Korea, Xu drafted a treaty consisting of fourteen articles. He commented that China had suffered from unfair treaties with other countries, in particular regarding extraterritoriality and tariff agreements, and would be rectifying these imbalances in its new treaties, starting with the one with Korea. Xu was determined to pursue an equal treaty with Korea for the sake of China's interests, but at the same time he revealed his traditional bias: "Korea was China's *fan* and *shuguo* in the past and it was not Korea's original wish to be autonomous. The country is small and surrounded by powerful neighbors. We should do our best to cherish it, rather than gain extra advantages from it." With this mindset, Xu wanted to make sure that both countries could enjoy the right of most-favored-nation status in trade with each other.[105]

While Xu was getting ready to embark on his trip to Korea, Wu Baochu (1869–1913), son of Gen. Wu Changqing, composed a preface to a book entitled *Three Stories of Korea* (Ch., *Aoyi Chaoxian sanzhong*), written by Zhou Jialu (1846–1909), who had served as an assistant to General Wu when the latter went to Hansŏng in 1882 to suppress the mutiny. In the preface, Wu Baochu reviewed China's humiliating defeat in Korea in 1895 and argued that China should have integrated Korea into China's household system in 1882 and converted the country into prefectures and counties of China (Ch., *jiqi tudi er junxian zhi*). He was dismayed that China now had to dispatch a representative to Korea for treaty negotiations, which made Korea "look like an enemy of China."[106] Wu offered a picture of China's presence in Chosŏn that was full of nostalgia, frustration, and uncertainty.

Negotiating with a Friendly Nation: The Sino-Korean Treaty of 1899

Xu arrived in Hansŏng on January 25, 1899, with the intention of "extending China's benevolence of cherishing the small" and was granted an audience with the Korean emperor on February 1. On the day of the audience, Xu was picked up by a sedan chair to be taken to the palace. When he entered the audience hall, he bowed once toward the emperor and bowed again as he approached the emperor. The emperor, wearing Western-style clothes, stood up to shake hands with Xu and to receive the Chinese letter of credence. Xu then read aloud a short tribute to the emperor, who in return showed his gratitude to the Chinese minister. After this, they shook hands again, and Xu bowed for the third time before he was escorted back to his legation.[107] The ceremony, conducted along the lines of "Western common rules" at the state-to-state level, was the first ritual performance between the Korean head of state and a state representative of China in the postwar period, and it marked the definitive end of centuries-long Zongfan rituals between the two countries.

Following the audience, Xu started treaty negotiations with Pak Che-sun (1858–1916), the minister of the Foreign Office. In September the two sides signed a trade treaty (K., *Tae Han'guk Tae Ch'ŏngguk t'ongsang choyak*) containing fifteen articles. Article 2 stated that each country would dispatch representatives to reside in the capital and treaty ports of the other and would enjoy most-favored-nation treatment. Article 5 endowed both with the right of consular jurisdiction. Article 12 allowed them to negotiate new regulations for border demarcation and to trade on the frontier in Manchuria. The agreement served as a replacement for the 1882 Sino-Korean Regulations as the first equal treaty between the two countries, but China made notable concessions. For example, China was forbidden to export opium to Korea, but similar restrictions did not apply to Korean exports to China. Xu explained to Emperor Guangxu that he did not challenge such items because he found that "the Korean monarch and subordinates still worship China in their minds, which contributed to the success of the negotiations."[108]

After signing the treaty, Xu commented that "Korea, China's *fan* and *shuguo* in the past, has now become a friendly nation of China, and nothing can change the situation. Recalling the past—what a pity it is!"[109] The two countries ratified the treaty in Hansŏng in December, and Xu was appointed by Beijing as the first Chinese minister to Korea. In stark contrast to Tang Shaoyi, who had struggled with reconciling China's past glory with the reality of the first years after the Sino-Japanese war, Xu in 1899 merely presented himself as a Western-style minister and quickly busied himself with reestablishing the Chinese diplomatic network in Korea in order to protect Chinese citizens and interests.

Korea would eventually send its minister to Beijing in reciprocity, but the dispatch was postponed because of China's deteriorating situation. The Boxer Uprising was sweeping across northwestern Shandong, and it began to spread toward Tianjin and Beijing. The anti-Christian uprising eventually resulted in a diplomatic and political disaster for China in August 1900, when the Eight-Nation Alliance occupied Beijing right after Emperor Guangxu and Empress Dowager Cixi had fled to Xi'an. In October, Li Hongzhang began to negotiate with Britain, the United States, Japan, Russia, Italy, France, Germany, and Austria-Hungary. In view of the dramatic changes in China, the Korean emperor, who was under close Japanese supervision, wrote a letter to the Meiji emperor asking Japan to protect Korean interests in China during the negotiations.[110] In January 1901 Beijing recalled Xu Shoupeng from Hansŏng to Beijing to assist Li in the peace negotiations. Before leaving Korea, Xu named one of his counselors, Xu Taishen, as acting minister.

In late July the Zongli Yamen changed its Chinese name to Waiwu bu, the Ministry of Foreign Affairs, legitimizing itself as China's sole foreign office. Xu Shoupeng was appointed as a minister of the ministry. On September 7, 1901, Li signed the final protocol with the foreign states, and the Chinese empire teetered on the edge of collapse. Li died two months later, leaving his lifelong dream of modernizing China and his many plans to protect Korea unfulfilled. With the return of Emperor Guangxu and Empress Dowager Cixi to the Forbidden City in January 1902, Korea was finally ready to send its first minister to take his place amid the rubble of the city of Beijing.

The Korean government appointed Pak Che-sun, Xu Shoupeng's treaty nego-tiation counterpart and the former commissioner in Tianjin, as the first Korean minister plenipotentiary to China.[111] On September 30, 1902, Pak presented his letter of credence to Emperor Guangxu in the Forbidden City following a tailored Western-style procedure.[112] The ceremony of kowtow, performed by Korean trib-utary emissaries to the emperor of China for centuries, had come to an end. Interestingly, the Chinese official records on the audience are very brief, exactly like those on the first meeting between Emperor Tongzhi and foreign ministers in 1873. Perhaps the court saw in the new rituals both a reminder of the Chinese empire's past glory vis-à-vis its outer *fan* and a complex challenge to China's dignity. After the audience, the Ministry of Foreign Affairs instructed Xu Taishen to send two Korean-language interpreters to Beijing to facilitate its further com-munications with Pak.[113] The Korean language thus joined the list of the official foreign languages of the Chinese foreign ministry. A new—if fleeting—bilateral relationship had begun.

Chinese Zongfanism and Korean Colonialism in the Borderland: Sino-Korean Contacts in South China and Manchuria

The transformation of the Sino-Korean relationship was not as clear-cut in China's provinces as it was in Beijing. In the coastal areas of South China, local officials still followed prewar routines to manage affairs regarding Korea. In December 1895, for instance, Governor Liao Shoufeng (1836–1901) in Zhejiang Province reported to Emperor Guangxu that officials in Wenzhou had rescued twenty-eight Koreans from a shipwreck in October and provided the victims with clothes and food, "following conventions," eventually returning them to Chosŏn via Shanghai. Liao called these Koreans "barbarians of the country of Chosŏn who had suffered from the shipwreck" (Ch., *Chaoxian guo nanfan*), using the same Zongfan wording as that used in the eighteenth century.[114] The Wenzhou case became a model for similar cases in the following years.

In May 1901 Governor Yu Lianyuan in Zhejiang reported that fifteen Korean fishermen had suffered a shipwreck on China's coast. After consulting the Wenzhou precedent, he followed the conventions of saving and taking care of them and sent them on to Shanghai.[115] Yu had been a pillar of the Pure Stream in the 1890s and had been among those who called for Beijing to protect Chosŏn for the sake of the integrity of the Great Qing. By this point, China had signed its new treaty with Korea and Yu had been promoted to governor, but in Yu's mind Chosŏn—the term he used, rather than "Great Korea" or "Han"—was still a *fan* of the Great Qing and the Korean fishermen belonged to the category of "barbarians." Yu's successors in Zhejiang from 1902 to 1908 embraced the same approach.[116] In almost all cases the Korean victims were referred to as "barbarians" who were beneficiaries of China's policy of "cherishing the small" or "cherishing the men from afar." In provincial practice, then, Zongfan norms were no weaker than they had been in the seventeenth and eighteenth centuries.

In contrast to the benign and almost imperceptible postwar transformation of the Sino-Korean relationship in South China, the shift in the border areas in Manchuria was manifested in blood, fire, and death. According to the reports of Chinese officials in Manchuria in 1907, Koreans started to attack and loot Chinese villages along the border of Jilin and Mukden in the late 1890s, and the situation deteriorated dramatically after 1901, when Beijing was occupied by the Eight-Nation Alliance and Manchuria was occupied by Russia.[117] Chinese bandits similarly attacked Korean villages on the border. The sharp rise in Sino-Korean border conflicts signaled the local disorder caused by the collapse of the Zongfan arrangement from the top down. For local and nonofficial forces on both sides of the border, impoverished peasants in particular, practical concerns and the pressures of daily needs, such as the search for fertile land, food, livestock, and energy resources, prevailed over national relationships and state interests. With the sudden absence of Chinese and Korean authority, the borderland in Manchuria became a perfect location for Chinese and Korean bandits and other illegal armed groups to build up their strength and extract goods from local farmers and settlers.

Between early 1901 and early 1905, officials in Mukden and Jilin reported to Beijing at least a dozen cases of serious cross-border crime committed by Koreans, including armed robberies, burglaries, shootings, homicides, rapes, kidnappings, and arson. Chen Zuoyan, a local Chinese official in Yanji in eastern Jilin, reported that a Korean attack against a Chinese area in March 1901 claimed eleven Chinese lives and caused a loss of 4,337.81 taels of silver.[118] As more Korean immigrants poured over the border into Chinese territory, the situation continued to worsen. In July 1903 Chen Zuoyan reported a series of misdeeds by Korean settlers and called on Beijing to take urgent measures to protect Chinese interests. A local report revealed that a Korean armed attack against four villages in Yanjin in the fall of 1903 had damaged 211 Chinese and Korean houses and cost more than 19,546.46 taels of silver.[119] In the meantime, Chinese bandits continued to cross the border rivers to pillage Korean villages, and on the Chinese side of the border the Chinese pawns of local officials extracted money from Korean immigrants. At least four instances of illegal logging or kidnapping on the Korean side, for example, were committed by Chinese bandits.[120] In August 1903, emphasizing that "Korea is different from what it was in the past," the Chinese minister in Hansŏng, Xu Taishen, suggested to Beijing that China should implement countermeasures to check Korean expansion into Chinese territory in Yanji, an area the Koreans and Japanese began to refer to as "Kando" (Ch., Jiandao). Britain and Japan, which had formed an alliance in 1902, informed Xu that Russian machinations were behind the attempt to settle Koreans in this area. In the following two years, the Chinese and Korean foreign ministries sought in vain to settle border disputes in Manchuria.[121]

Many historical and geopolitical factors contributed to the violent conflicts in the border areas. The absence of any demarcation of the point at which the Yalu and Tumen Rivers converged—marking the traditional boundary between the two countries—had been a problem since the Kangxi period in the eighteenth century. Although a borderline existed, it was not clearly or legally delineated, as it would be in modern times between two sovereign states. In the first half of the twentieth century, this issue evolved into a dispute that involved not just China and Korea but Japan as well. Border conflicts were also fueled by China's opening of Manchuria in the 1870s, when the Manchu court abolished the two-hundred-year-old policy of segregating Manchuria from inner China and encouraged people to immigrate to the area for cultivation. The new policy and the rich resources in the area also attracted thousands of poor Korean peasants, who crossed the Tumen River to cultivate the wilderness in the convergence zone, forcing China to deal with these foreign citizens.[122] Emperor Guangxu had instructed local officials in 1882 to tolerate the illegal Korean immigrants as long as they had no intention of encroaching on China's borders. Later, in order to solve the mounting problems, China started to assimilate Korean immigrants into the Chinese populace by ordering them to cut their hair in the Chinese style and to wear Chinese clothes. This policy provoked strong protest from Korea.[123]

The accumulating conflicts led to a skirmish in the spring of 1904, when Chinese forces under the command of the officer Hu Dianjia defeated a group of Korean soldiers who had crossed the Tumen River with the purpose of occupying more land and mobilizing the Korean immigrants to break away from Chinese governance. This was the first time that China used force to resolve a dispute with Korea in the post-1895 period. The skirmish resulted in China's resumption of territorial and administrative control over the area and forced Korea to return to peace talks. On June 15, 1904, Hu Dianjia, Chen Zuoyan, and three Korean officials signed an agreement with the title "Regulation on Sino-Korean Border Affairs with the Purpose of Solving Problems Arising from the Conflict" (Ch., Zhong-Han bianjie shanhou zhangcheng). Its name notwithstanding, the agreement primarily served to tie up remaining unresolved issues from the spring skirmish; it was not a state-to-state treaty for the long-term strategic goal of settling border disputes.[124]

At the time the Sino-Korean agreement was signed, Japan was fighting with Russia for control of Manchuria. After it finally prevailed over Russia, Japan publicly made Korea into its protectorate in November 1905. The Korean minister to Beijing was recalled, and all affairs regarding Korean contacts with China were transferred to the management of the Japanese legation in Beijing. In February 1906, with the closing of the American, British, and French legations in Hansŏng and the arrival of the first Japanese residential general, Itō Hirobumi, China also recalled its third minister to Korea, Zeng Guangquan.

In Manchuria Sino-Korean border conflicts continued to increase, and the local Chinese officials believed that Korea was aggressively expanding to the Chinese side, where Korean immigrants significantly outnumbered the Chinese population. In 1907 Wu Luzhen (1880–1911), the Chinese investigator in charge of Sino-Korean border affairs, reported that there were more than fifty thousand Koreans on the Chinese side of the Tumen River, compared to fewer than ten thousand Chinese residents. According to Wu's investigation of thirty-nine villages in the Helongyu area, the Korean settlers had established a total of 5,990 households in these villages, dwarfing the 264 Chinese households. Wu commented that this ancestral territory of the Qing had almost become "Chosŏn's colony" (Ch., Chaoxian zhimin zhi di).[125] Although Korea was falling victim to Japanese colonialism, Korean immigrants had served as the vanguard in the Korean colonization of Chinese territory in Manchuria. This type of Korean colonization subsequently served as a vehicle of Japan's colonial expansion into the vast inner land of Manchuria over the following three decades.

In order to protect the interests of Chinese merchants in Korea, Beijing appointed Ma Tingliang as the consul-general to Korea in 1909, a year after Emperor Guangxu and Empress Dowager Cixi died and the new emperor was inaugurated with the regnal title of Xuantong. China was in the throes of violent domestic upheaval through a series of reforms and rebellions, so the relationship with Korea was not a priority for the Beijing government. On August 22, 1910, Korea was annexed by Japan. Beijing made no official comment on the annexation. In Hansŏng, Ma instructed Chinese citizens to follow the new orders issued by the Japanese authorities, and he dismissed the police forces in Chinese settlements.

Beijing's silence notwithstanding, the Japanese annexation was alarming to many Chinese, who felt the same colonial threat hanging over China. Dai Jitao (1891–1949), who had been educated in Japan and would later become an assistant to Sun Yat-sen (1866–1925), published an editorial in a Shanghai newspaper in August 1910 criticizing Beijing's indifferent attitude to this tragic chapter in Korea's history. Invoking the time-honored Sino-Korean relationship since the Jizi period, Dai declared that "Korea has been China's *shuguo* for more than three thousand years, its lands lie within China's borders [Ch., *jiangyu*], its people belong to the same ethnic group as the Chinese, its characters are Chinese, and its political customs are Chinese legacies." Lamenting Korea's tragic fate, Dai warned that unless China roused itself, it too would soon suffer a Japanese invasion in the political, military, and industrial arenas.[126]

In Manchuria, the governor-general of the Three Northeastern Provinces, Xiliang (1853–1917), was alarmed by Japan's "colonial policy" (Ch., *zhimin zhengce*) toward China, enacted through the Koreans who continued to cross the border to occupy Chinese land. In September and October 1910, Xiliang reported, more than thirty thousand Korean immigrants were living among the Chinese residents on China's side of the border. The governor-general emphasized that since these Korean immigrants had become Japanese citizens upon the Japanese annexation of Korea in August, they were no longer subject to Chinese jurisdiction but rather answered to the Japanese consul. Xiliang argued that this change would "harm our sovereignty" (Ch., *sun wo zhuquan*), and that "the thousands of Korean immigrants would play the lead in Japan's annexation of Manchuria." He suggested that China use the newly issued *Nationality Regulations of the Great Qing* (Ch., *Da Qing guoji tiaoli*) to convert the Korean immigrants into Chinese citizens in order to make the territorial borderline distinct and secure.[127]

In August 1911 Zhao Erxun (1844–1927), Xiliang's successor, urged Beijing to heed Xiliang's proposal and to naturalize the Korean immigrants on Chinese soil. Stressing that "all the counties along the Yalu River, which are more than ten in number, belong to China's inner land [Ch., *neidi*]," Zhao proposed that China tell the Korean immigrants to "become civilized" (Ch., *guihua*) by applying for and obtaining Chinese citizenship.[128] Like Xiliang, Zhao was aware that the issue of the nationality of the considerable Korean immigrant population was inextricably linked to China's sovereignty. Zhao's observation reveals that in the early 1910s, Chinese officials—at least those in Manchuria—perceived Sino-Korean relations purely on the state-to-state level. However, before Beijing could respond to Zhao's proposal, the nationalist revolution broke out in Wuhan in October 1911, quickly leading to the collapse of the dynasty.

Conclusion

On February 12, 1912, the Manchu court issued an edict of abdication that announced the end of the Great Qing and acknowledged the Qing's loss of the Mandate of Heaven. The Qing declared that it was handing over China's "sovereignty" to "the entire people." The imperial court and a group of Han Chinese and Manchu ministers who had drafted the edict stressed that the post-Qing political system should guarantee that "the complete integrity of the territories of the five races, Chinese, Manchus, Mongols, Muhammadans, and Tibetans" be maintained for "a great state under the title 'the Republic of China.'"[1] According to their blueprint, the new China would integrate into its territory the outer subordinates, or outer *fan*, that had been administered by the Mongolian Superintendency, but it would not encompass those outer *fan* whose contacts with China had been under the jurisdiction of the Ministry of Rites. Most of the latter were already under foreign colonial rule. From then on, China, or Zhongguo, was principally defined by its state sovereignty and territorial borders, the connotations of the Chinese empire having shrunk sharply.

Yuan Shikai, the prime minister of the Imperial Cabinet of the Qing since November 1911 and the leader of the New Army in North China, was entrusted by the imperial court with organizing a provisional Republican government. Having started his political career in Chosŏn, Yuan was now the most powerful man in China and would soon become the first president of the republic. But Yuan's new China showed little concern for Korea's fate. In 1912 Japan entered the Taishō period and China underwent its transformation into a republic, but

Korea remained under the yoke of Japanese colonialism. Having witnessed the dramatic changes in East Asia and the rapid proliferation of ideas of national independence across the world, the Chinese in the 1910s held mixed views of colonial Korea. Although some Chinese visitors saw Korea as a positive model of modernization,[2] a greater number regarded the country as a negative example of colonialism and a vivid warning to China about the perils of falling under colonial rule. An anonymous Chinese visitor en route to Japan in 1918, for instance, commented that it was the blood of the Korean people that nourished the remarkable achievements in Korea. The visitor predicted that within a few decades the whole country of Korea and the ethnic Korean people would become extinct.[3] By underscoring the dangers of colonialism, he sought to mobilize his countrymen to save China from being subjugated by foreign powers such as Japan.

Passionate and patriotic Chinese nationalists such as the anonymous traveler may have been more or less relieved when the May Fourth Movement erupted in Beijing in 1919, the same year in which the March First Independence Movement swept Hansŏng in colonial Korea. Each of the two movements opened a new chapter in the modern history of its respective country. More importantly, the Korean nationalists who survived the Japanese suppression of the movement escaped to China and established a government in exile in Shanghai, calling it the Provisional Government of the Republic of Korea. Not only did China thus become a safe harbor for the overseas Korean nationalist movement, but the Sino-Korean relationship was transformed yet again in the twentieth century. The pre-1895 inner dual network between the two countries was resuscitated in 1919, this time linking the Korean Nationalist Party with the Chinese National-ist Party, on the one hand, and the Korean state—which for now existed only in imagined form because of Japanese colonialism—with the Chinese state, on the other. Informed by the age-old politico-cultural homogenization, this dual net-work remained the basic political arrangement between the two sides in main-land China throughout the Republican era, from 1912 to 1949, as well as after the establishment of the People's Republic of China in 1949.

By the end of the 1950s, the People's Republic of China had recovered the majority of the Qing's territory and begun to govern its vast expanse through a new kind of regime and a new set of political, cultural, and social norms imported from the West. By mining historical sources from late imperial and modern China for precedents, the new state sought to integrate into its terri-tory certain areas that had been governed by the Qing with various degrees of control, ranging from Manchuria to Mongolia, from eastern Turkestan to the Himalayas, and from the southwestern mountainous areas to Taiwan and the small islands of the South China Sea. The policy of absorbing these areas into

Chinese territory completely removed any ambiguity that might otherwise have been caused by patriarchal relationships or kinship ties between central political actors and their local agents or subordinates—connections reminiscent of those that had characterized the Zongfan era. For instance, Tibet, where the Qing court had maintained an imperial resident since 1727, was incorporated into the People's Republic in the 1950s despite the fact that it had enjoyed independence since 1913.[4] In this sense, the People's Republic succeeded in redrawing China's borders and realizing the thwarted ambitions of the Republic of China during the latter's continental period from 1912 to 1949. It was also during this frenzied time before the triumph of the Communist revolution that China ultimately failed to reclaim Outer Mongolia, although in 1916 the Republican government under Yuan Shikai successfully restored the Zongfan relationship with Outer Mongolia by reviving the convention of imperial investiture from the Qing.[5]

The Chinese state narrative since 1949 has oversimplified late imperial history, treating the Qing as a single dynasty in Chinese history rather than as the node of a Qing-centric cosmopolitan world. However, the historical record of events on Qing China's frontiers, especially events with implications concerning the autonomous positions of certain political units, has challenged the official Chinese narrative by revealing the existence and operation of a cross-border Chinese empire under the Qing.[6] Outside China, almost all of Qing China's former subordinate countries under the management of the Ministry of Rites separated themselves from China's orbit in the post–World War II movement for national independence and decolonization. Since then, these countries have played only a minor role in Chinese nationalist histories of China, including Qing China, even though they were regarded in late imperial times as part of the Chinese empire. In this sense, what the authoritarian regime of the People's Republic of China has encountered on its borders since 1949 is a series of post-Qing problems unleashed by China's late imperial transformations.[7]

Korea is a typical case. This book has demonstrated that Korea formed part of the Chinese empire in the politico-cultural sense in the late imperial period, their connection weakening precipitously after 1895 and finally giving way to Japanese domination. But the Chinese perception of Korea's position within the Chinese world crossed the 1911 divide. From the time of the March First Independence Movement in 1919, the nationalist government of China was enthusiastic in its support of Korea, in part because of Chinese nostalgia for the familistic Sino-Korean relationship. Many Chinese regarded Korea as a lost land of China. In 1929, for example, the Administration for Industry and Commerce of Hebei Province published a "Map of the National Humiliation of the Central Civilized Country" (Ch., Zhonghua guochi ditu). The map shows the territory of the Republic of China, including Outer Mongolia and Tibet, which at the time presented themselves as independent countries, as well as the lands that China lost between the Treaty of Nerchinsk of 1689 and Japan's Twenty-One Demands of 1915. Among the lost lands were China's previous *fan* and subordinate countries (Ch., *fanshu*) Korea, Ryukyu, Annam, Siam, Myanmar, Bhutan, and Nepal. All of these territories together constituted "the central civilized country" (Ch., *Zhonghua*), reflecting the reach of the politico-cultural Chinese empire in the Qing period. Citing Sun Yat-sen's 1924 comment that China was a "second-level colony," a status that was even worse than that of a "semi-colony," the map's authors rallied the Chinese to erase the national humiliation of China's loss of these territories and to fight for China's future.[8]

In March 1930 the Chinese Nationalist Party, the Guomindang, issued a proclamation supporting the Korean independence movement against Japan. The nationalists claimed that

> Korea used to be China's vassal and dependent country, and according to historical records the Koreans are descendants of the Shang and Zhou Dynasties and a branch of our Chinese people. Their political and cultural production primarily follows the ways of the Han and Tang Dynasties, so they are obviously a school of our Chinese culture, and they practice our Chinese rituals of worship. Thus, they should ally with us to survive and become prosperous together. In this way, they can make their ancestors proud and present their unusual achievements as part of the everlasting lineage of the Yan and Huang emperors [Ch., *Yan Huang zisun*].[9]

The Chinese Communist Party shared the Nationalist Party's perception of Korea. In April 1937, three months before the Marco Polo Bridge Incident between Japan and China in Beijing, Mao Zedong (1893–1976) composed an address on behalf of the Chinese Communist Party at Yan'an for the sacrificial ceremony for the Huang emperor, the legendary "ancestor of the Chinese peoples" (Ch., *Zhonghua minzu shizu*). Mao recalled that Qing China "lost Ryukyu and Taiwan, and Korea was ruined" (Ch., *Liu Tai bushou, Sanhan wei xu*), and he mourned the demise of the Chinese empire's glory, which had historically undergirded the Sino-Korean relationship.[10] Thirteen years later, Mao sent his troops to North Korea to, as he saw it, rescue a country that had become part of the newly constructed and transnational Communist world.[11]

In the 1960s, when the Great Cultural Revolution swept China and triggered various conflicts between China, the Soviet Union, and North Korea in the global Cold War, North Korea launched a movement to consolidate Kim Il-sung (1912–1994)'s Chuch'e ideology (K., *Chuch'e sasang*, "thought of autonomy"), as part of which the regime sharply criticized Korea's Sadaeism (K., *Sadae juŭi*, "the -ism of serving the great") and China's Taegukism (K., *Taeguk juŭi*, "the -ism of serving as the great") in history.[12] China's book of all-under-Heaven was finally and bitterly closed on the peninsula. This moment also marked the end of China's prospects of again treating Korea as an outlying province or even incorporating it into China as a province. In the same period, the Chinese state abandoned the hope of retrieving Outer Mongolia, yet it had fully integrated Manchuria, Inner Mongolia, Xinjiang, and Tibet into Chinese territory and laid claim to Taiwan.

Here, at the very end of this book, let us go back to Ch'oe Hyo-il, the Korean warrior who, as described in the introduction, sacrificed himself in front of Emperor Chongzhen's tomb in 1644. Ch'oe died for the Chinese empire, but his martyrdom has not been celebrated in either Chinese or Korean historical narratives since at least 1895. In the remade East Asia of the twentieth and twenty-first centuries, both China and Korea have chosen to forget, purposely and perhaps permanently, that Chosŏn was long enfolded within the Chinese empire.

Notes

The following abbreviations are used in the notes:

ADPP	*American Diplomatic and Public Papers*
FO	17 Foreign Office Record Group 17, China Correspondence
FRUS	*Foreign Relations of the United States*
GXZP	Zhongguo diyi lishi dang'an guan, *Guangxu chao zhupi zouzhe*
HKMS	*Ku Han'guk oegyo munsŏ*
JACAR	Japan Center for Asian Historical Records
JJCZ	Qingdai gongzhongdang zouzhe ji Junjichu dang zhejian
KARD	*Korean-American Relations: Documents Pertaining to the Far Eastern Diplomacy of the United States*
LBZL	*Libu zeli*
LFZZ	Junjichu hanwen lufu zouzhe
LHZQJ	Gu and Dai, *Li Hongzhang quanji*
LKSS	Neige Like shishu
MBRT	*Manbun rōtō*
MWLD	*Manwen laodang*
NHGB	Nihon Gaimushō, *Nihon gaikō bunsho*
QSCJ	Qinshi fengming qianlai ciji Chaoxian guowang mufei juan
QSL	*Qing shilu*
RCGK	Renchuan gangkou juan
TMHG	*Tongmun hwigo*
WJSL	*Chosŏn wangjo sillok*
WJZA	Neige waijiao zhuan'an, Chaoxian
WLGS	Chang and Yeh, *Qing ruguan qian yu Chaoxian wanglai guoshu huibian, 1619–1643*
ZCSLHB	Zhongguo diyi lishi dang'an guan, *Qingdai Zhong-Chao guanxi dang'an shiliao huibian*
ZCSLXB	Zhongguo diyi lishi dang'an guan, *Qingdai Zhong-Chao guanxi dang'an shiliao xubian*
ZRHGX	*Qingji Zhong-Ri-Han guanxi shiliao*
ZRJSSL	*Qing Guangxu chao Zhong-Ri jiaoshe shiliao*
ZRZZ	Qi, *Zhong-Ri zhanzheng*

INTRODUCTION

1. *Sohyŏn Simyang ilgi*, 354. Please see the bibliography for translations of non-English titles.

2. *Ŭpchi P'yŏngan do p'yŏn*, 531–32; *Chosŏn wangjo sillok* (hereafter cited as *WJSL*) (Sukchong), 40:552.

3. There is no scholarly consensus on a generic term to describe the Sinocentric political arrangements of late imperial times. I adopt the term *Zongfan*, as explained in the following sections of this chapter and in the next chapter. Among modern sources, my use of Zongfan primarily follows Shao Xunzheng in his *Zhong-Fa-Yuenan guanxi* and Chang

Tsun-wu in his *Qing-Han Zongfan maoyi*. Some scholars have also used Zongfan as an interpretive lens in their studies of the relationship between the Qing and Inner Asia; see, for example, Zha, *Qingdai Xizang yu Bulukeba*. For some recent works on the Sinocentric foreign-relations system from an East Asian perspective, see, for example, Chen, *Zhongguo chuantong duiwai guanxi*; Huang, *Songdai chaogong tixi*; Kim, *Han-Chung kwan'gye sa*; Lee, *China's Hegemony*; Li, *Chaogong zhidu shilun*; and Sun, *Qingdai Zhong-Yue Zongfan guanxi*. For the discrepancy between this Sinocentric system and the Western understanding of it, see Chang, "Dongxi guoji zhixu yuanli," 54–57; Chang, *Qing-Han Zongfan maoyi*, 2–15; Hevia, *Cherishing Men from Afar*, 9–15; Larsen, "Comforting Fictions"; Nelson, *Korea and the Old Orders*, 288–97; Okamoto, *Sōshuken no sekaishi*, 90–118; Shao, *Zhong-Fa-Yuenan guanxi*, 37–38; Song, "'Tributary' from a Multilateral and Multi-layered Perspective"; Wills, "Tribute, Defensiveness, and Dependency"; Zhang, "Rethinking the 'Tribute System,'" Zhou, "Equilibrium Analysis." For a review of the literature on the "tributary system" and Korea, see Wang, "Co-constructing Empire," 28–43.

4. In Chinese history, *Zhengtong* has two major intellectual sources: the circulation of the "Five Virtues" (Ch., *Wude*, namely, earth, wood, metal, fire, and water), a theory put forward by Zou Yan (ca. 305–240 BC), and the great unification raised by scholars of the Tang and Song Dynasties based on their interpretations of the classic *Gongyang Commentary on the Spring and Autumn Annals* (Ch., *Chunqiu Gongyang zhuan*). The former was used in a temporal sense and the latter in spatial and politico-cultural senses. Since the Mongolian conquest of the Song in the thirteenth century, Zhengtong was principally bound with the great unification; see Rao, *Zhongguo shixue*, 12–26, 81–86. Both the Mongols of the Yuan and the Manchus of the Qing based the orthodox legitimacy of their dynasties on the ideology of the great unification. For the influence of Zhengtong on the historiographical tradition and politics in late imperial China, see Liu, *Zhengtong yu Hua–Yi*; for a similar influence in Tokugawa Japan, see Koschmann, *Mito Ideology*. For more details on the Qing and Chosŏn Korea in this regard, see the following chapters of this book.

5. Wang, "Yinzhou zhidu lun."

6. Wang, "Early Ming Relations," 37–41.

7. For discussions on the story of Jizi/Kija, see, for example, Kim, *Han-Chung kwan'gye sa*, 1:87–103; Wang, "Co-constructing Empire," 342–96; Miao, "Jishi Chaoxian wenti." For the unified Chinese dynasties' perception of Korea, see Haboush, "Contesting Chinese Time," 118.

8. *Yuanshi*, 15:4621; Chŏng, *Koryŏ sa*, 1:564.

9. *WJSL* (T'aejong), 1:205.

10. *WJSL* (Sejong), 2:483, 4:699. For Ming-Chosŏn relations, see Clark, "Sino-Korean Tributary Relations"; Wang, "Co-constructing Empire."

11. *Mingshi*, 27:8279; Hong, *Tamhŏn yŏn'gi*, 42:18; Kye, "Huddling under the Imperial Umbrella."

12. For the introduction of Neo-Confucianism to Chosŏn, see Duncan, *Origins of the Chosŏn Dynasty*, 237–65; Palais, *Confucian Statecraft*, 25–47.

13. *WJSL* (Sŏnjo), 21:497, 531; 22:189, 294, 439, 617.

14. See, for example, Yun, "Rethinking the Tribute System," 6–17.

15. For more discussion on the complexity of outer *fan* under the Qing, see chapter 2. On the Qing-Siamese case, see Chuang, "Xianluo guowang "; Mancall, "Ch'ing Tribute System"; Masuda, "Fall of Ayutthaya."

16. Shao, *Zhong-Fa-Yuenan guanxi*, 38; Koo, *Ch'ŏng nara*, 211–16.

17. *Qing shilu* (hereafter QSL) (Qianlong), 17:680, 732–40; 18:12; *Da Qing huidian shili*, 502:8a–9b.

18. Chun, "Sino-Korean Tributary Relations."

19. For the former, see Huang, *Chaoxian de ruhua*; for the latter, see Em, *Great Enterprise*, 23–24; Larsen, "Comforting Fictions"; Lee, *China's Hegemony*; Lim, "Tributary Relations."

20. For recent research on the relationship between the civilized–barbarian discourse and identity in early modern East Asia, see Chang, "Han'guk esŏ taejungguk kwannyŏm"; Fuma, *Chōsen enkōshi*, 38–43, 328–90; Larsen, *Tradition, Treaties, and Trade*, 35–42; Rawski, *Early Modern China*, 188–224; Sun, *Da Ming qihao*; Wang, *Xiao Zhonghua*; Yamauchi, *Chōsen kara mita Ka–I*.

21. Gaimushō, *Nihon gaikō bunsho* (hereafter *NHGB*), 2(28): 363–72.

22. Burbank and Cooper, *Empires in World History*, 8; Cooper, *Colonialism in Question*, 27. For the rise of empire in Chinese history, see Puett, *Ambivalence of Creation*, 141–76.

23. Wong, "China's Agrarian Empire," 190.

24. *Treaties, Conventions, etc.*, 1:1–13.

25. Choi, "Nerchinsk choyak"; Zhao, "Reinventing China."

26. Chuang, *Man Han Yiyu Lu*, 11–12, 168.

27. Huang, *Riben guozhi*, 4:1; Liang, *Yinbingshi heji*, 5:15.

28. Grosier, *General Description of China*, 244; Curzon, *Problems of the Far East*, 158.

29. Guo and Zhang, *Yuenan tongshi*, 413–61; Woodside, *Vietnam and the Chinese Model*, 9–10, 18–22. For the independent status of Vietnam in the Ming period, see Baldanza, *Ming China and Vietnam*, 77–110.

30. Haboush, *Confucian Kingship in Korea*, 11–26.

31. Zhongyang yanjiuyuan lishi yuyan yanjiusuo, *Ming Qing shiliao*, ser. 7, 5:491b. For China's modern diplomacy, see Kawashima, *Chūgoku kindai gaikō no keisei*; Li, *Zhongguo jindai waijiaoguan*; Okamoto and Kawashima, *Chūgoku kindai gaikō no taidō*; Rudolph, *Negotiated Power*. For Korea's modern diplomacy, see Larsen, *Tradition, Treaties, and Trade*; Mori, *Chōsen gaikō no kindai*.

32. Sun, *Qingdai Zhong-Yue Zongfan guanxi*, 92–93.

33. For the politics of time inscription in Korea during the Qing, see Haboush, "Contesting Chinese Time," 128–33.

34. For the Qing's cartographic survey and its significance, see Kicengge, "Nibcu tiaoyue jiebei tu"; Li, "Ji Kangxi 'Huangyu quanlan tu'"; Perdue, "Boundaries, Maps, and Movement." For the Qing-Annam and Qing-Chosŏn juridical negotiations, see Kim, "The Rule of Ritual." For a study of Chosŏn's perception of borders and Qing power from 1636 to 1912, see Kim, *Ginseng and Borderland*.

35. For the Sino-Korean demarcation negotiations, see Chang, "Qingdai Zhong-Han bianwu"; Kim, *Han-Chung kwan'gye sa*, 2:885–95; Ledyard, "Cartography in Korea"; Li, *Cho-Ch'ŏng kukgyŏng munje yŏn'gu*; Song, *Making Borders*.

36. *WJSL* (Sŏnjo), 22:57.

37. *Mingshi*, 27:8307.

38. *QSL* (Qianlong), 24:297, 25:715.

39. *Da Qing tongli*, 28:4–5.

40. *Da Qing Shixian li/shu*, 1646, 1679, 1731, 1795, 1821, 1842, 1865, 1894, 1898, 1909; Neige Like shishu (hereafter LKSS), no. 2–8; Qintian jian tiben zhuanti shiliao, R4–R7.

41. Elverskog, "Mongol Time," 143.

42. See, for example, *Haedong chido*, 1:2–3; Hostetler, *Qing Colonial Enterprise*, 47–49; Smith, *Mapping China*, 48–88.

43. *Simyang janggye*, 574.

44. Zhongguo diyi lishi dang'an guan, *Guangxu chao zhupi zouzhe* (hereafter GXZP), 112:243.

45. Kim, *Ŭmch'ŏng sa*, 40–41.

46. *QSL* (Guangxu), 55:128.

47. Cooper, *Colonialism in Question*, 156.

48. For the term "outlying province," see Zeng (the Marquis Tseng), "China," 9.

49. Schmid, *Korea between Empires*, 11, 55–100, 257–60.

50. See, for example, Hobsbawm, *Age of Empire*, 56–83; Cohen, *Discovering History in China*, 97–147; Hevia, *English Lessons*, 4–26; Iriye, "Imperialism in East Asia"; Rowe, *China's Last Empire*, 231–43; Westad, *Restless Empire*, 53–86.

51. Pomeranz, *Great Divergence*.

52. Hu, *Diguo zhuyi*; Scott, *China and the International System*.

53. For the paradigm of "New Qing history," see Millward et al., *New Qing Imperial History*; Waley-Cohen, "New Qing History." For interpretations of the Qing empire from an Inner Asian and ethnic perspective, see, for example, Crossley, *Manchus*; Crossley, *Translucent Mirror*; Crossley, Siu, and Sutton, *Empire at the Margins*; Elliott, *Manchu Way*.

54. See, for example, Di Cosmo, "Qing Colonial Administration"; Herman, "Empires in the Southwest"; Hevia, *Cherishing Men from Afar*; Hevia, *English Lessons*, 18, 166–174; Hostetler, *Qing Colonial Enterprise*; Kim, *Borderland Capitalism*; Millward, *Beyond the Pass*; Perdue, *China Marches West*.

55. Kim Kwangmin has pointed out that the "dual expansions" of European maritime commerce in the Indian Ocean and Chinese power in Xinjiang in the eighteenth century "changed the economic and political landscapes of Central Asia significantly." See Kim, *Borderland Capitalism*, 45.

56. Champion and Echstein, "Introduction," 3.

57. See, for example, Lee, *Diplomatic Relations*, 136–42; Kim, "Chinese Imperialism in Korea"; Deuchler, *Confucian Gentlemen*, 220; Kim, *Last Phase*, 348; Larsen, *Tradition, Treaties, and Trade*, 11–19. For the term "informal empire," see Gallagher and Robinson, "Imperialism of Free Trade."

58. Nelson, *Korea and the Old Orders*, 294.

59. As R. Bin Wong points out, "The absence of apparent change suggests the reproduction of a set of relationships or conditions." See Wong, *China Transformed*, 3.

60. As Peter I. Yun has argued, "In reality, each state was guided in its foreign policy formulation by the principles of realism and pragmatism. It is necessary to examine actual political motives and imperatives such as trade, cultural imports, and especially the issue of border security." See Yun, "Rethinking the Tribute System," 6. In his examination of the Qing's frontier policy, Matthew W. Mosca emphasizes that "there were no absolute policy differences distinguishing the empire's borderlands. Rather, it was the nature of the threat perceived that guided the empire's foreign policy choices." See Mosca, *From Frontier Policy to Foreign Policy*, 8.

1. CONQUERING CHOSŎN

1. *Ming Shenzong shilu*, 541:10283.

2. Huang, *1587*.

3. *Manbun rōtō* (hereafter *MBRT*), 1:67; Kuang and Li, *Qing Taizu chao manwen*, 1:63; *QSL* (Nurhaci), 1:63–64.

4. Michael, *Origin of Manchu Rule*, 44; *WJSL* (Kwanghaegun), 29:501; Crossley, "Manzhou Yuanliu Kao."

5. *Da Ming huidian*, 107:7a, 113:6a; Meng, *Qingdai shi*, 105.

6. *WJSL* (Kwanghaegun), 29:433, 508–22; Yi, *Ja'am jip*, 5:5.

7. For the Jurchen-Korean hierarchy, see Kawachi, *Mindai Joshin shi no kenkyū*, 424–50.

8. *MBRT*, 1:143.

9. Chang and Yeh, *Qing ruguan qian yu Chaoxian wanglai guoshu* (hereafter *WLGS*), 3.

10. *WJSL* (Kwanghaegun), 30:126–28.

11. Yi, *Ja'am jip*, 5:18–19.

12. *WJSL* (Kwanghaegun), 30:169.

13. Wang, *Xu Guangqi ji*, 1:106–17; *Ming Shenzong shilu*, 584:11172–73.

14. *WJSL* (Kwanghaegun), 31:129, 165–67.

15. *WJSL* (Injo), 33:503, 34:244.

16. *WJSL* (Injo), 34:163, 168, 208.

17. *MBRT*, 4:51.

18. Liu, *Qingchao chuqi*, 15–16.

19. *WJSL* (Injo), 34:208.

20. *WJSL* (Injo), 34:251, 260, 262; Liu, *Qingchao chuqi*, 54–57.

21. Choi, *Myŏng Ch'ŏng sidae*, 107–8.

22. *WJSL* (Injo), 34:414.

23. Zhongyang yanjiuyuan lishi yuyan yanjiusuo, *Ming Qing shiliao*, ser. 3, 1:45.

24. *WLGS*, 100.

25. Suzuki, "'Manbun gentō' ni mieru Chōsen."

26. *MBRT*, 5:619–21.

27. *MBRT*, 5:803, 853.

28. Luo, *Tiancong chao chengong zouyi*, 2:1a–3b, 20b; *Qingshi gao*, 12:3282; *MBRT*, 5:825–26.

29. *MBRT*, 4:92–95; *Manwen laodang* (hereafter *MWLD*), 861–62.

30. *QSL* (Hongtaiji), 2:171. For *laichao*, see Chun, "Tongyang kodaesa"; Fairbank, "Tributary Trade."

31. For the issue of the tributes and Ming China's and the Central Asian states' different understandings of their relationship, see Fletcher, "China and Central Asia."

32. *MBRT*, 4:99–100; *QSL* (Hongtaiji), 2:190–91.

33. Luo, *Tiancong chao chengong zouyi*, 3(1):10a–11b, 35a–35b; 3(2):15b.

34. Luo, *Tiancong chao chengong zouyi*, 3(1):11b, 21b; 3(2):18a.

35. For Nurhaci's and Hongtaiji's construction of Manchu imperial authority and their integration of multiethnic subjects for a new identity under the Manchu regime, see Crossley, *Translucent Mirror*, 177–85.

36. Farquhar, "Origins," 199–200; Perdue, *China Marches West*, 122–27.

37. See Ho, "In Defense of Sinicization"; Rawski, "Reenvisioning the Qing"; Huang, *Reorienting the Manchus*.

38. Ch'en, *Manzhou congkao*, 1–9; Zhao, "*Jiu Qing Yu*" *yanjiu*, 69–70.

39. *MBRT*, 1:76–78, 159–60, 191–92. For the relationship between *gurun* and the Manchu perception of "nation," see Elliott, "Manchu (Re)Definitions."

40. Imanishi, *Man-Wa Mō-Wa taiyaku Manshū jitsuroku*.

41. *MBRT*, 1:159–60, 191–92.

42. *MBRT*, 4:125; *QSL* (Hongtaiji), 2:190–91.

43. *QSL* (Hongtaiji), 2:71.

44. *MBRT*, 5:792; *QSL* (Hongtaiji), 2:165.

45. Luo, *Tiancong chao chengong zouyi*, 3(1):35.

46. *MBRT*, 4:29–30, 7:1439–41; *QSL* (Hongtaiji), 2:404.

47. *WJSL* (Injo), 34:625; *MBRT*, 6:981.

48. Tong, *Chunqiu shi*, 277–79; Zhang, *Qinzhi yanjiu*, 39–51.

49. For discussion, see Ge, *Zhaizi Zhongguo*, 41–44.

50. *MBRT*, 4:92–95, 332.

51. *MBRT*, 4:28.

52. *MBRT*, 6:893–98; *WLGS*, 168–69.

53. *QSL* (Hongtaiji), 2:341–43.

54. *MBRT*, 6:904–11; *QSL* (Hongtaiji), 2:347–49; *WJSL* (Injo), 34:624–25.

55. *WJSL* (Injo), 34:625.

56. *MBRT*, 6:982, 993–94; *Qing Taizong shilu gaoben*, 17; *WJSL* (Injo), 34:631.

57. *QSL* (Hongtaiji), 2:369–72; *MBRT*, 6:1005–6.

58. *WJSL* (Injo), 34:649.

59. *Chosŏnguk raesŏ bu*, 2:21–22; *WLGS*, 199–200.

60. *Chosŏnguk raesŏ bu*, 2:26–29; *WLGS*, 207–9.

61. Yi Kŭng-ik, *Yŏllyŏsil gisul*, 3:491–98.

62. *Chosŏnguk raesŏ bu*, 2:29–32; *WLGS*, 210–12.

63. *WJSL* (Injo), 34:671; *Tongmun hwigo* (hereafter *TMHG*), 2:1488.

64. *QSL* (Hongtaiji), 2:432–33, 511.

65. *WJSL* (Injo), 34:674, 677.

66. *QSL* (Shunzhi), 3:363.

67. *QSL* (Shunzhi), 3:995. The practice of "dividing cogongrass," which was recorded in *The Classic of History* as "dividing soil and cogongrass," refers to a part of the Zhou Zongfan investiture ritual in which the Son of Heaven endowed the vassals with some soil from his ancestral shrine and the soil was wrapped in white cogongrass. The vassals would then use the soil for their own ancestral shrines on their own lands.

68. See *Cefeng Chaoxian guowang Li Qin fengtian gaoming*, March 6, 1725; the King's memorial dated August 28, 1735, in Neige waijiao zhuan'an, Chaoxian (hereafter WJZA), no. 564–2–190–4.

69. *T'ongmun'gwan ji*, 1:112.

70. See, for example, Guanming's memorial on November 20, 1811, in Junjichu hanwen lufu zouzhe (hereafter LFZZ), no. 3–163–7728–16.

71. *QSL* (Qianlong), 17:680, 732–40; *Da Qing huidian shili*, 502:8a–9b.

72. *Qingji Zhong-Ri-Han guanxi shiliao* (hereafter *ZRHGX*), 3:1072–75.

73. Li to Yuan, February 1, 1886, in Gu and Dai, *Li Hongzhang quanji* (hereafter *LHZQJ*), 21:655.

74. Rockhill, "Korea in Its Relations with China," 32.

75. For the critiques of reinterpretation, see Lin, "Tributary System," 507; for "Pax Sinica," see Huang, *Dongya de liyi shijie*.

76. For a study of China's tribute system from an international-relations perspective, see Lee, *China's Hegemony*.

77. Perdue, "Tea, Cloth, Gold, and Religion," 2.

78. See Wills, *Embassies and Illusions*, 173; Smith, "Mapping China." Iwai Shigeki argues that the practice of foreigners paying homage to China (J., *chōkō*; Ch., *chaogong*) began to be incorporated into the Sino-foreign trade system (J., *goshi*; Ch., *hushi*) after 1380, when the Ming abolished the Maritime Trade Superintendency (Ch., Shibo si), a long-standing institution for managing maritime trade, and that this policy endured until 1684, when Emperor Kangxi resumed maritime trade. See Iwai, "Chōkō to goshi." Danjo Hiroshi emphasizes the same change in the Ming period; see Danjo, *Mindai kaikin*, 181–82, 336–37.

79. *QSL* (Hongtaiji), 2:633–34, 777, 820–21, 876, 890; *QSL* (Shunzhi), 3:898.

80. *TMHG*, 2:1533.

81. Yi, *Pusim ilgi*, 445.

82. *QSL* (Hongtaiji), 2:459; *Chosŏnguk raesŏ bu*, 2:36–41.

83. *WJSL* (Injo), 34:709.

84. *QSL* (Shunzhi), 2:511, 3:586–87.

85. Wang, "Santiandu," 290–96. For recent discussions about the Samjŏndo stele, see Koo, *Ch'ŏng nara*, 44–47; Bae, *Chosŏn kwa Chunghwa*, 33–65. In 2007, the 370th anniversary of Chosŏn's surrender to the Manchus in 1637, a Korean nationalist painted "ch'ŏlgŏ Pyŏngja 370" in large characters on the stele (*ch'ŏlgŏ* means "remove"), demonstrating the event's strong psychological impact on modern Korean nationalism.

86. *WJSL* (Injo), 34:709.

87. *QSL* (Hongtaiji), 2:649.

88. *TMHG*, 1485:1497–98, 1503–11.

89. *TMHG*, 2:1700–1702, 1747–48.

90. See Han, *Chŏngmyo, Pyŏngja horan*, 383–87.

91. For Manchu-Mongol relations during this period, see Elverskog, *Our Great Qing*, 27–39.

2. BARBARIANIZING CHOSŎN

1. For the post-Ming process of decentering China among China's neighbors, see Haboush, "Constructing the Center"; Rawski, *Early Modern China*, 1–10, 225–34.

2. *QSL* (Shunzhi), 3:91–92.

3. *QSL* (Qianlong), 18:643.

4. Langkio's palace memorial, April 17, 1653, in LKSS, no. 2–3.

5. Zhongyang yanjiuyuan lishi yuyan yanjiusuo, *Ming Qing shiliao*, ser. 7, 5:404b.

6. *QSL* (Shunzhi), 3:363.

7. Millward, *Beyond the Pass*, 36–38.

8. *MBRT*, 5:790–92; *MWLD*, 1297–99; *QSL* (Hongtaiji), 2:165.

9. *Zhaofu Zheng Jing chiyu*.

10. Chuang, *Man Han Yiyu Lu*, 11–12, 168.

11. *Da Ming jili*, 32:7a–8b.

12. For example, the *MBRT*, the most important historical record of pre-1644 Manchu history, did not refer to the Manchu regime as *abkai gurun*. For this subtle philological explanation, I am also grateful to two prestigious archivists and scholars, Wu Yuanfeng at the First Historical Archives of China and Zhao Zhiqiang at the Beijing Academy of Social Sciences, whose mother tongue is Xibo, which is almost identical to Manchu.

13. *QSL* (Hongtaiji), 2:455.

14. *QSL* (Shunzhi), 3:530–54; Guo, "Wushi Dalai Lama rujin shulun."

15. *QSL* (Shunzhi), 3:376–77.

16. *Libu zeli* (hereafter *LBZL*), 173:6b–10a, 174:8a–13b, 175:5b–6a, 176:6b–8a.

17. See, for example, Huang, *Chaoxian de ruhua*.

18. Chang, *Qing-Han Zongfan maoyi*, 25–27.

19. *QSL* (Shunzhi), 3:251, 272; *Lidai baoan*, 1:107.

20. For the case of Siam, see LKSS, no. 2–3; for Ryukyu, see Wu, "Qingchu cefeng Liuqiu."

21. Jiang, *Taiwan waiji*, 175–207.

22. *Zhaofu Zheng Jing chiyu*.

23. *QSL* (Shunzhi), 3:363, 586–87.

24. Zhongguo diyi lishi dang'an guan, *Qinggong zhencang lishi Dalai Lama dang'an*, 10–19.

25. See Xizang zizhiqu dang'an guan, *Xizang lishi dang'an*, files 34–74.

26. See, for example, *Da Qing huidian* (1764), vols. 79–80; *LBZL*, vols. 171–87; *Lifan yuan zeli*, vol. 16. John King Fairbank and S. Y. Têng have also argued that the way in which the Qing controlled and managed these Mongol tribes was "all in the traditional forms of the tributary relationship"; see Fairbank and Têng, "On the Ch'ing Tributary System," 158–63. Recent scholarship has complicated this picture by examining how the Manchu and Mongol sides perceived each other's positions in the Qing-led empire; see Elverskog, *Our Great Qing*, 23–39.

27. *Da Qing huidian shili*, 975:9b–10a.

28. See, for example, *QSL* (Yongzheng), 8:388; Zhongguo diyi lishi dang'an guan, *Qingdai Junjichu manwen aocha dang*, 1:1123, 2:1476; *Xizang dang'an*, files 34–74; *Da Qing huidian* (1764), 80:26a.

29. Mark Mancall also points out that after 1644 the Mongolian Superintendency "used rites and forms of the traditional Confucian Chinese system to conduct relations with the 'barbarians'"; see Mancall, "Ch'ing Tribute System," 72–73.

30. *LBZL*, 171:1–14, 172:1–22, 181:1–7, 184:1–6, 185:1–3, 186:1–5. For the classic discussion on the regulations, see Fairbank, "Preliminary Framework," 10–11; Fairbank and Têng, "On the Ch'ing Tributary System," 163–73.

31. *Da Ming huidian*, vols. 105–8.

32. Hostetler, *Qing Colonial Enterprise*, 118–21.

33. For the Qing's expansion to the southwest, see Herman, "Empires in the Southwest"; Hostetler, *Qing Colonial Enterprise*; Gong, *Ming Qing Yunnan tusi*; Li, *Qingdai tusi zhidu*.

34. *Zhupi yuzhi*, 45:1a–81a.

35. *Da Ming huidian*, 105:1b; *Da Qing huidian* (1899), 39:2a–3a.

36. *Da Qing huidian* (1764), 56:1a–2b; *LBZL*, vols. 171–80; *Da Qing huidian* (1899), 39:2a–3a. The successive changes to the list over the course of the Qing period are highlighted by the five editions of *Da Qing huidian* (issued in 1690, 1732, 1764, 1818, and 1899, respectively). See Fairbank and Têng, "On the Ch'ing Tributary System," 174; Banno, *Kindai Chūgoku seiji gaikōshi*, 87.

37. *Da Qing huidian* (1764), 80:1a, 10b. Peter C. Perdue argues that this claim "was as much mythical as real"; see Perdue, *China Marches West*, 527.

38. *LBZL*, vols. 172–77. Siam sent emissaries once every three years until 1839 and once every four years thereafter.

39. *LBZL*, 172:1b–5b.

40. *TMHG*, 2:1700–1744; *Ch'ŏng sŏn go*, 2:404–502; Chang, *Qing-Han Zongfan maoyi*, 18–19; Liu, *Qingdai Zhong-Chao shizhe*, 154–251. In practice, the Korean tributary emissaries simultaneously gathered intelligence on the Qing and reported their findings to the king after they returned home in attachments to their palace memorials (K., *p'iltam*). Their intelligence-gathering activities helped the Korean court understand the dynamics of the Qing's domestic and international situation. For *p'iltam* from 1639 to 1862, see *Tongmun koryak*, 3:405–530. For a specific case of intelligence gathering, see Ding, "18 segi ch'o Chosŏn yŏnhaengsa."

41. *QSL* (Qianlong), 24:297, 25:715.

42. *LBZL*, 172–80:1a. The number of attendants in Sulu's missions was also open, but theoretically Sulu sent a mission only once every five years.

43. Langkio's memorial, February 9, 1653, in LKSS, no. 2–1; LFZZ, nos. 3–163–7728–8, 3–163–7730–25.

44. *T'ongmun'gwan ji*, 1:94–98; Yi, *Pugwon rok*, 707–9.

45. Langkio's memorial, May 28, 1653, in LKSS, no. 2–4.

46. *TMHG*, 1:903–1044, 2:1045–1245, 1747–71; Chun, "Sino-Korean Tributary Relations," 92–94, 101; Liu, *Qingdai Zhong-Chao shizhe*, 35–41, 154–251.

47. *QSL* (Shunzhi), 3:940; *T'ongmun'gwan ji*, 1:215–18.

48. Qingdai gongzhongdang zouzhe ji Junjichu dang zhejian (hereafter JJCZ), no. 072667; *LBZL*, 181:1b–2a. For the mission in 1845, see JJCZ, no. 076837; Huashana, *Dongshi jicheng*.

49. Ch'iksa ilgi, 17:14b; Chongli, *Fengshi Chaoxian riji*, 22b–23a.

50. Hong, *Tamhŏn yŏn'gi*, 42:29.

51. Akŭkton si, 5; Huang and Qian, *Fengshi tu*, nos. 9 and 11.

52. See Yi, *Yŏnhaeng kisa*, 58:256–388, 59:12–15; Kim, *Ŭmch'ŏng sa*, 21; Baijun, *Fengshi Chaoxian*.

53. For the palisade, see *Da Qing huidian shili*, 233:20a; *Shengjing tongzhi*, 11:5a–6a; Yang, *Liubian jilue*, 1:1; Yang, *Qingdai liutiao bian*, 27–53; Edmonds, "Willow Palisade."

54. Kim, *Tongyŏ do*, no. 16.

55. Boming xizhe, *Fengcheng suolu*, 2a.

56. Kang, *Yŏnhaeng noch'ong gi*, 447–50.

57. *WJSL* (Sukchong), 40:117.

58. See Yi, *Yŏnhaeng kisa*, 58:314–15; Kwon, "Chosŏn Korea's Trade," 163–70; Yi, *Chosŏn huki taechŏng muyŏk*, 63–79.

59. *TMHG*, 1:672; *T'ongmun'gwan ji*, 1:112–30; WJZA, no. 564–2–190–4.

60. *T'ongmun'gwan ji*, 1:112–13.

61. WJZA, no. 564–2–190–4.

62. LFZZ, no. 3–163–7729–42; *Chaoxian shiliao huibian*, 20:513–73.

63. *WJSL* (Injo), 34:709.

64. *QSL* (Shunzhi), 3:363; *QSL* (Kangxi), 4:678–79.

65. *Cefeng Chaoxian guowang Li Qin fengtian gaoming.*

66. *Jangsŏgak sojang gomunsŏ*, 3:20–21.

67. *Jangsŏgak sojang gomunsŏ*, 3:30–33.

68. LKSS, no. 2–3.

69. See Crossley, *Translucent Mirror*, 11–12.

70. See Chuang, "Xianluo guowang"; Mancall, "Ch'ing Tribute System"; Masuda, "Fall of Ayutthaya."

71. Rockhill, "Korea in Its Relations with China," 2.

72. See, for example, LFZZ, nos. 3–163–7729–16/17/26/27/29/31/33/45/46; for more on the Korean tributes, see *Qingdai Zhong-Chao guanxi dang'an shiliao huibian* (hereafter ZCSLHB); *Qingdai Zhong-Chao guanxi dang'an shiliao xubian* (hereafter ZCSLXB).

73. *LBZL*, 172:6a–7b; Zhongyang yanjiuyuan lishi yuyan yanjiusuo, *Ming Qing shiliao*, ser. 7, 5:469b.

74. Yi, *Yŏnhaeng ilgi*, 100–101.

75. Zhongyang yanjiuyuan lishi yuyan yanjiusuo, *Ming Qing shiliao*, ser. 7, 5:449b.

76. *LBZL*, 171:3b–4a, 11b–15a; *Da Qing tongli*, 43:1–6.

77. *Da Tang Kaiyuan li*, 386–92.

78. *Sadae mungwe*, 42:14b–15b.

79. As JaHyun Kim Haboush points out in the context of seventeenth-century Korea, "In the cultural matrix of the time, ritual was seen as the manifestation of order as well as a means through which order was preserved and restored." See Haboush, "Constructing the Center," 70–71.

80. *QSL* (Kangxi), 4:678.

81. See, for example, *QSL* (Qianlong), 26:9.

82. Hong, *Tamhŏn sŏ*, 108.

83. *Guanglu si zeli*, 23:4b–6a; *LBZL*, 299:7a–7b.

84. *LBZL*, vol. 1, illustration no. 5.

85. Wang, *Xiao Zhonghua*, 137–38.

86. Dong, *Xianqiao shanfang riji*, 18–27.

87. Pak, *Hwanjae sŏnsaengjip*, 6–7.

88. Kim, *Last Phase*, 12.

89. Hong, *Tamhŏn sŏ*, 72, 322.

90. Li and Ch'oi, *Hanke shicun*, 261–66; Hong, *Tamhŏn sŏ*, 392, 396.

91. *Manbu jich'ik sarye*, 12–37.

92. *Kwansŏ jich'ik jŏngnye*, 63–101.

93. Li, *Shi Liuqiu ji*, 4:14b–23a, 5:6b–17b.

94. *Ch'iksa ilgi*, 1:25b; 3:28a, 30b; 4:18; 5:10a; 7:18a; 8:17a; 9:19b; 10:24b; 11:26b; *Tumangang kamgye mundap ki*, 34.

95. Langkio's memorial, May 18, 1653, in LKSS, no. 2–4.

96. Chang, *Qing-Han Zongfan maoyi*, 36–37.

97. Iwai, "Chōkō to goshi," 137.

98. *LBZL*, 172:11a–12b.

99. Huang, *Chaoxian de ruhua*, 479–91.

100. *QSL* (Qianlong), 9:477.

101. Yi, *Yŏnhaeng ilgi*, 193–94.

102. *QSL* (Qianlong), 9:330–31, 477–79.

103. Hong, *Tamhŏn sŏ*, 176.

104. *QSL* (Qianlong), 9:633–34, 711.

105. *QSL* (Qianlong), 17:721–22, 857; Ch'iksa ilgi, 12:8a.

106. *QSL* (Yongzheng), 8:399–400, 458.

107. *QSL* (Qianlong), 12:527–74; *TMHG*, 1:913–18. For a study of the case of Mangniushao, see Kim, *Ginseng and Borderland*, 92–103.

108. For more on the case of Zeng, see Spence, *Treason by the Book*.

109. *QSL* (Yongzheng), 8:696–97.

110. See Hirano, *Shin teikoku to Chibetto mondai*, 71–112.

111. *Lidai diwang miao yanjiu*, 14–31.

112. See Crossley, *Translucent Mirror*, 261–62.

113. Kishimoto, "'Zhongguo' he 'Waiguo,'" 365–66.

114. The imperial envoys in 1729, 1731, 1736, 1748, and 1750 did so. See Ch'iksa ilgi, vols. 4–9.

115. *QSL* (Qianlong), 14:120–21.

116. *Jiu Tangshu*, 16:5274.

117. Millward, *Beyond the Pass*, 25.

118. *Guben Yuan Ming zaju*, 4:1–12.

119. *Siku quanshu zongmu tiyao*, 15:12.

120. *Huang Qing zhigong tu*, 40–41, 54–55, 58–59, 66–67.

121. Chuang, *Xie Sui Zhigong tu*, 60–61, 78–79; Hostetler, *Qing Colonial Enterprise*, 47; Smith, *Mapping China*, 75–76.

122. Zhu, *Qingshi tudian*, 6:197–98.

123. Crossley, "Manzhou Yuanliu Kao," 761.

124. *QSL* (Qianlong), 17:259–60.

125. Pritchard, *Anglo-Chinese Relations*, 133–43.

126. These reports can be found in *ZCSLXB* and *ZCSLHB*. As chapter 6 shows, in the 1900s Chinese provincial governors were still submitting similar reports to Beijing.

127. For *tianchao tizhi*, see Zhongguo diyi lishi dang'an guan, *Qingdai Zhong-Liu guanxi dang'an xubian*, 723.

128. *QSL* (Qianlong), 21:578; Zhongguo diyi lishi dang'an guan, *Qianlong chao manwen jixin dang yibian*, 12:117.

129. For further cases, see Kim, "Kŏllyung nyŏnkan Chosŏn sahaeng."

3. JUSTIFYING THE CIVILIZED

1. *WJSL* (Sukchong), 40:118; Wang, *Xiao Zhonghua*, 43–51.

2. *Cefeng Chaoxian wangshidi Li Qin fengtian gaoming*, May 24, 1722.

3. *Songja taejŏn*, 96; *WJSL* (Sukchong), 38:243–44, 265, 288; 39:92; 41:94.

4. Haboush, "Constructing the Center," 62–90.

5. Sin, *Ch'ŏngsaem jip*, 4:1a–2b, 8b–13a.

6. *WJSL* (Sukchong), 40:76, 108, 122, 124.

7. For the most comprehensive collection of these journals, see Lim, *Yŏnhaengnok jŏnjip*.

8. Hong, *Tamhŏn sŏ*, 11; *Ch'ŏng sŏn go*, 2:458.

9. Hong, *Tamhŏn sŏ*, 93.

10. Hong, *Tamhŏn sŏ*, 106–8.

11. Hong, *Tamhŏn sŏ*, 117.

12. Fuma, *Chōsen enkōshi*, 365–69.
13. Hong, *Tamhŏn sŏ*, 172–76.
14. Hong, *Tamhŏn sŏ*, 72, 322.
15. Pak, *Chŏngyu chip*, 109–15, 383–438.
16. Pak, *Chŏngyu chip*, 437–38.
17. Ch'ae, *Ham'in nok*, 335–81.
18. Pak, *Yŏlha ilgi*, 1:10b.
19. Pak, *Yŏlha ilgi*, 1:59b–65b.
20. Pak, *Yŏlha ilgi*, 2:1a–2a.
21. Pak, *Yŏlha ilgi*, 2:57b.
22. Pak, *Yŏlha ilgi*, 3:20b; Min, *Chungguk gŭndaesa yŏn'gu*, 4.
23. Pak, *Yŏlha ilgi*, 3:26a–32b, 85a–87b, 92a–92b.
24. Pak, *Yŏlha ilgi*, 3:75a.
25. The rules of Qing bureaucracy contributed to this paradox. The Ministry of Rites, describing the Koreans' meeting with the Panchen Erdeni in a memorial to the emperor, simply fabricated its account, saying that after receiving the gifts from the Panchen, the Koreans immediately performed kowtow to show their gratitude. See Pak, *Yŏlha ilgi*, 3:91b.
26. *QSL* (Qianlong), 22:872.
27. Pak, *Chŏngyu chip*, 380–81.
28. Sŏ, *Yŏlha kiyu*, 335.
29. Sŏ, *Yŏlha kiyu*, 342, 421–22.
30. Sŏ, *Yŏlha kiyu*, 442.
31. *QSL* (Qianlong), 25:817, 873–74, 973.
32. *QSL* (Qianlong), 25:874, 966–74.
33. *Qinding Annan jilue*, 21:14a.
34. *Qinding Annan jilue*, 23:24a, 26:18a.
35. *QSL* (Qianlong), 25:1049–50, 1198, 1201–28.
36. Some modern scholars have argued that the man who presented himself at the border was not Nguyễn Huệ himself but rather a double; see Lam, "Intervention versus Tribute in Sino-Vietnamese Relations." In any case, what mattered to Beijing was that Annam's sovereign demonstrated subordination to Qing authority.
37. *Qinding Annan jilue*, 28:21.
38. *QSL* (Qianlong), 26:174–75. By rendering the phrase *fengjian shizhong* as "centering," James Hevia, in his study of the Macartney mission, may have given the phrase a more extended meaning; see Hevia, *Cherishing Men from Afar*, 123.
39. *QSL* (Qianlong), 26:196–200.
40. For a review of this case, see Harrison, "Qianlong Emperor's Letter."
41. Mosca, *From Frontier Policy to Foreign Policy*, 69–160.
42. Zhongguo diyi lishi dang'an guan, *Yingshi Majiaerni fanghua dang'an*, 32–38.
43. Zhongguo diyi lishi dang'an guan, *Yingshi Majiaerni fanghua dang'an*, 51, 148–49.
44. Peyrefitte, *Immobile Empire*, 223–24; Durand, "Jianting zeming."
45. Zhongguo diyi lishi dang'an guan, *Yingshi Majiaerni fanghua dang'an*, 57–60, 162–75.
46. Chen, *Chinese Law in Imperial Eyes*, 8.
47. *QSL* (Qianlong), 27:257–64; Yi, *Yŏnhaeng ilgi*, 105–27.
48. *Qing Jiaqing chao waijiao shiliao*, 5:11a–12a, 37a–40b, 57a.
49. Staunton, *Narrative of the Chinese Embassy*, v–vi.
50. Peyrefitte, *Immobile Empire*, 524–25.
51. Baijun, *Fengshi Chaoxian*, 571–661.
52. LFZZ, no. 3–163–7729–44.
53. Huashana, *Dongshi jicheng*, 131–99.

54. Wang, *Xiao Zhonghua*, 140. For the story of Ye, see Wong, *Yeh Ming-Ch'en*.

55. *Chouban yiwu shimo* (Xianfeng), 2:610–19.

56. *Chouban yiwu shimo* (Xianfeng), 3:748–94.

57. *Chouban yiwu shimo* (Xianfeng), 3:938.

58. *Treaties, Conventions, etc.*, 1:715.

59. *Chouban yiwu shimo* (Xianfeng), 3:952–61.

60. *Treaties, Conventions, etc.*, 1:405.

61. *Treaties, Conventions, etc.*, 1:419.

62. Loch, *Personal Narrative of Occurrences*, 258, 274.

63. Loch, *Personal Narrative of Occurrences*, 286–89.

64. For the latest research on the Zongli Yamen, see Rudolph, *Negotiated Power*; Li, *Zhongguo jindai waijiaoguan*.

65. *Chouban yiwu shimo* (Xianfeng), 8:2708–15.

66. Frederick Low to Hamilton Fish, no. 77, January 13, 1872, in *Foreign Relations of the United States* (hereafter *FRUS*), *1872–'73*, 127–28.

67. *Ch'ŏng sŏn go*, 2:490–91; *ZCSLXB*, 315–17; *QSL* (Xianfeng), 44:1093.

68. See Mao, *Jindai de chidu*, 166–254.

4. DEFINING CHOSŎN

1. For the term "everyday familiarity," see Heidegger, *Being and Time*, 176.

2. For the translation of *Wanguo gongfa*, see Liu, *Clash of Empires*, 108–39; Okamoto, *Sōshuken no sekaishi*, 90–118.

3. Wheaton, *Wanguo gongfa*, vol. 1.

4. Fairbank, "Early Treaty System," 257.

5. *Kojong Sunjong sillok*, 1:121.

6. *Ilsŏngnok*, 66:199–201.

7. *ZRHGX*, 2:29; *FRUS, 1867–'68*, 1:420.

8. *FRUS, 1867–'68*, 1:420.

9. See, for example, Grosier, *General Description of China*, 244.

10. Nelson, *Korea and the Old Orders*, 292.

11. See, for example, Curzon, *Problems of the Far East*, 144–45.

12. Tamura, "Ejiputo kenkyu"; Em, *Great Enterprise*, 30.

13. Wheaton, *Wanguo gongfa*, 1:25a–28b; 2:2b–3a; Wheaton, *Elements of International Law*, 44–50, 79.

14. Nelson, *Korea and the Old Orders*, 289; Westad, *Restless Empire*, 81–82.

15. Aihanzhe, ed., *Dong Xi-yang kao meiyue tongji zhuan*, 91–92. Aihanzhe, literally "people loving China," might refer to a group of missionaries who were active in South China near Guangdong. For Gützlaff's contribution to the Chinese norms discussed here, see Mosca, *From Frontier Policy to Foreign Policy*, 218–19.

16. See Edward Hertslet, "Memorandum respecting Corea," December 19, 1882, in *Korea, the Ryukyu Islands, and North-East Asia*, 2–3; Frederick Low to Hamilton Fish, November 23, 1871, in Davids, *American Diplomatic and Public Papers* (hereafter *ADPP*), 9:184; Mori Arinori to the Zongli Yamen, January 15, 1876, in *ZRHGX*, 2:270.

17. Rockhill, "Korea in Its Relations with China."

18. Curzon, *Problems of the Far East*, 209–22.

19. *ZRHGX*, 2:33–34.

20. *Ilsŏngnok*, 66:614.

21. *Kojong Sunjong sillok*, 1:227–28.

22. *Ilsŏngnok*, 66:309, 582.

23. *Kojong sidae sa*, 1:263.

24. *FRUS, 1867–'68*, 1:416.

25. *Kojong Sunjong sillok*, 1:235.

26. Kuiling, *Dongshi jishi shilue*, 737.

27. *Ilsŏngnok*, 66:643–48.

28. *FRUS, 1867–'68*, 1:4224.

29. *ZCSLXB*, 344–60.

30. *FRUS, 1867–'68*, 1:426–28.

31. *ADPP*, 9:49.

32. Dennett, *Americans in Eastern Asia*, 418–19.

33. See Griffis, *Corea: The Hermit Nation*.

34. See Le Gendre's letter on June 21, 1867, in "Rishi shokan," Japan Center for Asian Historical Records (hereafter JACAR), ref. no. A03030060500. For Admiral Bell's expedition against the aborigines, see Carrington, *Foreigners in Formosa*, 156–57.

35. Davidson, *Island of Formosa*, 117–22.

36. Low to Fish, no. 225, July 16, 1870, in *FRUS, 1870–'71*, 362.

37. *ZRHGX*, 2:165–66.

38. Low to Fish, no. 29, April 3, 1871; no. 31, May 13, 1871, in *FRUS, 1871–'72*, 111–15.

39. *ZRHGX*, 2:175.

40. Low to Fish, dispatch 102, November 23, 1871, in *ADPP*, 9:184.

41. *Treaties, Conventions, etc.*, 2:508; Gaimushō jōyakukyoku, *Kyūjōyaku isan*, 1:394–95.

42. JACAR, ref. nos. A03023011000, A03023011700.

43. See Yen, *Taiwan*, 159–74; Mayo, "Korean Crisis of 1873," 802–5.

44. Li's palace memorial, May 3, 1873, in *LHZQJ*, 5:346–47.

45. Wade to Earl Granville, no. 118, confidential, May 15, 1873; no. 131, May 25, 1873; no. 143, June 4, 1873, in Foreign Office Record Group 17, China Correspondence (hereafter FO 17), 654.

46. *FRUS, 1873–'74*, 1:188.

47. Shima, *Soejima Taneomi zenshū*, 2:165–66, 456.

48. JACAR, ref. no. A03023011900.

49. Soejima to Sanjō, June 29, 1873, in *NHGB*, 6:160.

50. Tada, *Iwakurakō jikki*, 3:46–90; Mayo, "Korean Crisis of 1873."

51. In Tokyo, the British minister, Harry Parkes, clearly told the Japanese foreign minister, Terashima Munenori, "I really am not aware whether the territory in question is or is not beyond the jurisdiction of the Chinese Government. During a residence of upwards of twenty years in China, I always heard that the whole of Formosa was claimed by China." See Parkes to Terashima, April 16, 1874, in *NHGB*, 7:37.

52. *Chouban yiwu shimo* (Tongzhi), 10:3835–949.

53. Parkes to Earl of Derby, July 20, 1875, in *Korea, the Ryukyu Islands, and North-East Asia*, 39.

54. Tabohashi, *Kindai Nissen kankei*, 1:515.

55. Ōkubo, *Mori Arinori zenshū*, 1:779–80; Mori Arinori bunsho, R. 2–68.

56. Terashima to Tei, November 15, 1875, in *NHGB*, 8:138.

57. Wade to Earl of Derby, no. 5, January 12, 1876, in FO 17, 719.

58. Marquis of Zetland, *Letters of Disraeli*, 373.

59. Earl of Derby to Wade, no. 77, January 1, 1876, in *British Parliamentary Papers, China*, 107.

60. Wade to Earl of Derby, no. 6, confidential, January 12, 1876, in FO 17, 719.

61. Mori Arinori bunsho, R. 2–67.

62. Mori Arinori bunsho, R. 1–55–1.

63. Mori's letter to his father, January 13, 1876, Mori Arinori bunsho, R. 1–55–1.

64. Chen, *Weng Tonghe riji*, 3:1176.

65. Mori to the Zongli Yamen, January 15, 1876, in *ZRHGX*, 2:270.

66. *Qing Guangxu chao Zhong-Ri jiaoshe shiliao* (hereafter *ZRJSSL*), 1:1b–2a.

67. *Ch'ŏng sŏn go*, 2:495.

68. Mori to Terashima, February 3, 1876, in *NHGB*, 9:170–76; Li to the Zongli Yamen, January 23–24, 1876, in *LHZQJ*, 31:334–42.

69. Mori's original English report of the meeting on January 24 is missing, but the Japanese translation by the Gaimushō is still available in Tokyo; see JACAR, ref. no. B03030144000; Mori to Terashima, February 3, 1876, in *NHGB*, 9:170–76.

70. Li to the Zongli Yamen, January 23, 1876, in *LHZQJ*, 31:340; *NHGB*, 9:172.

71. Mori, "The Second Interview," JACAR, ref. no. B03030144000.

72. *ZRHGX*, 2:295.

73. Mori Arinori bunsho, R. 1–55–1.

74. *Ch'iksa ilgi*, 17:28b.

75. Quan, "Jianghua tiaoyue."

76. *ZRHGX*, 2:300.

77. Guo, *Guo Songtao riji*, 3:14–15.

78. *ZRHGX*, 2:316–18.

79. Bruce Cumings has also questioned whether this treaty can be seen as a modern one; see Cumings, *Korea's Place in the Sun*, 102.

80. Gaimushō jōyakukyoku, *Kyūjōyaku isan*, 3:2.

81. For affirmations of this view, see, for example, *ADPP*, 10:66–77; *British Parliamentary Papers, Japan*, 9–10; Deuchler, *Confucian Gentlemen*, 47; Hua, *Zhongguo bianjiang*, 121; Larsen, *Tradition, Treaties, and Trade*, 63; Morse, *International Relations*, 3:8. For challenges to it, see Hsü, *China and Her Political Entity*, 109–10; Kim, *Last Phase*, 252.

82. *NHGB*, 9:115.

83. Bingham to Fish, dispatch 364, March 22, 1876, in *ADPP*, 10:66–77; Parkes to Earl of Derby, no. 13, March 25 and 27, 1876, in *British Parliamentary Papers, Japan*, 9–11, 17.

84. For a review of Korea's modern sovereignty, see Em, *Great Enterprise*, 21–84.

85. Mori Arinori bunsho, R. 2–68.

5. SUPERVISING CHOSŎN

1. Yi to Li, December 24, 1879, in *ZRHGX*, 2:398–401.

2. *NHGB*, 13:435.

3. See Deuchler, *Confucian Gentlemen*, 110–13.

4. Shufeldt to R. W. Thompson, dispatch 21, August 30, 1880, in *ADPP*, 10:102–5; Li to Yu, August 28, 1880, in *LHZQJ*, 32:585; Paullin, "Opening of Korea," 483.

5. Yi, *Kawo koryak*, 11:436.

6. *Kojong Sunjong sillok*, 1:617; *QSL* (Guangxu), 53:726–27.

7. *ZRJSSL*, 2:31a–32a.

8. Li to the Zongli Yamen, March 2, 1881, in *ZRHGX*, 2:467–68.

9. Wu, Xu, and Wang, *Huang Zunxian ji*, 2:394, 400.

10. He to the Zongli Yamen, November 18, 1880, in *ZRHGX*, 2:441.

11. *Kojong Sunjong sillok*, 1:629; Chun, "T'ongni kimu amun."

12. For these secret reports and memorandums, see Hŏ, *Chosa sich'al dan*.

13. *Sŭngjŏngwŏn ilgi*, 7:262.

14. *Ilsŏngnok*, 73:450–53, 478–81, 534–35.

15. *Kojong Sunjong sillok*, 2:14–16; Yi, *Kawo koryak*, 7:271–72.

16. *Ilsŏngnok*, 73:578–82.

17. Kim, *Ŭmch'ŏng sa*, 1–2; Sim, *Mangi yoran chaeyong p'yŏn*, 701.

18. Kim, *Ŭmch'ŏng sa*, 3, 12–21.

19. Li's memorial, January 21, 1882, in *LHZQJ*, 9:539–44.

20. Kim, *Ch'ŏnjin tamch'o*, 2.

21. *QSL* (Guangxu), 53:1002–3.

22. Paullin, "Opening of Korea," 485–87.

23. Holcombe to Frederick Frelinghuysen, February 4, 1882, in *ADPP*, 10:163–71.

24. Kim, *Ch'ŏnjin tamch'o*, 12–13.

25. Kim, *Ch'ŏnjin tamch'o*, 20–21.

26. Kim, *Ch'ŏnjin tamch'o*, 17.

27. For China's struggle to abolish extraterritoriality as "the most important imperialist practice in China," see Kayaoğlu, *Legal Imperialism*, 149–90.

28. Kim, *Ch'ŏnjin tamch'o*, 23–26.

29. *ZRHGX*, 2:552–55.

30. *Ku Han'guk oegyo munsŏ* (hereafter *HKMS*), 10:12–14.

31. *HKMS*, 10:14–15.

32. T'ongsang Miguk silgi, 6a–9b; *HKMS*, 10:1–2; Okamoto, *Zokkoku to jishu no aida*, 35–69.

33. Ŏ, *Chongjŏng nyŏnp'yo*, 131.

34. Baoting's memorial, June 14, 1882, in *ZRJSSL*, 3:17b–18a.

35. Imperial edict, June 14, 1882, in *ZRJSSL*, 3:18b.

36. Baoting's memorial, June 28, 1882, in Gongzhong dang zouzhe, 4–1–30–0278–025.

37. *Kojong sidae sa*, 2:331–37.

38. Inoue Kaoru to Hanabusa, July 31, 1882, in *NHGB*, 15:221–23; Li Shuchang to Zhang Shusheng, July 31, 1882, in *ZRHGX*, 2:735–47.

39. Kim, *Ŭmch'ŏng sa*, 179–85; Kim's conversation with Zhou Fu, August 5, 1882, in *ZRHGX*, 2:769–72.

40. *ZRHGX*, 3:765, 789–805; Kim, *Ŭmch'ŏng sa*, 189–90.

41. *NHGB*, 15:226–30.

42. Li Shuchang to Yoshida, August 9 and 12, 1882, in *NHGB*, 15:164–65.

43. Inoue's conversations with Boissonade, August 9 and 13, 1882, in *NHGB*, 15:169–73; *Boissonade tōgi*, 140–62. For the Anglo-French joint action against the Egyptian revolt and the British conquest of Egypt in 1882, see Reid, "Urabi Revolution."

44. Hart to James Duncan Campbell, no. 370, Z/83, August 10, 1882, in Fairbank, Bruner, and Matheson, *I. G. in Peking*, 417.

45. For the African case, see Lewis, *Divided Rule*, 14–16.

46. Zhang Shusheng to the Zongli Yamen, August 9, 1882, in *ZRHGX*, 2:773; Li Shuchang to the Zongli Yamen, August 31, 1882, in *ZRHGX*, 3:836.

47. For the influence of virtue on China's statecraft, see Wang, "Early Ming Relations," 42–45.

48. Kim, *Tongmyo yŏngjŏp nok*.

49. *ZRHGX*, 3:863–79.

50. *ZRHGX*, 3:843, 867.

51. Yuan to Li, August 6, 1886, in *LHZQJ*, 22:77.

52. Kim, *Last Phase*, 1, 348.

53. *ZRJSSL*, 2:33a–34b.

54. *ZRHGX*, 3:967–76.

55. Kim, *Ŭmch'ŏngsa*, 212.

56. See Larsen, *Tradition, Treaties, and Trade*, 101–3.

57. *Treaties, Conventions, etc.*, 2:847–53; *ZRHGX*, 3:983–86.

58. *GXZP*, 112:243.

59. Yun, *Yun Ch'i-ho ilgi*, 1:4.

60. See Larsen, *Tradition, Treaties, and Trade*, 72–94. According to Larsen, the 1882 Sino-Korean Regulations "constitute the first time that the Qing Empire proactively sought to promote Chinese commercial interests beyond its borders through the use of treaties and international law" (90).

61. *GXZP*, 112:243.

62. For the Kangxi emperor's role in introducing his empire to Western knowledge, see Jami, *Emperor's New Mathematics*.

63. Mao, "Qingmo diwang jiaokeshu," 127–29.

64. Mao, "Qingmo diwang jiaokeshu," 147.

65. Chongqi's memorial, in *ZRHGX*, 3:1063–69.

66. Li to the Zongli Yamen, January 3, 1883, and the Ministry of Rites to the Zongli Yamen, January 18, 1883, in *ZRHGX*, 3:1072–75, 1085–88.

67. Chunggang t'ongsang changjŏng chogwan; Yŏ Chungguk wiwŏn hoesang sangse changjŏng.

68. *ZRHGX*, 3:1020–30; Hart to Campbell, no. 390, Z/100, December 10, 1882, in Fairbank, Bruner, and Matheson, *I. G. in Peking*, 436; Lensen, *Balance of Intrigue*, 1:31–53.

69. Frelinghuysen to Foote, no. 3, Washington, DC, March 17, 1883, in *Korean-American Relations* (hereafter *KARD*), 1:25–26.

70. Renchuan gangkou juan (hereafter RCGK), vol. 1, n.p.

71. Chen to Min Yŏng-muk, October 20, 1883, in *HKMS*, 8:5.

72. Yun, *Yun Ch'i-ho ilgi*, 1:14–16.

73. Li Hongzhang to the Zongli Yamen, January 2, 1884, in *ZRHGX*, 3:1314–15.

74. For the Korean mission of 1883 to the United States, see, for example, Walter, "Korean Special Mission."

75. Hart to Campbell, no. 518, Z/212, March 23, 1885, in Fairbank, Bruner, and Matheson, *I. G. in Peking*, 590; the Zongli Yamen to Parkes, November 22, 1884, in *ZRHGX*, 3:1494.

76. Li Nairong to Chen Shutang, December 12, 1883, and Chen Shutang to Chen Weikun, December 20, 1883, in RCGK, vol. 1, n.p.

77. Chen to Min, February 7, 1884, in RCGK, vol. 2, n.p.

78. Larsen, *Tradition, Treaties, and Trade*, 109.

79. For Chinese immigrants and their activities in Korea after the 1870s, see Yang and Sun, *Chaoxian huaqiao shi*, 107–63. For a study of the Chinese merchants in Inch'ŏn and their influence on modern Korean and East Asian financial markets through the case of Tongshuntai, see Kang, *Tongsunt'ae ho*. Tongshuntai was founded by Cantonese merchants, and by the mid-1880s it had developed into a leading Chinese firm in Korea. It later served as a financial agency for the Chinese government. The firm finally ended its operations in Korea in September 1937 after the outbreak of the Second Sino-Japanese War. See Kang, *Tongsunt'ae ho*, 59–112, 280–81; Larsen, *Tradition, Treaties, and Trade*, 263–66; Yang and Sun, *Chaoxian huaqiao shi*, 142–45.

80. The number of Chinese immigrants in Korea was 2,182 in 1893, 3,661 in 1906, and 11,818 in 1910. Chinese immigrants were far outnumbered by their Japanese counterparts. In 1892, for example, 1,805 Chinese and 9,340 Japanese were living in Hansŏng, Inch'ŏn, Pusan, and Wŏnsan. See Yang and Sun, *Chaoxian huaqiao shi*, 125–31.

81. Li Hongzhang to the Zongli Yamen, March 29, 1884, in *ZRHGX*, 3:1355–57.

82. Chen to Min, January 15, 1884, in *HKMS*, 8:21–22; Li to Chen, December 12, 1883, in RCGK, vol. 1, n.p.

83. Chen to Li, December 12, 1883, in RCGK, vol. 1, n.p.

84. Chen to Min, January 15, 1884, and Min to Chen, January 19, 1884, in *HKMS*, 8:21–23.

85. Chen to Min, March 7, 1884, in *HKMS*, 8:35–38.

86. Min to Chen and Chen to Min, December 14, 16, and 17, 1883, in *HKMS*, 8:14–15.

87. Li Shuchang to the Zongli Yamen, December 29, 1883, in *ZRHGX*, 3:1259.

88. See, for example, Larsen, *Tradition, Treaties, and Trade*, 2–17, 107–17.

89. Min to Chen, January 19, 1884, in *HKMS*, 8:23.

90. For the establishment of police forces in Inch'ŏn, see He, "Chaoxian bandao de Zhongguo zujie," 31–34.

91. Note of Langzhong County to Nanbu County, June 4, 1883, in Sichuan sheng Nanchong shi dang'anguan, *Qingdai Sichuan Nanbu xian yamen dang'an*, 58:402.

92. Sichuan sheng Nanchong shi dang'anguan, *Qingdai Sichuan Nanbu xian yamen dang'an*, 58:403–23; Chen to Min, March 11, 1884, in *HKMS*, 8:40–42.

93. Min to Chen, March 15, 1884, in *HKMS*, 8:45.

6. LOSING CHOSŎN

1. For the rise of the age of empires, see Hobsbawm, *Age of Empire*, 56–83.

2. Luo and Liu, *Yuan Shikai quanji*, 1:34–46.

3. Ōkubo, *Mori Arinori zenshū*, 1:195.

4. *Treaties, Conventions, etc.*, 2:588–89.

5. Ma, *Ma Xiangbo ji*, 1091–96.

6. *ZCSLHB*, 259; *ZRHGX*, 4:1957.

7. This title was a downgrade, imposed by Congress in July 1884, from the original "envoy extraordinary and minister plenipotentiary." See Frederick Frelinghuysen to Lucius Foote, no. 58, July 14, 1884, in *KARD*, 1:36.

8. Foulk to Thomas Bayard, no. 255, confidential, November 25, 1885, in *KARD*, 1:137–39.

9. Fisher, "Indirect Rule," 393–401.

10. Lewis, *Divided Rule*, 24–26.

11. Hugh Dinsmore to Thomas Bayard, no. 20, May 27, 1887, and Augustine Heard to James Blaine, no. 29, confidential, July 10, 1890, in *KARD*, 2:11, 21.

12. Li Hongzhang to the Zongli Yamen, January 30, 1886, in *ZRHGX*, 4:2002–4.

13. For the Port Hamilton incident, see Larsen, *Tradition, Treaties, and Trade*, 173–76; Zhang, *Zai chuantong yu xiandaixing*, 201–27.

14. Yuan to Li, August 6, 1886, in *LHZQJ*, 22:77.

15. Li to Yuan, February 1, 1886, in *LHZQJ*, 21:655.

16. Hugh Dinsmore to Thomas Bayard, no. 20, May 27, 1887, in *KARD*, 2:12; Horace Allen to Walter Gresham, no. 469, October 6, 1893, and no. 479, confidential, November 4, 1893, in *KARD*, 2:93–98; Larsen, *Tradition, Treaties, and Trade*, 192; Lensen, *Balance of Intrigue*, 1:92–93.

17. *Da Ming huidian*, 105:1b. The Ming conquered Annam in 1407 and divided it into fifteen prefectures, thirty-six subprefectures, and 181 counties, but it ended its colonial policy in 1428. See Guo and Zhang, *Yuenan tongshi*, 395–421.

18. He Ruzhang to the Zongli Yamen, November 18, 1880, in *ZRHGX*, 2:437–47; Li Shuchang to the Zongli Yamen, August 31, 1882, in *ZRHGX*, 3:836.

19. *Zhang Jian quanji*, 6:206–7.

20. Li to the Zongli Yamen, November 23, 1882, in *ZRHGX*, 3:1030–33.

21. Shengyu's memorial, December 6, 1885, in *ZRJSSL*, 9:16b–18b.

22. *Kang Youwei quanji*, 1:394–96.

23. Zeng, "China," 9. Zeng is referring here to the office of the Warden of the Marches of England against Scotland, which was created in 1309 in order to monitor and defend the marches (i.e., the border) of England and Scotland; see Reid, "Office of Warden."

24. Swartout, *American Adviser*, 142.

25. See, for example, Lee, *Diplomatic Relations*, 52–124.

26. Dinsmore to Thomas Bayard, no. 20, May 27, 1887, in *KARD*, 2:11–13.

27. See Larsen, *Tradition, Treaties, and Trade*, 176–89; Zhang, *Zai chuantong yu xiandaixing*, 227–74.

28. Yuan to Cho Pyŏng-sik, October 21 and November 8, 1887, in *HKMS*, 8:382, 384.

29. *HKMS*, 10:317; *ZRJSSL*, 10:37a.

30. Allen, *Things Korean*, 163–64.

31. Zhang, *Zhang Yinhuan riji*, 244–50, 279.

32. Zhang Yinhuan's palace memorial, March 6, 1888, in LFZZ, no. 3–5700–043.

33. Hart to Campbell, no. 651, Z/342, June 3, 1888, in Fairbank, Bruner, and Matheson, *I. G. in Peking*, 705.

34. 50 Cong. Rec. 8136 (August 31, 1888); italics in the original.

35. Dinsmore to Thomas Bayard, no. 20, May 27, 1887, in *KARD*, 2:12.

36. Foulk to Frederick Frelinghuysen, no. 229, October 10, 1884, in *FRUS 1885–'86*, 326. Foulk described the stele: "The front of the stone is closely filled entirely with an inscription deeply cut in what I took to be Manchu Tartar script characters; these closely resemble Sanscrit or Pali characters, but they are written in vertical lines, beginning on the left. Over the body of the inscription is a title line written horizontally from left to right. On the back of the stone is another inscription only partly covering it, in Chinese square characters" (326).

37. Rockhill, "Korea in Its Relations with China," 1.

38. Rockhill, "Korea in Its Relations with China," 1–2.

39. Min Chong-muk to Yuan, June 4, 1890, and Yuan to Min and Li Hongzhang, June 5, 1890, in Qinshi fengming qianlai ciji Chaoxian guowang mufei juan (hereafter QSCJ), n.p.

40. Yuan to Li Hongzhang, May 16, 1890, in *ZRJSSL*, 11:31a.

41. Yuan to Heard, June 5, 1890, in QSCJ, n.p.

42. Yuan to Li, June 6, 1890, in QSCJ, n.p.

43. Yuan to Li, June 6, 1890, in QSCJ, n.p; Li to the Zongli Yamen, June 13, 1890, in *ZRHGX*, 5:2785.

44. Li to Yuan, and Yuan to Chinese commercial commissioners in Chosŏn, June 6, 1890, in QSCJ, n.p.

45. Min Chong-muk to Yuan, June 10, 1890, in QSCJ, n.p.

46. Yuan to Heard, September 30, 1890, and Kim Yŏngsu to Yuan, October 11, 1890, in QSCJ, n.p.

47. Heard to Yuan, October 11, 1890, in QSCJ, n.p.

48. Heard to James Blaine, no. 13, June 7, 1890, in *KARD*, 2:124–26.

49. *LHZQJ*, 23:102–5.

50. For the 1890 imperial mission to Korea, see Okamoto, "*Fengshi Chaoxian riji* zhi yanjiu"; Van Lieu, "Politics of Condolence." Van Lieu's study also reveals the significant influence of the Chinese propaganda movement following the 1890 mission on Western historiography of Chosŏn-Qing relations; see Van Lieu, "Politics of Condolence," 103–10.

51. *LHZQJ*, 23:69–75.

52. Chongli, *Fengshi Chaoxian riji*, 2b–3a.

53. *Shihan jilue*, 3–7.

54. Li to Yuan, October 12, 1890, in QSCJ, n.p.

55. Chongli, *Fengshi Chaoxian riji*, 12b–13b.

56. *Notes on the Imperial Chinese Mission*, 8.

57. Ch'iksa ilgi, 19:1a–6a.

58. Chongli, *Fengshi Chaoxian riji*, 17b–18a.

59. Chongli, *Fengshi Chaoxian riji*, 26b–27a.

60. *China Imperial Maritime Customs Decennial Reports*, app. 2, 42.

61. *Shihan jilue*, 22–26.

62. Ch'iksa ilgi, 19:11a–12a.

63. For defenses of this argument, see Okamoto, *Sekai no naka no Nitsu-Shin-Kan*, 15–28; Larsen, *Tradition, Treaties, and Trade*, 190–91; Van Lieu, "Politics of Condolence."

64. Augustine Heard to James Blaine, no. 89, confidential, November 19, 1890, in *KARD*, 2:35.

65. Treat, "China and Korea," 506–43.

66. See, for example, Nelson, *Korea and the Old Orders*, 175–80; Lin, *Yuan Shikai yu Chaoxian*, 137–321; Kim, *Last Phase*, 350; Larsen, *Tradition, Treaties, and Trade*, 128–73; Zhang, *Zai chuantong yu xiandaixing*, 192–201. But Larsen has critically pointed out that "Yuan represented only one strand of Qing imperial strategy in Chosŏn Korea, and often not the most influential one at that"; see Larsen, *Tradition, Treaties, and Trade*, 173.

67. Chongli, *Fengshi Chaoxian riji*, 54b–55a.

68. *China Imperial Maritime Customs Decennial Reports*, app. 2, 42.

69. Nelson, *Korea and the Old Orders*, 202.

70. Chongli, *Fengshi Chaoxian riji*, 55b–60b.

71. Nie, *Dongyou jicheng*, 547–53.

72. Qi, *Zhong-Ri zhanzheng* (hereafter *ZRZZ*), 1:16.

73. *ZRZZ*, 1:23–24.

74. *ZRZZ*, 1:33–35.

75. *QSL* (Guangxu), 56:396.

76. *ZRZZ*, 1:61.

77. *ZRZZ*, 1:45–48.

78. *ZRZZ*, 1:155.

79. *ZRZZ*, 1:146–52, 199; Hong Liangpin's memorial, August 10, 1894, in LFZZ, no. 3–167–9115–5.

80. *Qinggong zhencang lishi Dalai Lama dang'an*, 387–88.

81. *NHGB*, 28(2):373.

82. *ZRZZ*, 3:188.

83. *ZRZZ*, 3:290.

84. *Ilsŏngnok*, 79:209; Koketsu, "Ni-Shin kaisen"; Em, *Great Enterprise*, 21–52.

85. Wang Wenshao to the Zongli Yamen, July 12, 1896, in *ZRHGX*, 8:4856–57.

86. The Zongli Yamen's memorial, July 27, 1896, in *ZRHGX*, 8:4871–74.

87. Wang Wenshao to the Zongli Yamen, August 7, 1896, in *ZRHGX*, 8:4899–900.

88. The Zongli Yamen's memorial, November 20, 1896, in *ZRHGX*, 8:4968.

89. In 1905 Tang Shaoyi brought his Korean experience to the treaty negotiations with Britain over Tibet; see Lu, *Xizang jiaoshe jiyao*, 17–20; Tang's telegrams to Beijing, July 2, July 14, and August 21, 1905, in Waiwu bu Xizang dang, 02–16–001–06–061/066, 02–16–003–01–007.

90. Tang Shaoyi to the Zongli Yamen, March 13, 1897, in *ZRHGX*, 8:4989.

91. Schmid, *Korea between Empires*, 11, 55–100.

92. *Ilsŏngnok*, 80:161–63; Lensen, *Balance of Intrigue*, 2:644–46.

93. *ZRJSSL*, 51:21a, 35b, 36b.

94. *ZRJSSL*, 51:40.

95. *ZRJSSL*, 52:1a–2b.

96. *ZRJSSL*, 52:2b.

97. Mao, "Wuxu bianfa," 45.

98. Tang Shaoyi to the Zongli Yamen, August 28, 1898, in *ZRHGX*, 8:5146–48.

99. Zhang, *Zhang Yinhuan riji*, 549.

100. Mao, "Wuxu bianfa," 48.

101. Zhongguo shixue hui, *Zhongguo jindaishi ziliao congkan, Wuxu bianfa*, 4:325–26.

102. Zhang, *Zhang Yinhuan riji*, 554.

103. *ZRJSSL*, 52:7a.

104. Imperial decree, October 11, 1898, in *ZRHGX*, 8:5160.

105. Xu Shoupeng to the Zongli Yamen, December 4, 1898, in *ZRHGX*, 8:5179.

106. Wu, "Chaoxian sanzhong xu," 1.

107. Xu's memorial, March 5, 1899, in *ZRHGX*, 8:5200; Han Ch'ŏng ŭiyak kongdok, 11–12.

108. Xu's memorial, July 19, 1899, in *ZRJSSL*, 52:38a–38b.

109. *ZRHGX*, 8:5246–47.

110. Giwadan jihen ni kanshi Kankoku kōtei.

111. *HKMS*, 9:534.

112. *GXZP*, 112:342–43.

113. *ZRHGX*, 8:5556.

114. *GXZP*, 112:332–33.

115. *GXZP*, 112:339.

116. *GXZP*, 112:241–42, 344–57.

117. Zhao Erxun quanzong dang'an, no. 125–2.

118. Chen Zuoyan's report, March 1901, in *ZRHGX*, 9:5839–44.

119. The Manchu general of Jilin to the Ministry of Foreign Affairs, July 29, 1903, in *ZRHGX*, 9:5680–82; Zhang Zhaolin's report, fall 1903, in *ZRHGX*, 9:5849–81.

120. Zhao Erxun quanzong dang'an, no. 125.

121. For the issue of Kando/Jiandao, see Song, *Making Borders*.

122. Kim, "Pugyŏ yosŏn," 253; Wu, *Yanji bianwu baogao*, chap. 4, 1–2.

123. Yuan Shikai to Li Hongzhang, August 30, 1890, in *ZRHGX*, 9:5703–5.

124. For the regulation, see *ZRHGX*, 9:5952–53.

125. Wu, *Yanji bianwu baogao*, chap. 4, 11.

126. Tang and Sang, *Dai Jitao ji*, 29.

127. Xiliang to the Ministry of Foreign Affairs, September 8 and 17, 1910, in *ZRHGX*, 10:7119, 7127. For the full text of the *Da Qing guoji tiaoli* issued on March 28, 1909, see Ding, "Qingmo yixing guoji guanli tiaoli."

128. Zhao to the Ministry of Foreign Affairs, August 15, 1911, in *ZRHGX*, 10:7202.

CONCLUSION

1. *China Mission Year Book, 1912*, app. C, 17.

2. Wang and Wan, *Chaoxian diaocha ji*; Chen, *Diaocha Chaoxian shiye baogao*.

3. *Chaoxian wenjian lu*, 2–3.

4. See Goldstein, *History of Modern Tibet*, 638–813; van Schaik, *Tibet*, 207–69.

5. Chang, *Waimeng zhuquan*, 269–303.

6. See, for example, Fiskesjö, "Rescuing the Empire"; Carlson, "Reimagining the Frontier"; Liu, *Recast All under Heaven*, 3–18, 171–241.

7. For an example, see Rawski, *Early Modern China*, 235–63.

8. *Zhonghua guochi ditu*.

9. *Zhongyang ribao*, Nanjing, March 15, 1930, in Hu, *Hanguo duli yundong*, 303.

10. Ji, *Mao Zedong shici*, 546.

11. For the relationship between Mao's "Central Kingdom" mentality and China's decision to enter the Korean War, see Chen, *China's Road*, 213–20. For the effect of this mentality on the Sino-Korean demarcation in Manchuria, see Shen, *Saigo no tenchō*, 2:144–47.

12. Shen, *Saigo no tenchō*, 2:181–82.

Glossary of Chinese Characters

ROMANIZATION OF CHINESE, KOREAN, AND JAPANESE	CHINESE CHARACTERS
a hwangje	我皇帝
Aoyi Chaoxian sanzhong	奧廙朝鮮三種
banshi dachen	辦事大臣
Bao Chaoxian ce	保朝鮮策
Beiyang tongshang dachen	北洋通商大臣
beiyi	北夷
benchao	本朝
bi Chaoxian shili, qingfeng wangwei, cong zhengshuo	比朝鮮事例, 請封王位, 從正朔
bianwai zhi guo	邊外之國
bianyi xingshi	便宜行事
biao / p'yo	表
biaozheng wanbang	表正萬邦
bici zhi fen	彼此之分
binzhu li	賓主禮
binzhu zhi li	賓主之禮
Bujun tongling yamen	步軍統領衙門
bukpŏl	北伐
buluo	部落
cefeng	冊封
chaejo	再造
chaje gungwan	子弟軍官
chajon t'ŭknip	自尊特立
chakan chishi	查勘敕使
ch'amho	僭號
chaogong / chōkō	朝貢
Chaogong tongli	朝貢通例
chaojin	朝覲
Chaoxian celue	朝鮮策略
Chaoxian gongshi yantu	朝鮮貢使宴圖
Chaoxian guo nanfan	朝鮮國難番
Chaoxian guo xi yuanren	朝鮮國系遠人
Chaoxian guo yiguan	朝鮮國夷官
Chaoxian guowang zhi yin	朝鮮國王之印
Chaoxian nai waiyi zhi ren	朝鮮乃外夷之人
Chaoxian shanhou liuce	朝鮮善後六策
Chaoxian shili	朝鮮事例
Chaoxian wei wo shuguo, pizai dongyi	朝鮮為我屬國, 僻在東夷
Chaoxian zhimin zhi di	朝鮮殖民之地
chehu / zhuhou	諸侯
chengchen nagong	稱臣納貢
chim / zhen	朕

(Continued)

(Continued)

duli banzhu	獨立半主
duo wo Chaoxian	奪我朝鮮
E yi	俄夷
Eluosi fanshu guo	俄羅斯藩屬國
erguo	爾國
fanbang / pŏnbang	藩邦
fanchen wu waijiao	藩臣無外交
fanfeng	藩封
fanfu	藩服
fanfu renmin	藩服人民
fanguo	蕃國 / 藩國
fangwu	方物
fanping	藩屏
fanshu	藩屬
fanwang	藩王
feng siyi	風四夷
fengjian shizhong	豐儉適中
fengshi	封諡
fengtian gaoming	奉天誥命
Fengtian yu Chaoxian bianmin jiaoyi zhangcheng	奉天與朝鮮邊民交易章程
fenmao	分茅
fu	福
gaijian xingsheng	改建行省
Gaimushō	外務省
gaitu guiliu	改土歸流
gaoming	誥命
ge menggu huibu	各蒙古回部
geguo gongshi fangci	各國貢使仿此
genben zhongdi	根本重地
gesheng	各省
gongshi guanshe	貢使館舍
gongwu	貢物
goshi	互市
gu	孤
gu fanshu, bao bianjiang	固藩屬, 保邊疆
Guanglu si	光祿寺
guiguo	貴國
guihua	歸化
guochao	國朝
guojia gongdiao	國家公帑
guoshu / kuksŏ	國書
guoti	國體
Guozi jian	國子監
haesang chi iin	海上之夷人
haibang	海邦
hama yŏn	下馬宴
Ham'in nok	含忍錄
han [ref. Japanese domain]	藩
handi	漢地
hanghu	行戶
hanguan weiyi	漢官威儀
hanjie	漢節

(Continued)

(Continued)

ROMANIZATION OF CHINESE, KOREAN, AND JAPANESE	CHINESE CHARACTERS
Hanlin yuan	翰林院
hanyi	漢夷
hanzi	漢字
hanzoku	藩屬
hasa	下士
he wo tianchao tizhi	合我天朝體制
Hongbŏm	洪範
hosŏ	胡書
houfu	侯服
houwang bolai	厚往薄來
huairou dongtu	懷柔東土
huairou yuanren	懷柔遠人
huamin	華民
huangchao	皇朝
huangdi	皇帝
huangfu xian bin	荒服咸賓
Huangqing zhigong tu	皇清職貢圖
huangshang	皇上
huangtian wu qin, wei de shi fu	皇天無親, 惟德是輔
huashang shiwu guan	華商事務官
Huashang dijie	華商地界
Huaxia	華夏
Hua Yang zujie	華洋租界
Hua–Yi zhi bian shenyan	華夷之辨甚嚴
Hugŭm ch'ŏnmyŏng hwangje	後金天命皇帝
Huitong siyi guan	會同四譯館
hushi	互市
Hwa–I bungye	華夷分界
Hwa–I il ya	華夷一也
Hwa–I ju	華夷主
Hwa–I ŭi chai	華夷差異
hwangbok hambin	荒服咸賓
ich'u	夷酋
insin mu oegyo	人臣無外交
iyang sŏn	異樣船
iyong husaeng	利用厚生
ji wuyi neidi junxian	幾無異內地郡縣
jiafu yu huangjia	夾輔於皇家
jiangyu	疆宇
jianhu	監護
jianjiu Zhongguo zhi zhi	漸就中國之制
jiaohua	教化
jiasheng	家聲
jiayu waifan zhi dao	駕馭外藩之道
jiazhang	家長
Jilin Chaoxian shangmin suishi maoyi zhangcheng	吉林朝鮮商民隨時貿易章程
Jindian	金典
jingong	進貢
Jingshan qingli si	精膳清吏司
Jinguo waifan menggu	金國外藩蒙古

jiqi tudi er junxian zhi	籍其土地而郡縣之
jishi Yun Gui, buke shi Chaoxian	即失雲貴, 不可失朝鮮
Jizi / Kija	箕子
Junjichu	軍機處
junxian qi di	郡縣其地
Juren	舉人
Kaiping kuangwu ju	開平礦務局
Kamni amun	監理衙門
Kando / Jiandao	間島
Kapsin jŏngbyŏn	甲申政變
kimi	羈縻
kŏ a chungwŏn	據我中原
koguk	故國
Kŏmundo	巨文島
kongmul	貢物
kongsa	貢使
Kŏnjuwi mabŏp / Jianzhouwei mafa	建州衛馬法
Kŏnyang	建陽
kosŏn kwan	考選官
kuan wen ren sheng huangdi	寬溫仁聖皇帝
kūmei / kongming	空名
Kwangmu	光武
Kyŏngsa	京師
kyorin	交鄰
laichao	來朝
laigui	來歸
laihua	來化
Lanwang zouxie. Zhidao liao. Gaibu zhidao.	覽王奏謝. 知道了. 該部知道.
Li yishi zhi mingfen, ding wanzai zhi gangchang	立一時之名分, 定萬載之綱常
Liangyi shuiwu jiandu	兩翼稅務監督
liaoyin jiaoqing	僚寅交情
Libu	禮部
Lidai diwang miao	歷代帝王廟
Lifan yuan	理藩院
Liji	禮記
lingshi	領事
lishang	例賞
lishi	理事
Liu Tai bushou, Sanhan wei xu	琉臺不守, 三韓為墟
Liutiao bian	柳條邊
Luhuan huijing tu	臚歡薈景圖
Lunchuan zhaoshang ju	輪船招商局
lunji	倫紀
Lunyu	論語
manzi difang	蠻子地方
maoyi	貿易
Menggu yamen	蒙古衙門
mingfen	名分
Mingguo jiuli	明國舊例
mingzheng yishun	名正義順
Mohwa gwan	慕華館
Muwiyŏng	武衛營

(Continued)

(Continued)

naebuk	內服
Nambyŏl gung	南別宮
Nanyang zhuguo	南洋諸國
nei zhuhou	內諸侯
neichen	內臣
neidi shangmin	內地商民
neifan	內藩
neifu	內服
Neige	內閣
neiguo zhi zhengzhi, waiguo zhi tiaoyue	內國之政治, 外國之條約
neishu	內屬
neiwai miaoyi, waiyi fanzhong	內外苗夷, 外夷番眾
neiwai zhi bie	內外之別
Neiwu fu	內務府
nianhao	年號
noch'u	奴酋
paijie	排解
panggi	房妓
peichen	陪臣
Pibyŏnsa	備邊司
p'iltam	筆談
pingfan	屏藩
pingfu	屏輔
pinghan dongfan	屏翰東藩
pinghan tianchao	屏翰天朝
pingli	平禮
pingxing	平行
p'ŏnbi	褊裨
Pukhak p'ae	北學派
Pukhak pyŏl	北學辨
Pukhak ŭi	北學議
Puma Koryŏ kugwang	駙馬高麗國王
pumo chi pang	父母之邦
Pyŏlgi gun	別技軍
pyŏltan	別單
Pyŏngja horan	丙子胡亂
Qi dahen	七大恨
qiangong zhengshuo	虔恭正朔
qianshi rugong	遣使入貢
qin Zhongguo, jie Riben, lian Meiguo	親中國, 結日本, 聯美國
Qingchao	清朝
Qingliu	清流
qingxin xianghua, chengchen rugong	傾心向化, 稱臣入貢
qinjunwang	親郡王
Qinming zhuzha Chaoxian zongli jiaoshe tongshang shiyi	欽命駐紮朝鮮總理交涉通商事宜
Qintian jian	欽天監
qinwang	親王
qishuang saixue	欺霜賽雪
queting	闕庭
Renchuan kou huashang dijie zhangcheng	仁川口華商地界章程

rijiang	日講
roch'u	老酋
rouhui yuanren, yishi bu yiwen	柔惠遠人, 以實不以文
ru zhisheng zhi yi	如直省之儀
sadae / shida	事大
Sadae juŭi	事大主義
Sadae sa	事大司
sahak	邪學
saiken sen	歲遣船
san gui jiu koutou	三跪九叩頭
san jugong	三鞠躬
sangma yŏn	上馬宴
sangmu wiwŏn	商務委員
sangsa	上士
sanyi	三揖
Seikan ron	征韓論
seja / shizi	世子
sep'ye	歲幣
shangguo	上國
shangshu / Shangshu	尚書
shangwu weiyuan	商務委員
shanhu wansui	山呼萬歲
shaoshu minzu	少數民族
shengchao	聖朝
shengfan jie	生番界
Shengjing jiangjun	盛京將軍
Shibo si	市舶司
shilang	侍郎
Shinkoku	清國
shisun	世孫
Shixian li / Shixian shu	時憲曆 / 時憲書
shiyi changji yi zhiyi	師夷長技以制夷
shizai zhi mingfen	實在之名分
shouru bantu	收入版圖
shouwei neidi er zhi qizheng	收為內地而執其政
shu qi nan, jie qi fen, qi qi anquan	紓其難, 解其紛, 期其安全
shubang (shu-pang)	屬邦
shufan	屬藩
shuguo	屬國
shuken	主權
shunfu	順付
shuoli	朔曆
shu yu tizhi youguan	殊與體制有關
sihai yi er wanguo laiwang	四海一而萬國來王
Siku quanshu zongmu tiyao	四庫全書總目提要
sin / chen	臣
sinsa	信使
Sinsa yuram dan	紳士遊覽團
siqing	私情
Sirhak	實學
sisŏ Chungguk	詩書中國
siyi	四夷 / 四裔

(Continued)

(Continued)

siyi xianfu	四夷咸服
So Chunghwa	小中華
sobang	小邦
songsŏ	上書
sui Zhongguo	綏中國
sun wo zhuquan	損我主權
suoshu bangtu	所屬邦土
Susin sa	修信使
Taebodan	大報壇
taeguk	大國
Taeguk juŭi	大國主義
Tae Han'guk Tae Ch'ŏngguk t'ongsang choyak	大韓國大清國通商條約
Taehan	大韓
Taewŏn'gun	大院君
taguk in	他國人
taotai / daotai	道臺
tianchao jiahui yuanren fuyu siyi zhi dao	天朝加惠遠人撫育四夷之道
tianchao tizhi	天朝體制
tianchao zhi chizi	天朝之赤子
tiandao shenyuan	天道深遠
tianfo zhi zi	天佛之子
tianjia	天家
tianming	天命
tianshi	天室
tianxia guojia zhi zhu	天下國家之主
tianxia yijia	天下一家
tianzi	天子
tiaoyue	條約
titong	體統
tizhi youguan	體制攸關
T'ongni kimu amun	統理機務衙門
T'ongni kyosŏp t'ongsang samu amun	統理交涉通商事務衙門
Tonghak	東學
Tongnim mun	獨立門
Tongshuntai hao	同順泰號
tot'ong	道統
tuguan	土官
Tushang heqi, haowu liyi	徒傷和氣，毫無利益
tusi	土司
ŭibun	義分
ŭidae Chungguk	衣帶中國
Ŭijŏngbu	議政府
uri yŏk Chunggukin	我亦中國人
wai zhuhou	外諸侯
waifan	外藩
Waifan zhi yu zongfan, shi shu xiangtong	外藩之與宗藩，事屬相同
waijiao	外交
waishu	外屬
Waiwu bu	外務部
waiyi shuguo	外夷屬國
wanghua buji	王化不及

wanghua zhi wai	王化之外
wangshi	王室
Wanguo gongfa	萬國公法
wanguo laichao	萬國來朝
wanguo suozong	萬國所宗
wanquan wuque zhi duli zizhu	完全無缺之獨立自主
weisuo	猥瑣
wenwu zhi bang	文物之邦
wijŏng ch'ŏksa	衛正斥邪
wo Chaoxian	我朝鮮
wo guojia yi zhong xiao ren yi xin wei genben	我國家以忠孝仁義信為根本
wo Zhongguo	我中國
wochao	我朝
Wude	五德
wufu	五服
Wukou tongshang dachen	五口通商大臣
xiaguo	下國
xiahuang	遐荒
xianghua zhi cheng	向化之誠
xianru bantu	咸入版圖
xiao hansu	效漢俗
xiaobang	小邦
xifan shengseng	西蕃聖僧
Xishi jiangyi	西史講義
Xiyang	西洋
Xiyu	西域
Yan Huang zisun	炎黃子孫
yangban	兩班
yang'i	洋夷
yang'i poguk	攘夷保國
yangren	洋人
yeak ŭigwan	禮樂衣冠
yemul	禮物
yiguan liyue zhi zu, yi yu qinshou	衣冠禮樂之族, 夷於禽獸
yiguo	異國
yijia	一家
yimu	夷目
Yingguo zizhu zhi bang, yu Zhongguo pingdeng	英國自主之邦, 與中國平等
Yingjili guo gongshi	唤咕唎國貢使
yiren	夷人
yisa kŏchi	以死拒之
yongfu yu Zhongguo	永輔于中國
Yŏngsŏn sa	領選使
Yŏngŭn mun	迎恩門
Yŏnhaengnok	燕行錄
Yŏlha ilgi	熱河日記
you yu neidi xingsheng wuyi	尤與內地行省無異
youbang	友邦
youru junxian	有如郡縣
yu Chaoxian yiti youdai	與朝鮮一體優待
yu hubi zhi zhong yu kongzhi zhi dao	於護庇之中寓控制之道
yuan bushi woguo guanxia zhi di	原不是我國管轄之地

(Continued)

ROMANIZATION OF CHINESE, KOREAN, AND JAPANESE	CHINESE CHARACTERS
yuanfu	遠服
yuanguo	遠國
yuanren laigui	遠人來歸
yuanyi	遠夷
yuguo	與國
yunei	域內
zaofeng nanyi	遭風難夷
Zhamen / ch'akmun	柵門
zhangcheng	章程
zhao Chaoxian shili	照朝鮮事例
zhao Chaoxian zhi li	照朝鮮之例
zhao shuguo tongwen zhi yi	昭屬國同文之誼
zhao Taixi yili	照泰西一例
zhao tianchao rouyuan shenren	昭天朝柔遠深仁
zheng shubang mingfen	正屬邦名分
zhengda	正大
zhenggong	正貢
zhengming dingfen	正名定分
zhengshi	正史
Zhengtong	正統
Zhengtong lun	正統論
zhengzhi zhi dao	正直之道
zhi fei qiwang er junxian zhi	直廢其王而郡縣之
Zhigao zhi bao	制誥之寶
zhigong qinxiu	職貢勤修
zhimin zhengce	殖民政策
Zhimin zhuyi	殖民主義
zhisheng	直省
Zhong Wai tifu	中外褆福
zhong yijia gongzhu zhi qing	重一家共主之情
Zhonggao	忠告
Zhongguo Chaoxian shangmin shuilu maoyi zhangcheng	中國朝鮮商民水陸貿易章程
Zhongguo / Zhongyuan zhi dao	中國 / 中原之道
Zhongguo gongguan	中國公館
Zhongguo lun	中國論
Zhongguo ren	中國人
Zhongguo wei tianxia gongzhu	中國為天下共主
Zhongguo yiguan	中國衣冠
Zhongguo zhi ren	中國之人
Zhongguo zhi zhi	中國之制
Zhongguo zhuzha Chaoxian zonglingshi	中國駐紮朝鮮總領事
Zhong-Han bianjie shanhou zhangcheng	中韓邊界善後章程
Zhonghua diguo	中華帝國
Zhonghua guochi ditu	中華國恥地圖
Zhonghua minzu shizu	中華民族始祖
Zhonghua zhi tu	中華之土
Zhongtu	中土
Zhong Wai yijia	中外一家
Zhong Wai zhi dafang	中外之大防
Zhongxia	中夏

Zhongyong	中庸
Zhongyuan	中原
zhu Zhongguo	主中國
Zhuchi Chaoxian waijiao yi	主持朝鮮外交議
zhuguo zhi zhang	諸國之長
Zhuke qingli si	主客清吏司
Zhuzha Chaoxian guo qinchai dachen	駐紮朝鮮國欽差大臣
Ziben zhuyi	資本主義
zidi jia	子弟家
Ziguang ge	紫光閣
ziwen	咨文
zixiao	字小
Zizhi tongjian	資治通鑒
zizhu / chaju / jishu	自主
Zongban Chaoxian gekou jiaoshe tongshang shiwu	總辦朝鮮各口交涉通商事務
Zongban Chaoxian shangwu weiyuan	總辦朝鮮商務委員
zongfa fengjian	宗法封建
Zongfan	宗藩
Zongli geguo shiwu yamen	總理各國事務衙門
zoushi	奏事
zunshou Zhongguo guiju	遵守中國規矩
zunzhou rangyi	尊周攘夷
zuoyi	作揖
zuzhi	祖制

Bibliography

UNPUBLISHED SOURCES

Zhongguo diyi lishi dang'an guan [The First Historical Archives of China], Beijing

Gongzhongdang zouzhe [Palace memorials with emperors' comments]. Catalog no. 4.
Junjichu hanwen lufu zouzhe [Chinese copies of the palace memorials of the Grand Council]. Catalog no. 3.
Neige Like shishu [Chronicle of the Ministry of Rites censorate section of the Grand Secretariat]. Catalog nos. 2–1 to 2–8.
Neige waijiao zhuan'an, Chaoxian [Diplomatic cases concerning Chosŏn at the Grand Secretariat]. Catalog no. 564–2–190.
Qintian jian tiben zhuanti shiliao [Documents pertaining to the routine memorials of the Imperial Astronomical Bureau]. Catalog nos. R1–R7.
Shuntian fu quanzong dang'an [The complete archives of Shuntian prefecture]. Catalog no. 28–4.
Zhao Erxun quanzong dang'an [The complete archives of Zhao Erxun]. Catalog no. 125/137/566.

Kyujanggak han'guk'ak yŏn'guwŏn [Kyujanggak Institute for Korean Studies], Seoul National University, Seoul

Akŭkton si [Akdun's poems]. Catalog no. 3442–21.
Ch'iksa ilgi [Diaries of welcoming the imperial envoys]. 19 vols. Catalog no. 73-101-5.
Chorok kuksŏ ko [Copies of letters of credence]. Catalog no. 80-103-318-O.
Chosŏnguk raesŏ bu [Records of the letters from Chosŏn]. 3 vols. Catalog no. Ko-5710-5-1/2.
Chunggang t'ongsang changjŏng chogwan [Rules for trade at Chunggang]. Catalog no. 80-103-137-B.
Han Ch'ŏng ŭiyak kongdok [Official documents regarding Korean-Qing negotiations]. Catalog no. 83-16-16-N.
Kakyu gobu [Records of miscellaneous documents]. Catalog no. Ko-5710-5-4.
Kim Ch'ang-hŭi. Tongmyo yŏngjŏp nok [Diaries of welcoming the Chinese generals]. Catalog no. 76-103-15-H.
Kim Yun-sik. Ch'ŏnjin tamch'o [Records of the written conversations in Tianjin]. Catalog no. 75-103-27-K.
Kwansŏ jich'ik jŏngnye [Regulations on supporting imperial envoys in P'yŏngan Province]. Catalog no. 75-103-27-B-Ea10.
Manbu jich'ik sarye [Regulations on accommodating imperial envoys in Ŭiju]. Catalog no. 73-103-27-B-Ea11.
Plan of Settlements in Chemulpo. Map, ca. 1892. Catalog no. 26644-2-2.
Renchuan kou huashang dijie zhangcheng [Regulations for the Chinese merchants' settlement]. Catalog no. 80-103-137-F.
Tae Han'guk Tae Ch'ŏngguk t'ongsang choyak [The trade treaty between the Great Korea and the Great Qing]. Catalog no. 80-103-137-N.

T'ongsang Miguk silgi [The original record of negotiations with the United States on the treaty of trade and amity]. Catalog no. 80-103-319-B.

Tumangang kamgye mundap ki [Minutes of the negotiations over the demarcation of the borderline along the Tumen River]. Catalog no. 75-103-27-N.

Yŏ Chungguk wiwŏn hoesang sangse changjŏng [Negotiations with Chinese representatives over the details of the treaty]. Catalog no. 80-103-137-B.

Yŏji to [Map of Korea]. Catalog no. 4709-78-v.1-03.

Zhongyang yanjiuyuan jindaishi yanjiusuo dang'an guan [Archives of the Institute of Modern History, at Academia Sinica], Taipei

Qinshi fengming qianlai ciji Chaoxian guowang mufei juan [The imperial envoys came to Chosŏn to express the emperor's condolences on the king's mother]. Catalog no. 01-41-016-08.

Renchuan gangkou juan [Archives on Inch'ŏn]. 2 vols. In Zhu Chaoxian shiguan dang, Chen Shutang [Archives of the Chinese legation to Chosŏn on Chen Shutang]. Catalog no. 01-41-004.

Shihan jilue [Notes on the imperial mission to Korea]. 1892. Catalog no. 01-41-016-08.

Waiwu bu Xizang dang [Archives of the Ministry of Foreign Affairs on Tibet]. 1905. Catalog no. 02-16-001/003.

Zhu Chaoxian shiguan dang, Yuan Shikai [Archives of the Chinese legation to Chosŏn on Yuan Shikai]. Catalog no. 01-41-016.

Other institutions in Japan, Korea, Taiwan, and the United States

Cefeng Chaoxian guowang Li Qin fengtian gaoming [The imperial mandate to invest Yi Gŭm as king of Chosŏn]. 1725. Jangseogak, the Academy of Korean Studies, Sŏngnam, Korea.

Cefeng Chaoxian wangshidi Li Qin fengtian gaoming [The imperial mandate to invest Yi Gŭm as crown brother of the king of Chosŏn]. 1722. Jangseogak, the Academy of Korean Studies, Sŏngnam, Korea.

Dai Shin kōtei kudoku hi [Stele of the honors and virtues of the emperor of the Great Qing]. Photographs, VI-1-269. Tōyō Bunko, Tokyo.

Foreign Office Record Group 17, China Correspondence. Public Record Office, London.

Giwadan jihen ni kanshi Kankoku kōtei yori Nihon kōtei heika ni shinsho [The autographic letter of the Korean emperor to his Japanese emperor regarding the Boxer Uprising in China]. Archive catalog no. 7-3-1-11. Gaimushō gaikō shiryō kan, Tokyo, Japan.

Japan Center for Asian Historical Records. Accessed December 17, 2017. http://www.jacar.go.jp/.

Mori Arinori bunsho [Mori Arinori papers]. Kokuritsu kokkai toshokan, Tokyo.

Qingdai Gongzhongdang zouzhe ji Junjichu dang zhejian [The palace memorials and the Grand Council of the Qing]. Guoli gugong bowuyuan, Taipei.

Soejima Taneomi bunsho [Soejima Taneomi papers]. Kokuritsu kokkai toshokan, Tokyo.

Zhaofu Zheng Jing chiyu [The imperial edict to persuade Zheng Jing to surrender]. 1669. Catalog no. 038209. Institute of History and Philosophy, Academia Sinica, Taipei.

PUBLISHED SOURCES

Aihanzhe, ed. *Dong Xi-yang kao meiyue tongji zhuan* [Eastern-Western monthly magazine]. Compiled by Huang Shijian. Beijing: Zhonghua shuju, 1997.

Allen, Horace N. *Things Korean: A Collection of Sketches and Anecdotes Missionary and Diplomatic*. New York: Fleming H. Revell, 1908.

Al-Sayyid Marsot, Afaf Lutfi. *A Short History of Modern Egypt*. Cambridge: Cambridge University Press, 1985.

Bae, Woo-sung. *Chosŏn kwa Chunghwa: Chosŏn i kkum kkugo sangsang han segye wa munmyŏng* [Chosŏn and China: The world and civilization that Chosŏn dreamed of and imagined]. Paju, Gyeonggi: Dolbegae, 2014.

Baijun. *Fengshi Chaoxian yicheng riji* [Diary of the journey of the imperial mission to Chosŏn]. In *Shi Chaoxian lu* [Records of imperial missions to Chosŏn], edited by Yin Mengxia and Yu Hao, vol. 2, 547–661. Beijing: Beijing tushuguan chubanshe, 2003.

Baldanza, Kathlene. *Ming China and Vietnam: Negotiating Borders in Early Modern Asia*. Cambridge: Cambridge University Press, 2016.

Banno Masataka. *Kindai Chūgoku seiji gaikōshi: Vasuko da Gama kara Goshi Undō made* [Modern Chinese political and diplomatic history: From Vasco da Gama to the May Fourth Movement]. Tokyo: Tōkyō daigaku shuppankai, 1973.

Bartlett, Beatrice S. *Monarchs and Ministers: The Grand Council in Mid-Ch'ing China, 1723–1820*. Berkeley: University of California Press, 1991.

Boissonade tōgi [Conversations with Boissonade]. Vol. 8 of *Kindai Nihon hōsei shiryōshū* [A collection of historical materials on Japan's modern law]. Tokyo: Kokugakuin daigaku, 1986.

Boming xizhe. *Fengcheng suolu* [Miscellaneous records of Fenghuang City]. N.p., 1801.

British Parliamentary Papers, China, No. 1 (1876). London: Harrison and Sons, 1876.

British Parliamentary Papers, Japan, No. 1 (1876). London: Harrison and Sons, 1876.

Burbank, Jane, and Frederick Cooper. *Empires in World History: Power and the Politics of Difference*. Princeton, NJ: Princeton University Press, 2010.

Byington, Mark E. *The Ancient State of Puyŏ in Northeast Asia: Archaeology and Historical Memory*. Cambridge, MA: Harvard University Asia Center, 2016.

Carlson, Allen. "Reimagining the Frontier: Patterns of Sinicization and the Emergence of New Thinking about China's Territorial Periphery." In *Sinicization and the Rise of China: Civilizational Processes beyond East and West*, edited by Peter J. Katzenstein, 41–64. London: Routledge, 2012.

Carrington, George Williams. *Foreigners in Formosa, 1841–1874*. San Francisco: Chinese Materials Center, 1978.

Ch'ae Che-gong. *Ham'in nok* [Records of enduring contempt and insults]. In Lim, *Yŏnhaengnok jŏnjip*, vol. 40.

Champion, Craige B., and Arthur M. Echstein. "Introduction: The Study of Roman Imperialism." In *Roman Imperialism: Readings and Sources*, edited by Craige B. Champion, 1–15. Malden, MA: Blackwell, 2004.

Chang Chi-hsiung. "Dongxi guoji zhixu yuanli de chayi: 'Zongfan tixi' dui 'zhimin tixi'" [A comparison of Eastern and Western principles of international order: "Zongfan system" vs. "colonial system"]. *Zhongyang yanjiuyuan jindaishi yanjiusuo jikan* 79 (2013): 47–86.

——. *Waimeng zhuquan guishu jiaoshe, 1911–1916* [Disputes and negotiations over Outer Mongolia's sovereignty, 1911–1916]. Taipei: Academia Sinica, 1995.

Chang Hyun-guen. "Han'guk esŏ taejungguk kwannyŏm ŭi pyŏnhwa: Chunghwa juŭi, so Chunghwa juŭi, t'al Chunghwa juŭi" [The changes in the Korean concept of

China: Sinocentrism, small-Sinocentrism, and post-Sinocentrism]. *At'ae yŏn'gu* 18, no. 2 (2011): 97–123.

Chang Tsun-wu. "Qingdai Zhong-Han bianwu wenti tanyuan" [A study of Sino-Korean border issues during the Qing Dynasty]. *Zhongyang yanjiuyuan jindaishi yanjiusuo jikan* 2 (1971): 463–503.

——. *Qing-Han Zongfan maoyi, 1637–1894* [Sino-Korean tributary trade, 1637–1894]. 2nd ed. Taipei: Zhongyang yanjiuyuan jindaishi yanjiusuo, 1985.

Chang Tsun-wu and Yeh Chuan-hung, eds. *Qing ruguan qian yu Chaoxian wanglai guoshu huibian, 1619–1643* [A collection of sovereign letters exchanged between the Manchus and Chosŏn, 1619–1643]. Taipei: Guoshiguan, 2000.

Chaoxian shiliao huibian [A collection of historical materials about Chosŏn Korea]. 20 vols. Beijing: Quanguo tushuguan wenxian suowei fuzhi zhongxin, 2004.

Chaoxian wenjian lu [Records of the journey to Chosŏn]. Beijing, 1918.

Chen, Jian. *China's Road to the Korean War: The Making of the Sino-American Confrontation*. New York: Columbia University Press, 1994.

Chen, Li. *Chinese Law in Imperial Eyes: Sovereignty, Justice, and Transcultural Politics*. New York: Columbia University Press, 2016.

Ch'en, Ta-tuan. "Investiture of Liu-Ch'iu Kings in the Ch'ing Period." In Fairbank, *Chinese World Order*, 135–64.

Ch'en Chieh-hsien. *Manzhou congkao* [Studies of the early Qing Dynasty]. Taipei: Guoli taiwan daxue wenxueyuan, 1963.

Chen Linzhi. *Diaocha Chaoxian shiye baogao* [A report on the investigation of the industry of Chosŏn]. Baoding, 1917.

Chen Shangsheng. *Zhongguo chuantong duiwai guanxi yanjiu* [A study of China's traditional foreign relations]. Beijing: Zhonghua shuju, 2015.

Chen Yijie, ed. *Weng Tonghe riji* [Weng Tonghe's diary]. 6 vols. Beijing: Zhonghua shuju, 1989–98.

Chien, Frederick Foo. *The Opening of Korea: A Study of Chinese Diplomacy, 1876–1885*. Hamden, CT: Shoe String, 1967.

China Imperial Maritime Customs Decennial Reports, 1882–91. Shanghai: Statistical Department of the Inspectorate General of Customs of China, 1893.

China Mission Year Book, 1912. Shanghai: Christian Literature Society for China, 1912.

Choi Hak-kŭn, trans. *Mongmun Manju sillok* [The veritable records of the Manchus written in Mongolian]. Seoul: Tongmun'gwan, 1976.

Choi Hyong-won. "Nerchinsk choyak ŭi manjumun koch'al" [On the Manchu text of the Treaty of Nerchinsk]. *Altai hakpo* 12 (2002): 81–94.

Choi So-ja. *Myŏng Ch'ŏng sidae Chung-Han kwan'gye sa yŏn'gu* [A study of Sino-Korean relations in the Ming-Qing transitional period]. Seoul: Ihwa yŏja taehakkyo ch'ulp'ansa, 1997.

Chŏng In-ji. *Koryŏ sa* [History of the Koryŏ Dynasty]. 3 vols. Seoul: Asia munhwasa, 1973.

Ch'ŏng sŏn go [Selected items on Chosŏn institutions]. 3 vols. Seoul: T'amgudang, 1972.

Chongli. *Fengshi Chaoxian riji* [Diary of the journey to Chosŏn as an envoy]. Beijing, 1893.

Chongzhen lishu [A treatise on calendrical science during the Chongzhen period]. 2 vols. Shanghai: Shanghai guji chubanshe, 2009.

Chongzhen shilu [The veritable records of Emperor Chongzhen]. Taipei: Zhongyang yanjiuyuan, 1962.

Chosŏn wangjo sillok [The veritable records of the kings of the Chosŏn Dynasty]. 48 vols. Seoul: Kuksa p'yŏnch'an wiwŏnhoe, 1984.

Chouban yiwu shimo (Tongzhi chao) [Complete records of the management of barbarian affairs during the Tongzhi period]. 10 vols. Beijing: Zhonghua shuju, 2008.

Chouban yiwu shimo (Xianfeng chao) [Complete records of the management of barbarian affairs during the Xianfeng period]. 8 vols. Beijing: Zhonghua shuju, 1979.

Chuang Chi-fa. *Man Han Yiyu Lu jiaozhu* [Annotations to *Yiyu Lu* published in the Manchu and Chinese languages]. Taipei: Wenshizhe chubanshe, 1983.

——. "Xianluo guowang Zheng Zhao rugong qingting kao" [A study of King Taksin's tributary mission to the Qing court]. *Dalu zazhi* 51, no. 3 (1975): 126–41.

——. *Xie Sui Zhigong tu manwen tushuo jiaozhu* [Interpretations and annotations on the Manchu characters in *Zhigong tu* drawn by Xie Sui]. Taipei: Guoli gugong bowuyuan, 1989.

Chun Hae-jong. *Han-Chung kwan'gye sa yŏnggu* [Studies in the history of Korean-Chinese relations]. Seoul: Ilchogak, 1970.

——. "Sino-Korean Tributary Relations in the Ch'ing Period." In Fairbank, *Chinese World Order*, 90–111.

——. "T'ongni kimu amun sŏlch'i ŭi gyŏngui e taehayŏ" [On the establishment of the T'ongni kimu amun]. *Yŏksa hakpo* 17/18 (1962): 687–702.

——. "Tongyang kodaesa e issŏsŏ ŭi 'kwihwa' ŭi ŭiŭi" [Some notes on "naturalization" in early East Asian history]. In *Tonga munhwa ŭi pigyosa ŭi yŏn'gu* [Comparative studies of East Asian culture], 21–45. Seoul: Ilchogak, 1976.

Clark, Donald N. "Sino-Korean Tributary Relations under the Ming." In *The Cambridge History of China*, vol. 8, part 2, *The Ming Dynasty, 1368–1644*, edited by Denis Twitchett and Frederick W. Mote, 272–300. Cambridge: Cambridge University Press, 1998.

Cohen, Paul A. *Discovering History in China: American Historical Writing on the Recent Chinese Past*. New York: Columbia University Press, 1984.

Cooper, Frederick. *Colonialism in Question: Theory, Knowledge, History*. Berkeley: University of California Press, 2005.

Crossley, Pamela Kyle. *The Manchus*. Malden, MA: Blackwell, 1997.

——. "*Manzhou Yuanliu Kao* and the Formalization of the Manchu Heritage." *Journal of Asian Studies* 46, no. 4 (1987): 761–90.

——. *A Translucent Mirror: History and Identity in Qing Imperial Ideology*. Berkeley: University of California Press, 1999.

Crossley, Pamela Kyle, Helen F. Siu, and Donald S. Sutton, eds. *Empire at the Margins: Culture, Ethnicity, and Frontier in Early Modern China*. Berkeley: University of California Press, 2006.

Cumings, Bruce. *Korea's Place in the Sun: A Modern History*. New York: W. W. Norton, 2005.

Curzon, George N. *Problems of the Far East: Japan–Korea–China*. 2nd ed. London: Longmans, Green, 1894.

Da Ming huidian [The collected statutes of the Great Ming]. 228 vols. Beijing, 1587.

Da Ming jili [The collected rituals of the Great Ming]. 53 vols. Beijing, 1530.

Da Qing huidian [The collected statutes of the Great Qing]. 100 vols. Beijing, 1764, 1899.

Da Qing huidian shili [The collected statutes and precedents of the Great Qing]. 1220 vols. Beijing, 1899.

Da Qing Shixian li/shu [The annual calendar of the Great Qing]. Beijing: Qintian jian, 1646, 1658, 1679, 1731, 1769, 1795, 1821, 1842, 1865, 1894, 1898, 1909.

Da Qing tongli [The comprehensive rites of the Great Qing]. 6 vols. Taipei: Taiwan shangwu yinshuguan, 1978.

Da Tang Kaiyuan li [The rituals of the Great Tang]. Beijing: Minzu chubanshe, 2000.

Danjo Hiroshi. *Mindai kaikin: Chōkō shisutemu to Ka–I chitsujo* [The system of maritime exclusion: The tribute for the Chinese court and the civilized–barbarian order in the Ming Dynasty]. Kyoto: Kyoto daigaku gakujutsu shuppankai, 2013.

Davids, Jules, ed. *American Diplomatic and Public Papers: The United States and China, 1861–1893*. 18 vols. Wilmington, DE: Scholarly Resources, 1979.

Davidson, James W. *The Island of Formosa, Past and Present: History, People, Resources, and Commercial Prospects*. London: Macmillan, 1903.

Dayi juemi lu [Great righteousness resolving confusion]. Beijing, 1729.

Dennett, Tyler. *Americans in Eastern Asia: A Critical Study of the Policy of the United States with Reference to China, Japan and Korea in the Nineteenth Century*. New York: Macmillan, 1922.

Deuchler, Martina. *Confucian Gentlemen and Barbarian Envoys: The Opening of Korea, 1875–1885*. Seattle: University of Washington Press, 1977.

Di Cosmo, Nicola. "Qing Colonial Administration in Inner Asia." *International History Review* 20, no. 2 (1998): 287–309.

Ding Chennan. "18 segi ch'o Chosŏn yŏnhaengsa ŭi Chen Shangyi haejŏk chiptan kwanlyŏn chŏnbo sujip hwaltong" [Chosŏn's tributary emissaries' intelligence gathering activities among Chen Shangyi's pirate group in the early eighteenth century]. *Tongbang hakchi* 178 (2017): 27–58.

Ding Jinjun, ed. "Qingmo yixing guoji guanli tiaoli" [On the late Qing's discussions and the issue of nationality regulations]. *Lishi dang'an*, no. 3 (1988): 53–56.

Dong Wenhuan. *Xianqiao shanfang riji* [Dong Wenhuan's diary]. Beijing: Beijing tushuguan chubanshe, 1996.

Duncan, John B. *The Origins of the Chosŏn Dynasty*. Seattle: University of Washington Press, 2000.

Durand, Pierre-Henri. "Jianting zeming: Majiaerni shihua zaitan" ("De la confrontation naît la lumière: Nouvelles considérations sur l'ambassade Macartney") [The confrontation of light is born: New considerations on the Macartney embassy]. Translated by Xu Minglong. In Zhongguo diyi lishi dang'an guan, *Yingshi Majiaerni fanghua dang'an shiliao huibian*, 89–148.

Edmonds, Richard L. "The Willow Palisade." *Annals of the Association of American Geographers* 69, no. 4 (1979): 599–621.

Elliott, Mark C. "Manchu (Re)Definitions of the Nation in the Early Qing." *Indiana East Asian Working Papers Series on Language and Politics in Modern China* 7 (1996): 46–78.

——. *The Manchu Way: The Eight Banners and Ethnic Identity in Late Imperial China*. Stanford, CA: Stanford University Press, 2001.

Elverskog, Johan. "Mongol Time Enters a Qing World." In *Time, Temporality, and Imperial Transition: East Asia from Ming to Qing*, edited by Lynn A. Struve, 142–78. Honolulu: University of Hawaii Press, 2005.

——. *Our Great Qing: The Mongols, Buddhism, and the State in Late Imperial China*. Honolulu: University of Hawaii Press, 2006.

Em, Henry H. *The Great Enterprise: Sovereignty and Historiography in Modern Korea*. Durham, NC: Duke University Press, 2013.

Fairbank, John King, ed. *The Chinese World Order: Traditional China's Foreign Relations*. Cambridge, MA: Harvard University Press, 1968.

———. "The Early Treaty System in the Chinese World Order." In Fairbank, *Chinese World Order*, 257–75.

———. "A Preliminary Framework." In Fairbank, *Chinese World Order*, 1–19.

———. *Trade and Diplomacy on the China Coast, 1842–1854*. Cambridge, MA: Harvard University Press, 1951.

———. "Tributary Trade and China's Relations with the West." *Far Eastern Quarterly* 1, no. 2 (1942): 129–49.

Fairbank, John King, Katherine Frost Bruner, and Elizabeth MacLeod Matheson, eds. *The I. G. in Peking: Letters of Robert Hart, Chinese Maritime Customs, 1868–1907*. Cambridge, MA: Belknap Press of Harvard University Press, 1975.

Fairbank, John King, and S. Y. Têng, eds. *Ch'ing Administration: Three Studies*. Cambridge, MA: Harvard University Press, 1960.

Fairbank, John King, and S. Y. Têng. "On the Ch'ing Tributary System." *Harvard Journal of Asiatic Studies* 6 (1941): 135–246.

Farquhar, David M. "The Origins of the Manchus' Mongolian Policy." In Fairbank, *Chinese World Order*, 198–205.

Fisher, Michael H. "Indirect Rule in the British Empire: The Foundations of the Residency System in India (1764–1858)." *Modern Asian Studies* 18, no. 3 (1984): 393–428.

Fiskesjö, Magnus. "Rescuing the Empire: Chinese Nation-Building in the Twentieth Century." *European Journal of East Asian Studies* 5, no. 1 (2006): 15–44.

Fletcher, Joseph F. "China and Central Asia, 1368–1884." In Fairbank, *Chinese World Order*, 206–24.

Foreign Relations of the United States, 1867–'68. 2 vols. Washington, DC: U.S. Government Printing Office, 1867–68.

Foreign Relations of the United States, 1871–'72. 6 vols. Washington, D.C.: U.S. Government Printing Office, 1871–72.

Foreign Relations of the United States, 1872–'73. Washington, D.C.: U.S. Government Printing Office, 1872–73.

Foreign Relations of the United States, 1873–'74. 3 vols. Washington, D.C.: U.S. Government Printing Office, 1873–74.

Foreign Relations of the United States, 1875–'76. 3 vols. Washington, D.C.: U.S. Government Printing Office, 1875–76.

Foreign Relations of the United States, 1885–'86. 3 vols. Washington, D.C.: U.S. Government Printing Office, 1885–86.

Foreign Relations of the United States, 1890–'91. Washington, D.C.: U.S. Government Printing Office, 1890–1891.

Foreign Relations of the United States, 1891–'92. Washington, D.C.: U.S. Government Printing Office, 1891–1892.

Fuma Susumu. *Chōsen enkōshi to Chōsen tsūshinshi* [Korean embassies to Beijing and Korean embassies to Japan]. Nagoya: Nagoya daigaku shuppankai, 2015.

Gaimushō jōyakukyoku, ed. *Kyūjōyaku isan* [A compilation of old treaties]. 3 vols. Tokyo: Gaimushō jōyakukyoku, 1930–36.

Gallagher, John, and Ronald Robinson. "The Imperialism of Free Trade." *Economic History Review* 6, no. 1 (1953): 1–15.

Ge Zhaoguang. *Zhaizi Zhongguo: Chongjian youguan "Zhongguo" de lishi lunshu* [Residing in Zhongguo: Reconstructing the historical narrative about "Zhongguo"]. Beijing: Zhonghua shuju, 2011.

Goldstein, Melvyn C. *A History of Modern Tibet, 1913–1951: The Demise of the Lamaist State*. Berkeley: University of California Press, 1989.

Gong Yin. *Ming Qing Yunnan tusi tongzuan* [A general compilation of the indigenous chieftains in Yunnan over the Ming and Qing periods]. Kunming: Yunnan minzu chubanshe, 1985.

Griffis, William Elliot. *Corea: The Hermit Nation*. 4th ed. New York: Charles Scribner's Sons, 1894.

Grosier, Jean-Baptiste. *A General Description of China*. London: Paternoster-Row, 1788.

Gu Tinglong and Dai Yi, eds. *Li Hongzhang quanji* [The collected works of Li Hongzhang]. 39 vols. Hefei, Anhui: Anhui jiaoyu chubanshe, 2008.

Guanglu si zeli [Regulations and cases of the Court of Imperial Entertainments]. Hong Kong: Fuchi shuyuan, 2004.

Guben Yuan Ming zaju [The only existing copy of the Yuan and Ming operas]. 4 vols. Shanghai: Shangwu yinshuguan, 1949.

Guo Meilan. "Wushi Dalai Lama rujin shulun" [The account of the fifth Dalai Lama's visit to Beijing]. *Zhongguo bianjiang shidi yanjiu* 2 (1997): 33–41.

Guo Songtao. *Guo Songtao riji* [Guo Songtao's diary]. 4 vols. Changsha: Hunan renmin chubanshe, 1981–83.

Guo Zhenduo and Zhang Xiaomei, eds. *Yuenan tongshi* [A general history of Vietnam]. Beijing: Zhongguo renmin daxue chubanshe, 2001.

Guy, R. Kent. *Qing Governors and Their Provinces: The Evolution of Territorial Administration in China, 1644–1796*. Seattle: University of Washington Press, 2013.

Haboush, JaHyun Kim. *The Confucian Kingship in Korea: Yŏngjo and the Politics of Sagacity*. New York: Columbia University Press, 2001.

——. "Constructing the Center: The Ritual Controversy and the Search for a New Identity in Seventeenth-Century Korea." In *Culture and the State in Late Chosŏn Korea*, edited by JaHyun Kim Haboush and Martina Deuchler, 46–90. Cambridge, MA: Harvard University Asian Center, 1999.

——. "Contesting Chinese Time, Nationalizing Temporal Space: Temporal Inscription in Late Chosŏn Korea." In *Time, Temporality, and Imperial Transition: East Asia from Ming to Qing*, edited by Lynn A. Struve, 115–41. Honolulu: University of Hawaii Press, 2005.

Haedong chido [Maps of Korea]. 3 vols. Seoul: Kyujanggak, 1995.

Haeoe han'guk'ak charyo ch'ongsŏ [Series of overseas materials regarding Korea]. Seoul: Sŏngkyunkwan taehakkyo dongasia haksulwŏn, 2004.

Hakoda Keiko. *Gaikōkan no tanjō: Kindai Chūgoku no taigai taisei no hen'yō to zaigai kōkan* [The birth of diplomats: The change in China's foreign relations and China's overseas consulates in modern period]. Nagoya: Nagoya daigaku shuppankai, 2012.

Hamashita Takeshi. *Chōkō shisutemu to kindai Ajia* [The tributary system and modern Asia]. Tokyo: Iwanami shoten, 1997.

——. *Kindai Chūgoku no kokusai teki keiki: Chōkō bōeki shisutemu to kindai Ajia* [The international opportunities of modern China: The tribute trade system and modern Asia]. Tokyo: Tokyo daigaku shuppankai, 1990.

Han Myŏng-gi. *Chŏngmyo, Pyŏngja horan kwa Tongasia* [Studies of Manchu's invasions of Chosŏn Korea in 1627 and 1636 with East Asian perspectives]. Seoul: P'urŭn yŏksa, 2009.

Harrison, Henrietta. "The Qianlong Emperor's Letter to George III and the Early-Twentieth-Century Origins of Ideas about Traditional China's Foreign Relations." *American Historical Review* 122, no. 3 (2017): 680–701.

He Jiangfeng. "Chaoxian bandao de Zhongguo zujie: Yi 1884 zhi 1894 nian Renchuan Huashang zujie wei gean yanjiu" [The Chinese settlement on the Korean

Peninsula: A case study of the Chinese merchants settlement in Inch'ŏn from 1884 to 1894]. *Shilin* 131 (2012): 26–35.

Heidegger, Martin. *Being and Time*. Translated by Joan Stambaugh. Albany: State University of New York Press, 1996.

Herman, John E. "Empires in the Southwest: Early Qing Reforms to the Native Chieftain System." *Journal of Asian Studies* 56, no. 1 (1997): 47–74.

Hevia, James L. *Cherishing Men from Afar: Qing Guest Ritual and the Macartney Embassy of 1793*. Durham, NC: Duke University Press, 1995.

——. *English Lessons: The Pedagogy of Imperialism in Nineteenth-Century China*. Durham, NC: Duke University Press, 2003.

Hirano Satoshi. *Shin teikoku to Chibetto mondai: Taminzoku tōgō no seiritsu to gakai* [The Qing empire and the Tibet issue: The formation and collapse of the multiethnic unification]. Nagoya: Nagoya daigaku shuppankai, 2004.

Ho, Pingti. "In Defense of Sinicization: A Rebuttal of Evelyn Rawski's 'Reenvisioning the Qing.'" *Journal of Asian Studies* 57, no. 1 (1998): 123–55.

——. "The Significance of the Ch'ing Period in Chinese History." *Journal of Asian Studies* 26, no. 2 (1967): 189–95.

Hŏ Donghyŏn, ed. *Chosa sich'al dan kwan'gye charyojip* [The collected materials of the inspection mission of the Korean officials to Japan]. Seoul: Kukhak charyo yŏn'guwŏn, 1999.

Ho Takushu. *Meiji shoki Nikkan-Shin kankei no kenkyū* [Relations between Japan, Korea, and China in the early Meiji period]. Tokyo: Hanawa shobō, 1969.

Hobsbawm, Eric. *The Age of Empire, 1875–1914*. New York: Vintage Books, 1989.

Hong Tae-yong. *Tamhŏn sŏ* [The collected writings of Hong Tae-yong]. Seoul: Taeyang sŏjŏk, 1980.

——. *Tamhŏn yŏn'gi* [Hong Tae-yong's journey to Beijing]. In Lim, *Yŏnhaengnok jŏnjip*, vols. 42–43.

Hostetler, Laura. *Qing Colonial Enterprise: Ethnography and Cartography in Early Modern China*. Chicago: University of Chicago Press, 2001.

Hsü, Immanuel C. Y. *China's Entrance into the Family of Nations: The Diplomatic Phase, 1858–1880*. Cambridge, MA: Harvard University Press, 1960.

Hsu, Shuhsi. *China and Her Political Entity: A Study of China's Foreign Relations with Reference to Korea, Manchuria and Mongolia*. New York: Oxford University Press, 1926.

Hu Ch'un-hui. *Hanguo duli yundong zai Zhongguo* [The Korean independence movement in China]. Taipei: Zhonghua minguo shiliao yanjiu zhongxin, 1976.

Hu Sheng. *Diguo zhuyi yu Zhongguo zhengzhi* [Imperialism and Chinese politics]. 7th ed. Beijing: Renmin chubanshe, 1996.

Hua Qiyun. *Zhongguo bianjiang* [China's borderlands]. Nanjing: Xin Yaxiya xuehui, 1933.

Huang, Pei. *Reorienting the Manchus: A Study of Sinicization, 1583–1795*. Ithaca, NY: Cornell University East Asia Program, 2011.

Huang, Ray. *1587, A Year of No Significance: The Ming Dynasty in Decline*. New Haven, CT: Yale University Press, 1981.

Huang Chih-lien. *Chaoxian de ruhua qingjing gouzao: Chaoxian wangchao yu Man Qing wangchao de guanxi xingtai lun* [The construction of the Confucian context in Chosŏn: Comments on Qing-Chosŏn relations]. Beijing: Renmin daxue chubanshe, 1995.

——. *Dongya de liyi shijie: Zhongguo fengjian wangchao yu Chaoxian bandao guanxi xingtai lun* [The ritual worlds of East Asia: Comments on the relations between Chinese and Korean dynasties]. Beijing: Renmin daxue chubanshe, 1994.

Huang Chunyan. *Songdai chaogong tixi yanjiu* [A study of the tributary system of the Song Dynasty]. Beijing: Shangwu yinshuguan, 2014.

Huang Ming zuxun [The ancestral injunctions of the imperial Ming]. Nanjing, ca. 1395.

Huang Qing zhigong tu [Illustrations of subordinate peoples of the imperial Qing]. Shenyang: Liaoshen shushe, 1991.

Huang Xingtao. "Qingdai manren de 'Zhongguo' rentong" [The Manchus' "Zhongguo" identity in the Qing period]. *Qingshi yanjiu* 1 (2011): 1–12.

Huang Youfu and Qian Heshu, eds. *Fengshi tu* [Pictures of the imperial mission to Chosŏn]. Shenyang: Liaoning minzu chubanshe, 1999.

Huang Zunxian. *Riben guozhi* [History of Japan]. 40 vols. Guangzhou: Fuwen zhai, 1890.

Huashana. *Dongshi jicheng* [Diary of the imperial mission to Chosŏn]. In *Haeoe han'guk'ak charyo ch'ongsŏ* [Series of overseas materials regarding Korea], vol. 7, 114–246.

Ilsŏngnok [Records of daily reflections]. 86 vols. Seoul: Kyujanggak, 1982–96.

Imanishi Shunjū. *Man-Wa Mō-Wa taiyaku Manshū jitsuroku* [Comparative translation of Manchu-Japanese and Mongolian-Japanese Manchu records]. Tokyo: Tōsui shobŏ, 1992.

Iriye, Akira. "Imperialism in East Asia." In *Modern East Asia: Essays in Interpretation*, edited by James B. Crowley, 122–50. New York: Harcourt, Brace, and World, 1970.

Iwai Shigeki. "Chŏkŏ to goshi" [Tribute and trade]. In *Higashi Ajia sekai no kindai: 19 seiki* [Modern East Asia: The nineteenth century], edited by Wada Haruki, 134–53. Tokyo: Iwanami shoten, 2010.

Jami, Catherine. *The Emperor's New Mathematics: Western Learning and Imperial Authority during the Kangxi Reign (1662–1722)*. New York: Oxford University Press, 2012.

Jangsŏgak sojang gomunsŏ daegwan [The collection of Jangseogak's archives]. 7 vols. Seongnam, Gyeonggi: Han'guk'ak chungang yŏn'guwŏn ch'ulp'anbu, 2010–16.

Ji Shichang, ed. *Mao Zedong shici jianshang daquan* [A comprehensive appreciation of Mao Zedong's poems and lyrics]. Nanjing: Nanjing chubanshe, 1994.

Jiang Risheng. *Taiwan waiji* [The supplementary history of Taiwan]. Fuzhou: Fujian renmin chubanshe, 1983.

Jiu Tangshu [Old history of the Tang Dynasty]. 16 vols. Beijing: Zhonghua shuju, 1975.

Kang, David. *China Rising: Peace, Power, and Order in East Asia*. New York: Columbia University Press, 2007.

Kang Baek-nyŏn. *Yŏnhaeng noch'ong gi* [A journal of the stations along the journey to Beijing]. In Lim, *Yŏnhaengnok jŏnjip*, vol. 19.

Kang Chin-a. *Tongsunt'ae ho: Tong Asia hwagyo chabon kwa kŭndae Chosŏn* [Tongshuntai: Chinese merchant network in East Asia and modern Korea]. Taegu Kwangyŏksi: Kyŏngbuk taehakkyo ch'ulp'anbu, 2011.

Kang Youwei quanji [The collected works of Kang Youwei]. 3 vols. Shanghai: Shanhai guji chubanshe, 1987–92.

Katzenstein, Peter J., ed. *Sinicization and the Rise of China: Civilizational Processes beyond East and West*. New York: Routledge, 2012.

Kawachi Yoshihiro. *Mindai Joshin shi no kenkyū* [A study of the history of the Jurchen tribes in the Ming Dynasty]. Kyoto: Dŏhŏsha, 1992.

Kawashima Shin. *Chūgoku kindai gaikō no keisei* [The formation of China's modern diplomacy]. Nagoya: Nagoya daigaku shuppankai, 2004.

Kayaoğlu, Turan. *Legal Imperialism: Sovereignty and Extraterritoriality in Japan, the Ottoman Empire, and China*. New York: Cambridge University Press, 2010.

Kicengge. "Nibcu tiaoyue jiebei tu de huanying: Manwen 'Heilongjiang liuyu tu' yanjiu" [The illusion of the Nerchinsk Treaty boundary stone: The *Map of the Amur Region* in Manchu]. *Gugong xueshu jikan* 29, no. 1 (Fall 2011): 147–236.

Kim, Dal Choong. "Chinese Imperialism in Korea: With Special Reference to Sino-Korean Trade Regulations in 1882 and 1883." *Journal of East and West Studies* 5, no. 2 (1976): 97–110.

Kim, Jaymin. "The Rule of Ritual: Crimes and Justice in Qing-Vietnamese Relations during the Qianlong Period (1736–1796)." In *China's Encounters on the South and Southwest: Reforging the Fiery Frontier over Two Millennia*, edited by James A. Anderson and John K. Whitmore, 288–321. Leiden: Brill, 2015.

Kim, Key-hiuk. *The Last Phase of the East Asian World Order: Korea, Japan, and the Chinese Empire, 1860–1882.* Berkeley: University of California Press, 1980.

Kim, Kwangmin. *Borderland Capitalism: Turkestan Produce, Qing Silver, and the Birth of an Eastern Market.* Stanford, CA: Stanford University Press, 2016.

Kim, Seon-min. *Ginseng and Borderland: Territorial Boundaries and Political Relations between Qing China and Chosŏn Korea, 1636–1912.* Berkeley: University of California Press, 2017.

——. "Kŏllyung nyŏnkan Chosŏn sahaeng ŭi ŭn bunsil sagŏn" [Studies of cases of silver loss by Chosŏn's emissaries in the Qing during the Qianlong period]. *Myŏngch'ongsa yŏn'gu* 33 (2010): 139–66.

Kim Chŏng-ho. *Tongyŏ do* [Map of the East Land]. Seoul: Kyujanggak, 2003.

Kim Han-gyu. *Han-Chung kwan'gye sa* [A history of Korean-Chinese relations]. 2 vols. Seoul: Marŭk'e, 1999.

Kim No-kyu. "Pugyŏ yosŏn" [A selection of documents on the northern area]. *Paeksan hakpo* 17 (1974): 230–68.

Kim Yun-Sik. *Ŭmch'ŏng sa* [Cloudy and sunny diary]. Seoul: Kuksa p'yŏnch'an wiwŏnhoe, 1958.

Kishimoto Mio. "'Zhongguo' he 'Waiguo': Ming Qing liangdai lishi wenxian zhong sheji guojia yu duiwai guanxi de yongyu" ["China" and "foreign barbarians": Diction of national and foreign relations in Ming and Qing historical records]. In *Fu'an de lishi: Dang'an kaojue yu Qingshi yanjiu* [Exploring the archives and rethinking Qing studies], edited by His-yuan Chen, vol. 2, 357–93. Taipei: Academia Sinica, 2013.

Kojong sidae sa [The chronicle of the period of King Kojong]. 4 vols. Seoul: Kuksa p'yŏnch'an wiwŏnhoe, 1967–70.

Kojong sillok [The veritable records of King Kojong]. Seoul: T'amgudang, 1970.

Kojong Sunjong sillok [The veritable records of King Kojong and King Sunjong]. 3 vols. Seoul: T'amgudang, 1970.

Koketsu Satoko. "Ni-Shin kaisen zengo no Nihon gaikō to Shin-Kan shūshoku kankei" [Japan's diplomacy and Sino-Korean tributary relations before and after the outbreak of the Sino-Japanese War]. In *Sōshuken no sekaishi: Tōzai Ajia no kindai to honyaku gainen* [A world history of suzerainty: Modern East and West Asia and the translation of concepts], edited by Okamoto Takashi, 207–31. Nagoya: Nagoya daigaku shuppankai, 2014.

Koo Bum-jin. *Ch'ŏng nara, k'imera ŭi cheguk* [The Qing, a chimera of an empire]. Seoul: Minŭmsa, 2012.

——. "Ch'ŏng ŭi Chosŏn sahaeng insŏn gwa 'dae Ch'ŏng cheguk ch'eje'" [A study of the personnel appointments of Qing imperial envoys to Korea and the "system of the Great Qing empire"]. *Inmun nonch'ong* 59 (2008): 179–228.

——. "Chosŏn ŭi ch'ŏng hwangje sŏchŏl ch'uka wa Kŏnllyung ch'ŏlsun 'chinha oegyo'" [Chosŏn's congratulations on the Qing emperor's birthday and the special mission for Emperor Qianlong's seventieth birthday]. *Han'guk munhwa* 68 (2014): 215–48.

———. "Chosŏn ŭi Kŏllyung ch'lsun chinha t'ŭksa wa 'Yŏlha ilgi'" [The special mission for Emperor Qianlong's seventieth birthday and the *Rehe Diary*]. *Inmun nonch'ong* 70 (2013): 3–60.

Korea, the Ryukyu Islands, and North-East Asia, 1875–1888. Vol. 2 of *Asia, 1860–1914*, part 1, series E of *British Documents on Foreign Affairs, Reports and Papers from the Foreign Office Confidential Print*. Frederick, MD: University Publications of America, 1989.

Korean-American Relations: Documents Pertaining to the Far Eastern Diplomacy of the United States. Vol. 1 edited by George McAfee McCune and John A. Harrison. Vol. 2 edited by Spencer J. Palmer. Berkeley: University of California Press, 1951 and 1963.

Koschmann, J. Victor. *The Mito Ideology: Discourse, Reform, and Insurrection in Late Tokugawa Japan, 1790–1864*. Berkeley: University of California Press, 1987.

Ku Han'guk oegyo munsŏ [The records of the foreign affairs of old Korea]. 20 vols. Seoul: Koryŏ taehakkyo ch'ulp'anbu, 1965–69.

Kuang Lu and Li Hsüeh-chih, comp. and trans. *Qing Taizu chao manwen yuandang* [The Manchu records about the Qing during the Nurhaci period]. 2 vols. Taipei: Zhongyang yanjiuyuan lishi yuyan yanjiusuo, 1970.

Kuiling. *Dongshi jishi shilue* [Some poems on the visit to Chosŏn]. In *Shi Chaoxian lu* [Records of imperial missions to Chosŏn], edited by Yin Mengxia and Yu Hao, vol. 2, 663–789. Beijing: Beijing tushuguan chubanshe, 2003.

Kwon Naehyun. "Chosŏn Korea's Trade with Qing China and the Circulation of Silver." *Acta Koreana* 18, no. 1 (2015): 163–85.

———. "Chosŏn-Qing Relations and the Society of P'yŏngan Province during the Late Chosŏn Period." In *The Northern Region of Korea: History, Identity, and Culture*, edited by Sun Joo Kim, 37–61. Seattle: University of Washington Press, 2010.

Kye, Seung-Beom. "Huddling under the Imperial Umbrella: A Korean Approach to Ming China in the Early 1500s." *Journal of Korean Studies* 15, no. 1 (2010): 41–66.

Lam, Truong Buu. "Intervention versus Tribute in Sino-Vietnamese Relations, 1788–1790." In Fairbank, *Chinese World Order*, 165–79.

Larsen, Kirk W. "Comforting Fictions: The Tributary System, the Westphalian Order, and Sino-Korean Relations." *Journal of East Asian Studies* 13, no. 2 (2013): 233–57.

———. *Tradition, Treaties, and Trade: Qing Imperialism and Chosŏn Korea, 1850–1910*. Cambridge, MA: Harvard University Asia Center, 2008.

Ledyard, Gary. "Cartography in Korea." In *The History of Cartography*, edited by J. B. Harley and David Woodward, vol. 2, *Cartography in the Traditional East and Southeast Asian Societies*, 235–345. Chicago: University of Chicago Press, 1987.

Lee, Ji-Young. *China's Hegemony: Four Hundred Years of East Asian Domination*. New York: Columbia University Press, 2017.

Lee, Yur-Bok. *Diplomatic Relations between the United States and Korea, 1866–1887*. New York: Humanities, 1970.

Lensen, George Alexander. *Balance of Intrigue: International Rivalry in Korea and Manchuria, 1884–1899*. 2 vols. Tallahassee: University Presses of Florida, 1982.

Lewis, Mary Dewhurst. *Divided Rule: Sovereignty and Empire in French Tunisia, 1881–1938*. Berkeley: University of California Press, 2014.

Li, Gertraude Roth. "The Manchu-Chinese Relationship, 1618–1636." In *From Ming to Ch'ing: Conquest, Region, and Continuity in Seventeenth-Century China*, edited by Jonathan D. Spence and John E. Wills Jr., 2–38. New Haven, CT: Yale University Press, 1979.

Li Dingyuan. *Shi Liuqiu ji* [A journal of the mission to Ryukyu]. 6 vols. Beijing, 1802.

Li Huazi. *Cho-Ch'ŏng kukgyŏng munje yŏn'gu* [A study of the border between Chosŏn and the Qing]. Seoul: Jipmundang, 2007.

Li Shiyu. *Qingdai tusi zhidu lunkao* [Research on the indigenous chieftains system in the Qing period]. Beijing: Zhongguo shehui kexue chubanshe, 1998.

Li Wenjie. *Zhongguo jindai waijiaoguan qunti de xingcheng, 1861–1911* [The emergence of modern Chinese diplomats, 1861–1911]. Beijing: Shenghuo dushu xinzhi sanlian shudian, 2017.

Li Xiaocong. "Ji Kangxi 'Huangyu quanlan tu' de cehui jiqi banben" [A study of the mapping of the Kangxi Atlas with editions]. *Gugong xueshu jikan* 30, no. 1 (2012): 55–85.

Li Yu and Ch'oi Yŏng-hŭi, eds. *Hanke shicun* [The poems of Korean guests]. Beijing: Shumu wenxian chubanshe, 1995.

Li Yunquan. *Chaogong zhidu shilun: Zhongguo gudai duiwai guanxi tizhi yanjiu* [History of the Chinese tributary system: A study of the foreign relations system of premodern China]. Beijing: Xinhua chubanshe, 2004.

Liang Qichao. *Yinbingshi heji* [The collected works of Liang Qichao]. 40 vols. Shanghai: Zhonghua shuju, 1936.

Libu zeli [The regulations and cases of the Ministry of Rites]. 202 vols. Beijing, 1844.

Lidai baoan [Historical archives of the Ryukyu Kingdom]. 15 vols. Taipei: Guoli taiwan daxue, 1972.

Lidai diwang miao yanjiu lunwen ji [A collection of essays on the Temple of Ancient Monarchs]. Hong Kong: Xianggang guoji chubanshe, 2004.

Lifan yuan zeli [The regulations and cases of the Mongolian Superintendency]. Hong Kong: Fuchi shuyuan, 2004.

Lim Jongtae. "Tributary Relations between the Chosŏn and Ch'ing Courts to 1800." In *The Cambridge History of China*, vol. 9, part 2, *The Ch'ing Dynasty to 1800*, edited by Willard J. Peterson, 146–96. Cambridge: Cambridge University Press, 2016.

Lim Key-zung, ed. *Yŏnhaengnok jŏnjip* [A comprehensive collection of records of Chosŏn's emissaries to Beijing]. 100 vols. Seoul: Tongguk taehakkyo ch'ulp'anbu, 2001.

Lin, Hsiao-Ting. "The Tributary System in China's Historical Imagination: China and Hunza, ca. 1760–1960." *Journal of the Royal Asiatic Society*, 3rd ser., 19, no. 4 (2009): 489–507.

Lin Ming-te. *Yuan Shikai yu Chaoxian* [Yuan Shikai and Chosŏn]. Taipei: Zhongyang yanjiuyuan lishi yuyan yanjiusuo, 1970.

Liu, Lydia H. *The Clash of Empires: The Invention of China in Modern World Making.* Cambridge, MA: Harvard University Press, 2004.

Liu, Xiaoyuan. *Recast All under Heaven: Revolution, War, Diplomacy, and Frontier China in the 20th Century.* New York: Continuum, 2010.

Liu Jiaju. *Qingchao chuqi de Zhong-Han guanxi* [Sino-Korean relations in the early Qing period]. Taipei: Wenshizhe chubanshe, 1986.

Liu Pujiang. *Zhengtong yu Hua-Yi: Zhongguo chuantong zhengzhi wenhua yanjiu* [Orthodox legitimacy and the civilized–barbarian distinction: A study of traditional Chinese politics and culture]. Beijing: Zhonghua shuju, 2017.

Liu Wei. *Qingdai Zhong-Chao shizhe wanglai yanjiu* [A study of Sino-Korean envoys in the Qing period]. Harbin: Heilongjiang jiaoyu chubanshe, 2002.

Liu Xiaomeng. *Manzu cong buluo dao guojia de fazhan* [The development of the Manchus from a tribe to a country]. Shenyang: Liaoning minzu chubanshe, 2001.

Loch, Henry B. *Personal Narrative of Occurrences during Lord Elgin's Second Embassy to China in 1860*. London: John Murray, 1869.

Lu Xingqi, ed. *Xizang jiaoshe jiyao* [A brief history of China's negotiations over Tibet]. Taipei: Mengzang weiyuanhui, 1954.

Luo Baoshan and Liu Lusheng, eds. *Yuan Shikai quanji* [The collected works of Yuan Shikai]. 36 vols. Zhengzhou: Henan daxue chubanshe, 2013.

Luo Zhenyu, ed. *Shiliao congkan chubian* [The first collection of historical materials]. 10 vols. Beijing: Dongfang xuehui, 1924.

——. *Tiancong chao chengong zouyi* [Officials' palace memorials during the Tiancong period]. Vols. 2–3 of *Shiliao congkan chubian* [The first collection of historical materials]. Beijing: Dongfang xuehui, 1924.

Ma Xiangbo. *Ma Xiangbo ji* [The collected works of Ma Xiangbo]. Shanghai: Fudan daxue chubanshe, 1996.

Manbun rōtō [Old records written in Manchu]. 7 vols. Tokyo: Tōyō bunko, 1955–63.

Mancall, Mark. "The Ch'ing Tribute System: An Interpretive Essay." In Fairbank, *Chinese World Order*, 63–89.

Manwen laodang [Old records written in Manchu]. 2 vols. Beijing: Zhonghua shuju, 1990.

Manzhou shilu [The veritable records of the Manchus in the Nurhaci period]. 8 vols. Shenyang: Liaoning tongzhiguan, 1930.

Mao Haijian. *Jindai de chidu: Liangci yapian zhanzheng junshi yu waijiao* [A measure of modernity: China's military and diplomacy during the two Opium Wars]. Shanghai: Shanghai sanlian chubanshe, 1998.

——. "Qingmo diwang jiaokeshu" [Textbooks for the emperors of the late Qing]. In *Yiran rujiu de yuese* [The moonlight as old as before], 123–64. Beijing: Shenghuo dushu xinzhi sanlian shudian, 2014.

——. *Tianchao de bengkui: Yapian zhanzheng zai yanjiu* [The collapse of the Heavenly Dynasty: A reconsideration of the Opium War]. Beijing: Shenghuo dushu xinzhi sanlian shudian, 1995.

——. "Wuxu bianfa qijian Guangxu di duiwai guannian de tiaoshi" [Changes in Emperor Guangxu's worldview during the Reform Movement of 1898]. *Lishi yanjiu* 6 (2002): 23–50.

Marquis of Zetland, ed. *The Letters of Disraeli to Lady Chesterfield and Lady Bradford*. Vol. 1, *1873–1875*. New York: D. Appleton, 1929.

Masuda, Erika. "The Fall of Ayutthaya and Siam's Disrupted Order of Tribute to China (1767–1782)." *Taiwan Journal of Southeast Asian Studies* 4, no. 2 (2007): 75–128.

Mayo, Marlene J. "The Korean Crisis of 1873 and Early Meiji Foreign Policy." *Journal of Asian Studies* 31, no. 4 (1972): 793–819.

Meng Sen. *Qingdai shi* [History of the Qing Dynasty]. Taipei: Zhengzhong shuju, 1960.

Miao Wei. "Jishi Chaoxian wenti de zai sikao" [A reconsideration of the issue of Jizi Chosŏn]. *Zhongguo bianjiang xue* 2 (2014): 220–42.

Michael, Franz. *The Origin of Manchu Rule in China*. New York: Octagon Books, 1965.

Miles, Gary B. "Roman and Modern Imperialism: A Reassessment." *Comparative Studies in Society and History* 32, no. 4 (1990): 629–59.

Millward, James A. *Beyond the Pass: Economy, Ethnicity, and Empire in Qing Central Asia, 1759–1864*. Stanford, CA: Stanford University Press, 1998.

Millward, James A., Ruth W. Dunnell, Mark C. Elliott, and Philippe Forêt, eds. *New Qing Imperial History: The Making of Inner Asian Empire at Qing Chengde*. London: RoutledgeCurzon, 2004.

Min, Tu-ki. *Chungguk gŭndaesa yŏn'gu* [A study of modern Chinese history]. Seoul: Ilchogak, 1970.

Ming jingshi wenbian [Collected essays about the statecraft of the Ming]. 6 vols. Beijing: Zhonghua shuju, 1962.

Ming Shenzong shilu [The veritable records of Emperor Wanli of the Ming]. Taipei: Zhongyang yanjiuyuan, 1962.

Mingshi [History of the Ming]. 28 vols. Beijing: Zhonghua shuju, 1974.

Mori Mayuko. *Chōsen gaikō no kindai: Shūzoku kankei kara Dai Kan teikoku e* [Chosŏn's modern diplomacy: From tributary relations to the Great Korean Empire]. Nagoya: Nagoya daigaku shuppankai, 2017.

Morse, Hosea Ballou. *The International Relations of the Chinese Empire*. 3 vols. New York: Longmans, Green, 1910–18.

Mosca, Matthew W. *From Frontier Policy to Foreign Policy: The Question of India and the Transformation of Geopolitics in Qing China*. Stanford, CA: Stanford University Press, 2013.

Needham, Joseph. *Science and Civilisation in China*. Vol. 3. Cambridge: Cambridge University Press, 1959.

Neige cangben manwen laodang [Old records written in Manchu, edition preserved at the Grand Secretariat]. 20 vols. Shenyang: Liaoning minzu chubanshe, 2009.

Nelson, M. Frederick. *Korea and the Old Orders in Eastern Asia*. Baton Rouge: Louisiana State University Press, 1945.

Nicolet, Claude. *Space, Geography, and Politics in the Early Roman Empire*. Ann Arbor: University of Michigan Press, 1991.

Nie Shicheng. *Dongyou jicheng* [Notes on the journey to the eastern areas]. In *Haeoe han'guk'ak charyo ch'ongsŏ* [Series of overseas materials regarding Korea], vol. 7, 247–719.

Nihon Gaimushō, ed. *Nihon gaikō bunsho* [Documents on Japanese foreign policy]. Vols. 3–36. Tokyo: Nihon kokusai renkō kyōkai, 1938–57.

Notes on the Imperial Chinese Mission to Corea, 1890. Shanghai, 1892.

Ŏ Yun-jung. *Chongjŏng nyŏnp'yo* [The chronology of a political career]. Seoul: Kuksa p'yŏnch'an wiwŏnhoe, 1958.

Okada Hidehiro, ed. *Shinchō towa nanika* [What is the Qing Dynasty?]. Tokyo: Fujiwara shoten, 2009.

Okamoto Takashi. *Chūgoku no tanjō: Higashi Ajia no kindai gaikō to kokka keisei* [The birth of China: International relations and formation of a nation in modern East Asia]. Nagoya: Nagoya daigaku shuppankai, 2017.

——. "*Fengshi Chaoxian riji zhi yanjiu*" [Studies on *Diary of the Journey to Chosŏn as an Envoy*]. In *Jindai Zhongguo, Dongya, yu shijie* [China, East Asia, and the world in modern times], edited by Wang Jianlang and Luan Jinghe, 15–28. Beijing: Shehui kexue wenxian chubanshe, 2008.

——. *Sekai no naka no Nitsu-Shin-Kan kankei shi* [History of relations between Japan, the Qing, and Korea in the world]. Tokyo: Kodansha, 2008.

——, ed. *Sōshuken no sekaishi: Tōzai Ajia no kindai to honyaku gainen* [A world history of suzerainty: Modern East and West Asia and the translation of concepts]. Nagoya: Nagoya daigaku shuppankai, 2014.

——. *Zokkoku to jishu no aida: Kindai Shin-Kan kankei to higashi Ajia no meiun* [Between the tributary state and self-rule: Modern Qing-Korean relations and East Asia's fate]. Nagoya: Nagoya daigaku shuppankai, 2004.

Okamoto Takashi and Kawashima Shin, eds. *Chūgoku kindai gaikō no taidō* [Emerging diplomacy in modern China]. Tokyo: Tokyo daigaku shuppankai, 2009.

Ōkubo Toshiaki, ed. *Mori Arinori zenshū* [The collected works of Mori Arinori]. 3 vols. Tokyo: Senbundō shoten, 1972.

Pak Che-ka. *Chŏngyu chip* [The collected works of Pak Che-ka]. Seoul: T'amgudang, 1971.

Pak Chi-wŏn. *Yŏlha ilgi* [Rehe diary]. 6 vols. Taipei: Taiwan shudian, 1956.

Pak Kyu-su. *Hwanjae sŏnsaengjip* [The collected works of Pak Kyu-su]. 11 vols. Seoul: Unyang sanbang, 1911.

Palais, James B. *Confucian Statecraft and Korean Institutions: Yu Hyŏngwŏn and the Late Chosŏn Dynasty*. Seattle: University of Washington Press, 1996.

Paullin, Charles Oscar. "The Opening of Korea by Commodore Shufeldt." *Political Science Quarterly* 25, no. 3 (1910): 470–99.

Perdue, Peter C. "Boundaries, Maps, and Movement: Chinese, Russian, and Mongolian Empires in Early Modern Central Eurasia." *International History Review* 20, no. 2 (1998): 263–86.

———. *China Marches West: The Qing Conquest of Central Eurasia*. Cambridge, MA: Harvard University Press, 2005.

———. "Tea, Cloth, Gold, and Religion: Manchu Sources on Trade Missions from Mongolia to Tibet." *Late Imperial China* 36, no. 2 (2015): 1–22.

Peyrefitte, Alain. *The Immobile Empire: The First Great Collision of East and West*. Translated by Jon Rothschild. New York: Alfred A. Knopf, 1992.

Pomeranz, Kenneth. *The Great Divergence: China, Europe, and the Making of the Modern World Economy*. Princeton, NJ: Princeton University Press, 2000.

Pritchard, Earl H. *Anglo-Chinese Relations during the Seventeenth and Eighteenth Centuries*. New York: Octagon Books, 1970.

Puett, Michael. *The Ambivalence of Creation: Debates concerning Innovation and Artifice in Early China*. Stanford, CA: Stanford University Press, 2001.

Qi Qizhang, ed. *Zhong-Ri zhanzheng* [The Sino-Japanese War]. 12 vols. Beijing: Zhonghua shuju, 1989–96.

Qi Yunshi. *Huangchao fanbu yaolue* [A general survey of the subordinates of the imperial dynasty]. Taipei: Chengwen chubanshe, 1968.

Qinding Annan jilue [A brief record of the appeasement of Annam, imperially ordained]. 20 vols. Beijing: Shumu wenxian chubanshe, 1986.

Qing Guangxu chao Zhong-Ri jiaoshe shiliao [Historical materials on Sino-Japanese negotiations in the Guangxu period of the Qing]. 88 vols. Beijing: Gugong bowuyuan, 1932.

Qing Jiaqing chao waijiao shiliao [Historical archives on diplomatic affairs in the Jiaqing period]. 6 vols. Beijing: Gugong bowuyuan, 1932.

Qing ruguan qian shiliao xuanji [Selections of historical materials on the Qing before 1644]. Beijing: Zhongguo renmin daxue chubanshe, 1989.

Qing shilu [The veritable records of the emperors of the Qing]. 60 vols. Beijing: Zhonghua shuju, 1985–87.

Qing Taizong shilu gaoben [The draft veritable records of Hongtaiji]. Shenyang: Liaoning daxue lishixi, 1978.

Qingji Zhong-Ri-Han guanxi shiliao [Historical materials on the relationship between China, Japan, and Korea in the late Qing]. 11 vols. Taipei: Zhongyang yanjiuyuan jindaishi yanjiusuo, 1972.

Qingshi gao [Manuscript on the history of the Qing]. 48 vols. Beijing: Zhonghua shuju, 1977.

Quan Hexiu. "Jianghua tiaoyue yu Qingzhengfu guanxi wenti xinlun" [A new study of relations between the Treaty of Kanghwa and the Qing government]. *Shixue jikan* 4 (2007): 20–26.

Rao Zongyi. *Zhongguo shixue shang zhi Zhengtong lun* [The narratives of orthodox legitimacy in Chinese historiography]. Beijing: Zhonghua shuju, 2015.

Rawski, Evelyn S. *Early Modern China and Northeast Asia: Cross-Border Perspectives.* Cambridge: Cambridge University Press, 2015.

———. "Reenvisioning the Qing: The Significance of the Qing Period in Chinese History." *Journal of Asian Studies* 55, no. 4 (1996): 829–50.

Reid, Donald Malcolm. "The Urabi Revolution and the British Conquest, 1879–1882." In *The Cambridge History of Egypt*, vol. 2, edited by M. W. Daly, 217–38. Cambridge: Cambridge University Press, 1998.

Reid, R. R. "The Office of Warden of the Marches: Its Origin and Early History." *English Historical Review* 32, no. 128 (1917): 479–96.

Ren Zhiyong. *Wanqing haiguan zaiyanjiu: Yi eryuan tizhi wei zhongxin* [A reconsideration of Chinese customs in the late Qing: Focusing on the dual system]. Beijing: Zhongguo renmin daxue chubanshe, 2012.

Rockhill, William Woodville. "Korea in Its Relations with China." *Journal of the American Oriental Society* 13 (1889): 1–33.

Rowe, William T. *China's Last Empire: The Great Qing.* Cambridge, MA: Belknap Press of Harvard University Press, 2009.

Rudolph, Jennifer. *Negotiated Power in Late Imperial China: The Zongli Yamen and the Politics of Reform.* Ithaca, NY: Cornell University East Asia Program, 2008.

Sadae mungwe [Records of serving the great]. 24 vols. Seoul, 1935.

Schmid, Andre. *Korea between Empires, 1895–1919.* New York: Columbia University Press, 2002.

Schwartz, Benjamin I. "The Chinese Perception of World Order, Past and Present." In Fairbank, *Chinese World Order*, 276–88.

Scott, David. *China and the International System, 1840–1949: Power, Presence, and Perceptions in a Century of Humiliation.* Albany: State University of New York Press, 2008.

Shao Xunzheng. *Zhong-Fa-Yuenan guanxi shimo* [The ins and outs of relations among China, France, and Vietnam]. Beijing: Guoli qinghua daxue chuban shiwusuo, 1935.

Shen Zhihua. *Saigo no tenchō: Mō Takutō Kimu Iruson jidai no Chūgoku to Kita Chōsen* [The last Heavenly Dynasty: China and North Korea under Mao Zedong and Kim Il-sung]. 2 vols. Tokyo: Iwanami shoten, 2016.

Shengjing tongzhi [Comprehensive history of Shengjing]. 32 vols. Beijing, 1684.

Shima Yoshitaka, ed. *Soejima Taneomi zenshū* [The collected works of Soejima Taneomi]. 2 vols. Tokyo: Keibunsha, 2004.

Sichuan sheng Nanchong shi dang'anguan, ed. *Qingdai Sichuan Nanbu xian yamen dang'an* [Archives of Nanbu County of Sichuan during the Qing Dynasty]. 308 vols. Anhui: Huangshan shushe, 2016.

Siku quanshu zongmu tiyao [Essentials of complete books of the four storehouses catalog]. 40 vols. Shanghai: Shangwu yinshuguan, 1931.

Sim Sang-kyu. *Mangi yoran chaeyong p'yŏn* [A collection of cases relating to the finances of Chosŏn]. Seoul: Kyŏng'in munhwasa, 1972.

Simyang janggye [Reports from Shenyang]. Seoul: Kyŏngsŏng cheguk taehak pŏpmunhakbu, 1935.

Sin Yu-han. *Ch'ŏngsaem jip* [A collection of the green spring]. 6 vols. Seoul: Kyŏng'in munhwasa, 1997.

Smith, Richard J. *Mapping China and Managing the World: Culture, Cartography and Cosmology in Late Imperial Times.* New York: Routledge, 2013.

———. "Mapping China and the Question of a China-Centered Tributary Trade System." *Asia-Pacific Journal* 11, no. 3 (2013): 1–22.

Sŏ Ho-su. *Yŏlha kiyu* [Records of the journey to Rehe]. In Lim, *Yŏnhaengnok jŏnjip*, vol. 51.

Sohyŏn Simyang ilgi [Crown Prince Sohyŏn's diary in Shenyang]. Seoul: Minsogwŏn, 2008.

Song, Nianshen. *Making Borders in Modern East Asia: The Tumen River Demarcation, 1881–1919.* Cambridge: Cambridge University Press, 2018.

———. "'Tributary' from a Multilateral and Multi-layered Perspective." *Chinese Journal of International Politics* 5, no. 2 (2012): 155–82.

Songja taejŏn [The collected works of Song Si-yŏl]. Seoul: Taeyang sŏjŏk, 1980.

Spence, Jonathan D. *Treason by the Book.* New York: Viking, 2001.

Staunton, George Thomas. *Narrative of the Chinese Embassy to the Khan of the Tourgouth Tartars in the Years of 1712, 13, 14, & 15.* London: John Murray, 1821.

Sun Hongnian. *Qingdai Zhong-Yue Zongfan guanxi yanjiu* [A study of Sino-Vietnamese Zongfan relations during the Qing Dynasty]. Harbin: Heilongjiang jiaoyu chubanshe, 2004.

Sun Weiguo. *Da Ming qihao yu xiao Zhonghua yishi, 1637–1800* [The Great Ming and the ideology of Little China, 1637–1800]. Beijing: Shangwu yinshuguan, 2007.

Sŭngjŏngwŏn ilgi [The daily records of the Royal Secretariat of the Chosŏn Dynasty]. 92 vols. Seoul: Kuksa p'yŏnch'an wiwŏnhoe, 1961–68.

Suzuki Kai. "'Manbun gentō' ni mieru Chōsen kokuō no koshō" [The names of the king of Chosŏn in "Original records written in Manchu"]. In *Chōsen chō kōki no shakai to shisō* [Society and thought of the late Chosŏn Dynasty], edited by Kawahara Hideki, 83–98. Tokyo: Bensei shuppan, 2015.

Swartout, Robert R., Jr., ed. *An American Adviser in Late Yi Korea: The Letters of Owen Nickerson Denny.* Tuscaloosa: University of Alabama Press, 1984.

Tabohashi Kiyoshi. *Kindai Nissen kankei no kenkyū* [A study of modern Japanese-Korean relations]. 2 vols. Keijo: Chōsen sōtokufu, 1940.

Tada Kōmon. *Iwakurakō jikki* [The true records of Iwakura Tomomi]. 3 vols. Tokyo: Iwakurakō kyōseki hozonkai, 1927.

Tamura Airi. "Ejiputo kenkyū kara mita kindai Nihon no Ajia kan" [Modern Japanese views of Asia with reference to Egyptian studies]. *Gakushūin shigaku* 9 (1972): 59–64.

Tang Wenquan and Sang Bing, eds. *Dai Jitao ji, 1909–1920* [The collected works of Dai Jitao, 1909–1920]. Wuhan: Huazhong shifan daxue chubanshe, 1990.

Tong Shuye. *Chunqiu shi* [History of the spring and autumn period]. Shanghai: Shanghai guji chubanshe, 2003.

Tongmun hwigo [A collection of diplomatic materials]. 4 vols. Seoul: Kuksa p'yŏnch'an wiwŏnhoe, 1978.

Tongmun koryak [A brief collection of Chosŏn's diplomatic materials]. 5 vols. Seoul: Kyujanggak, 2012.

T'ongmun'gwan ji [Records of the Bureau of Interpreters]. 2 vols. Seoul: Kyujanggak, 2006.

Treat, Payson J. "China and Korea, 1885–1894." *Political Science Quarterly* 49, no. 4 (1934): 506–43.

———. *The Far East: A Political and Diplomatic History.* New York: Harper and Brothers, 1928.

Treaties, Conventions, etc., between China and Foreign States. 3 vols. 2nd ed. Shanghai: Statistical Department of the Inspectorate General of Customs of China, 1917.

The Treaties, Regulations, etc., between Corea and Other Powers, 1876–1889. Shanghai: Statistical Department of the Inspectorate General of Customs of China, 1891.

Ŭpchi P'yŏngan do p'yŏn [The gazetteer of P'yŏngan province]. 4 vols. Seoul: Asia munhwasa, 1986.

Van Lieu, Joshua. "The Politics of Condolence: Contested Representation of Tribute in Late Nineteenth-Century Chosŏn-Qing Relations." *Journal of Korean Studies* 14, no. 1 (2009): 83–116.

van Schaik, Sam. *Tibet: A History.* New Haven, CT: Yale University Press, 2011.

Wakeman, Frederic, Jr. *The Great Enterprise: The Manchu Reconstruction of Imperial Order in Seventeenth-Century China.* Berkeley: University of California Press, 1985.

Waley-Cohen, Joanna. "The New Qing History." *Radical History Review,* no. 88 (2004): 193–206.

Walter, Gary D. "The Korean Special Mission to the United States of America in 1883." *Journal of Korean Studies* 1, no. 1 (July–December 1969): 89–142.

Wang, Sixiang. "Co-constructing Empire in Early Chosŏn Korea: Knowledge Production and the Culture of Diplomacy, 1392–1592." PhD diss., Columbia University, 2015.

Wang, Yuanchong. "Civilizing the Great Qing: Manchu-Korean Relations and the Reconstruction of the Chinese Empire, 1644–1761." *Late Imperial China* 38, no. 1 (2017): 113–54.

——. "Claiming Centrality in the Chinese World: Manchu-Chosŏn Relations and the Making of the Qing's 'Zhongguo' Identity, 1616–1643." *Chinese Historical Review* 22, no. 2 (2015): 95–119.

——. "Santiandu 'Da Qing huangdi gongde bei' man han beiwen zai yanjiu" [A reconsideration of the Chinese and Manchu inscriptions of the "Stele of the Honors and Virtues of the Emperor of the Great Qing"]. *Zhongguo bianjiang xue* 3 (2015): 271–308.

Wang Gungwu. "Early Ming Relations with Southeast Asia: A Background Essay." In Fairbank, *Chinese World Order,* 34–62.

Wang Guowei. "Yinzhou zhidu lun" [A discussion of the systems of the Shang and Zhou Dynasties]. In *Guantang jili* [The collected works of Wang Guowei], vol. 2, 451–80. Beijing: Zhonghua shuju, 1959.

Wang Yangbin and Wan Baoyuan. *Chaoxian diaocha ji* [Notes on the investigation of Chosŏn]. Beijing, 1915.

Wang Yuanzhou. *Xiao Zhonghua yishi de shanbian: Jindai Zhong-Han guanxi de sixiangshi yanjiu* [Transformations of the ideology of Little China: A study of modern Sino-Korean relations from the perspective of intellectual history]. Beijing: Minzu chubanshe, 2013.

Wang Zhongmin, ed. *Xu Guangqi ji* [The collected works of Xu Guangqi]. 2 vols. Beijing: Zhonghua shuju, 1963.

Westad, Odd Arne. *Restless Empire: China and the World since 1750.* New York: Basic Books, 2012.

Wheaton, Henry. *Elements of International Law.* London: Humphrey Milford, 1836.

——. *Wanguo gongfa* [International law]. 4 vols. Translated by Ding Weiliang (W. A. P. Martin). Beijing: Chongshiguan, 1864.

Wills, John E., Jr., ed. *China and Maritime Europe, 1500–1800: Trade, Settlement, Diplomacy, and Mission.* New York: Cambridge University Press, 2011.

——. *Embassies and Illusions: Dutch and Portuguese Envoys to K'ang-I, 1666–1687.* Cambridge, MA: Harvard University, Council on East Asian Studies, 1984.

——. "Tribute, Defensiveness, and Dependency: Uses and Limits of Some Basic Ideas about Mid-Ch'ing Foreign Relations." *American Neptune* 48, no. 4 (Fall 1988): 225–29.

Wong, J. Y. *Yeh Ming-Ch'en: Viceroy of Liang Kuang, 1852–8.* New York: Cambridge University Press, 1976.

Wong, R. Bin. *China Transformed: Historical Change and the Limits of European Experience*. Ithaca, NY: Cornell University Press, 1997.

——. "China's Agrarian Empire: A Different Kind of Empire, a Different Kind of Lesson." In *Lessons of Empire: Imperial Histories and American Power*, edited by Craig Calhoun, Frederick Cooper, and Kevin W. Moose, 189–200. New York: New Press, 2006.

Woodside, Alexander Barton. *Vietnam and the Chinese Model: A Comparative Study of Vietnamese and Chinese Government in the First Half of the Nineteenth Century*. Cambridge, MA: Harvard University Press, 1988.

Wright, Mary C. *The Last Stand of Chinese Conservatism: The T'ung-Chih Restoration, 1862–1874*. Stanford, CA: Stanford University Press, 1957.

Wu Baochu. "Chaoxian sanzhong xu" [Preface to Three Stories of Korea]. In *Aoyi Chaoxian sanzhong* [Three stories of Korea], by Zhou Jialu. Wuchang, 1899.

Wu Luzhen. *Yanji bianwu baogao* [Reports on border affairs in Yanji]. Taipei: Wenhai chubanshe, 1969.

Wu Yuanfeng. "Qingchu cefeng Liuqiu guowang Shang Zhi shimo" [The ins and outs of the Qing investiture to Shang Zhi, King of Ryukyu, in the early Qing]. *Lishi dang'an* 4 (1996): 75–83.

Wu Zhenqing, Xu Yong, and Wang Jiaxiang, eds. *Huang Zunxian ji* [The collected works of Huang Zunxian]. 2 vols. Tianjin: Tianjin renmin chubanshe, 2003.

Xizang zizhiqu dang'an guan, ed. *Xizang lishi dang'an huicui* [A collection of Tibetan historical archives]. Beijing: Wenwu chubanshe, 1995.

Yamauchi Kōichi. *Chōsen kara mita Ka–I shisō* [The civilized–barbarian ideology observed from the perspective of Chosŏn]. Tokyo: Yamakawa shuppansha, 2010.

Yang, Lien-sheng. "Historical Notes on the Chinese World Order." In Fairbank, *Chinese World Order*, 20–33.

Yang Bin. *Liubian jilue* [Records of the Willow Palisade]. Shanghai: Shangwu yinshuguan, 1936.

Yang Shusen, ed. *Qingdai liutiao bian* [The Willow Palisade in the Qing period]. Shenyang: Liaoning renmin chubanshe, 1978.

Yang Zhaoquan and Sun Yumei. *Chaoxian huaqiao shi* [A history of the Chinese in Korea]. Beijing: Zhongguo huaqiao chuban gongsi, 1991.

Yen, Sophia Su-fei. *Taiwan in China's Foreign Relations, 1836–1874*. Hamden, CT: Shoe String, 1962.

Yi Chae-hak. *Yŏnhaeng ilgi* [Diary of the journey to Beijing]. In Lim, *Yŏnhaengnok jŏnjip*, vol. 58.

Yi Ch'ŏl-sŏng. *Chosŏn huki taechŏng muyŏk yŏn'gu* [A study of the history of Korean trade with the Qing in the late Chosŏn period]. Seoul: Kuk'ak charyo wŏn, 2000.

Yi Kon. *Yŏnhaeng kisa* [Records of the mission to Beijing]. In Lim, *Yŏnhaengnok jŏnjip*, vols. 58–59.

Yi Kŭng-ik, ed. *Yŏllyŏsil gisul* [A history of Chosŏn compiled by Yi Kŭng-ik]. 3 vols. Seoul: Kyŏngmun sa, 1976.

Yi Kyŏng-am. *Pusim ilgi* [Diary of the journey to Shenyang]. In Lim, *Yŏnhaengnok jŏnjip*, vol. 15.

Yi Min-hwan. *Ja'am jip* [The collected works of Yi Min-hwan]. Vol. 82 of *Han'guk munjip ch'onggan* [Collection of Korean literature]. Seoul: Minjok munhwa chujinhoe, 1992.

Yi Sang-bong. *Pugwon rok* [Record of the journey to the Qing]. In *Yŏnhaengnok sŏnjip boyu* [Addenda to the selected collection of records of Chosŏn's emissaries to Beijing], vol. 1, 705–934. Seoul: Tongasia haksulwŏn, Taedong munhwa yŏn'guwŏn, 2008.

Yi Yu-wŏn. *Kawo koryak* [The collected works of Yi Yu-wŏn]. 2 vols. Seoul: Minjok munhwa chujinhoe, 2003.

Yin Mengxia and Yu Hao, eds. *Shi Chaoxian lu* [Records of the imperial missions to Chosŏn]. Beijing: Beijing tushuguan chubanshe, 2003.

Yuanshi [History of the Yuan Dynasty]. 15 vols. Beijing: Zhonghua shuju, 1976.

Yun, Peter I. "Rethinking the Tribute System: Korean States and Northeast Asian Interstate Relations, 600–1600." PhD diss., University of California, Los Angeles, 1998.

Yun Ch'i-ho. *Yun Ch'i-ho ilgi* [Yun Ch'i-ho's diary]. 11 vols. Seoul: T'amgudang, 1973.

Zeng Jize [Marquis Tseng]. "China: The Sleep and the Awakening." *Asiatic Quarterly Review* 3 (January 1887): 1–10.

Zha Luo. *Qingdai Xizang yu Bulukeba* [Tibetan-Bhutanese relations in the Qing Dynasty]. Beijing: Zhongguo shehui kexue chubanshe, 2012.

Zhang, Feng. "Rethinking the 'Tribute System': Broadening the Conceptual Horizon of Historical East Asian Politics." *Chinese Journal of International Politics* 2, no. 4 (2009): 545–74.

Zhang Jian quanji. [The collected works of Zhang Jian]. 7 vols. Nanjing: Jiangsu guji chubanshe, 1994.

Zhang, Xiaomin, and Xu Chunfeng. "The Late Qing Dynasty Diplomatic Transformation: Analysis from an Ideational Perspective." *Chinese Journal of International Politics* 1, no. 3 (2007): 405–45.

Zhang Jinguang. *Qinzhi yanjiu* [Studies on the institutions of the Qin Dynasty]. Shanghai: Shanghai guji chubanshe, 2004.

Zhang Liheng. *Zai chuantong yu xiandaixing zhijian: 1626–1894 nianjian de Zhong-Chao guanxi* [Between tradition and modernity: Sino-Korean relations, 1626–1894]. Beijing: Shehui kexue wenxian chubanshe, 2012.

Zhang Shuangzhi. *Qingdai chaojin zhidu yanjiu* [A study of the pilgrimage system of the Qing Dynasty]. Beijing: Xueyuan chubanshe, 2010.

Zhang Yinhuan. *Zhang Yinhuan riji* [Zhang Yinhuan's diary]. Shanghai: Shanghai shudian, 2004.

Zhao, Gang. "Reinventing China: Imperial Qing Ideology and the Rise of Modern Chinese National Identity in the Early Twentieth Century." *Modern China* 32, no. 1 (2006): 3–30.

Zhao Zhiqiang. "*Jiu Qing Yu*" *yanjiu* [A study of Old Manchu Language]. Beijing: Beijing yanshan chubanshe, 2002.

Zheng Hesheng. *Jinshi Zhong Xi shiri duizhao biao* [Cross-reference lists of modern Chinese and Western historical dates]. Beijing: Zhonghua shuju, 1981.

Zhongguo diyi lishi dang'an guan, ed. *Guangxu chao zhupi zouzhe* [Palace memorials with Emperor Guangxu's instructions]. 120 vols. Beijing: Zhonghua shuju, 1996.

——. *Junjichu manwen Zhungaer shizhe dang yibian* [The Chinese translations of the Manchu records preserved at the Grand Council regarding the emissaries of the Zunghar Mongols]. Beijing: Zhongyang minzu daxue chubanshe, 2009.

——. *Qianlong chao manwen jixin dang yibian* [A collection of Chinese translations of the Manchu record books of imperial edicts]. 24 vols. Changsha, Hunan: Yuelu shushe, 2011.

——. *Qingdai Junjichu manwen aocha dang* [The records preserved at the Grand Council regarding the emissaries of the Zunghar Mongols to Tibetan temples for donations in the Qing Dynasty]. 2 vols. Shanghai: Shanghai guji chubanshe, 2010.

——. *Qingdai Zhong-Chao guanxi dang'an shiliao huibian* [A collection of archives on Sino-Korean relations in the Qing Dynasty]. Beijing: Guoji wenhua chuban gongsi, 1996.

——. *Qingdai Zhong-Chao guanxi dang'an shiliao xubian* [A continuing collection of archives on Sino-Korean relations in the Qing Dynasty]. Beijing: Zhongguo dang'an chubanshe, 1998.

——. *Qingdai Zhong-Liu guanxi dang'an xubian* [A continuing collection of archives on Sino-Ryukyu relations in the Qing Dynasty]. Beijing: Zhonghua shuju, 1994.

——. *Qinggong zhencang lishi Dalai Lama dang'an huicui* [The treasure collection of the Dalai Lama from the archives of the Qing Dynasty]. Beijing: Zongjiao wenhua chubanshe, 2002.

——. *Yingshi Majiaerni fanghua dang'an shiliao huibian* [A collection of archives on the Macartney embassy to China]. Beijing: Guoji wenhua chuban gongsi, 1996.

Zhongguo shixue hui. *Zhongguo jindaishi ziliao congkan, Wuxu bianfa* [A collection of materials on modern Chinese history, the reform of 1898]. 4 vols. Shanghai: Shanghai renmin chubanshe, 1957.

Zhonghua guochi ditu [Map of the national humiliation of the Central Civilized Country]. Hebei: Hebei sheng gongchang ting, 1929.

Zhongyang yanjiuyuan lishi yuyan yanjiusuo, ed. *Ming Qing shiliao* [Historical documents on the Ming and Qing Dynasties]. Ser. 7. 10 vols. Taipei: Zhongyang yanjiuyuan lishi yuyan yanjiusuo, 1962.

Zhou Fangyin. "Equilibrium Analysis of the Tributary System." *Chinese Journal of International Politics* 4, no. 2 (2011): 147–78.

Zhu Chengru, ed. *Qingshi tudian* [Illustrated history of the Qing Dynasty]. 9 vols. Beijing: Zijincheng chubanshe, 2002.

Zhupi yuzhi [Palace memorials with emperor's comments]. 60 vols. Shanghai: Dianshizhai, 1887.

Index

Akdun, 62

Algeria, 15

Allen, Horace N., 187

all-under-Heaven (*tianxia*), 4, 8–10, 13, 38, 53, 79, 87, 163–64, 181–82, 199, 218–19

amba gurun, 23, 31, 48, 85. *See also* China

Amherst, Lord, 106–7

Amin, 25, 26

Anhui Province, 103, 155

An Ki-yŏng, 149

Annam, 6, 55, 58–61, 64, 70, 72, 82, 99–101, 104, 107, 163, 201, 218. *See also* Vietnam; Zongfan system

Baber, Edward C., 179

Baijun, 107–8

Bandi, 79

Bao Chengxian, 29

Baoding negotiations, 138–40

Baoting, 155–56

Bao Xinzeng, 201

barbarians: changing meaning of, from Yongzheng to Qianlong, 80–81; Chosŏn's status as, 82–85, 87–88, 156, 164, 210; defined as *yi*, 7, 72; Hongtaiji's understanding of, 38–39; Jin's description of Ming as, 30, 32; under Qing Dynasty, 58–60, 82–84; in Zongfan framework, 33. *See also* civilized-barbarian distinction and discourse

Beijing: British and Korean missions in 1860 and 1861 to, 109–17; Chosŏn emissaries as residents in, 156; emissaries to, and Korean antipathy toward Qing, 89; Fifth Dalai Lama's visit to, 54; Hong Tae-yong's visit to, 90–92; Korean tributary missions of 1866 and 1867 to, 127–28; Manchu takeover of, 1–2; Nurhaci's visit to, 22; Pak Che-ka's visit to, 92–94; Pak Chi-wŏn's visit to, 94–96; permanent residence of British representatives in, 109–13, 121; reception of emissaries in, 71–74

Beijing-Hansŏng overland route, 62–65

Beiyang superintendent, 42, 146–47, 156, 165

Bell, Henry H., 128

Bellonet, Henri de, 123, 126, 127

Bingham, John, 143, 145

Boissonade, Gustave, 159

borders: under Qing Dynasty, 62–65; Qing emperors and Sino-Korean disputes concerning, 14–15, 78–80, 163; Sino-Korean demarcation of, 211; Sino-Korean treaties regarding, 164–68; Sino-Korean violent conflicts at, 209–14; Sino-Vietnamese disputes concerning, 13, 163

Boxer Uprising, 208

British East India Company, 106, 113

British Empire: as barbarian, 84; and British mission of 1793, 103–6; expansion of, into India, 179–80; and First Opium War, 106–7; permanent residence of representatives in Beijing, 109–13, 121; tributary mission to Beijing, 113–17

Brown, John M., 206

Burlingame, Anson, 128

Burma, 51, 55, 59, 60, 61, 64, 70, 82, 99, 103, 111, 116, 136, 137, 155, 156, 176, 181, 198, 201

Cahar, 10, 31

calendar, Qing, 14, 58, 101–2, 184

Central Asia, 29, 82, 92, 135, 176, 224n55

"central civilized country" (*Huaxia*; *Zhonghua*), 52, 62, 75, 82, 87, 90, 91, 101, 108, 127, 217, 218

Ch'ae Che-gong, 93–94

Chang Bok, 94–95

Changlin, 198

Chen Rui, 112

Chen Shutang, 168, 169–74, 177

Chen Zhilin, 54

Chen Zuoyan, 210–11

"cherishing men from afar," 48–49, 72, 85, 98, 198, 210

"cherishing the small," 4, 45, 48, 49, 61, 79, 101, 158, 198, 210

China: channels of communication between Korea and, after 1883, 179*fig.*; and debate concerning Chosŏn's sovereignty, 186–88; establishes imperial resident in Chosŏn, 177–81; first minister of, to Korea, 204–7;